The building on the corner of Brick Lane and Fournier Street which has been a Huguenot Church, a synagogue and is now a mosque.

Strangers, Aliens and Asians

For centuries Spitalfields in East London has been a first point of settlement for new immigrants to Britain. Proximate to the affluence of the City of London and the poverty of what is now the London Borough of Tower Hamlets, Spitalfields has been, and still is, an area 'on the edge'. This book examines the settlement, integration and assimilation processes undergone by three different immigrant groups over a period of almost 350 years, assessing the relative successes and failures. The groups looked at are the French Huguenots who arrived in significant numbers in the closing decades of the seventeenth century; Eastern European Jews coming from the Russian Empire in the last third of the nineteenth century; and Bangladeshis whose large-scale settlement began in the late 1950s.

Strangers, Aliens and Asians sets out to investigate at grass-roots level the migrant experience and the processes by which the outsider may become the insider. The book explores the dynamics which drive the processes of immigrant settlement and assimilation and looks at whether these are solely the outcome of the temporal setting, cultural background and the contemporaneous socio-economic and political conditions, or whether there are factors which, irrespective of the prevailing environment, are constant features in the symbiosis between the outsider and the insider. The central themes under discussion include the reconstruction of home in an alien environment; migrant religiosity in an alien society; the role of the mother tongue in the assimilation process; and the expressions of xenophobia, anti-alienism and racism that emerged over the centuries in Spitalfields.

Anne J. Kershen is the Director of the Centre for the Study of Migration at Queen Mary, University of London. Although starting out as an Anglo-Jewish historian she has now broadened her ethnic and temporal framework to embrace more general patterns of immigration and settlement in London.

British politics and society
Series Editor: Peter Catterall
ISSN: 1467–1441

Social change impacts not just upon voting behaviour and party identity but also the formulation of policy. But how do social changes and political developments interact? Which shapes which? Reflecting a belief that social and political structures cannot be understood either in isolation from each other or from the historical processes which form them, this series will examine the forces that have shaped British society. Cross-disciplinary approaches will be encouraged. In the process, the series will aim to make a contribution to existing fields, such as politics, sociology and media studies, as well as opening out new and hitherto neglected fields.

The Making of Channel 4
Edited by Peter Catterall

Managing Domestic Dissent in First World War Britain
Brock Millman

Reforming the Constitution
Debates in twenty-first century Britain
Edited by Peter Catterall, Wolfram Kaiser and Ulrike Walton-Jordan

Pessimism and British War Policy, 1916–1918
Brock Millman

Amateurs and Professionals in Post-war British Sport
Edited by Adrian Smith and Dilwyn Porter

A Life of Sir John Eldon Gorst
Disraeli's awkward disciple
Archie Hunter

Conservative Party Attitudes to Jews, 1900–1950
Harry Defries

Strangers, Aliens and Asians

Huguenots, Jews and Bangladeshis in
Spitalfields 1660–2000

Anne J. Kershen

Routledge
Taylor & Francis Group

LONDON AND NEW YORK

**942.
15
KER**

First published 2005
by Routledge
2 Park Square, Milton Park, Abingdon, Oxon OX14 4RN

Simultaneously published in the USA and Canada
by Routledge
711 Third Avenue, New York, NY 10017

Routledge is an imprint of the Taylor & Francis Group

First issued in paperback 2011

Typeset in Garamond by Wearset Ltd, Boldon, Tyne and Wear

British Library Cataloguing in Publication Data
A catalogue record for this book is available from the British Library

Library of Congress Cataloging in Publication Data
A catalog record for this book has been requested

ISBN 978-0-714-65525-3 (hbk)
ISBN 978-0-415-51542-9 (pbk)

For my grandson,
Alexander Fisher

Contents

Acknowledgements

Writing a book which covers four centuries of history and three different diasporic groups has built up a considerable number of thank yous. I must first acknowledge the debt I owe to my undergraduate and postgraduate students at Queen Mary, University of London, whose exhilarating participation in my courses on East London and immigration was the stimulus for this volume. I am also indebted to the indomitable Bill Fishman, whose fellowship I inherited and in whose giant footsteps I have attempted to tread. I must thank my colleagues in the Department of Politics at Queen Mary, particularly Wayne Parsons and Ken Young, and our supportive secretary Jasmin Salucideen, together with those from other departments including, Elza Adamowicz, Alison Blunt, Jenny Cheshire, Simon Harvey, Roger Mettam, Parvati Nair, Philip Ogden and Prakash Shah, all of whom contributed valued advice. An enormous thank you to Queen Mary subject librarian Eilis Rafferty for her endless patience in responding to my desperate emails and phone calls and for her ability to conjure up texts from the depths of the archives and references that seemed impossible to find. I also owe a debt to Chris Lloyd and his team at the Tower Hamlets Local History Library for all their help in bringing forward maps, books and documents which have enriched this volume. Thanks also to Sarah Gillings and Carol Segal from the Jewish Museum London, Stephen Massil and David Pohl at the Huguenot Library and librarians at the Guildhall Library. A special thank you also to Peter Catterall for his helpful and incisive comments on the manuscript.

I have been particularly fortunate in having had Todd Endelman read and comment on draft chapters and make constructive suggestions – his wise and speedy responses have been invaluable. I must record particular thanks to my colleague Shompa Lahiri, research fellow at the Centre for the Study of Migration and to David Garbin for casting his eye over the sections which relate to life in the Bengali community and for correcting errors in Old French. I have also received invaluable help from many others including Ayub Ali, Gerry Black, Bob Brett, Yousuf Choudhury, Peter Corbishley, John Eade, Nicholas Evans, Cathy Gardner, Mike Goodmaker, Robin Gwynn, Colin Holmes, Michael Keating, John Klier, Kenneth Leech,

Carolyn Lougee, Ceri Peach, Mafijur Rafique, Immam Shafique Rahman, Jonathan Romain, Maxine Seller, Marlena Schmool, Nazneen Uddin, Laura Vaughan, John Webber, Jerry White, Veronica White and James Lloyd Williams.

The writing and researching of this book would not have been possible without Martin Paisner; and I am most grateful for his continuing support for my academic work and for the bonus of having his, and his wife Susan's, friendship. I have to thank my children, Deborah and Paul, and James and Mandy, for tolerating my absent-mindedness while the writing of the book was underway, and my grandson Alexander for ensuring that there were times when 'bowling just a few balls' took precedence over theories and patterns of migration. Finally, I have to thank my husband Martin for his love, forbearance, willingness to read innumerable drafts and, most importantly, for always being there.

Anne J. Kershen
Queen Mary, University of London
Summer 2004

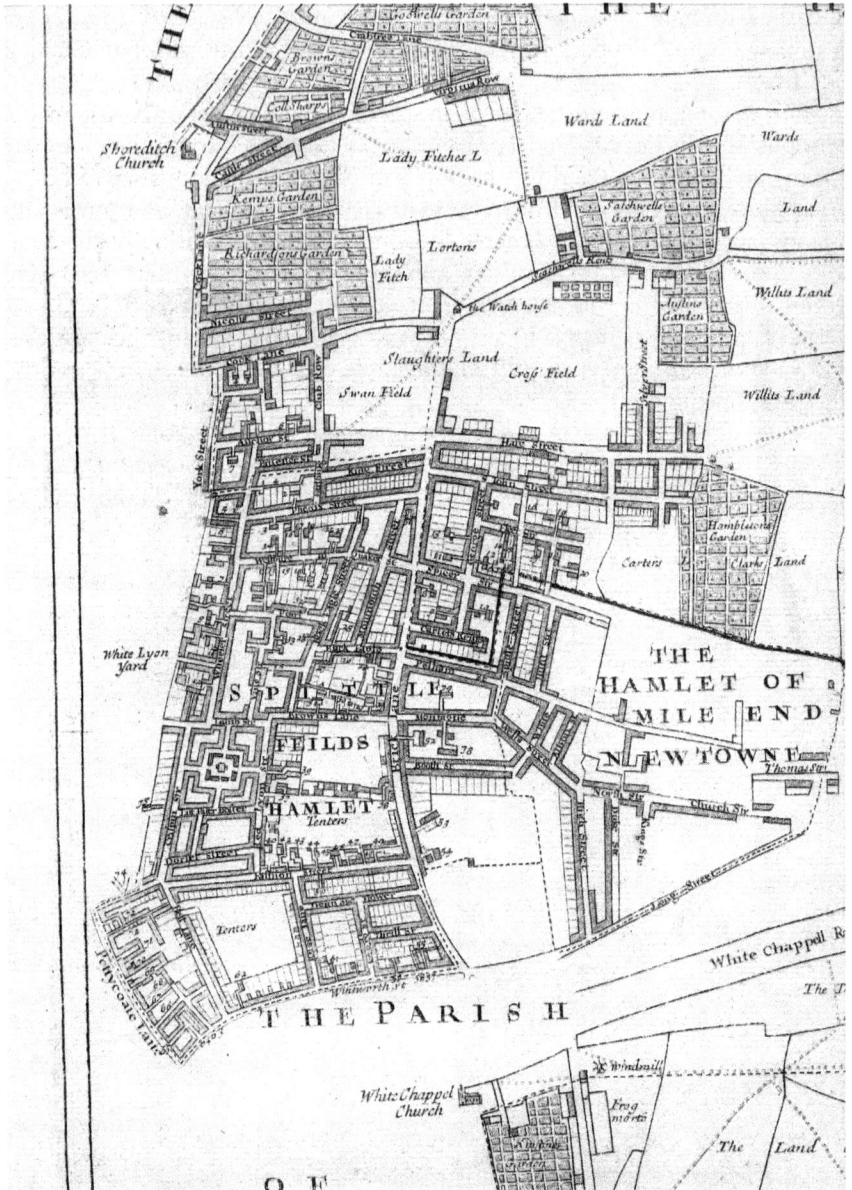

Figure 1 Gascoyne's 1703 map of Spitalfields in Stepney.

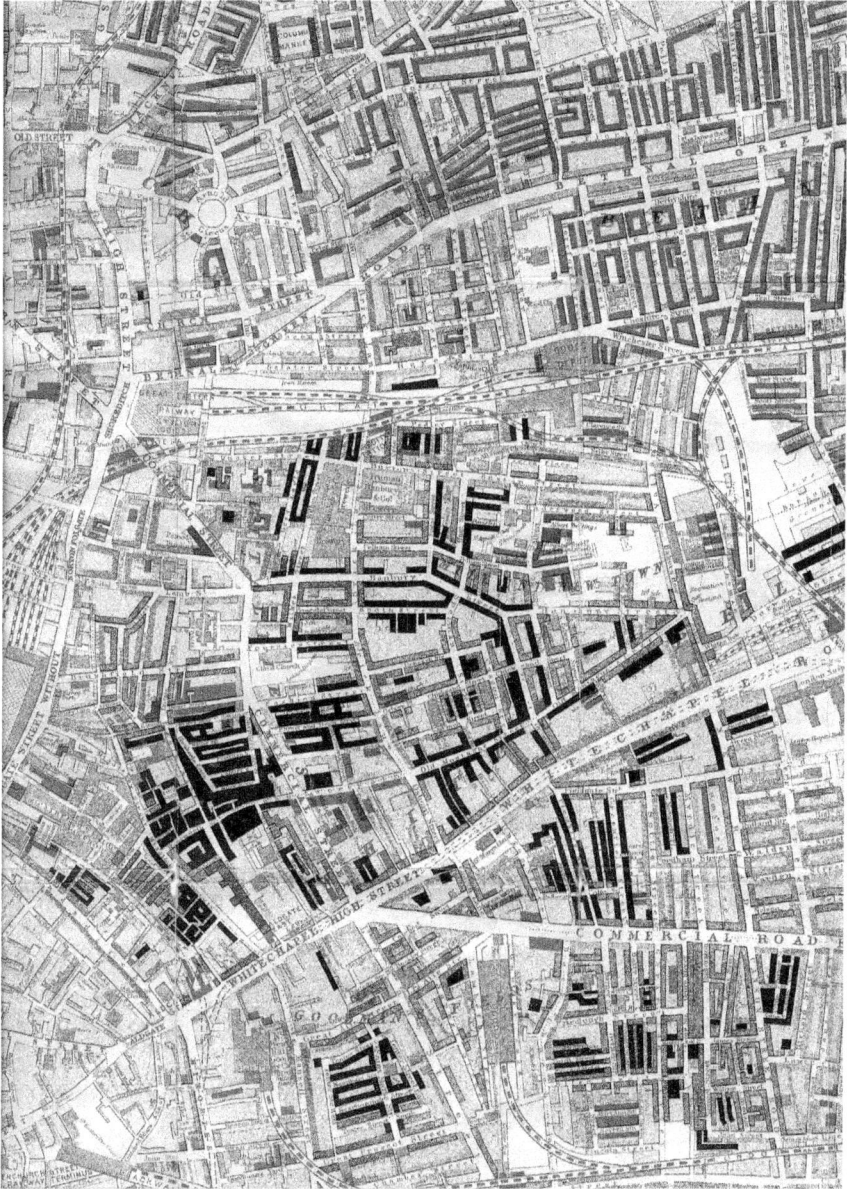

Figure 2 The East End of London *c.*1900 (source: adapted from C. Russell and H.S. Lewis, *The Jew in London: A Study of Racial Character and Present-day Conditions*, London, T. Fisher Unwin, 1900).

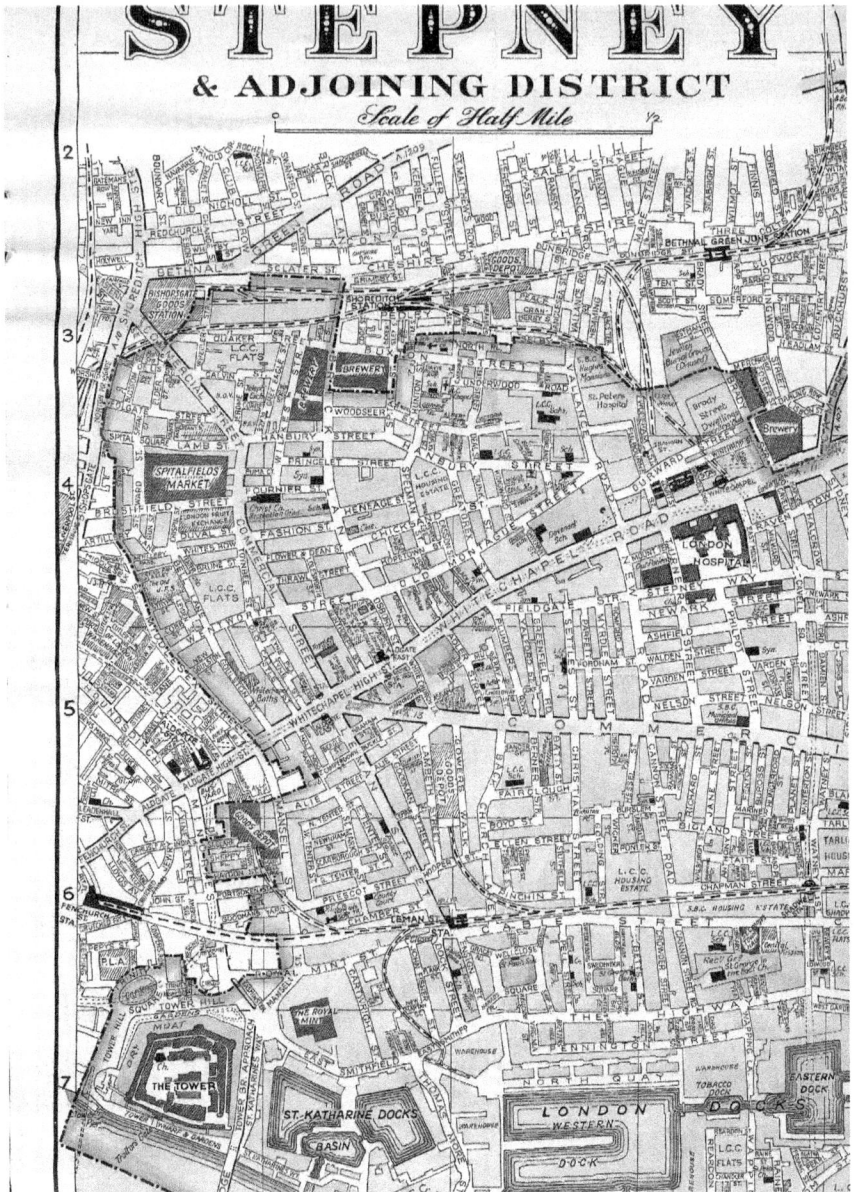

Figure 3 1950 Stepney Borough Council map showing Spitalfields.

Introduction

Spitalfields has been peripheral to the mosaic of London since Roman times. It was then, and has remained ever since, a place on the edge, a bridge between the included and the excluded. A twilight 'zone of transition'[1] in which the culture and economy of the native and the stranger have evolved, at times merging, at other times competing. Through metaphor Spitalfields has been presented as deprived, dangerous and exotic. It has been called, variously, 'the city of darkest night', 'a jungle', 'a bazaar', 'an abyss', words which instantly conjure up images of poverty, violence and otherness. It is encrusted with diversity and a history of tolerance living side-by-side with intolerance. Spitalfields has vibrated with the sights, sounds and smells of the minority groups who have inhabited it over the centuries and has been known as Petty France, Little Jerusalem and, now, Banglatown. Yet it is also part of the cockney East End and home to Petticoat Lane market. An area on the edge, yet only minutes from the heart of the nation, it presents the perfect geographic and temporal framework in which to undertake a comparative and thematic study of immigration in a metropolis.

The subject groups of this book are the Huguenots who arrived from France in the seventeenth and eighteenth centuries; Eastern European Jews who immigrated to Britain in considerable numbers during the last third of the nineteenth century; and Bangladeshis, whose large-scale settlement began in the late 1950s. All made Spitalfields their first point of settlement. As such it was the location for the most important stage in the migrant rite of passage.

The movement of peoples is as old as the Bible. Whilst the Hebrews were searching for the 'land flowing with milk and honey',[2] Hittites and Kassites were on the move. In later centuries the Romans, Goths and Mongols also crossed geographic and territorial boundaries. All were looking for 'the promised land', though its form differed from group to group. Some sought a peaceful haven, others land and its natives to subordinate. Migrants have not always found their utopia – many have had to work at creating it, the successful being those who, in Machiavellian fashion, recognised the potential and used initiative and ability to create good fortune. The phenomenon of the immigrant presence and the resultant impact on the receiving society is not new. People have been arriving on British soil for more than two millennia. Some settled permanently, some stayed for just a short while and then moved on, while others returned to their roots. Whatever the duration of the sojourn, that presence forms a part of British history and, whilst immigrants continue to arrive, it will go on doing so.

In 2002, 513,000 immigrants arrived in the United Kingdom with the intention of living in the country for more than one year.[3] Economic migrants and asylum-seeking refugees, they came from sending societies that covered the globe, from Europe – both inside and outside the European Union – North America, Africa, South Asia, the Middle East and countries recorded by the Home Office simply as 'other'.[4] In addition to those whose presence was legal, there were entrants with no right of admission but who had gained access by illegal means and therefore were not accounted for in government statistics.[5] In each case, as willing or unwilling emigrants, they had selected Britain as the destination, if not as a promised land then as a place which, for them, offered hope and opportunity.

The statistics and macro-based discourses on the movements of people often ignore completely, or diminish, the individual or group in favour of the big picture of migration and its patterns and flows. The aim of this book is to examine at grass-roots level, the migrant experience and the processes by which the outsider may become the insider. The objectives are twofold: first, to identify the dynamics which drive the processes of immigrant settlement and assimilation; second, to determine whether these are solely the outcome of temporal setting, cultural background and contemporaneous socio-economic and political conditions or whether other factors, irrespective of the prevailing environment, constantly feature in the symbiosis taking place between the outsider and the insider. In order to inform the future as well as illuminate the past, the study incorporates three temporally, geographically and culturally diverse groups that settled in the same space but at different times. The selected spatial focus is the Spitalfields district of London, a quarter which has been a first point of settlement for immigrants since before the mid-sixteenth century.

The volume avoids the more traditional, chronological structure but rather follows a thematic approach which, it is hoped, may be of benefit to future migrants and their sending and receiving societies. I do not claim to cover all features of migrant life in the chapters that follow. Instead I have selected those aspects which affected the lives of a majority of the immigrants living in Spitalfields in the periods under the microscope.[6] In particular, I have focused upon those facets which will enable me to pinpoint the differences as well as the similarities in the processes of settlement undergone by the three groups.

Outline by chapter

Chapter 1 offers a brief excursion into methodology and theory. It considers the variations in migrant typologies; the representation of immigration flows and patterns through cartography; and the way in which these can be used to put meat on the bones of migration studies. After analysing the significance of the ghetto as a place of migrant settlement, the chapter concludes with an evaluation of some of the theories of migration currently in use. These include the classical, liberal neo-classical, historical-structuralist and global-transnational. It would be impractical, indeed impossible, to draw any conclusions about the immigrant rite of passage without knowledge of the sending society, its socio-economic structure, political regime and religious and cultural norms. Accordingly, Chapter 2 travels back to sixteenth- and seventeenth-century France to acquaint readers with the origins of Calvinism and the life of the Huguenots in their country of birth. It explores Eastern Europe, more specifically the regions of Russia and Russia–Poland which, by the early decades of the nineteenth century, had become the Pale of Settlement. This was the area where the majority of the Empire's Jews were required to live and eke out a living. Finally, Chapter 2 surveys Bangladesh, in order to familiarise the reader with that country and the region of Sylhet, the area from which 95 per cent of those living in Spitalfields emigrated.

Having been introduced to 'over there', Chapter 3 aims to familiarise the reader with 'over here', most specifically with the landscape of Spitalfields. It is one which has been subjected to change yet in many ways remains unaltered, a landscape multi-layered with a patina representing an amalgam of the memories and experiences of all those immigrants who arrived, stayed for a while and then moved on. Chapter 4 examines the role of religion in the lives of the Huguenots, Eastern European Jews and Bangladeshis in Spitalfields. It is often assumed that religion binds the marginalised and threatened. However, the chapter demonstrates that, whilst in most instances the migrants maintained their religiosity, in some cases new arrivals eschewed religion in order to enjoy a secular existence. With few exceptions, newly arrived immigrants to Spitalfields were, if not paupers, then in need of charity and welfare in the first few days or weeks following arrival. The distribution of charity was co-ordinated by the houses of religion and Chapter 5 provides details of the way in which members of each group were, on arrival, assisted by their co-patriots, co-religionists and the state, by all three, by two, or just one, of these bodies.

Language is one of the main pillars of society and lack of articulacy in the majority language alienates the immigrant more than any other aspect of the settlement process. Chapter 6 examines the role of the mother tongue in the integration process, questioning whether it is a source of marginalisation or a bridge to assimilation. Each of the three groups imported their mother tongue. In the seventeenth and eighteenth centuries French was the language of the English elite, its use denoting education and affluence. The established British Jewish community considered Yiddish, the mother tongue of the Eastern European Jew, a dialect of the peasantry, one used by the uneducated and poor and, as such, to be eschewed with all rapidity.

Sylheti, the dialect of the immigrants from the region of Sylhet is not the official, national language. Even if favoured by members of the Bengali community in Spitalfields, it is considered a lower-class, peasant dialect by Bangladesh's urban, educated population.

Immigrants to Spitalfields were drawn by the economic opportunities they believed it offered. Chapter 7 measures their entrepreneurial spirit and economic activities against Weber's definition of the spirit of capitalism, testing his assumption that the Huguenots were the progenitors of the hard-work ethic. In Chapter 8 we confront what is a perennial problem, that of the negative reaction of the receiving society to the immigrant, the outsider. The chapter considers the ways in which verbal and physical expressions of antipathy – of xenophobia, anti-alienism and racism – have persisted and questions whether levels of physical violence have increased over the centuries. Finally, the book's Conclusion assesses the foregoing chapters in order to establish whether it is people, or the time and place they inhabit, which determine the processes of settlement and assimilation undergone by immigrants in an alien environment.

Terminology

It has become common practice to use the terms diaspora and diasporic to describe immigrants and their groups. The word diaspora originates from the Greek *speiro* (to sow) and the preposition *dia* (over). According to Robin Cohen, when the Greeks used the word in regard to humans it was within the context of migration and colonisation.[7] It subsequently took on a more sombre meaning and became linked with the Jews and others such as the Armenians, whose migrations were spurred by violence, threat and death. More recently, the noun has been used to describe those peoples who are 'spread' globally, as a result of war, trade or culture. It is in this sense that the words diaspora and diasporic appear in this book and as such can be applied without qualm to the three protagonist groups. Each of them were part of a movement that spread itself transcontinentally. The Huguenots who left France went to England, Switzerland, Holland, Germany and to the New World. The Jewish diaspora has had a global spread for centuries, while Bangladeshi migrants are now to be found in North America, the Middle East and various countries in Europe as well as in Britain.

The term 'assimilation' appears throughout the book. There are various kinds of assimilatory behaviour, which operate at different levels and can be interpreted in different ways. The word can be used to describe absorption and integration into mainstream society, or conformity with the dominant group. It can also be applied to the process of acculturation, or adaptation to an alien culture. I have been mainly concerned with the processes of acculturation and integration and this is the way the word assimilation should be read in the book.

I have used the terms 'Bengali' and 'Bangladeshi' interchangeably throughout this book to refer to the most recent settlers in Spitalfields. Whilst the term Bengali can be applied both to those who come from what is now Bangladesh[8] and to those living in West Bengal, in India, it is the way most of the Bangladeshi residents of Spitalfields choose to refer to themselves. I have been told, with pride by several of those I interviewed for this volume, that it is because Bengali is the official language of their country, one that they or their kin fought for, that they choose this nomenclature.

When writing about the Huguenots and their arrival in what we now call the United Kingdom, for any events preceding 1707 and the Act of Union, I have referred to England as the sovereignty. Anything taking place after that date occurs in Britain.

Finally, I should stress that, as the following chapters will illustrate, this book is an empirical as opposed to theoretical study. However, no such work can be presented without some form of theoretical anchor. That is the role of Chapter 1.

Notes

1 See J. Rex, *Race, Colonialism and the City*, London, Routledge and Kegan Paul, 1973, p. 12.
2 *The New English Bible*, Swindon, Bible Society, 1995 edition, 'Exodus', Chapter 3, verse 10, p. 45.
3 http://www.census2001.gov.uk/cci/nugget.asp?id.-260 (accessed 2 June 2004).
4 Ibid. According to government statistics, the number of 'in-migrants' to the UK from Bangladesh, India and Sri Lanka, from the Middle East and from African Commonwealth countries (excluding South Africa), was higher in 2002 than in any other year over the ten-year period 1992–2002.
5 By their very nature, it is impossible to quantify the number of illegal migrants present in the United Kingdom, with estimates varying from 100,000 to 750,000.
6 The most obvious omission is that of politics. The Huguenots, though active in English trade and economy, did not involve themselves in the national politics of the time, though they were engaged in local parish politics and for this see R. Gwynn, *Huguenot Heritage: The History and Contribution of the Huguenots in Britain*, Brighton, Sussex Academic Press, 2001 edition. Eastern European Jews, as a result of their national and economic status, played little part in national politics, though members of the established community had been, by the late 1880s, admitted both to the Commons and the Lords, the Member of Parliament for Whitechapel being Samuel Montagu, later Lord Swaythling. In the area of Spitalfields, the most vocal political activists were the anarchists and for this see W.J. Fishman, *East End Jewish Radicals 1875–1914*, London, Duckworth, 1975. There was also engagement in local politics and for this see, G. Alderman, *London Jewry and London Politics 1889–1986*, London, Routledge, 1989. For the Bangladeshi community the politics of the *desh* (homeland) were often interwoven with those of the *bidesh* (overseas), in this instance Spitalfields. For a detailed and seminal account, see J. Eade, *The Politics of Community*, Aldershot, Avebury, 1989.
7 See R. Cohen, *Global Diasporas*, London, University College Press, 1997, p. ix.
8 The nation-state created after the civil war with Pakistan ended in 1971.

1   People, place and a phenomenon

This is a book about people, place and a phenomenon. The people in chronological order of their arrival in England are Huguenots, the strangers;
Eastern European Jews, the aliens; and Bangladeshis, the Asians. The place
is Spitalfields, an area of 250 acres, lying in the western part of the East End
and bordering the eastern edge of the City of London. The phenomenon is
migration, in this context the movement of people from one country to
another with the intention of settling in the host country for a significant
period or permanently. The subjects of this book were all migrants, essentially people who moved from their country of birth to London. There much
of the similarity would appear to end. The migrant groups came in different
centuries, were of different religions and, at first sight, appear to fall into
different categories: those of refugees, immigrants and sojourners. However,
the realities of life can never be painted in black and white; there is always
shading. It is thus with the Huguenots, Eastern European Jews and
Bangladeshis. They would appear to fit comfortably into specific and separate temporal, typological and theoretical compartments, but do they really?
Before examining the empirical data enabling us to respond to this question,
we need to explore some of the methodologies employed in the study of
migrations and migrants.

People

Typologies

Migrants, as opposed to travellers or holidaymakers, are individuals or
groups who, for whatever reasons, move from one place to another for a
period of at least a year. Whilst the noun 'migrant' can be used in a variety
of spatial contexts, it is usually assumed that those it is describing have
covered some distance, either within one country or between one or more
nations. International migration is acknowledged as a permanent or semi-
permanent crossing of national boundaries.[1] However, one of the earliest
migration theorists, the late nineteenth-century geographer Ernest George
Ravenstein, initially focused his attention on the internal movements of

people in Britain, only subsequently enlarging his studies to assume an international perspective.[2] This book's protagonists were all transnational migrants who immigrated with the intention of remaining for a period of years, if not permanently. Having now established their migrant status, the next step is to establish under which typological headings the Huguenots, Eastern European Jews and Bangladeshis appear.

The primary category of migration is that which separates those who emigrate willingly from those who are forced to leave. However, it is not always possible to recognise the dichotomy. The catalytic issues are rarely clear-cut and it is imperative to incorporate this factor into any analysis. As the Lucassen brothers recorded at the end of the 1990s, 'The rapid reduction of . . . typologies to fixed dichotomies often causes the dividing and isolating capacity of an analytical framework to overshadow its clarifying and explanatory potential.'[3] Thus, we have to be cautious how we define and where we locate the Huguenots, Eastern European Jews and Bangladeshis within the framework of migration.

Migrants can be listed under three main typological classifications: voluntary, involuntary and those on the borderline, the grey area between the positives. The category 'voluntary' accommodates the broadest band of migrants. It includes all those who have made the decision to leave home of their own free will in search of a more favourable, if not perfect, economic, meteorological, political, religious or sexual environment – or a combination of some, if not all. It is regularly accepted that the majority of free migrants are, or were, what the late twentieth century denominated 'economic' migrants – people who leave home for elsewhere with the specific intention of enhancing their economic prospects. Both skilled and unskilled emigrants fall into this broad-based voluntary category, one which has a number of sub-sectors accommodating, amongst others, professionals, artisans, white-collar workers and blue-collar or manual workers. Once the emigrant becomes an immigrant, the receiving societies' preferences and sub-classifications tend to be imposed. Though the skilled are most frequently perceived as 'good' migrants, this form of acceptance is subject to prevailing political and socio-economic biases. In the 1930s, German refugee doctors found it almost impossible to gain entry to Britain in their professional capacity, the BMA arguing that their admission would endanger British jobs.[4] One of the few means of access for Jewish men and women seeking to leave Nazi Germany was through employment as domestic servants and gardeners, sectors where there was a paucity of home labour. More recently, Alison Bloch has shown that, in the late 1990s, 'Many refugees arrive in Britain with high levels of education and qualifications. Nevertheless, they seem unable to use their skills in paid employment'.[5] At the same time, unskilled immigrants, usually plugging gaps in the labour market, are perceived as wage-undercutters, job-stealers or social-benefit fraudsters. In spite of the benefits some may provide, they are labelled 'bad' migrants and parasites on a national economy.

The first peacetime Aliens Act to be passed in Britain appeared on the Statute Book at the end of 1905. It sought to prohibit the entry of pauper aliens and was a direct response to the significant increase of Eastern European alien immigrants in London and the main provincial cities.[6] The introduction of immigration control introduced a new type of migrant to the United Kingdom: the illegal, as opposed to the legal, immigrant. Yet, even though the status of illegal has existed for almost a century, it is only in the past few decades, with the introduction of increasingly restrictive immigration legislation, that the noun 'illegal' has become common parlance and, standing alone can be used to describe an undesirable and unwanted entrant to Britain. In peacetime, the determining of who is a 'legal' or 'illegal' immigrant is dependent on the response of governments to the economic or social threat posed by outsiders. Tensions over the consequences of a widening pool of immigrant labour at times of financial uncertainty and growing unemployment encourages the closing of borders and an increasing selectivity in the admittance of aliens. At the time of writing, existing legislation[7] makes it almost impossible for an 'economic' migrant to gain entry into Britain without guaranteed employment or considerable personal financial resources. So obsessed are governments and the public with the threat and presence of 'illegals'[8] that even the word immigrant is taken as a pejorative. It is now rarely used to describe the pioneering individual who seeks to contribute to the receiving society and improve the quality of life for self and family, thus building a future which offers hope and security. Instead the immigrant has become the scrounger, a being that imperils native jobs, homes and the traditional British way of life.

The Huguenots immigrated to England at a time when there were no entry controls. In modern parlance, the French Calvinists would have been legals. Eastern European Jews were arriving both before and after the Aliens Act of 1905 came into operation.[9] Once immigration controls were in place, those unable to demonstrate an ability to earn a living and who did not have £5 for themselves and £2 for each dependent, as a means of maintenance prior to taking up employment, were denied entry. Even before the Act was in operation, access was denied to any would-be immigrant with a criminal record, anyone showing evidence of insanity, or those suffering from a contagious disease. Doubtless some slipped through the net at the specified ports of entry, but it would be impossible to quantify them. Even though Bengali migrants have been arriving in Britain since the eighteenth century, large-scale immigration has only taken place since the 1950s. In the half century following, immigrant entry to Britain has been increasingly policed and contained. Almost certainly there are illegal Bangladeshi immigrants now working in the curry restaurants and leather workshops of Spitalfields. However, as in the case of their Eastern European alien predecessors, it would be impossible to provide details of their age, gender or exact location.

The antithesis of voluntary is, of course, involuntary, a tragic heading under which too many migrants are listed. Involuntary migration incorporates the victims of colonial expansion and slavery, of forced labour into the gulags of the Soviet Union and the concentration camps of Nazi Germany as well as refugees from ethnic cleansing, religious persecution and natural disasters. According to the *Shorter Oxford English Dictionary*, the noun refugee, an anglicised version of the word *réfugié*, first appeared in the English language in 1685, and was used to refer to Huguenots who had escaped from France after the revocation of the Edict of Nantes.[10] In contrast with those forcibly expelled from their countries of residence, for example Huguenot clergy in the seventeenth and eighteenth centuries and Asian Ugandans two centuries later, lay Calvinists were not ejected from France but, in the years leading up to, and following, the 1685 revocation of the Edict of Nantes, were forbidden to leave. Those escaping to England and other Protestant countries risked all because they refused to subjugate religious beliefs to national loyalty.

It is the grey area between voluntary and involuntary migrants which requires particular analysis. The researches of Jan Lucassen, Diana Kay and Robert Miles have revealed that what may, in the past, have been perceived as free movement was in fact coerced. Lucassen provides the example of one group of seasonal migrants who decided to risk their health, and sometimes their lives, because they needed the proceeds of work to pay their debts to landowners who had provided them with food in the winter in return for their labour during harvest time.[11] European Voluntary Workers, who were recruited from refugee camps in Europe, were moved around and treated as 'virtual slaves',[12] whilst indentured labourers freely signed up for work, though some, for example, Chinese workers in the early twentieth century, were misled as to what exactly they were signing up for.[13] Robin Cohen has shown that 'most indentured labourers were recruited from India',[14] their treatment closely resembling that of the African slaves they were replacing. Indentureds, those who were bound by contract to their masters, enjoyed virtually no freedom of movement, were subjected to physical and financial punishment and rarely ended up with more than the cost of their fare home.[15] They had, however, made a free decision to sign up and consequently, however enslaved, could not be bought or sold. They inhabit a middle place on the free/unfree chart. And how free a decision is that of the twenty-first-century relocated worker who, if he or she does not move with the company, might well be forced into unemployment and financial hardship? The decision to move in the case of commercial and professional relocation might be one rationally taken, but how *free* is it? In contrast, writing about nineteenth-century Russian Jewry, John Klier[16] has proved that it is a misconstruction to believe that, in order to escape the pogroms, Eastern European Jews left their homes as refugees or unwilling migrants. Research has shown that the majority had made a rational choice to seek economic mobility in the west. The Huguenots cover the spectrum from voluntary through to involuntary. Some, as will be shown below, were genuine economic migrants; others were clergy forced to leave, even if free to determine their destination; but the majority comprised those who would have preferred not to leave France but did so rather than succumb to the will of the Catholic monarch and clerics. It is generally assumed that the Bengali immigrants came for economic reasons and were voluntary emigrants. There was, however, a minority of anti-government activists who would have preferred to stay but had to leave for reasons of personal safety.

Up until this point, I have considered the movement of migrants under the categories of free, unfree or in that middle place. I have also surveyed the kaleidoscope of skills and reasons for departure of those who migrate. In his book, *Global Diasporas*,[17] Robin Cohen takes the notion of diaspora as the basis for his typological discourse. Eschewing an individualist approach, he lists migrants as diasporic groups, locating them under the following headings: victim, labour, trade, imperial and culture.[18] Using this methodology, the Huguenots and Jews would appear predominantly in the victim (religious) column, though a small number of each could be considered under trade, or even labour, while the Bengalis would be cross-indexed under labour and imperial with a minority under victim and possibly trade.

There is one typology which can only be applied after several decades, or even generations, of immigrant settlement have passed. It has been used by Alejandro Portes and Robert Bach and classifies according to totality of migrant assimilation. As their exemplar, Portes and Bach put forward the Eastern European Jew who arrives in America with 'different cultural values and norms then gradually absorbs those of the host society'.[19] This approach cannot be used indiscriminately, since the pace of absorption varies with the individual and is inevitably tempered by colour, creed and cultural heritage. Evaluation can only take place with the passage of time and the benefit of hindsight. Therefore, while we can use this methodology for the Huguenots and Eastern European Jews who settled in Spitalfields and state that they conformed to the assimilationist type, it is far too early in the process of settlement and integration to classify the Bangladeshi immigrants. Additionally, with Britain's apparent transition from a mono-cultural to a multi-cultural society, the definition of assimilation has altered: it is no longer mandatory to eschew all forms of 'difference'. However, the process of absorption is still in its early days and we will have to wait at least a generation before we can make an informed judgement as to the level of assimilation achieved by the Bangladeshi immigrants of the second half of the twentieth century.

Flows and patterns

Flows and patterns are the dynamics of migration, manifestations of the movement of people. A flow can be registered on a map when it becomes apparent that there is a significant movement of people from point A, the 'source', to point B, the 'destination' or first point of settlement. Flow systems can be charted at regional, national, continental and global levels.

The cartography enables us to identify volume and direction; the flow may narrow or widen as the movement increases or decreases in size and pace. Flows are not always mono-directional. History has shown us that they can be circular, counter- or progressive. A circular flow is a phenomenon manifested in seasonal and return migration. It can span generations and can be applied to a group, even if the eventual returnees are not the original migrants but their descendants, as in certain instances with Huguenot return after the French Revolution and some returnees to the Caribbean Islands. A circular flow is not to be confused with a counterflow, whereby the arrival of immigrants, or departure of emigrants, results in the outward or inward movement of others. This latter can be an internal movement – from ghetto to suburb – or transnational from core to periphery, or from periphery to periphery. An example of an internal counterflow is the current movement of Bangladeshis out of west Spitalfields, their replacements being affluent professionals. Transnational counterflows occurred in Portugal and Greece during the second half of the twentieth century when, following the emigration of native labour, it became necessary to replenish the depleted workforce from poorer non-European countries. Migrant Eastern European Jews from Russia or Lithuania created a progressive flow when, while some made London their permanent place of settlement, others, after a temporary stay, dispersed to North America, South America or South Africa.

Patterns of migration are what constitute the flow. A simplified way of describing the coalition of flows, patterns and typologies is to represent the flow as a tunnel or cable, the pattern as the rhythm and form of movement inside the tunnel or cable, the typologies as those individuals or groups creating the pattern. A pattern may be regular or irregular, and may be composed of individuals or groups of varying sizes. What neither the pattern nor the flow can tell us is whether the group or individual moves from one region or country to another for reasons of economic amelioration, political and/or religious freedom or to achieve an improved lifestyle. Without the typological data, we cannot establish whether the migrants are pioneers, part of a pre-existing movement, or a single exodus such as the mass displacement arising from natural disaster, ethnic cleansing or war.

Patterns of migration which recur either spasmodically or regularly over a significant period of time, evolve from information relayed back from the place of settlement to the point of departure. It is the information from the pioneer settlers, transmitted along the networks maintained by families, trade organisations and town and village communities, that initiates a pattern of movement that has been called chain migration.[20] As the threat to religious freedom increased, some sixteenth-century French Calvinist merchants, with established trading connections and a knowledge of England, transferred families and resources across the Channel. Though some returned home in 1598, when the Edict of Nantes was pronounced,[21] others remained, creating links in the chain and the nuclei of future communities. The network and tenuous chain proved lifelines when conditions in France became intolerable. The one-way flow of Calvinists was facilitated by information transmitted along the human network that stretched from England to France. Long before the days of the mass media, mobile phone and World Wide Web, an efficient means of broadcasting life-saving knowledge was activated and a pattern of chain migration put in place. Once the pressure was on, and the decision to leave taken, wherever possible men preceded their wives and families. However, this was not always possible and there are many examples of desperate and destitute entire families, as well as women without their menfolk, arriving in England seeking refuge.

Examining the Eastern European Jewish experience, we can detect similar patterns of chain migration though, in temporal terms, a far more prolonged flow. Jews were readmitted to England in 1656 and, from that date onwards, with the exception of the period of the French wars, there was a steady trickle of Jewish immigrants into Britain from Central and Eastern Europe as well as from Southern Europe and the tip of North Africa. The early networks were serviced by a Jewish diaspora which had been circulating information in, and even beyond, Europe for almost two millennia. By the second half of the nineteenth century, there was an efficient information system operating between Western and Eastern Europe forwarding news about communities and jobs. What was transmitted acted as a beacon for those seeking the promised land, not in spiritual but in economic terms. The message was simple, the *golde medineh*,[22] lay westward. The first point of settlement was often a decisive factor in the lives of migrants. A commentator writing in the late nineteenth century explained that

> the immigrant's future is more or less determined by the sort of trade done at the town where he lands or arrives. He may become a tanner or a dyer in Hull, and have a different ambition from what he would have if he landed at, say Liverpool, Glasgow or London.[23]

By the closing decades of the nineteenth century, the regular stream of migrants moving from east to west had developed into a flood. The pace had accelerated and the flow had broadened. So heavy was the one-way traffic that leaders of the Anglo-Jewish community sought to staunch it, informing those in the Pale of Settlement by all available networks – letter, word of mouth and items in the Yiddish press – that life in England was harsh and that only the fortunate, or ruthless few, made it out of the ghetto. In common with other chains of migration, it was normally young Jewish males who 'came ahead of their families to establish themselves economically'.[24] Yet here, as in the case of the Huguenots, there were exceptions. Single females seeking to escape the hopeless future on offer in the *shtetl* made the journey to England alone, at times falling into the hands of pimps and white-slave traffickers. But neither the threat of the brothel nor the ruthlessness of the ghetto checked the flow. It had become self-sustaining and did not significantly reduce[25] until the combined effects of the First

World War, the short-lived optimism that followed the Russian Revolution and the anti-alien legislation of 1920, brought immigration from Eastern Europe to Britain to a virtual halt.

The network linking the villages of Sylhet with East London can be traced back to the eighteenth century when lascar seamen temporarily spent time in the local seamen's hostel close to the Pool of London. The link between core and periphery became more firmly established during the two world wars. What developed was a perfect example of post-colonial patterns of migration; migrants from the colonies making their way to the 'mother country' metropolis in search of jobs. There is no doubting that the early post-Second World War Bangladeshi arrivals came to Britain as temporary migrants or sojourners, intending to remain for only as long as it would take to earn enough money to return home and buy their piece of land. As we will see below, though some were able to buy the land, few could afford to return and live on it. This conforms to a pattern drawn by Castles and Miller in the early 1990s.[26] In this the short-term migrant comes to recognise that the 'stay' has to be extended and, accordingly, institutes the process of family reunion. Gradually, as wives and children begin to flow in, a new pattern emerges. Once the family unit is established a (more) secure domestic and economic model is created; enlarged family, schooling and, imperceptibly, the transition from sojourner and sojourner's family to resident family. The short term or temporary becomes the permanent. The flow has continued, the pattern alters slightly, but the typologies that create the more recent pattern have changed completely.

The structure of the extended family in the villages of Bangladesh made it most unlikely that unattached women would migrate to Britain as economic pioneers. Those Bengali women who have settled in Spitalfields have been the wives, daughters, at times even mothers, of the pioneers. However, during the past decade, as Bangladeshi women have become more liberated and educated, they have begun to perform as independent players and have themselves become sojourners, carrying out a variety of economic activities, predominantly in the Middle East. In so doing they have initiated female networks which are the engines of a specific gender-based chain of migration.

Place

A sense of place is essential to an understanding of the migrant experience. It is not simply place as the point of departure, as opposed to the point of arrival, but place as the dynamic and organic, changing its nature and superficial appearance and adding layers to its landscape. The following two chapters will examine in detail the points of departure and Spitalfields, the place of arrival. In this section, I wish to consider the abstract point of arrival, most specifically the place that is the migrants' first point of settlement, a space which, because of the peoples that inhabit it, metamorphoses from an integral part of the indigenous local to a self-contained, self-created ethnic ghetto.

In 1928, writing in the introduction to *The Ghetto*, the seminal work by Louis Wirth,[27] one of the founders of the Chicago School of Sociology, Robert Park, described the city as a 'mosaic of segregated peoples', a 1920s' depiction of what we today call a multi-cultural society.[28] Doubtless Park was thinking of Chicago and its diverse ethnic groups, each of which he believed was 'seeking to preserve its peculiar cultural forms and to maintain its individual and unique conceptions of life'.[29] Each group had created its own, self-imposed ghetto, one which was culturally, and often spatially, segregated, marginalised and peripheral to mainstream activity, although frequently a part of it. As Wirth suggests, it was a place of 'transition between old and new world',[30] one in which the inhabitants too often looked only inward and became dependent on their own community, thus voluntarily prolonging their ghettoisation. This is not to suggest that during this period the residents did not undergo a transformation. Change takes place imperceptibly as leakage from outside influences the internal up to the point at which assimilation replaces isolation.

In an alien environment, the outsider will turn inwards, taking comfort and security from the familiar, while attempting to become familiarised with what is strange. Gradually the internalisation will become externalised, as a natural ghetto evolves. The minority group's occupation of a specific space, usually but not always, in a marginalised area of a town or city, is confirmed. Ghettoes, by their form and nature are an urban phenomenon. Once solely associated with diasporic Jews,[31] they are now recognised as spaces where ethnic minorities cluster and where the basic infrastructure is formulated by the ethos of self-help. Over three-quarters of a century ago, Park wrote that the ghetto met a need and performed a social function.[32] His analysis is as true in the first decade of the twenty-first century as it was then, the ghetto of the modern day providing for the cultural, physical and religious needs of those who create and inhabit it. One has only to take a walk through Spitalfields to see the proof. Though the smells, sounds and places of worship are of a different ethnic minority, as Chapter 3 in this volume illustrates, within the ghetto the outsider becomes the insider, the evidence as tangible now as it was in the past.

Wirth suggested that the place and space that was the ghetto represented a prolonged case of social isolation from mainstream society.[33] Yet, in London's East End, as in the Pale of Settlement,[34] the ghetto was rarely completely cut off from the outside world. In order to produce a common economic benefit, interaction between native and immigrant took place. As a result, seepage of language and cultural awareness was inevitable, especially whilst the native (or member of the receiving society) was under no pressure to absorb more than absolutely necessary for any transaction. The immigrant could, and did, determine the pace and extent by which the ghetto walls came down. The ghetto is also a moveable space. As the first- or second-generation immigrants make the move from initial to second point of settlement so their ghetto moves and re-establishes itself. Its outward appearance may change, may exhibit greater affluence and the seeds of integration, but it is still a ghetto. Once again the evidence is to be seen on the streets of the cities and towns of Britain. The Jewish exodus from the East End of London, which was well nigh complete by the late 1950s, did not mark the end of Jewish clustering in the capital. Jewish communities reassembled to the north and northwest of London, predominantly to the boroughs of Barnet and Redbridge and, whilst the differences were not as resonant as those of seventy-five years before, these suburban ghettoes were marked by the food shops and religious centres which served the ethnic minority. Until the twenty-first century, the Jewish ghettoes of Britain had no formal external markers but, in the summer of 2002, for the first time on British soil, though a feature of a number of other metropolitan centres including New York, Washington and Sydney, an *eruv*[35] was erected in the London Borough of Barnet. Constructed according to religious tradition, so as to enable the sick, the elderly, the child-bearing and those with young children to access synagogues and other communal centres on the Sabbath, opposition to the *eruv* was voiced by some Jews opposed to what they believed publicly pronounced an (albeit middle-class) Northwest London Jewish ghetto.

It is too early to comment on the transportation of the Bangladeshi ghetto, but the signs are there as the secondary settlements of Bangladeshi families begin to appear on the routes out of the East End. The Huguenots' story differs; they did not take their 'place' with them. Unencumbered by differences of colour and religion, the exodus from Spitalfields and East London was almost invisible, its process one which demonstrated ongoing assimilation with the mainstream through trade, marriage and church. Clustering was neither necessary nor a feature. Huguenots today are recognisable by their French-sounding surnames.[36] Otherwise there is no means of tracing group progression beyond Spitalfields.

As the pioneer immigrant settles, the seeds of the ghetto are sown. But whilst a physical space is essential, a specified place may not be. For it is the group that occupies place and temporarily transforms the landscape into what it wants it to be. It is the migrants that cluster. Without the immigrant presence, the place that becomes the ghetto remains just another urban space.

The phenomenon

Historians, by tradition, have been more concerned with extracting the phenomena which depict the 'how and why' than in constructing the theories which result from the empirical data.[37] Although the major part of this book is devoted to people, the beef in the sandwich of history, the diversity and complexity of migratory patterns at the dawning of the twenty-first century, together with increasing international concern about the growing numbers of those on the move and their impact on receiving societies, make it essential that we familiarise ourselves with at least some of the theories that attempt to explain the cause and effect of the movement of people. No longer is it possible to concur with Everett Lee's view, published in 1966 that, subsequent to Ravenstein originally presenting his Laws of Migration in 1885 and 1889, 'This [twentieth] century has brought no comparable excursion into migration theory.'[38] Within ten years[39] of Lee's article appearing in the journal *Democracy*, world migratory patterns had undergone significant change, with the result that theorists from a variety of ideological and disciplinary stances had begun formulating hypotheses in an attempt to explain what was happening and why.

Following gently on the heels of the disintegrating old world-occupying empires was the forerunner of their modern counterpart, colonisation by commerce. This was heralded by the arrival of mercantilism during the fifteenth and sixteenth centuries, a system marked by the international movement of goods, funds and people. The transportation of raw materials from the periphery to the core, which enabled the rich in the civilised metropolises of England and the Low Countries to enjoy such delicacies as tea, sugar, nutmeg and cinnamon from the East and West Indies, was accompanied by the movement of people. Some went willingly, from core to periphery to run the sugar and tea plantations, to administrate and teach 'natives' the ways of the civilised western world. Others went unwillingly, forcibly moved from periphery to periphery, occasionally from periphery to core, as slaves. It was a structure, a world system, that enabled England and the Low Countries to benefit economically from the presence of diasporic religious groups such as the Huguenot International and the Jews, particularly Sephardi merchants and bankers.[40] In the 1970s, Immanuel Wallerstein set out to explain what had occurred and its contemporary relevance, comparing and contrasting the earlier world systems with nineteenth- and twentieth-century world economies. Coming from a Marxist or historical-structuralist perspective, he proposed that 'world empires' were single political systems with 'boundaries, structures, member groups, rules of legitimation and coherence'. He considered them self-control systems which, 'held within [themselves] a multiplicity of cultures and an extensive division of labour'.[41] By contrast, the contemporary world economies were operating in 'an area larger than that any political entity can totally control',[42] what in modern parlance tends to be referred to as globalisation. Migration was a major factor, in many ways both cause and effect, of the emergence of world systems in the age of mercantilism and beyond and in the creation and survival of world economies. However, it was not until the penultimate decade of the nineteenth century that a theory was put forward to explain the phenomenon. That early theory, as befitted the prevailing ideology, was liberal in nature and explanation, dealing with the individual, the micro, as opposed to the meso (intermediate agencies operating between the individual and the state, national and supra-national commercial organisations)[43] and the macro, the national economies and empires that were, in reality, the propelling forces.

Classical theory

On 15 March 1885 Ravenstein, in a lecture to the Royal Statistical Society, put forward his 'Laws of Migration'. These have become simplified into what is now known as the classic 'push and pull' theory. Essentially, Ravenstein sought to explain what drove an individual from home or the sending society (point A) to the place of settlement or receiving society (point B). In other words, what were the forces that made 'elsewhere' appear more attractive than 'here'. His individualistic theory assumed that would-be migrants rationally compared the benefits of point B to those of point A. If these proved greater, then the decision must be to migrate. For this reason, according to Ravenstein's theory, the migrant was 'pushed' from home and 'pulled' towards the receiving society. Ravenstein was the first person to attempt to make sense of the phenomenon of migration and did so in response to a chance remark by a member of the Royal Statistical Society, namely that migration appeared to have no laws. Ravenstein's initial set of laws were based on his analysis of the United Kingdom's 1881 Decennial Census. This held no immigration-related demographic shocks, as only 350,800 of the population were recorded as overseas-born, thus leaving 98.99 per cent of the population as native British. Although there had been a gradual increase in the number of Eastern European arrivals,[44] there was no indication of the flood that would burst forth from the pages of the 1891 Census. Ravenstein's interest was in those who had migrated internally as a result of industrial and agricultural innovation and change. It was not until the final decade of the nineteenth century that the alien presence, by that time visibly concentrated in East London, the Leylands of Leeds and the Red Bank district of Manchester, started to arouse tensions and the articulation of concerns about the impact of the Eastern European immigrants on native jobs and homes.

It was the perceptible westward movement of Europeans during the 1880s that encouraged Ravenstein to extend his original study to include Europe and America. In 1889 he produced the follow-up paper.[45] Using the same analytical framework as before, he incorporated some important additional factors. This time he used national population gains and losses as a means of determining whether a country was one of net emigration or immigration. For example, he concluded that between 1851 and 1886 Russia experienced a net population inflow; 1,733,441 immigrants creating as he put it a 'cross-current outflow of 846,931 emigrants'.[46] Taking these facts in isolation, it might have been assumed that Russia was, 'a promised land', for the geographer made no reference to the totalitarian nature of Russian society or its political and religious intolerance, all, as will be shown below, determining factors in the emigration of that Empire's Jews. And it is for his ahistorical approach, his disregard for the socio-political context, political barriers and boundaries in the geography of movement and for analysis based on individualism, that Ravenstein has been criticised.[47]

In spite of the criticisms, Ravenstein does provide us with a starting point from which to evaluate the causes and consequences of migration. Though a number of his 'laws' are no longer of relevance in the post-industrial world, others, such as the phenomenon that, though migrants travel long distances by rail or sea, they tend to settle close to their points of disembarkation, confirm repeated migratory patterns. For example, Spitalfields, only half a mile from the Pool of London and the Docks, has been a first point of settlement for a range of immigrants, including Huguenots, Jews, Indian lascars in the eighteenth and nineteenth centuries as well as later emigrants from the Indian subcontinent arriving by sea. Though Ravenstein informs us that this pattern was not unusual, he provides no historical linkages or data to explain the phenomenon. In spite of theoretical weaknesses and omissions, Ravenstein is most remembered, and indeed most criticised, for what has become known as – though not so labelled by him – the 'push and pull' theory. This was based on the principle of individual rational choice whereby the advantages and disadvantages of staying home were measured against those of moving elsewhere. Ravenstein described the process as follows; if a discontented individual living in an overpopulated region or country with scant resources – the push – identified underdeveloped resources elsewhere which held out the 'promise of remunerative labour' and the possibility of men 'bettering themselves' – the pull – then the rational decision would be to leave home and travel abroad. He further suggested that the pull of economic expectation proved even more powerful than the push of 'oppressive laws, heavy taxation, unattractive climate, congenial surroundings ... even compulsion (slavery)'.[48] In other words, without a positive elsewhere, even under the worst conditions, the individual would not move. This is a questionable thesis. Push and pull in its most basic Ravensteinesque form was homocentric, grounded in economic liberalism, apparently blind to the history of slavery and colonisation and unaware of the immigration controls recently imposed in the United States of America. It presumed that the migratory flow would be from overpopulated to underpopulated regions. The simplistic process of rationally weighing up the good and bad points of home and away and the subsequent physical response has become known as the classic, 'push and pull', theory of migration. Though discounted by some, I would suggest that it at least provides a viable basis from which to start an analysis of the movement of people.

Although basic, we can test the theory against the experiences of our three subject groups. The Huguenots were pushed out of France because of their religious beliefs and drawn, or pulled, to England because of its religious tolerance. However, there is an economic dimension to this equation, that of the knowledge of the financial potential of developing nascent trades such as silk production or starting new ones such as the manufacture of scientific instruments. Jews left Eastern Europe to escape religious persecution and lack of political freedom but most of all because of limited economic expectations. There is no disputing the view that, with the exception of a tiny minority, the migrants from Bangladesh, predominantly from the impoverished region of Sylhet, came to London to 'make their fortunes' and return home 'rich men of high status'. Therefore, in each case, irrespective of the push, economic opportunity exerted a powerful pull and, when economic factors are introduced, classical migration theory moves on to its neo-classical form.

Liberal neo-classical theory

Liberal neo-classical migration theory[49] is Ravenstein taken one, economic, step further. As used by economic theorists such as George Borjas, it retains the individualistic dimension but factors in contingencies such as national boundaries and barriers, individual financial needs and resources, existing national and international immigration policies and would-be host incentives. Borjas suggests that 'individuals migrate because it is in their benefit' [either in terms of physical satisfaction or income] to do so'. He assumes that individuals regard potential host societies as existing in a marketplace where they, the would-be migrants, shop around in order to 'maximize their utility'[50] by making the most effective use of their human capital. Under this theory, state-imposed restrictions on emigration and immigration are perceived as distortions of what is otherwise a rational balance of costs and benefits. Neo-classical migration theory might be described as rational-positivist. It combines the micro and the macro, focusing on the nation-versus-nation advantages and disadvantages of wage and employment conditions, with emigration perceived as an 'individual decision for income maximisation'.[51]

Neo-classical economic theories of migration based on individual rational choice can be criticised for being simplistic and unreliable in forecasting future patterns of migration. In addition, Castles and Miller maintain that they are ahistorical and take no account of networks established by colonisation or the movement and settlement of earlier migrants. Nor do they account for the unpredictability of migratory flows as, for example, the counterflow of migrants to countries such as Greece and Portugal after native labour had emigrated to Western Europe. According to neo-classical theory, the poorest would move to the richest countries and those from densely populated areas would move to more sparsely peopled regions. This has clearly not been the case. The brain drain was a movement from core to core, purely based on economic maximisation, while it was young Sylheti pioneers with access to financial resources that migrated from a severely overpopulated Bangladesh to the overcrowded streets of Spitalfields.

Though the physical act of migration may be singular, carried out by a male member of the household – husband, son, brother or father – the decision to migrate will invariably be collective, taken at family, extended household or village level. For example, in the case of Eastern European Jews and young Bangladeshis, the travel costs would be borne by the family and/or the community. In reality the very poor are rarely amongst those who migrate for economic gain. They move only when there is no option, at the point of a gun or in the aftermath of floods, earthquakes or other natural disasters. It is the very poorest in the most deprived countries that we see on our television screens walking hundreds of miles in the desert in the hope of finding, not jobs and homes, but food and water. For them there are clear push and pull factors, the former starvation, the latter, survival.

The main points of neo-classical migration theory can be summarised as follows:

- International migration of workers resulting from wage differentials between countries;
- Labour markets being the primary mechanism for individual labour flows;
- Control of migration regulated by labour markets in both the sending and receiving societies;
- International free trade;
- Opposite labour flows, skilled, from core to periphery and unskilled from periphery to core;
- Factors in the individual decision-making process including: boundaries, barriers, individual financial needs and resources and receiving-society incentives.[52]

Neo-classical theory appears to operate in a Panglossian, harmonious world in which everything functions in the best possible manner for the potential migrant, even barriers and boundaries. How did the three protagonist groups of this volume perform within the framework of this theory? Irrespective of the barriers imposed by the French monarchy, the economic potential and religious sanctuary offered by England made escape across the Channel worthwhile for some 40,000 Huguenots. Similarly, in spite of the risks, hardship, heartache and policed borders which accompanied the journey from the Pale of Settlement to London, Eastern European Jews still considered it desirable. Eager young Bengali men sought to maximise their economic potential by migrating to a space which, in spite of the colonial ties, was alien and in complete contrast to the rural environment of their home villages. For the French Calvinists, the pull factor was not an opportunity to maximise their economic potential but freedom of religious worship, though the positive prospects for developing skills and industries were not overlooked. For the Jews, Spitalfields was a place of settlement that offered economic prospects and, in addition, freedom of speech and freedom of religion. In each case there was also a clear push factor. However, an economic model is not sufficient. The phenomenon of migration needs to be explored within a much broader framework, one that incorporates the past and the present, the individual and the group, capital and labour.

Historical-structuralist theory

Historical-structuralist migration theory is primarily concerned with labour migrants. It has its roots in Marxist and neo-Marxist theories of political economy and the iniquitous distribution of money and power. It promotes the view that the movement of labour, be it voluntary or involuntary, is the result of capitalist imperialism; the discourse used to describe the phenomenon vested in colonial and post-colonial terminology. Portes and Bach suggest that Marxist migration theory is the 'Analysis of labour migration within the framework of the growth of the capitalist economy . . . part of the struggle between labour and capital that goes beyond national boundaries.'[53] It is a class-based internationalist theory and can only exist within an historical framework. As Wallace has said, 'Understanding the past is crucial to interpreting the present.'[54] As such it is the antithesis of Ravenstein's laws.

The historical-structuralist perspective of migration works best when it is applied in the context of colonial and post-colonial flows. Used as a lens through which to examine the Bangladeshi experience, it explains the movement of labour from periphery to core as the product of the British presence in India. As such it does not take account of the established networks which existed outside of empires and colonies or those which pre-dated colonisation, nor does it incorporate the rational decision-making process based on the maximisation of individual utility. For those who conform to the historical-structuralist approach, these factors would all be a smoke-screen for capitalist string-pulling.

To neo-Marxists the phenomenon of migration is premised on the following principles:

- that labour is human capital and migration is always labour related;
- that all countries of emigration have at some time had colonial links or been a part of that system;
- that analytical and theoretical emphasis is on the historical but restricted to the spheres of empire-building, in either the political or economic form, with the temporal focus predominantly on the colonial and post-colonial eras, i.e. world empires or world economies.

Certain inconsistencies can be elicited from the above. As we know from the section on typologies, migration is not always labour-related. Other causal factors can include religion, sexuality, climate, politics and natural wanderlust. Though Nikolinokas states that 'All emigrant countries were dependent on colonial powers at some time',[55] it is not possible to reconcile the migration of French Calvinists or Eastern European Jews with direct, or even indirect, colonisation by the receiving society, in this instance Britain. What can be agreed is that Marxist theories of migration are most commonly found in discourses on world empires, colonialism and post-colonialism and the movement of those colonised.

Global-transnational theory

According to Wallerstein, the modern world system, that is a capitalist world economy, began in Europe in the sixteenth century with the Dutch and British domination of world trade through shipping. From this came flows of raw material, goods and people from periphery to core, core to periphery and, as previously stated, in the case of the slave trade, from periphery to periphery. The systems became more widespread and complex as the centuries passed. As the post-colonial periphery-to-core migration consolidated, there was the growth of multi-culturalism as well as the fusing of cultures, the latter most evident in the province of food, fashion and music. Political empires wilted and supra-national commercial empires grew in power and influence. Individuality was sacrificed as McDonaldisation took over. The damaging effect of this form of commonality was forecast as early as 1913 by the social scientist and commentator Joseph Jacobs. He was concerned that individual ethnic identity would be lost, pointing to, 'the deadly monotony of dress and furniture which is becoming more and more international'. As he wrote,

> The growth of intercommunication is giving a common set of ideas and ideals to the whole world, and making it more and more difficult for any special culture like the Irish, Japanese or Jewish to hold its own. . . . There would be nothing gained for the world . . . if all were tomorrow to become indistinguishable from their neighbours.[56]

The development of sophisticated means of communication and the growth of corporate power has resulted in the emergence of recent theories relating to the transnational[57] movement of people and the global spread of corporate power. These movements, of high-powered government and corporate actors as well as 'more modest individuals' occur with regularity across national borders.[58] Within this context 'workers are propelled by the dynamics of the transnational capitalist economy'.[59] Castles and Miller[60] suggest that the most important component of transnational migration is human agency, often operating at the meso level, linking the macro with the micro.[61] In recent decades the intermediaries have satisfied both the legal and the illegal, the latter including people-traffickers and smugglers, players who can transform the voluntary, rational decision-making migrant into an involuntary human slave. Members of the transnational community are not those who move elsewhere and send remittances home, sojourners whose migratory experience is intended as impermanent. Nor are they the ones who cross national boundaries in order to arrive at their intended point of –

permanent – settlement. In the lives of transnational players, the actual movement back and forth across borders is central. National boundaries and loyalties are of minor importance. For them the global is the local.

Conclusion

Migrants are people who for one reason or another have moved from a settled environment to one they believe to be preferable and more beneficial. The movement can be voluntary or involuntary, the decision made at leisure or under duress, influenced by any one of a number of factors, the most common being economic enhancement. Those who migrate encompass a spectrum of abilities, from the scientist attracted by the most up-to-date research facilities and funding, the labourer seeking work on building sites in the City of London, through to the desperate prepared to do anything, even pick cockles on the beaches of Morecambe Bay.[62] However, though we may attempt to typecast the immigrant, we must also remember that typologies must not be cast in stone. The legal migrant can easily become the illegal by staying on after the work permit or student visa has expired or holiday terminated. The skilled arrival may, within days, become the unskilled as it becomes apparent that the only work available is cleaning in restaurants and hospitals.

The flow of migrants may be part of a regular pattern, or represent a one-off. It might involve players in a long-running chain of migration or pioneers who may, or may not, initiate a network which will feed yet another chain. What this chapter has shown is that, only by examining the typologies, flows and patterns, is it possible to begin to evaluate the experiences and processes that those migrants have to undergo. For example, from the records of the French churches in London[63] we are able to chart the flow of Huguenot refugees, their patterns of migration and, at the micro and personal level, gender, names, occupations, towns and cities of origin, even dates of departure and size of families. Not all immigrant records are as helpful or as detailed. Yet by using whatever data is available, it should be possible to humanise the statistics and begin to comprehend the processes and pace of settlement and assimilation.

It is clear from above that no one theory can in itself account for the variations in typologies, patterns and flows of migration that have occurred over the centuries. The migration of any one person or group has to be analysed within a broad framework which takes account of the historical and contemporary conditions in both sending and receiving societies. In many instances, this will reveal links which explain the choice of destination. These connections may be diasporic networks, for example those established by the Jews and Huguenots, both of whom were victims of religious persecution. Or they might be the outcome of colonisation which, as in the case of Britain, led to the arrival in the metropolis of labour recruited in the 1950s and 1960s to work on the buses, trains, in the hospitals and in the textile factories of the midlands and north of England. A study of the three subject groups of this book confirms that, in order to understand the migrant experience from sending to receiving societies, we have to be flexible in our approach. With very few exceptions, perhaps slavery or transportation to the death camps, there is always a push factor to counterbalance the pull. The relevant strengths of each and their causal factors represent vital ingredients in our understanding of outcomes.

As this chapter illustrates, the Huguenots, Jews and Bangladeshis form part of a history of migration which began in biblical times and will continue as long as the human race has ambition and mobility. From the above brief outline of the methodologies of migration study, it has become clear that, irrespective of temporal, cultural and religious differences, each group has something in common with the other, as well as characteristics which set it apart. To recognise what the similarities and differences are, and how they affected the process of settlement in Spitalfields, we must start at the beginning, at the point of departure.

Notes

1 See for example J. Samuel, *Migration and Development*, Ottawa, International Development Information Centre, 1998, p. 1.
2 See below, this chapter.
3 J. and L. Lucassen, 'Migration, Migration History, History: Old Paradigms and New Perspectives', in J. and L. Lucassen (eds), *Migration, Migration History, History*, Bern, Peter Lang, 1997, p. 10.
4 See C. Holmes, *Anti-Semitism in British Society 1876–1939*, London, Edward Arnold, 1979, p. 206.
5 A. Bloch, 'It's Not Working: Refugee Employment and Urban Regeneration', in A. Kershen (ed.), *Language, Labour and Migration*, Aldershot, Ashgate, 2000, p. 218.
6 See Chapter 8 below.
7 http://www.ind.homeoffice.gov.uk/default.asp?pageId=3784 (accessed 20 May 2004).
8 It is impossible to quantify the number of illegals in Britain at the time of writing, estimates varying from 100,000 to 750,000.
9 The Aliens Act of 1905 came into operation on 1 January 1906.
10 *Shorter Oxford English Dictionary*, Oxford, Oxford University Press, 2002 edition, p. 2510.
11 J. and L. Lucassen, op. cit., p. 12.
12 Ibid.
13 Ibid., p. 13.
14 R. Cohen, *Global Diasporas*, London, University College Press, 1997, p. 60.
15 Ibid., p. 61.
16 J. Klier, 'What Exactly Was the *Shtetl?*', in G. Estraikh and M. Krutikov (eds), *The Shtetl: Image and Reality*, Oxford, Legenda, published by the European Humanities Research Centre, 2000, pp. 32–3.
17 Cohen, op. cit.
18 Ibid., p. x.
19 A. Portes and R. Bach, *Latin Journey*, Berkeley, University of California Press, 1985, p. 4.

20 See D. Hoerder, 'Segmented Macrosystems and Networking Individuals' in J. and L. Lucassen, op. cit., pp. 73–84.

21 The Edict of Nantes offered Huguenots 'toleration, limited freedom of worship, physical protection and guarantees of a normal social life'. See R. Gwynn, *Huguenot Heritage: The History and Contribution of the Huguenots in Britain*, Brighton, Sussex Academic Press, 2001 edition, pp. 22–4.

22 The golden land.

23 J. Smith, 'The Jewish Immigrant', *Contemporary Review*, LXXXVI, London, 1899, p. 426.

24 L. Vaughan, 'Clustering, Segregation and the "Ghetto": The Spatialisation of Jewish Settlement in Manchester and Leeds in the 19th century', unpublished Ph.D. thesis, Bartlett School of Architecture, University of London, 1999, p. 164.

25 There was a slowing down of arrivals from Eastern Europe in the years following the Aliens Act of 1905 but numbers had started to increase at the beginning of the second decade of the twentieth century, only to be brought to a sudden halt at the outbreak of war in 1914.

26 S. Castles and M. Miller, *The Age of Migration*, New York and Basingstoke, Palgrave Macmillan, 2003 edition, p. 25.

27 L. Wirth, *The Ghetto*, Chicago, University of Chicago Press, 1928.

28 Ibid., p. vii.

29 Ibid.

30 Ibid., p. 129.

31 It is believed that the use of the word ghetto, as an area in which Jews were confined, was derived from a quarter of the city of Venice where Jews lived in the fifteenth century. See Wirth, op. cit., p. 1.

32 Ibid., p.viii.

33 Ibid., p. 4.

34 See Chapter 2 below.

35 An *eruv* is created by selecting a specific area and pinpointing its physical boundary with posts linked by a very fine wire many feet above ground level.

36 For example Bosanquet, Dollond, Olivier and Vigne.

37 See the Lucassens' view of this in J. and L. Lucassen, op. cit., p. 10.

38 E. Lee, 'A Theory of Migration', which appeared in *Democracy* 1966 and is reprinted in R. Cohen, *Theories of Migration*, Cheltenham, Edward Elgar, 1996, p. 15.

39 It is generally accepted that the changes were attitudinal and Eurocentric, largely the result of the 1973 oil crisis.

40 For an account of the readmission of Jews to England in the mid-seventeenth century, see C. Roth, *A History of the Jews of England*, Oxford, Clarendon Press, 1979 edition, Chapter VIII.

41 I. Wallerstein, *The Modern World System*, Vol. 1, New York and London, Academic Press, 1974, p. 347.

42 Ibid.

43 See Castles and Miller, op. cit., p. 28.

44 It should be pointed out that it was not until 2001 that a question regarding religion (and that subject to self-selection) appeared in the Decennial Census. Thus statistics regarding Jews in Britain were collated from figures of synagogue membership and associated births, deaths and marriages and, in the case of those born overseas, between 1871 and 1914, those who were recorded as having been born in Eastern Europe. Thus the figures have to be regarded with caution.

45 E.G. Ravenstein, 'Laws of Migration', *Journal of the Royal Statistical Society*, 52, 1889, pp. 241–305.

46 Ibid.
47 A.R. Zolberg, 'The Next Waves: Migration Theory for a Changing World', *International Migration Review*, 23 (3), 1989, p. 405.
48 Ravenstein, op. cit., p. 286.
49 See G. Borjas, 'Economic Theory and International Migration', *International Migration Review*, 23 (3), 1989, p. 458.
50 Ibid.
51 D.S. Massey *et al.* 'Theories of International Migration: A Review and Appraisal in Population and Development', quoted in Cohen, *Theories*, op. cit., p. 182.
52 See Zolberg, op. cit., p. 407.
53 Portes and Bach, op. cit., 1985, p. 26.
54 I. Wallace, *The Global Economic System*, London, Unwin Hyman, 1990, p. 98.
55 M. Nikolinokas, 'Notes towards a General Theory of Migration in Late Capitalism', *Race and Class*, XVII (1), 1975, pp. 5–17, 10.
56 Quoted in L. Wirth, op. cit., p. 46.
57 See S. Vertovec, 'Conceiving and Researching Transnationalism', *Ethnic and Racial Studies* 22 (2), 1999.
58 A. Portes, 'Conclusion: Towards a New World: The Origins and Effects of Transnational Activities', *Ethnic and Racial Studies*, 22 (2), 1999, p. 464.
59 Zolberg, op. cit., p. 407.
60 In the 2003 edition of their book *The Age of Migration*, Castles and Miller acknowledge the current trend of interdisciplinary theorising and its contemporary relevance. See Castles and Miller, op. cit., p. 27.
61 Ibid., pp. 27, 29–30.
62 In April 2004 some twenty-three illegal Chinese immigrants died whilst picking cockles at Morecambe Bay, Lancashire.
63 Available in the Huguenot Library which is now located in London, NW1.

2 Home

For migrants, even more than for those who do not move far from their place of origin, home is a contested metaphor; a carpet bag of memories, emotions and experiences. It is now but it is then. It is over here yet over there. It is days filled with laughter, love and sunshine but it can also be darkness and threat. Real and tangible yet imagined and mythologised, home is deconstructed on departure and then constantly reconstructed as the migrant experience and lifecycle evolve. Home is all about belonging. It is about being rooted, having a focal point at which to direct hopes, fears, ambitions and the myth of return. But is it? There is also the concept of home at its most powerful in 'absence or negation'.[1] However, if we follow Eric Hobsbawm's contrary precept, we must then ask whether is it only in the diaspora, when distance softens the harshness of reality, that the construction process can begin?

The word home is not easy to define, for in the game of semantics it has a multiplicity of connotations. In feminist literature home is frequently a private place, one concerned with the 'intimate, personal, emotional, domestic and familial'.[2] For some women it is a place of subjugation and exclusion where they live out their hidden and other lives, a place which those used to life in a liberal and egalitarian society may find shocking and oppressive. For example, young Bengali women from Spitalfields may discover on their (temporary) 'return' to Bangladesh that, rather than the dream relayed to them by their parents, home is a place where the female is marginalised and subservient. Both male and female Bengali teenagers are reported as having been disillusioned by what they have found on returning 'home'. As Gardner and Shukur revealed in the early 1990s, 'The myth of beauty, food and trees heavy with fruit' was not quite the reality, instead the young people were faced with 'a lack of privacy, insects and mud',[3] a place, where now, in the twenty-first century, many homes have no electricity or running water and television sets run on car batteries. Others, visiting for the first time have, 'loved it absolutely. . . . After this first trip I've changed, I don't know, it's like I've discovered new things about myself, about my roots, my identity'.[4] Even the older Bangladeshis find on return that home, as they remembered it, no longer exists; both it and they have changed, and can never be the same again. For others, home was, and is, a place where colonial subjection left the indigenous, colonised population with no rights.[5] The act of colonisation alienated its subjects and removed them, metaphorically, from their roots, thus fusing the colony and, what would become for many in the future, the receiving society.

Conversely, there is the construction of home in the public space: a territorial concept, as for example, home(land) as a metaphor for nation or region, *mon pays* as the Huguenots would have recognised it. Thus home may become a fusion of myths accumulated in a remembered landscape which may itself be more imagined than real. Following this theme, it is possible to suggest that, for the Huguenots, *their* France was an 'imagined community' and, as such, one that could be deterritorialised and spatially and temporally transported elsewhere.

Rapport and Dawson have referred to home as the 'normality',[6] but this only begs the questions, which home and what normality? Is it that which has been left behind due to religious persecution, as in the case of the Huguenots, or as the result of the combination of economic and religious persecution, as was the case for many late nineteenth-century Eastern European Jews? In this context the experience of these two groups necessitates further clarification. Is their normality to be defined as peace and security or threat and hardship? In addition, we must determine whether 'home' was the family collective recently departed or, as in the case of religious Jews, the mythologised spiritual homeland exited more than 2,000 years ago. It is clear from the above that there is no single, or simple, definition of home. It is a term of reference which is still under debate and, though all of us experience it, we cannot always accurately define what it means to us in either the real or the imagined world.

Myths and realities

The common denominator in the experience of all emigrants is the departure from home that begins the journey from that which is familiar to that which is foreign. Stowed away in the baggage is a remembrance of that which has been left behind. Over time this becomes an edited memory which may soften, or eventually exclude, all that is harsh, cruel and disagreeable, leaving the gentle, the happy and the kind in the forefront of the mind. These memories are transported by the individual and, as home and community evolve, incorporated by the group.

Joly and Cohen, writing in 1989, suggested that 'Immigrants cherish the myth of return . . . for refugees the possibility of returning home is less feasible.'[7] But this should not presuppose that refugees do not cherish the myth of return. For the dispossessed and persecuted the myth is based on a land free from persecution and persecutors. Who could doubt the Huguenot longing to return to *leur patrie, leur pays, leur foyer*,[8] their land, their hearth, their home, an idealised *pays* where Calvinists would not be persecuted for their religious beliefs. However, the Catholic French monarchy maintained its ban on Calvinism until the year before the Revolution. During this time the Huguenot myth of return faded and, as the decades passed, many French Calvinists living in London transferred their national and religious allegiance to the British crown and the English church.

For late nineteenth-century Eastern European Jewry, diaspora was its middle name. Accordingly, the location and definition of home is not straightforward. Was it to be found in the towns, villages and cities of the Pale of Settlement or in the biblical land from which Jews were exiled almost two millennia before? Wherever they were in the diaspora, Jews prayed for a return to their spiritual homeland. Until the emergence of political Zionism towards the end of the nineteenth century, the myth of return was solely a religious construct. Even after Herzl had called for a Jewish state, ultra-orthodox Jews believed (and still believe) that the true 'return' would follow the coming of the Messiah; then, and only then, could a religious homeland be constructed. Ultra-orthodox Jews gave little credence to the concept of a secular political state. For them the myth of return was a sacred dream.[9] Accordingly, the majority of Eastern European Jews migrating westward carried two myths with them, one of return and one of home, the latter incorporating a selection of religious, domestic and economic ingredients which could be fused into a fulfilling existence in the elsewhere. Whatever the dreams of the emigrants, home, in its material and physical form, was the *shtetl*, for those who settled in East London, it became a *shtetl* called Spitalfields. As the journey west began, so did the construction of the myth, not from bricks and cobblestones but from

> The people who live in it, not the place or the buildings or the street. 'My home is the family and the family activities, not the walls or the yard or the broken-down fence … essentially the house remains a temporary dwelling, inhabited for a brief moment of history.'[10]

Once settled in the west, the myth of return became, for some Eastern European Jews, a remote dream, for others it remained a religious imperative. For all, the myth of home was a building block in the process of assimilation and settlement.

The mythologised *desh*[11] was the space in which the material proceeds of the pioneering Bangladeshis' short sojourn in the *bidesh*[12] would become manifest. Land ownership is a vital status symbol for Bangladeshis and 'is held in an almost mystical regard'.[13] In the early years of their overseas settlement, for many migrants from the Indian subcontinent, the myth of home was inseparable from the myth of return. Muhammad Anwar's *The Myth of Return*[14] records that Pakistani immigrants initially perceived themselves as sojourners who would soon earn enough money to enable them to return home and 'buy land [and] build better houses and to raise their social status'.[15] For the Bangladeshis who came to Britain in the late 1950s and

1960s, the myth of return was structured with economic bricks. The commitment to send regular remittances to Bangladesh[16] combined with low wages and/or unemployment in Britain meant that few of the pioneers were able to transform the myth into reality. The *bidesh*, the elsewhere, became another home, a pluralised home, one which was, at the same time, a stone-built house in Sylhet and an overcrowded flat in a high-rise block, or multi-occupancy, in Spitalfields.

All those who make the journey from the 'place of one's dwelling and nurturing, with its associations'[17] to elsewhere, carry with them memories and images which are packaged in semantics. For those in the English-speaking world, the predominant word is *home*, a derivative from the Old High German *heim*, thus the Yiddish *heim*.[18] For Bangladeshis the word is *desh*. As with the English word home, both *heim* and *desh* incorporate a multiplicity of meanings and emotions: the habitual family dwelling, the household, a place of nurturing, a village, a region or a state; the essence of rootedness. The words conjure up memories of childhood and, invariably, feelings of mothering, tenderness, warmth and security; experiences both real and imagined. *Der heim* was not just a basic dwelling in a *shtetl* in the Pale of Settlement, it was where 'being Jewish' happened. It was reality, but also part of a myth, one encrusted with a patina gathered during hundreds of years of dispersal. Eastern Europe encapsulated the myth and reality for the deracinated Ashkenazi Jews who found themselves in Spitalfields. In the minds of dispersed Bangladeshis, particularly those who had made the journey from Sylhet, the *desh* summoned up similar images and emotions. These were dominated by powerful kinship relations, the network of dwellings and the nexus of support. Yet there is one overwhelming difference between the Jewish arrivals of the late nineteenth century and those coming from the Indian sub-continent almost 100 years later. Unlike the wandering Jews who would never own the land upon which their *shtetleich* stood, or truly belong to the nation that did, for Bangladeshis, after 1971, the *desh* was their nation and their state. One for which they had fought a very bloody civil war.

Within the French language there is no singular equivalent to the word home. Instead the language offers a range of nouns from which the speaker or writer can select the most appropriate for the job in hand, including *patrie, pays, foyer, maison*. Such variety acts as a barrier to the creation of the emotional image that is projected from 'home'. As a result we are forced to question the semantic wrapping of the Huguenots' transported emotions and memories. Was there a clear-cut differentiation between the territorialised yet mythologised homeland? Between 'The cultural hearth ... and geographic cradle', as described by an unknown late twentieth-century Uzbek poet,[19] and the private and personal space in which the day-to-day living and nurturing took place? Sadly, little evidence remains to enable us to provide an accurate answer. We can only suppose that, irrespective of language, in common with the other subject groups in this book, the emotions conjured up by the thoughts and descriptions of 'home' are global.

The migrant experience does not begin with disembarkation, nor embarkation, with the first point of settlement or even the point of departure – it starts in the heart of the sending society and is linked to that country's prevailing economic, political and religious climate and culture. The decision-making process may take months or minutes, be made under duress or after a period of relaxed rational thought allowing for a calm consideration of the advantages and disadvantages of emigration. It is rooted in past memories and experiences, in future expectations, and, at times, in fear. In attempting to comprehend and analyse the processes of assimilation as experienced by Huguenots, Jews and Bangladeshis in London's Spitalfields district, it is imperative to provide an impression of the ambience of the sending society. We need to acquire a basic knowledge of life 'over there' in order to make some sense of the migrants' choice of destination and patterns of settlement in the elsewhere. That is what this chapter sets out to do.

Profitable strangers?

Calvinism evolved out of Martin Luther's Wittenberg Challenge of 1517. In 1521 Lutheranism was declared 'pernicious' by the Sorbonne in Paris and subsequently French religious reformers began to look towards Switzerland where Zwingli, Farel and John Calvin had settled. In 1536 Calvin published his *Institutes of the Christian Religion* and brought discipline and direction to what, at the time, was a somewhat disorganised sectarian Protestant alternative. The doctrine was a 'discipline of life' and embraced the religious, social and economic. It was one which would be powerfully manifest in the development of Huguenot society in England. Calvinism was a puritanical form of religion which taught reverence, chastity, sobriety, frugality, industry and honesty. It encouraged the glorification of God through good works and achievements. As such it was the progenitor of the 'Protestant work ethic'. The Puritan ethos extended to sobriety of dress, though, as suggested by William Hogarth's 1736 caricature painting, *Noon, L'Église des Grecs, Hog Lane, Soho*, this ordinance was not always followed.[20] However, for those disillusioned with the lavishness, laxity and controls of Catholicism in France, Protestantism, most particularly that propounded by John Calvin, was perceived as a viable and valid alternative for Frenchmen for whom religion was an intrinsic part of their lives.

Nine years after the *Institutes* first appeared, the first French Calvinist community was established in Meaux. By 1559 there were seventy-two Calvinist temples in France, a sufficient number to warrant the calling of a national Calvinist synod. By the the next year, the French followers of John Calvin had been given the epithet Huguenot. The origins of the title are unclear. Nicola Sutherland suggests that it devolved from the Swiss word *Eidguenot*, the name given to the Swiss alliance formed to oppose the Savoyard prince-bishop,[21] accordingly becoming associated with independence from Catholicism. In France, the application of the word Huguenot, even as late as the nineteenth century, was intended as a pejorative, and at times was used as a direct insult.[22] By contrast, in England, the title was intended to imply respect for a God-fearing, hard-working people, 'profitable strangers' as they were sub-titled.

By the time of the national synod, Calvinist communities had been established in Normandy, Ile de France, Languedoc and Gascogny. French Calvinists covered the spectrum of social classes, the sole exception being the peasantry who remained staunchly Catholic. The French nobility were well represented amongst the RPR or *Religion Prétendue Reformée* (a name given to Calvinism). Members of the houses of Bourbon, Condé and Chatillon all supported the teachings of Calvin. And it was the nobility who, in the last half of the sixteenth century, were responsible for Calvinism becoming politicised and, as such, the catalyst for the thirty years of a civil war that raged on and off from the mid-1560s until the 1590s. It was the controls imposed upon them during this time, and most particularly the shocked outrage which followed the Massacre of St Bartholomew's Day in 1572, which drove the earliest religious refugees across the Channel to seek sanctuary from the Protestant English monarch. From the beginning of the 1560s, with Elizabeth I on the throne, England was seen as a place of sanctuary for Protestants fleeing the Low Countries and France (in the context of the Protestant refugees, in those early days, it was difficult to separate one nationality from the other).[23] Those who arrived prior to the proclamation of the Edict of Nantes in 1598, established nuclear communities in London, Canterbury, Dover, Norwich and Southampton. It was these early arrivals who laid down religious and communal foundations for the French men, women and children, who, from 1670 onwards, would look to England as a refuge from the increasingly severe persecutions of the monarchy and church in their beloved France.

The Peace of Monsieur in 1576 was the herald of a shortlived, but more equable, time for the French Calvinists. Accordingly, emigration slowed down, some immigrants even returning to France. In 1598, Henri IV, the king some referred to as the Huguenots' protector, issued the Edict of Nantes.[24] This gave religious equality to the dissenters who, by this time, had established their own garrison towns and general assembly. The Edict was arguably not so much a peace as 'an armistice',[25] which pulled together the various privileges guaranteed the Huguenots following outbreaks of fighting during the thirty years of civil war. The Edict provided complete civil equality, i.e. no exclusions from institutions, guilds, trades or professions on the basis of religion. In addition, it stipulated in which nobles' castles and churches religious meetings could be held and also imposed certain controls on the printing and publishing of religious works. In reality, the Edict created a 'Protestant state within a state',[26] one controlled by the nobles who had adopted Calvinism. By the end of the sixteenth century, Calvinism in France had become a political entity with the religious dimension subjugate. The twenty-five years that followed the death of

Henri IV saw a reversion of the status of the Huguenots. A series of unsuccessful rebellions under the Regency and the subsequent rule of Louis XIII, resulted in a deterioration of the political and military situation of the Calvinists. In 1626, following the siege of La Rochelle, the Catholics gained control of what had been a Calvinist stronghold. Defeat was a signal for those aristocrats who had seen Calvinism as a political tool to leave the sinking ship and transfer their loyalties to the king and Catholicism. Once the political threat was out of the way, the tensions subsided and there followed thirty years of what has been called the 'halcyon period' for the French Protestants. It was during those three decades that the Huguenot population of France prospered in commerce and industry.

The most popular commercial activity for the French Calvinists was silk production. Huguenots were engaged at all economic and skill levels of the industry, from designing to advances in weaving which included lustring, alamoles and flowered silks, down to the most basic manufacturing processes. Patterned silks were produced in Lyons and Tours and lustrings in Nîmes. In addition, Calvinists manufactured felt hats in Caudebec in Normandy. They were also gunsmiths, bootmakers, hairdressers, watchmakers, clockmakers, goldsmiths and silversmiths, furniture-makers and soldiers. Huguenot economic activity covered a spectrum of skills, trades and professions integral to the French way of life and seemingly essential to the economic structure of the country. 'In towns such as Nîmes, La Rochelle, Caen and Rouen, Calvinist notables and businesses dominated urban life',[27] many growing influential and wealthy. Working harder and playing less than their Catholic counterparts, they built up businesses and homes which were the temporal manifestations of their glorification of God. At the same time they aroused antagonisms which would, in less than three decades, make their lives as Calvinists unendurable. As German Jews would 300 years later, the Huguenots believed themselves to be secure in their well-being, convinced it was the natural right of those who saw no conflict between nationality and religion. But this was not the French Catholic view, for though in reality the religious minority was harmless, as the years passed and their wealth and piety increased, the Huguenots of France became objects of fear.

The thirty years of tolerance, which have been called '*le protestantisme en léthargie*',[28] ended in 1661 with the death of Mazarin. Louis XIV personally took over the governance of France. According to Mettam, the transition began slowly, for though Louis 'took an interest in the question of Huguenots', they were not perceived as a primary problem and, initially, a policy of gentle conversion to Catholicism was pursued, the objective being a nation that was universally French Catholic.[29] However, by the end of the 1660s, warning lights had come on. Forty-nine new regulations inhibiting RPR activity were published. Few Huguenots took defensive or protective action. It is easy for historiographers, with the benefit of hindsight, writing long after the events, to criticise or wonder why those being persecuted for

their race or religion do not escape before it is too late. In spite of discrimi-
natory restrictions, Huguenots showed a reluctance to relinquish their
quality and style of life. Many stayed put. There were, however, some perspicacious Huguenots. They departed for England, Holland, Germany or
Switzerland, taking with them family and property. It was they who created
the commercial, religious and charitable infrastructures needed to support
the impoverished co-religionist immigrants who came later.

By 1679, King Louis's supporters had come to believe that the Calvinists
were a threat to the monarch and to Catholic France. The consensus was that
their wings must be clipped. This begs the question, if they were economically essential and unconfrontational, why were the Huguenots persecuted?
Cataloguing the 'rationalization of intolerance', Geoffrey Adams has singled
out the different aspects of Huguenot behaviour which gave rise, at times, to
understandable opposition.[30] They were varyingly perceived by their opponents as: advocating republicanism; being heretical, fanatical, intolerant and
self-righteous; being engaged in treason and sedition; having excessive
wealth. Those who found their way to England later provided ample evidence of the inaccuracy, if not treachery, of those scare-mongering assess-
ments. However ill founded the accusations, the king and his supporters
were determined to eliminate the Huguenot presence. As Louis became
increasingly absorbed with religion and 'French Catholicism', in a climate of
increasing terror, monarch and state adopted a policy of aggressive proselytisation, or exclusion. From 1679 onwards, Huguenots were gradually
excluded from public employment, the legal professions, medicine, mid-
wifery and the publishing and selling of books. Mixed marriages – between
Catholics and Calvinists – were forbidden and previous legal guarantees
given by Richelieu were withdrawn. Huguenot temples were ordered to be
destroyed and conversion to Catholicism rewarded. The conversion of children of seven and under was particularly encouraged. Still worse was to
come. By 1681, the Dragonnades had begun. This was a system under
which French soldiers were billeted exclusively with the Huguenot section
of society. The pressures were financial and physical. The cost to Calvinist
families was crippling and brutality was officially encouraged. Emigration
was forbidden. If discovered, punishment for men was virtual slavery on
board French naval galleys and, for women, imprisonment. Although the
general date for the mass movement of Huguenots from France to England
and other destinations is usually taken to be that of the formal revocation of
the Edict of Nantes in 1685, in reality Calvinists were seeking refuge from
1679 onwards.

For true believers the pressures applied by the French king and his army
on the Huguenots reinforced their faith that Calvinism was the only way to
live a rewarding temporal, as well as spiritual, existence. In the face of such
divinely led determinism, Louis saw the only option as being the cancella-
tion of the Edict of Nantes. The revocation of 1685 was, in reality, a
summary of all the prohibitions that had been put in place piecemeal in the

preceding six years, plus a few extra touches. Under the revocation, there were to be no Protestant services held in public or in private and laymen were forbidden to emigrate and/or remove their property from France. All those who had already left the country illegally were 'invited to return'. If they did not, their property would be confiscated. All ministers who refused to convert were exiled. All children born to Huguenot parents were to be forcibly baptised. There was one concession, all Calvinists who chose to remain in France could do so freely, providing they did not hold any religious services or meet for any religious purposes. As with other outlawed religions there were three options: escape, proselytise or go underground.

This book is concerned with those Huguenots who, either with the time to make a rational decision, or with the Dragonnades at their door, found their way to England, to London and thence to Spitalfields. What pull did England have? Once Queen Elizabeth I was on the throne, Protestant England became a beacon in a Catholic world. Elizabeth Labrousse suggests that the French Calvinists were not fully aware of the degree of antipathy felt by the Protestant Church of England towards Calvinism. She writes that, 'they were blissfully unaware of the fact that the Church of England was far from feeling towards them an unqualified friendliness'.[31] However, even if the Huguenots were unaware of the hostility felt towards them by certain members of the English Protestant church, we can still question why London, which was at the end of a perilous and often unpleasant journey by sea and land, was selected as a place of refuge. In other words, why cross the Channel? The answer lies in the economics of migration. Perceived economic opportunity undoubtedly played a significant part in the decision-making process. In the Huguenot world, religion and economic activity were intertwined.[32]

The Royal Charter for the establishment of the French 'Strangers' church in Threadneedle Street was issued in 1550. This enabled the early French Calvinists who settled in England in the second half of the sixteenth century to lay down the future community's religious foundations. With these in place they could, with confidence, put down communal and economic roots. French and Walloon Protestants established textile manufacturing centres along the east and south coasts of England and, by so doing, began the transformation of the English clothing industry.[33] Queen Elizabeth I's Privy Council was quick to recognise the advantages of a Huguenot presence and so was eager to grant concessions to those who might prove beneficial to the country's economy, most particularly those engaged in silk-weaving in London. Indeed, it was the nascent, and basic, English silk-weaving industry which attracted merchants and weavers from the regions of Normandy, Tours, Poitou and Lyons. We can only assume that entrepreneurs recognised the potential in introducing the more complex methods of production while artisans saw job opportunities.

By the mid-seventeenth century, the English economy again needed revitalising. The readmission of the Jews to England by Cromwell in 1656 was a decision as much motivated by an awareness of the benefits Sephardi Jewish merchants could bring to the country's international trading status as by the Lord Protector's belief in the second coming of the Messiah.[34] Further confirmation of the country's weak industrial infrastructure came from an Act of Parliament passed in 1665 to encourage the entry of skilled immigrants from overseas. For Huguenots in France who could read the writing on their domestic walls, an opportunity to develop nascent industries in a country that was sympathetic to a dissenting religion was a powerful draw. Linguistic familiarity was another feature of the 'pull' towards England. A number of merchants in Bordeaux and Normandy were 'exceptional in their knowledge of English; they often exchanged their sons for a year or two with their London counterparts, so that each had a second language'.[35] Therefore, not only did the Huguenots have established trading links with England, but also one of the major stumbling blocks to assimilation, that of language disability, had been removed in advance.

As stowaways or hidden passengers on board a ship crossing the Channel, the actual mechanics of escape were relatively easy. As religious discrimination increased, some prescient Calvinists sent family and property to England, to lay the foundations for their future comfort and security. The image of England as a safe and welcoming haven was formally confirmed in 1680 when Charles II, upon learning of the bestiality of the Dragonnades, proclaimed England a 'place of refuge for the Huguenots'. In the following year, he issued a Brief for the collection of monies for those needy French refugees. In November 1685, following the revocation, a further Brief was issued, albeit 'with extreme reluctance' by the Catholic King James II, who had come to the throne only nine months earlier.[36] It might be argued that these Royal interventions were forerunners of state aid for (welcome) asylum seekers.

Some Huguenots, with the benefit of time on their side and an opportunity to consider all options rationally, resolved to emigrate. Others made the same decision but in fear and haste. Whichever the case, the reality was that England was foreign but not that foreign; the culture was different but not that different; while the immigrants' language was dissimilar but one English nobility respected and valued. Amongst the refugees were those who found work as French tutors to the sons and daughters of the gentry. (An ability to speak French was, and remained for centuries to come, a manifestation of social status and gentility.) Economically, England offered commercial, manufacturing and professional opportunities. Refugee French soldiers, homesick for service but no longer willing, or able, to serve the country of their birth, were welcomed into the English army. English sympathisers offered charity to those forced to leave all behind them and, most significantly, England offered refugees the freedom to practise Calvinism. To Huguenots on the other side of the Channel, England was a beacon of promise, a land in which they would find a welcome. However, as the refugees would discover, at times that welcome wore very thin.[37]

As with any migratory flow, it is impossible to provide an accurate estimate of the numbers of Huguenots who fled France for England in the sixteenth and seventeenth and indeed eighteenth centuries, for it was not until the Edict of Toleration in 1787 that Huguenots felt safe in France. Some 10,000 to 15,000 settled in England between 1550 and the end of the sixteenth century whilst, in the seventeenth and eighteenth centuries, it is estimated that between 35,000 and 40,000 sought refuge, the largest volume of migrants arriving some eighteen months after the revocation. Of the total number of Calvinist arrivals, it has been estimated that some 20,000 settled in Spitalfields. As the chapters ahead will illustrate, the 'frogs', as they were pejoratively called, initially established their economic, domestic and religious bases at the eastern edges of the City of London. As the decades passed, these strangers gradually assimilated into the receiving society, Calvinism fusing with, and then being suffused by, English Protestantism. Parish records reveal that the third and fourth generations of Huguenots began giving their children English first names, some even anglicised their surnames for ease of use.[38] Spoken French all but disappeared, and the second phase of migration, the movement out of the ghetto that was Spitalfields, began.

By the second half of the nineteenth century, the manifest French character of Spitalfields had all but disappeared, though the landscape retained the Huguenot signature. The French Strangers had moved on and, by the 1850s, all that remained of the once despised noise of the frogs was a patois used by old women in Bethnal Green 'which was scarcely recognisable as French'.[39] The Gallicans, who had chosen religion as opposed to country, had gone through the painful experience of self-deracination and transferred their Protestant work ethic, high moral standards and love of *pays* to the land which gave them refuge.

A *shtetl* state of mind?

The next major wave of migrants into Spitalfields came from Eastern Europe. They were not the first Jews to settle in East London since King Edward I expelled the Jews in 1290.[40] Jews had been readmitted to England by Oliver Cromwell in 1656 and, since that date, there had been a steady inward trickle of both Sephardim and Ashkenazim.[41] Whilst the immigration of Sephardic Jews had slowed down almost to a halt by the mid-eighteenth century, there had been a continuing inflow of Ashkenazim, their migration disturbed only by the French wars. During the closing decades of the nineteenth century, the trickle developed into a flood as Jews from Eastern Europe, part of the great, late nineteenth-century westward migration, looked for their promised land. They sought a destination which offered financial opportunity in an environment of religious and political freedom. For the majority, the *golde medineh* was America, for a small minority, Britain was, if not the golden land, then the silver land. The accelerated movement of Russian and Russo-Polish Jewry was not, as some have suggested, principally because of the terror of the pogroms. As John Klier explains, 'It is another myth of Jewish history that the substantial outmigration of Jews from the Russian Empire was caused primarily by physical pogroms and "legislative pogroms".... It was demographic and economic pressure.'[42] In reality, the Eastern European Jews were escaping hunger, reduced economic opportunity and, for many, unemployment. They left behind them poverty and hopelessness; they brought with them a mythical construction of *der heim* and memories of a life which can only have existed through the lens of rose-tinted glasses. In truth, for all but a small, elite bourgeoisie, the quality of life for the Jews of Eastern Europe in the nineteenth century – 60 per cent of the world's Jewish population – was one of continuing deterioration. In order to appreciate the downward spiral of misery, disillusion and despondency that marked life in the Pale of Settlement in the nineteenth century, we have to look back more than 200 years.

During the middle ages, Ashkenazi Jews migrated eastward from central Europe. By the middle of the seventeenth century, the Jewish population of Poland and Lithuania totalled some 300,000.[43] For those living in Commonwealth Poland, it was 'Heaven for Jews, Paradise for nobles, hell for serfs.'[44] In an atmosphere of benevolent tolerance, Jews were encouraged to interact commercially with their Christian neighbours whilst retaining their socio-religious separatism. The golden period ended with the Khmelnitskii massacre of 1648, when the Cossacks rose up against their Polish (Catholic) overlords. To the Cossacks, Jews were no different to the Poles and thus to be given no quarter.

In the century that followed, Jews in Lithuania enjoyed continuing autonomy and tolerance. However, the Jewish population of the Polish Commonwealth was subject to conflict and disruption. Stability was gone, its successor economic and physical insecurity. The cracks in the Polish kingdom which had opened up in the seventeenth century enlarged until, in the closing decades of the eighteenth century, the Commonwealth disintegrated. In 1772, 1793 and again in 1795, it was partitioned, each time the spoils being shared by Russia, Austria and Prussia. As a result of the partitions, the major portion of the Jewish population was absorbed by a somewhat reluctant Russian Empire. For a brief honeymoon period, the Jews of Russia enjoyed equality with their Christian counterparts. Unsurprisingly, tolerance was rapidly replaced by fear and oppression and the century that followed became one of physical and economic constriction, increasing urbanisation, and government policies which combined ethnic separation with Russification. The status of Russian Jews was confusing. They were 'recognised in law as Russian subjects, although technically they were classed with the category of subjects known as *inorodtsy* (aliens), most of whom were pastoral and semi-nomadic peoples in Siberia and Central Asia'.[45] As such, they enjoyed none of the rights or responsibilities of subjects or citizens of enlightened democracies. But then neither did many of the Russian-Christian population who were subjects of the tsar, even though some had more privileges than others. In spite of their rather dubious status, Klier suggests that 'Russian Jews made a show of loyalty to the Empire ... the more acculturated they became, the more patriotic.'[46] This form of patriotism, and loyalty to the tsar, was manifested by some right up until the 1917 revolution. It was a pattern of behaviour condemned by many Russian Jewish leaders. Irrespective of their loyalties, from the reign of Empress Catherine through to the fall of the House of Romanoff, Russian Jews were perceived as a problem. Throughout the nineteenth century, the solution to the problem was sought by a combination of carrot-and-stick tactics with, inevitably, the emphasis on the latter.

Between 1797 and 1917, 140 restrictive statutes were passed regarding the Jews in Russia, statutes which 'were not based on race or nationality but solely on religion'.[47] Under Empress Catherine, autonomous self-government was limited; the use of Yiddish and Hebrew prohibited; and the Jewish population confined to an area, predominantly to the south and west of Russia which, by 1835, covered 362,000 square miles and included Lithuania, Vilna, Volhynia, Podolia, Ukraine, Crimea, Lublin and Lodz.[48] However, the day-to-day administration of controls was poor and there were opportunities for evasion. There were also exceptions. An elite class, including certain favoured merchants and industrialists, was permitted access to cities such as Moscow and St Petersburg. It should be noted however that, whilst the creation of the Pale of Settlement features high on the list of Russian-Jewish disadvantages, it spread over a prosperous area and contained the important fairs and trade routes of Western Russia.[49]

Tsar Nicholas I, Catherine's grandson, who succeeded his elder brother Alexander I in 1825, adopted an even harsher policy towards the Jewish population. In 1836, he ordered all Hebrew printing presses to be closed down and, nine years later, banned the wearing of traditional Jewish dress. Under Nicholas's rule, in the period from 1827 until 1856, Jewish military service was at its most severe. Young Jewish boys, arbitrarily conscripted to the army from the age of twelve, could be forced to serve for anything up to twenty-five years in conditions under which adherence to Jewish religious practice was virtually impossible.

As we will see below, both directly and indirectly, Russian government policy adversely affected the economic life of the Jewish population. And it was not only the lower classes who suffered. During the 1870s, controls were imposed upon those who engaged in legal and military careers. The assassination of Alexander II in 1881 and the discovery that a young Jewish girl had been one of those involved in the plot, resulted in a series of pogroms which, though not organised by the state, found very little official opposition. The state's reaction to the so-called 'Jewish involvement' was the issuing of the May Laws in 1882. These were a series of prohibitions further restricting Jewish movement and activity. The traditional rural/urban split of the Jewish population was no longer to be tolerated. Even though for some time Jews had been restricted to living at least thirty-five miles from the borders of the Pale, they were now to be urbanised and no longer permitted to live outside the limits of small towns and cities. They were banned from renting or purchasing rural properties and, in specified cities, certain categories of Jews could only obtain temporary residence. In other cases, Jews could only live on one side of a street. By the last decades of the nineteenth century, nearly all Russian Jewry was living in 'a pale within a pale' but, unlike the Huguenot state within a state, this was not of Russian Jewry's choosing and certainly not to their benefit.

The urbanisation of the Jews of the Russian Empire has been recorded by Ezra Mendelsohn. He shows that, between 1802 and 1897, the urban Jewish population of Belorussia-Lithuania, which included cities such as Minsk, Kovno, Pinsk and Grodno, grew from 16,802 at the beginning of the nineteenth century to 200,152 at the century's close. The largest increase took place in the closing decades.[50] The remainder of the Jewish population lived in the *shtetls* and it was the immigrant's mental construction of the *shtetl* that was exported. As Klier defines it, the *shtetl* was 'any settlement inhabited by Jews' except for the big cities.[51] In a recent article, he explores the complexity of the construct of the *shtetl*, one which defied geographic parameters or specific locations. It was a myth created by those who had lived in it. They packaged it, took it overseas and passed it down to future generations. The *shtetl* was not simply a dot on a map – it was 'a state of mind', a stronghold of Ashkenazi culture incorporating both the rural and the urban. It was where Jews 'spoke Yiddish, wrote and read Hebrew and bargained in broken Polish and Ukrainian'.[52] It represented the essence of the memories transported by migrants to the modern cities of the Pale, such as Odessa, Warsaw and Lodz, and to the East End of London and New York's Lower East Side.

Those who lived outside the Pale believed the *shtetl* to be a ghetto[53] where little interaction took place between different religions and races. In other words, it was an enclosure of Jews. As a consequence, it was thought that the interaction which occurred between Jews and non-Jews in the towns and cities of Britain and America was something novel, something Jews had not experienced before. This was not the case. *Shtetl* life served both Jews and non-Jews. In the *shtetl*, 'Jews were never isolated from the non-Jewish population'.[54] Even when Jews were in the majority, there was a frequent influx of Christians from outside for markets and fairs and, though the language of the Pale was Yiddish, there were Jews who spoke Russian and Polish. In addition, there were Russians and Poles who could communicate in Yiddish. Linguistic interface was a fact of life for many Jews in the Pale. In spite of this local interaction, some commentators believe that the Jews of Eastern Europe were essentially a village people. For example, Zborowski and Herzog state that 'until the late nineteenth century a very large proportion of the *shtetl* population grew up in ignorance of the world beyond'.[55] The veracity of this statement is questionable as, by the last quarter of the century, the prospects for socio-economic mobility in London and New York were well known to those living in the Pale of Settlement. Such knowledge was a powerful magnet for those whose life in the *shtetl* was one of misery and despair.

In reality, domestic life for the poorer members of the Jewish *shtetl* community was little different to that which the immigrants would find on arrival in London. In both places dirt, dust and overcrowding prevailed. Most *shtetl* homes consisted of one or perhaps two rooms, with plastered and whitewashed interiors and floors which were at best made of boards, more often of earth. Bed-sharing was the rule. Children shared with siblings and often with mother as well, father occupying a sofa. Sleeping and eating quarters were separated by a curtain. It is a description of life which would have been as easily recognised by the occupants of Hanbury Street in Sptialfields, as by those in Minsk. The myth of home carefully censored the reality of filthy, uncobbled streets paved with upturned wooden boxes serving as stepping stones and streets covered with dirty snow in winter and swamped with muddy water in spring. In summer, pedestrians had to manoeuvre around

> the dust piles in thick layers which the rain changes to mud so deep that wagon wheels stick fast and must be pried loose by the sweating driver. . . . After rain, streams and puddles of muddy water . . . when the mud gets too bad, boards are put down over the black slush so that people can cross the street.[56]

By comparison, Whitechapel Road and Brick Lane must have seemed, if not the promised land, then certainly the gateway to it.

The architecture of religion dominated the *shtetls*. Churches and synagogues of 'imposing size and design . . . their black wood exteriors hiding a riot of colour'[57] on the inside commanded, indeed demanded, the attendance of their congregants. Other public buildings included *mikvahs* (religious bathhouses) and *cheders* (religious schools). Secular schools were a late arrival on the Russian education scene and standards of education were poor for both Jew and Gentile.

The poverty and hardship of life in the *shtetl* was compensated for by a sense of community which was manifest in the nexus of support. Though *shtetl* Jews were not full citizens of the Russian Empire, they were 'full citizens of the Jewish community',[58] a community constructed out of their own system of beliefs and practices, rights and obligations. However, that self-governing Jewish community was not homogeneous. It was stratified by jealousies, social and economic layers and corruption, all of which would surface in the Jewish community in Spitalfields.

The urbanisation and impoverishment of the Jewish population of the Russian Empire was not accidental. It was the result of government policies which, over the period of the nineteenth century, gradually removed from Jewish hands occupations and activities which had enabled them to live outside the towns and cities. As early as 1804, the traditional Jewish association with the provision and sale of alcohol had come under attack and Jews were banned from maintaining and/or residing in inns and taverns. In 1845 they were forbidden to manufacture or sell liquor in rural areas. Even under the so-called enlightened rule of Alexander II, whose stated intention was to Russify and integrate Russian Jews, they fared poorly. The emancipation of the serfs following the Crimean War eliminated the intermediary role between landlord and peasants which the Jews had played for almost half a century. The Jews of the Pale were increasingly pushed into *shtetls* and cities to find work. The result was that not only the artisan, semi-skilled and unskilled sought jobs in urban areas but, 'by the 1880s and 1890s many teachers, rabbinical students and ritual slaughterers as well as petty merchants, faced the prospect of joining the ranks of the poorest proletariat'.[59] This was not the only source of financial hardship. In spite of restricted economic activity and opportunity, government ministers sought to grind the Jewish population down even further by extracting as much money as possible through the imposition of a system of local and national taxation.

Jewish economic life became one of low wages, interspersed by long periods of unemployment, in an environment of increasing hopelessness. Urbanisation created a large semi-skilled and unskilled proletariat, which was 'poverty-stricken, diseased and slum ridden'.[60] Ninety per cent lived from hand to mouth.[61] Writing about urban life in Belorussia in 1875, the founding father of Jewish socialism, Aaron Liberman, recorded that Jewish workers lived in 'the semi-darkness of cellars and similar hovels that had wet under floors ... crammed together in an oppressive stupefying atmosphere'.[62] For the majority, increasing economic hardship was the main characteristic of Jewish life in the Russian Empire in the second half of the nineteenth century.

The economic profile of the Jews of Russia, and indeed of Eastern Europe generally, though deteriorating, was not narrow. A minority of Russian and Russian-Polish Jewry were bankers, railroad developers, mill and factory owners. By the second half of the nineteenth century, Jews were active at most levels of the economy, the majority, approximately 74.3 per cent, engaged in unskilled, artisanal and petty trades. A further 3.5 per cent (179,400) worked in agriculture.[63] As the urban working class expanded in the closing decades of the nineteenth century, it created a surplus of labour in certain trades, particularly in tailoring, a traditional Jewish economic activity, dating back to biblical times.[64] In the Pale of Settlement, it was an occupation carried out in cramped and unhealthy conditions at a very low wage. Not surprisingly in a culture which revered learning and study, the unskilled and semi-skilled earned little respect. Unlearned men lacked 'prestige, respect, authority and status ... it was they who thronged the market place'.[65] To be a tailor was to be stigmatised and, for many forced to turn to the production of clothing, it was a condition 'which brought shame [to] my family'.[66] In contrast, poverty on the part of a prospective bridegroom was unimportant if the future son-in-law was a budding rabbi. In spite of this, in the promised land of Spitalfields, tailoring as an economic activity occupied five-sevenths of the Jewish male immigrant population,[67] while few of the immigrants became rabbis. Only a minority of Jewish workers in the Pale of Settlement found employment in factories. Religious practices and high holy days all too frequently conflicted with the working week. The one exception was the tobacco factories. Seventy-five per cent of these were Jewish owned and 78 per cent of the workforce in them was Jewish.[68] This possibly explains the fact that, 'Hardly one per cent of the arrivals [to London] mentioned the tobacco trade as their livelihood.'[69]

It was the ever increasing urban proletariat that provided the source of migrants. Even though it was 'technically illegal',[70] emigration was increasingly perceived as the solution to the ongoing hardships. In spite of the bureaucratic and financial difficulties involved, the young men (and women) of the Pale of Settlement emigrated. They travelled westward to find a new and better life, if not for themselves, then for their children and grandchildren. Not all found the *golde medineh* and not all stayed. In spite of the myths of Jewish success, in the early years of immigrant settlement there were those, some 50,000, who returned to Eastern Europe, having found London too hard and too cruel. By doing this they were not fulfilling the accepted 'myth of return' – rather they had been let down by the myth of elsewhere. For the reality was that, in the early years of Eastern European settlement and assimilation, only a ruthless few made it out of the East End Jewish ghetto.

From *desh* to *bidesh*

Given the freedom to worship, find employment and live a life free from state-imposed restraints, there would have been far fewer emigrations from France in the seventeenth and eighteenth centuries and from Eastern Europe in the nineteenth and early twentieth centuries.[71] History has shown that the majority of people prefer to remain secure within the familiar rather than confront the unknown. The pioneering young Bangladeshi migrants were not 'pushed' overseas by political denials of freedom[72] but rather by a desire for the acquisition of land in their Sylheti villages, what has been called the 'specific target'.[73] In rural Bangladesh, land ownership is the great aspiration, bringing with it the rewards of respect and 'a sense of self'.[74] Landholding is a vital tool in the construction of the identity of success. However, money to purchase the land could only be acquired in the elsewhere. For young Bengali men in the late 1950s and 1960s, the migratory pull was the availability of jobs in Britain. Employment in a textile factory, curry restaurant or leather workshop would enable them to save money and, after not too long a period, return home as 'rich men of high status'. For ambitious sojourners, the myth of return was uppermost, though, as with all travellers, the myth of home was in their luggage. As the Bengalis began to realise that return was at best a distant dream, the construction of home in Spitalfields began. For the majority of Bengalis, return became 'a dream maintained'.[75] It was at this point that the myth of home was reconfigured into a *desh* in the *bidesh*.

The Bangladeshi link with Britain goes back at least as far as 1757 and the British occupation of the Indian subcontinent. However Sylhet, the region from which 95 per cent of the Bangladeshi population of Tower Hamlets originates, did not come under British control for another eight years. Foreign rule was not new to the people of Sylhet; it dated back to 1612 and the Moguls. They put in place a system of small-scale land owner-ship, creating an infrastructure that, centuries later, gave credibility to the dream of land ownership and facilitated the raising of funds to cover the cost of migration. Even before British colonial rule, Indian seamen – lascars – found employment on ships bound for Britain as replacements for sailors who had either died or deserted.[76] In 1795, the connection with East London was established when, grudgingly, the East India Company provided a shelter in Kingsland Road for the 'wretched men' to use between their travels.[77] Lascars were poorly treated by their British employers and, once aboard the merchant vessels, were subjected to mental and physical exploita-tion. Lahiri's research has highlighted the strategies of resistance adopted by these sailing men to counteract both their harsh treatment and British mis-sionaries' unceasing attempts at proselytisation.[78] In the middle of the nine-teenth century, the link with East London was further cemented when a sailors' lodging house was established in West India Dock Road.[79] In her book, *Across Seven Seas and Thirteen Rivers*, Adams provides a detailed account of the experiences of men who made their way from Sylhet to Calcutta, in order to find employment as lascars on British merchant ships during the nineteenth and twentieth centuries. The early Bengali arrivals established a fragile network of transcontinental knowledge that evolved into an estab-lished chain of migration. The communal or family tradition of migration provides an explanation for the way in which some villages in Sylhet have become *Londoni*[80] while others have not.

Bangladesh occupies an area of 144,000 sq. km. (55,598 sq. miles), and is bounded almost entirely by India, with a southern coastline facing the Bay of Bengal. It is a densely populated, extremely poor country, with a popu-lation estimated, in 2001, to total 131,269,860, the majority – 61 per cent – aged between fifteen and sixty-four.[81] Between 1961 and 2001, the popu-lation grew by more than 150 per cent.[82] The terrain is mostly flat and subject to flooding during the summer monsoon season. As nearly two-thirds of the working population is employed in the production of rice, the natural hazards of cyclones, interspersed with droughts, create major imped-iments for anyone seeking to secure their future. Attempts have been made to encourage and develop overseas investment, but 'political infighting and corruption at all levels of government', plus 'opposition from the bureau-cracy, public-sector unions and other interested groups',[83] has slowed down development and opportunity. For the majority of the population, and this includes the people of Sylhet, quality of life is poor. In the late 1950s and 1960s, the period of large-scale male movement to the United Kingdom, (women and children arrived in the 1970s and 1980s), infant mortality was 111.9 per 1,000 and life expectancy was fifty-six years. Levels of literacy were as low as 17 per cent in rural areas such as Sylhet, though somewhat higher, at 19.7 per cent, in the towns.[84] By the end of the 1980s, when family reunions were still taking place, literacy was estimated to stand at 18 per cent for women and 39 per cent for men.[85] Dry as these statistics may be, they provide us with a tangible appreciation of the literacy problems facing the early male migrants to the United Kingdom and their wives and children in the decades that followed.

Sylhet, the region from which most of the Bangladeshi population in Spitalfields originates, covers an area of 12,714 sq. km. In 1985, the density of population was estimated at 512 people per sq. km. Sylhet lies to the northeast of Bangladesh and its predominantly flat terrain is given over to rice fields. The landscape is broken up by the hills to the east upon which tea estates were developed by the British in the second half of the nineteenth century.[86] Monsoon rains, which in the summer cut off the villages both from Sylhet town and from each other, are also responsible for the region's beauty. As a recent visitor described it:

> Sylhet is lovely, the countryside is different, more hills and we are staying close to the tea gardens that were originally planted ... in the nineteenth century. They are very beautiful and a change from the paddy fields. ... The countryside here is amazing, very fertile and green. This contrasts with the poverty that you see everywhere.[87]

For the men who made the journey from the rural beauty and semi-isolation of Sylhet to the chaos and grime of inner-city Spitalfields, the physical and topographical transition must indeed have been disorientating. But it was not only the changed landscape with which the migrants had to cope. Family, in nearly every case the nuclear as well as extended, was left behind and, in the early days of the men's Spitalfields existence, life was of the bachelor variety. The latter was not always unpopular, as Katy Gardner's research has shown for, while some men recall only the hardships, others remember that, 'It was a happy time', and the bachelor life was lived to the full.[88] Liked or loathed, it was certainly very different to life in the *desh*. However, although the young males experienced the traumas of migration, the experience in itself was not new to Sylhetis. The 'population of Sylhet has never been static, but instead has evolved from a constant flow of people moving into and out of the district'.[89] Perhaps the heritage of migration has made the long distances and long partings easier to bear.

Family and kinship are the essence of life in the villages of Sylhet. Families are of the extended variety, consisting of husband, wife, children and/or parents, the married children (sons and their wives as, upon marriage, a woman normally moves into the household of her husband), their families and any unmarried daughters. This extended family forms the household, the definition of which is 'a group of people who eat food from the same hearth'.[90] The family nexus is manifest in a number of ways and provides a support mechanism for the poorer kin and for those who want to migrate in order to provide more financial security for self and family. Thus, those who remain would often be the recipients of one or more remittances from the *bidesh*, and in receipt of what is known colloquially as *bideshi taka*. In the 1950s, 1960s and early 1970s this came predominantly from Britain but, in the closing decades of the twentieth century, the destination of sojourners increasingly became the Middle East. Sending a member of the family over-seas is both a pleasurable and a painful experience. Pleasure is experienced through becoming a *Londoni* family. Families and villages are given the title of *Londoni* as a means of identifying the fact that they have members who have migrated to Britain. The material improvements to homes, mosques, schools and land in these villages form the tangible manifestation of the benefits and also the facilitators of upward social mobility. Pain is suffered most by mothers and wives whose sons and husbands might be gone for years or, as in some cases, for a lifetime.

The nuclear family households live in a *ghor*, which is the effective and functional economic unit. The extended family occupies a cluster of *ghors* in proximity, and this is known as a *bari*, or a 'segment of patrilineage'. The *bari* is never static but changes in accordance with the domestic cycle.[91] Extent of landholding, location, structure and style of homes are the baro-meters of poverty and affluence. A poor family, even in the twenty-first century, will live in a mud-built home, 'with walls at least a foot thick and the roof made of thatch ... these homes are warm in winter and cool in summer'.[92] A far cry from the overcrowded, poorly constructed high-rise towers or nineteenth-century-built multi-occupancies of London's East End. Mud homes lack the modern essentials such as electricity, televisions often being run on car batteries.[93] The telephone remains a luxury that even many of the comparatively well-off seem not to have acquired. A report published in the year 2000 revealed the existence of only 500,000 landline telephones in the whole of Bangladesh. However, there were a reported 283,000 mobile cellular phones,[94] and, if the youth of the country follow the global trend, it is more than likely that the mobile phone will leapfrog its landline equival-ent and within a very short while become ubiquitous. The more affluent inhabitants of the villages, usually those with the *Londoni* tag, tend to have stone-built houses in which are to be found radios, televisions and other material manifestations of kinsmen who have made the journey to the *bidesh* and are repaying the debt through their remittances.

In spite of Bangladesh having elected a woman, Khaleda Zia, as prime minister in 2001, the country has been, and remains, a patriarchal society. Women occupy the maternal/domestic sphere and men the economic. The divisions are clearly defined, women inhabiting the private domain, males the public. Within the homestead, women are separated from the men, their quarters being to the rear in the kitchen area which only the closest male kin may enter. Whilst in the confines of the *bari*, women do not don full *purdah*. However, the veil or full *purdah* will be worn for longer trips. The wearing of *purdah* provides both freedom and separation and is a strategy often employed by Muslim women in Britain. The wearing of the veil by young unmarried women enables them to leave the domestic sphere and enter college or even work whilst, for newly reunited wives who have to venture forth from the seclusion of home into public space, the veil provides anonymity and security in an alien and often hostile environment.

Gardner asserts that in Sylhet, 'no women ever work outside in the fields no matter how destitute they are'.[95] In contrast, White's research has shown that, although it is culturally unacceptable, very poor women are often forced to find employment rice-husking and thus do work in the fields. However, as frequently the case in the Jewish Spitalfields community of the late nineteenth century, the village males, conscious of the stigma of poverty manifested by the labouring activities of women, boldly assert that 'it does not happen'.[96] In spite of these beliefs – or dreams – estimates reveal that, in the 1980s, nearly 70 per cent of women living in rural Bangladesh were impoverished and forced to work as labourers for payment in kind or for a very low wage.[97] Those from landless households often had no alternative but to rely on casual labour or begging to survive.

In rural Bangladesh females marry at an early age. In 1981 the mean was 16.9 years. This accounts for the broad age differential within Bangladeshi families living in London where, in one instance, a husband was found to be fifty years senior to his wife.[98] In all but the most elevated and informed levels of society, a Bangladeshi female has no say in the choice of her marriage partner. This tradition was transported to the *bidesh* but now many young Bangladeshi women living in Britain find the practice unacceptable.[99] Marriage in Bangladesh is of a less bureaucratic nature than in Britain and is seen as much as anything else as a financial transaction forming part of a civil contract between families. There is no required religious documentation. In the villages there is a paucity of legal certification, as 'marriage laws in South Asia are not premised on regulated systems; although such systems exist they are not mandatory and thus informal, customary marriages are invariably recognised.'[100] In order for Bangladeshi wives to gain access to the United Kingdom, it is necessary to produce documentary proof of marriage. The absence of this in many cases has created a backlog in the provision of entry permits. In some cases the wait for reunification has been as long as twenty years.

Islam in Bangladesh is syncretic, drawing on both Sunni and Sufi, the spiritual element of the latter a powerful factor with rural Muslims. The country has an 85 per cent Muslim population which includes a small number of urban Shiites. Although constituted as a democratic 'People's

Republic' in 1971, the role of Islam has become increasingly significant and there are some 190,000 mosques in Bangladesh. In 1988, an 'Islamic way of life' was proclaimed in a constitutional amendment which made Islam the state religion. The politicians stopped short of creating an Islamic state, fearful of the political repercussions. In Sylhet, as elsewhere, Islam permeates all elements of daily life. As is evident in the *bari* and in the mosque, Islam clearly separates the genders. The female maintains the domestic sphere and, though permitted to attend public worship, women are segregated from men and generally pray at home. Though often the hidden other, in reality the female frequently proves to be a powerful religious force within the family, reinforcing the cultural and domestic elements. Within the villages of rural Bangladesh, the mosque has a central role, as much a community centre as a place of prayer. In keeping with the demands of *zakat* (religious tax/charity), villagers often give up 2.5 per cent of their crop to the mosque to ensure its financial support. In the name of charity, those who are able to afford it provide for their poorer kin and give alms to beggars, in return for the unfortunates' prayers to Allah on their behalf. The syncretic nature of Islam in the villages of Sylhet where, as one religious (non-Muslim) commentator has explained, 'To be a Muslim in rural Bangladesh is more a statement of which group you belong to than of how you understand the word',[101] is most clearly demonstrated by the Sylhetis' strongly held belief in the spirits and the cult of the *pir* (saint). As Gardner explains, 'The poor in the villages accept their poverty by believing that is what Allah has ordained' and that 'Allah helps those who help themselves.'[102] In Islam a belief in the evil eye is acceptable and the transportation of the belief in spirits and ghosts to Tower Hamlets is most powerfully manifest in the treatment and diagnosis of mental and physical health disorders. Practising physician Veronica White has noted that, 'These spirits are strongly felt to be the cause of psychiatric problems and the afflicted are regarded as possessed.'[103] John Eade has illustrated how the health needs of the Muslim immigrants have been met by non-medically qualified religious community leaders, for example a *mullah* might attempt to treat severe wind pains by recommending the patient place a piece of paper containing written verses of the Quran on the affected part of the body.[104]

Most young male sojourners setting out for Britain in the 1950s and 1960s would have been given a copy of the Quran (written in Arabic), a prayer mat and other religious texts. Armed with these, as much spare money as their village or family could afford, the myth of return and the constituents of the myth of home, the young men made their way westward, as had the Huguenots and Eastern European Jews before them. They were on their way to a promised land called Spitalfields.

Conclusion

The three groups forming the subject of this book originated from geographically disparate sending societies and different centuries. Even with the inevitable grey areas of overlap, the migrant groups fall into separate categories: those of refugees, immigrants and sojourners. All chose the same destination and, when their backgrounds are explored, can be seen to share a number of common experiences and practices. In spite of differences in religious ideology and practice, the immigrant Huguenots, Eastern European Jews and Muslim Bangladeshis adhered to religions which were prescriptive, even if of varying strengths. Each group believed in a 'hard work ethic' and that charity, morality, sobriety and providence should play a central role in their lives. Each subscribed to the view that material achievement should manifest the glory of God. Within their houses of prayer, each group believed in the separation of the genders[105] and, particularly in the Jewish and Muslim creeds, in their delineated responsibilities in public and private space.

Although strangers in their chosen promised land, Huguenot, Jew and Bangladeshi had earlier links, however tenuous, with the metropolis of settlement. A minority of Huguenots had put in place a network which was to prove an invaluable conduit of escape. The impecunious Eastern European Jews entered a city within which earlier Jewish arrivals, some who were a part of the 1656 readmission, had set up an infrastructure of charitable support,[106] which would provide for their co-religionists and keep them out of the English Poor House. Bengalis could trace their association with the mother country back to the early years of Empire and, by seeking their fortunes in Britain, were following an established paradigm. The coincidental similarity extends into the workplace and trade which, in Spitalfields, gave employment to all three groups. The clothing industry represents a constant – the buildings which housed the Huguenot silk workshops became home to Jewish tailors who, in the 1950s and 1960s, as their involvement in the trade faded, stood at the interface of minority groups when Pakistani and Bengali workers and middlemen transformed tailoring and furriery workshops into leather-garment workshops.

However, as will become evident in the chapters ahead, there were differences as well as similarities. Some of the disparities were, and are, the outcome of the innate characteristics of each group; others were caused by exogenous factors over which the immigrant community had, and has, no control. The chapters that follow will compare and contrast the religious and socio-economic experiences of Huguenots, Jews and Bangladeshis in Spitalfields in order to ascertain whether the immigrants made Spitalfields what it is or whether Spitalfields made the migrants what they were and are. But first we need to familiarise ourselves with the location that provides the canvas for this study – one which was a terminal for many of the indigenous and indigent population of London, yet a starting point for our strangers, aliens and Asians.

Notes

1 E. Hobsbawm, 'Introduction', in A. Mack (ed.), 'Home a Place in the World', *Social Research*, 58 (1), 1991, p. 63.
2 See W. Webster, *Imagining Home: Gender, Race' and National Identity, 1945–64*, London, UCL Press, 1998.
3 K. Gardner and A. Shukur, 'I'm Bengali, I'm Asian and I'm Living Here: The Changing Identity of British Bengalis', in R. Ballard (ed.), *Desh Pardesh: The South Asian Presence in Britain*, London, Hurst, 1994, p. 150.
4 David Garbin, 'Migration, territories diasporiques et politiques identitaires: Bengalis musulmans entre "Banglatown" (Londres) et Sylhet (Bangladesh)', unpublished Ph.D. thesis, University of François Rabelais de Tours, 2004, p. 154.
5 Webster, op. cit., p. x.
6 N. Rapport and A. Dawson (eds), *Migrants of Identity: Perceptions of Home in a World of Movement*, Oxford, Berg, 1998, p. 7.
7 D. Joly and R. Cohen, *Reluctant Host*, Aldershot, Avebury, 1989, p. 6.
8 Unlike in English, Yiddish (derived clearly from the Hebrew/German) and Bengali, there is no one French word for home. The writer or speaker thus chooses the one most relevant to the sense of the conversation/theme. See this chapter below for further discussion.
9 This accounts for the lack of support given by ultra-orthodox Jewry to the establishment of a political Jewish state.
10 M. Zborowski and E. Herzog, *Life Is with People: The Culture of the Shtetl*, New York, Schocken, 1970 edition, p. 158.
11 Home or homeland.
12 Abroad.
13 Sarah C. White, *Arguing with the Crocodile*, London, Zed Books, 1992, p. 53.
14 M. Anwar, *The Myth of Return: Pakistanis in Britain*, London, Heinemann Educational, 1979.
15 Ibid., p. 21.
16 In 1995 it was estimated that Bangladesh was receiving $1 bn per annum in remittances. See K. Gardner, *Global Migrants, Local Lives*, Oxford, Clarendon Press, 1995, p. 23.
17 Definition in *The Shorter Oxford English Dictionary*, 2002 edition, Oxford, Oxford University Press, p. 976.
18 For the evolution of the Yiddish language, see Chapter 6 below.
19 C. Walker, 'The Impact of Homelands upon Diaspora', in G. Sheffer (ed.), *Modern Diasporas in International Politics*, Beckenham, Croom Helm, 1986, p. 17.
20 The painting shows an excessively dressed, powdered and rouged French couple leaving the French church.
21 N.M. Sutherland, *The Huguenot Struggle for Recognition*, New York and London, Yale University Press, 1980, p. 101.
22 R. Gwynn, *Huguenot Heritage: The History and Contribution of the Huguenots in Britain*, Brighton, Sussex Academic Press, 2001 edition, p. 3.
23 Ibid., pp. 36–8.
24 Henri of Navarre (crowned Henri IV) was originally a Protestant and at one time leader of the Huguenot armies. However, in 1593, having become heir to the throne of France, he rejected Calvinism, having taken 'instruction' from a group of Catholic bishops. In 1594 he was crowned king of France.
25 N.M. Sutherland, 'The Huguenots and the Edict of Nantes 1598–1629', in I. Scouloudi (ed.), *Huguenots in Britain and Their French Background 1550–1880*, Basingstoke, Macmillan, 1987, p. 160.

26 Ibid.
27 M. Prestwich, 'The Huguenots under Richelieu and Mazarin', in Scouloudi, op. cit., p. 177.
28 Ibid., p. 176.
29 R. Mettam, 'Louis XIV and the Persecution of the Huguenots', in Scouloudi, op. cit., pp. 198–216, 200–2.
30 See G. Adams, *The Huguenots and French Opinion 1685–1787*, Waterloo, Ontario, Wilfred Laurier University Press, 1991, pp. 9–12.
31 E. Labrousse, 'Great Britain as Envisaged by the Huguenots', in Scouloudi, op. cit., p. 144.
32 See Chapter 7 below.
33 Gwynn, op. cit., p. 75.
34 The readmission of the Jews has been said to have been agreed by Cromwell as a result of his belief that, once Jews inhabited all parts of the world (following the expulsion of 1290 the practice of Judaism had been forbidden in England), the second coming of the Messiah would take place, and he, Oliver Cromwell, would have facilitated this miracle. However, a more pragmatic view is that the trading benefits from the Jewish presence were considerable. See C. Roth, *A History of the Jews in England*, Oxford, Clarendon Press, 1979, Chapter VII.
35 Labrousse, op. cit., p. 144.
36 R. Smith, 'Financial Aid to French Protestant Refugees 1681–1727: Briefs and the Royal Bounty', *Proceedings of the Huguenot Society of London*, Vol. XXII, London, Huguenot Society of Great Britain and Ireland, 1976, p. 249. See Chapter 5 below for further details of charities established to benefit destitute Huguenots.
37 See Chapter 8 below.
38 As would the Jews after them, many Huguenots changed their surnames to the English equivalent and, within several generations, were giving their children English Christian names.
39 *East London Observer*, 4 March 1911.
40 In July 1290 King Edward I, knowing that they had no funds left to extort by taxation and under pressure from knights and barons who supported the Crusade, ordered the departure of all Jews from England within three months.
41 The nomenclature *Sephardi* is applied to the descendants of those who, following the fall of the Second Temple, settled in Iberia and North Africa. The Sephardim who arrived in England following the readmission of 1656 originated from the Iberian peninsula (Spain and Portugal) and the Mediterranean countries. The nomenclature *Ashkenazi* is applied to the descendants of those who, after the fall of the Temple, migrated eastward into Central and Western Europe, subsequently moving into Eastern Europe. Though both Ashkenazi and Sephardi Jews held (and continue to hold) the same beliefs, there were subtle differences in the rituals and liturgies and, whilst the dialect of the Sephardim was the infrequently used Ladino, that of the Ashkenazim was the almost universal Yiddish.
42 J. Klier, 'What Exactly Was the *Shtetl?*', in G. Estraikh and M. Krutikov (eds), *The Shtetl: Image and Reality*, Oxford, Legenda: published by the European Humanities Research Centre, 2000, pp. 32–3.
43 R. Spiro, 'Post-biblical Jewish History – the London Vista', in D. Englander (ed.), *The Jewish Enigma*, Milton Keynes, Open University, 1992, p. 41.
44 Quoted in C. Abramsky, M. Jachimczk and A. Polonsky (eds), *The Jews in Poland*, Oxford, Blackwell, 1986, p. 3.
45 Information provided by John Klier, 13 March 2001.
46 Klier, 13 March 2001.

47   A. Goldenweiser, 'Legal Status of Jews in Russia', in J. Frumkin, G. Aronson and A. Goldenweiser (eds), *Russian Jewry 1860–1917*, New York and London, Thomas Yoseloff, 1966, pp. 85 and 87.
48   A. Kershen, *Uniting the Tailors*, Ilford, Frank Cass, 1995, p. 9.
49   J. Klier, *Imperial Russia's Jewish Question: 1855–81*, Cambridge, Cambridge University Press, 1995, p. 10.
50   E. Mendelsohn, *Class Struggles in the Pale*, Cambridge, Cambridge University Press, 1970, p. 4.
51   Klier, 'What Exactly Was the *shtetl*', op. cit., p. 27.
52   Zborowski and Herzog, op. cit., p. 34.
53   See previous chapter for Louis Wirth's description of the ghetto and its role in the lives of the immigrant and marginalised.
54   Klier, 'What Exactly Was the *shtetl?*', p. 25.
55   Zborowski and Herzog, op. cit., p. 158.
56   Ibid., p. 61.
57   Ibid.
58   H. Kosak, *Cultures of Opposition: Jewish Immigrant Workers*, New York, State University of New York Press, 2000, p. 23.
59   Ibid., p. 22.
60   Mendelsohn, op. cit., p. 26.
61   Kosak, op. cit., p. iv.
62   Mendelsohn, op. cit., p. 13.
63   It was from amongst the Jewish agricultural class that recruits were found for Palestine and the farmlands of Argentina, Canada and America. J. Dijur, 'Jews in the Russian Economy', Frumkin *et al.*, op. cit., p. 124.
64   See Kershen, op. cit., Chapter 1.
65   Zborowski and Herzog, op. cit., p. 83.
66   Kosak, op. cit., p. 22.
67   Kershen, op. cit., p. 111.
68   Dijur, op. cit.
69   L. Gartner, *The Jewish Immigrant in England 1870–1914*, London, George Allen and Unwin, 1960, p. 73.
70   Klier, 13 March 2001.
71   This is not to suggest that there would not have been those who sought to leave both France and Eastern Europe in search of what they perceived as greater economic opportunity elsewhere.
72   The Home Office Immigration and General Unit believed that the number of applications for asylum lodged by Bangladeshis in the 1970s and 1980s was 'negligible', totalling no more than ten each year. In the absence of recorded statistics, the estimate was provided by Nick Hooper of the Home Office Immigration and General Unit, 26 March 1998.
73   V. Robinson, 'Indians', in C. Peach (ed.), *Ethnicity in the 1991 Census*, Vol. 2, London, HMSO, 1996, p. 96.
74   White, op. cit., p. 53.
75   This fact was confirmed to the author in a conversation held with Immam Shafique Rahhmad of the East London Mosque on 25 June 2002.
76   C. Adams, *Across Seven Seas and Thirteen Rivers*, London, Thap Books, 1987, p. 15.
77   Ibid., p. 17.
78   S. Lahiri, 'Patterns of Resistance: Indian Seamen in Imperial Britain', in A. Kershen, *Language, Labour and Migration*, Aldershot, Ashgate, 2000, pp. 162–5.
79   See Lahiri, op. cit. and R. Visram, *Ayahs, Lascars and Princes*, London, Pluto Press, 1985, p. 50.

80 Villages which had sent migrants to Britain and had benefited from their remittances.

81 http://www.odci.gov/cia/publications/factlook/geos/bg.html (accessed 17 June 2002).

82 In 1961, at the height of the migratory outflow, the population numbered 50,840,000. See http://icweb2.loc.gov/frd/cs.Bangladesh/bde_appen.html (accessed 17 June 2002).

83 http://www.odci.gov/cia/publications/factlook/geos/bg.html (accessed 17 June 2002).

84 In the past two decades standards have improved, with life expectancy at the beginning of the twenty-first century estimated at sixty years and the literacy level now standing at 56 per cent, as schooling, particularly in the villages, is of a higher standard.

85 http://www.odci.gov/cia/publications/factlook/geos.bg.html (accessed 17 June 2002).

86 See Adams, op. cit., pp. 10–12.

87 V. White, 'Postcards from Bangladesh', email to the author, 6 November 2000.

88 K. Gardner, 'Identity, Age and Masculinity amongst Bengali Elders in East London', in A. Kershen (ed.), *A Question of Identity*, Aldershot, Ashgate, 1998, p. 165.

89 Gardner, *Global Migrants*, op. cit., p. 37.

90 Ibid., p. 101.

91 I am thankful to David Garbin for pointing this out to me.

92 V. White, op. cit., 6 November 2000.

93 V. White to the author, 5 December 2003.

94 http://www.odci.gov/cia/publications/factlook/geos.bg.html (accessed 17 June 2002).

95 Gardner, *Global Migrants*, op. cit., p. 70.

96 S. White, op. cit., pp. 122–3.

97 Ibid.

98 V. White, 5 December 2003.

99 The issue of forced marriages in British Asian families is now on the British political agenda.

100 P. Shah, 'Bangladeshis in English Law', unpublished paper presented at 'Bangladeshis in Britain' workshop, 25 May 2002.

101 J. Webber, 'Islam in Bangladesh', Introductory notes for CCBI's Conference, 'Movements in Islam' undated, unpublished paper.

102 Gardner, *Global Migrants*, op. cit., p. 234.

103 V. White, 'Health Advocacy in Medicine', in Kershen, *Language*, op. cit., p. 83.

104 See J. Eade, 'The Power of the Experts: The Plurality of Beliefs and Practices concerning Health and Illness among Bangladeshis', in L. Marks and M. Worboys (eds), *Migrants, Minorities and Medicine*, London, Routledge, 1997.

105 In the Calvinist chapels men and women sat separately. See Chapter 4 below.

106 See Chapter 5 below.

3 Spitalfields

A place on the edge

The city is a mosaic of places and people; it is a multi-layered organism, its strata variegated by socio-economic status, race, gender and religion. The city is a tangible entity recognisable by sight, smell and sound. It contains a multiplicity of real and imagined communities and boundaries which co-exist within the whole. As Saskia Sassen suggests, 'each city contains many cities'.[1] Amongst the 'many' lies the immigrant quarter(s) which Sassen describes as, 'third world space' within a first-world context. The city is a crucible of equality and inequality within which interaction and interface, separation and marginalisation, ceaselessly take place. London is such a city. Its roots deeply embedded in a past created by natives and invaders, immigrants and refugees, citizens and outsiders, the assimilated and the marginalised. Its present fashioned by the local, national and global. Its future a fusion of all that has gone before and what is yet to come. Within this complex metropolis lies Spitalfields. Frequently viewed as a terminal, it is rarely referred to as a taking-off point, though that is what it has been for the Huguenots and Jews and, in time, may well become for the Bangladeshis who now fill its streets.

Our strangers, aliens and Asians not only inhabited the space that is Spitalfields, they also created demarcated zones within which were fashioned an ambience familiar to the outsider yet foreign and exotic to the natives of the metropolis. The Huguenots turned the cobbled streets and alleyways into 'Petty France'; the Eastern European Jews transformed them into a 'Little Jerusalem'; whilst the Bangladeshis have facilitated the most recent metamorphosis into 'Banglatown'. Each designation broadcasts the presence of an alien culture in the heart of one of the essential sites of Englishness, the East End, the home of the cockney.[2] As each wave of incomers marked out their ghetto boundaries, tensions at the edge, where the insider and outsider confronted each other, heightened as threats to native territory were constantly reinforced.

Over the centuries the real and imagined boundaries of Spitalfields have been juxtaposed with those of poverty and wealth. Beyond the restraints of the City of London, with its stipulations of citizenship and its demands for taxes,[3] the space that was Spitalfields provided a receptacle for the hopeless and the hopeful, the dispossessed and the dissident. In this small sector of the great metropolis, our strangers, aliens and Asians confronted their identity as other and made their first tentative steps towards the future and the challenges and opportunities it posed.

Location, location, location

In order for a location to take on the traditional role of first point of settlement,[4] a part Spitalfields has played for centuries, it has to conform to certain specifications. Primarily, it has to be close to the point of immigrant disembarkation; offer some form of economic activity if possible, accompanied by a promise of upward mobility; and provide basic living accommodation. In addition, the area has to be free from any legal, political and religious constraints which would make the incomer's life untenable. When such an area is marked out by pioneering immigrants, a pattern of chain migration often follows as networks are established between the place of settlement and 'home'. Gradually, ethnic enclaves or ghettoes evolve as 'voluntarily selected . . . local cultural areas'.[5] In the history of Spitalfields, the Huguenots and the Jews[6] were the first migrant pioneers in modern history to settle in any numbers at the eastern edge of the City of London. Unable to live within the city's walls they elected Spitalfields as first point of settlement and their launching pad to socio-economic mobility.

The area known as Spitalfields is within thirty minutes' walking distance of the London Docks, a distance of some two and a half miles, and less than half that distance from the City of London. At the time of writing its boundaries are formed by: to the west, Bishopsgate/North Folgate/ Middlesex Street; to the north, Shoreditch/ Bethnal Green/ Quaker Street/ Buxton Street through to Vallance Road; to the east, southwards down Brady Street to Whitechapel Road, the latter forming the district's southern boundary. Though the street names may have changed, the locale can be identified on maps dating back to the sixteenth century. A map of 1560 shows the 'Spital Fields', or the *Spittle Fyeld* as an undeveloped rural area bordering Bishopsgate and Aldgate. Even at that time, it is possible to distinguish a direct route running from the brick fields to the north, southwards to the river and Pool of London.[7] This track was later to become Brick Lane, the main artery of Spitalfields. In 1724, Daniel Defoe, in his *Tour of England and Wales*, described the 'numberless ranges of buildings' which were to be found in the area, 'called Spittle Fields, reaching from Spittle Yard, at Northern Folegate, and from Artillery Lane in Bishopsgate Street . . . to Brick Lane and the end of Hare Street, on the way to Bethnal Green'.[8]

The upgrading of Brick Lane,[9] the area's main thoroughfare, provides an insight into the transformation of the space that is the spine of Spitalfields. In the sixteenth century it was little more than a country track. In 1671, Christopher Wren deemed it almost impassable, 'an area remote and inaccessible'. One hundred years later it had become a major thoroughfare for coaches and a meeting place for radical weavers.[10] A change of century brought a change of ethnic minority but no variation in function. Brick Lane remained at the heart of Spitalfields, home to people of diverse occupations and a focal point for political dissent. In the closing decades of the nineteenth century, its street corners and open spaces were assembly points for Jewish socialists and anarchists.[11] In the mid-1930s it bore witness to battles between Mosley's fascist disciples and the communists and Jews. Through the 1970s, 1980s and into the early 1990s, the social landscape of Brick Lane remained one of intermittent violence between racist and anti-racist groups. However, by the beginning of the twenty-first century, it had taken on a more peaceful, and overtly ethnic, character. The central stretch of Brick Lane is now 'Banglatown'. This latest incarnation is visually announced by a banner which straddles the east and west sides of the street, fifty yards north of the junction of Osborne Street and Brick Lane. Yet the political tension has not gone. Just beyond the northern edge of Banglatown, under the railway arches of the East Coast line, where ethnic and native territory converge, members of the British National Party and National Front continue to propagate their racist response to the migrant presence.

The scramble for land

Though the hamlet of Spitalfields was created by an Act of Parliament in 1729, its place on the edge, as a home for those unable to settle within the boundaries of the City of London, can be traced back to the building of the White Tower by William the Conqueror in 1078. Those who served the Tower were required to live outside its, and the city's, walls in small hamlets – thus Tower Hamlets. By the middle of the thirteenth century, the New Hospital, previously St Mary's Priory, had become known locally as *spittle*, and the surrounding grounds, *spittle fields*. Peter Ackroyd considers that the sound of the word spittle 'suggests something spat out, violently ejected ... thus it became a haven for refugees'.[12] When the earliest Huguenot immigrants and refugees crossed the Channel in the sixteenth century, the area was barely developed. However, the dissolution of the monasteries by Henry VIII in 1534 created a scramble for land and the beginning of what Alan Palmer has referred to as the 'greatest land revolution ... [as] social climbers from court and city scrambled for advantage'.[13] This heralded the development (or redevelopment) of the district, the old St Mary's Priory being one of those suppressed by the Tudor king. John Stow's survey of 1598 recorded the changes taking place in and around the area of St Mary Spittle, which once had 'fair hedge rows of elms trees, with bridges and easy stiles to pass over into the pleasant fields'. He bemoaned the fact that the Tudor property developers were ruining the rural idyll by the continual building throughout of garden-houses and small cottages; and the fields on either sides be turned into garden-plots, tenter yards, bowling alleys, and such like, from Houndes Ditch in the west, as far as White Chappell, and further towards the east.[14]

Then, as do his successors now, Stow complained about, the 'bad and greedy men of spoil', who charged high rents. He condemned the ruthless developers who turned out the poor and the elderly in order to make way for the more affluent. Traffic congestion was another woe: according to Stow, 'the world runs on wheels with many whose parents were glad to go on foot'.[15]

By the mid-seventeenth century, Spital Square was home to a small Huguenot community, some of whom could trace their roots back to silk-weavers who had arrived from Rouen as early as 1532. In the early part of the seventeenth century, they had been joined by others, among them Flemings, who formed the nucleus from which the Huguenot community would grow. Almost as though anticipating the influx of refugees, the area bordering the City of London underwent intensive development and, by 1675, more than 1,366 two-storey tenement houses, with frontages measuring no more than twelve feet across, had been constructed. These small, mean houses were crowded into narrow streets and alleyways mainly at the southern end of Spitalfields, in and around Dean and Flower Street[16] and Thrall Street. At the same time, houses were built further north in Hare Street and Browns Lane which bordered on Cock Lane, now known as Bethnal Green Road. The properties attracted 'poor, indigent, idle and loose persons'[17] and, according to Sheppard, 'formed a humdrum network designed to give the maximum frontage, with little regard to access from the adjoining areas'.[18] Spitalfields soon became a magnet for the poor and dispossessed. Overcrowding became endemic. There were no attempts to control the growth or architecture of East London and building continued apace. Fashion Street and Whites Row were built up by the end of the 1650s. By 1683, two years before the revocation of the Edict of Nantes, the French weavers in Spitalfields were considered as 'sufficiently numerous'.[19] Although the southern part of the area was being developed as rapidly as possible, selected fields to the north were reserved as tenter land,[20] and remained as such until the nineteenth century. A 1686 map of the area clearly shows Spitalfields as a developed area with Petticoat Lane, Dean and Flower Street, Thrall Street and Brick Lane clearly identifiable.

The eighteenth century was one in which the Huguenots made their mark on the landscape of Spitalfields. Between 1718 and 1728, Charles Wood and Simon Michell built homes for silk masters in Church (later Fournier) Street, Princes (later Princelet) Street, Hanbury Street and Wood (later Wilkes) Street. However, it was Spital Square which was considered the best address and which was home to some of the more successful 'silk families'. (One hundred and fifty years on workshops and mantle-making factories[21] would replace the affluence and elegance.) While not having any particularly 'French influence in the building',[22] the properties of the more affluent reflected the Calvinists' prosperity and their owners' desire to glorify God through the architectural manifestation of their material success. The Wood Michell estate was an oasis of Huguenot success surrounded by a desert of poverty.

The French were also making an impact in the somewhat less salubrious area of Hog Lane (later Petticoat Lane, now Middlesex Street). Writing in 1759, John Strype recorded that 'French Protestants . . . many planted themselves here, . . . to follow their trades, [there] became a contiguous row of buildings on both sides of the street.'[23] North of Wilkes Street, homes for 'poorer weavers', many of whom were Huguenots, were also being constructed.[24] By the 1770s, John Noorthouck could write that 'A great number of streets, lanes and alleys [are] inhabited by Huguenots.'[25] A map of 1799 shows many of these homes to be as small and as mean as any. In 1743 the completion of *La Neuve Église*, the French church on the corner of Church Street and Brick Lane, provided Spitalfields with a spiritual edifice that would play host to subsequent waves of migrants through the centuries. As French church, ultra-orthodox synagogue or mosque, it became a religious landmark that encapsulated the sense and place of Spitalfields.

For many Huguenots prosperity died with the century's end. The Spitalfields Acts of the 1770s[26] and the end of the war with France seriously affected the silk-weaving industry. Following the passage of the Acts, a number of weavers moved out of the demarcated zone into Bethnal Green where there were no restrictions on wage rates for silk-weaving and, accordingly, more work. As a result, by 1807, Spitalfields was 'inhabited almost entirely by poor persons'.[27] In 1806, in a letter to the MP Samuel Whitbread, on the subject of the 'Distress Peculiar to the Poor of Spitalfields', William Hale described the area as one in which, 'almost all the poor of the City of London are congregated'.[28] By the 1830s, tens of thousands of Spitalfields weavers were unemployed. In the region of 1,100 were crammed into the poor house where they slept five or six to a bed. Six thousand more were in receipt of parochial relief.[29] Within fifty years, the ambience of Spitalfields had changed from one which combined middle-class comfort with lower-class unease, to one which was dominated by the impoverished and exploited poorer working classes. All remaining open ground had been built upon and the gracious Huguenot residences converted into multi-occupancies housing a never-ending stream of alien arrivals. Writing in 1894, J.H. Scott described the landscape of Spitalfields as one that had become 'a portion of London teeming with a population of poor Jews, criminals and unemployed always on the verge of crime'. From Scott's perspective, 'there is nothing here to invite visitors in the small and crowded streets and alleys'.[30] The pattern of overcrowding, poverty and marginalisation which Stow had detected at the end of the sixteenth century persisted, and would continue throughout the century to come.

A question of space

'By the 1880s overcrowding had reached a crisis point in central London.'[31] Many put the blame on the alien, the Eastern European Jew. In reality the root cause of the housing shortage, and the resultant multi-occupancy of the residences of the Huguenots, was the combined forces of industry and empire that had served to make London the greatest capital city in the world. Roads, railways, canals, indeed the very Docks themselves, had had to be built. A transport network had been needed to facilitate the swift transportation of imported raw materials from the London Docks to the centres of industry in the north and midlands and then convey the finished goods to markets at home and overseas. But omelettes cannot be made without breaking eggs and the eggs in this case were the slum dwellings of the capital's poor. It was so much cheaper and easier to knock down slums than to demolish the homes and businesses of the more affluent classes. In a century that was governed by the ethos of self-help, there was little or no thought given to the rehousing of the dishoused. Indeed the Charity Organisation Society was opposed to such a practice on the grounds that it would encourage self-indulgence and sloth.[32]

East London suffered particularly badly from the demolitions. Lacking the concern or control of the landed property owners who were to be found in the West End, there was little opposition to the demands of transport. In the 1840s, Spitalfields was bisected by Commercial Street from north to south (1848) and by the Eastern Counties Railway from east to west (1846). Overall, it is estimated that in the great railway boom some 76,000 people living in central London were displaced.[33] As the railway and road-building slowed, the conversion of houses into workshops and offices accelerated. Once again the residents of Whitechapel, particularly those living in and around Spitalfields, were severely affected. In 1881 the Charity Organisation Society reported that in 'large parts of Swan Street, Rosemary Lane, Mansell Street, Commercial Road and Commercial Street, warehouses have been continually displacing dwellings and tenement houses'.[34] It is ironic that 100 years on, it has been the young and affluent that have moved into the warehouses and reconverted them into desirable domestic dwellings.

It was not only the so-called benefits of industry and empire which forced the poor and disempowered out of their homes. Concerns about the dangers of unsanitary dwellings and lodging houses resulted in the passing of legislation which gave municipal authorities the power to demolish slum dwellings. The 1875 Cross Act included no compensatory rehousing clauses and thus, as demolition went on apace, overcrowding was inevitable. Model dwellings designed for artisans, such as those erected by Peabody and Waterlow in the 1860s and 1870s, did little to alleviate the housing needs of the poor and casual workers who, forced to live close to their work, were unable to guarantee a week's rent in advance. They had little choice but to move in with kith and kin and/or sublet in the surrounding streets. The overcrowding was not solely due to local migrations, the poor and criminal classes had flooded in from other parts of London also undergoing conversions and demolitions. The capital's underclass was drawn to an area renowned for accommodating criminals, prostitutes and drunks. By the 1870s, Flower and Dean and Thrall Streets had become notorious for their threatening, or promising, ambience. Into this 'labyrinth of reeking slums'[35] poured the aliens. As previously noted, there had been Jews living in Spitalfields since the readmission of 1656. By the 1870s, the colony of Dutch and Polish Jews, many housed in and around what was ironically called Fashion Street, was expanding in all directions as fresh waves of immigrants from Russia and Russia-Poland arrived. The area had become a cauldron on the point of bubbling over. At the close of the century it was reported that, within a close radius of Bell Lane, population density had reached 600 persons per acre.[36] Close by, in the area of Christ Church, density was said to be 286 persons per acre. To appreciate the implication of these statistics, it should be noted that the population density mean for London was fifty-six persons per acre.

Even though there were those who remarked on the respectability of the Jews and their clean habits, the majority of the native population was all too ready to point the finger at the 'foreign Jews', who lived in filthy conditions and exacerbated an already severe housing problem. As early as 1885, sixteen years before the Decennial Census for 1901 would reveal that the number of Eastern Europeans in London had virtually doubled in a decade,[37] established British Jewry was expressing unease about the conditions in which the new arrivals were living and the image they were projecting. Certain eminent Anglo-Jews took positive action and set up a Commission of Enquiry which was chaired by Lord Rothschild. The Commission's report found that 'The houses occupied by the Jewish poor . . . are for the most part barely fit, and many utterly unfit, for human habitation.'[38] The report went on to recommend that 'steps must be taken to cause the foreign poor upon arrival to imbibe notions proper to civilised life in this country'.[39] Improved housing was a prerequisite for ironing out the ghetto bends. This latter philosophy of Anglo-Jewry was deployed in all aspects of its involvement with the immigrant community, embracing education, youth clubs, social provision and, if possible, politics and labour organisation. The mantle of the *shtetl* had to be shed.

The recommendations of the Commission and the influence of its chairman changed the landscape of Spitalfields. A decision was promptly taken to provide 'More commodious and healthy lodgings and dwellings than those which they [those living in poor housing] now inhabit.'[40] As Jerry White describes, Rothschild Buildings, as the dwellings became known, were developed along the same lines as the earlier philanthropic buildings erected by Peabody and Waterlow. Whilst providing accommodation for artisans in the poorer districts, they were developed on a profit-making basis, usually offering those who, *philanthropically*, invested, a 4 or 4.5 per cent annual return. Accordingly, on completion, the rent had to be set at a level which would satisfy this requirement. As the regular payment of rent was mandatory, tenants were required to have a steady income. In 1886, when Rothschild Buildings were completed, rents were set at five shillings per week for two rooms and a scullery, rising to seven shillings and sixpence per week for four rooms and a scullery. At these levels it was deemed the investors' return could be satisfied. As was so often the case the, so-called, philanthropic industrial dwellings were out of the reach of those who needed decent housing most, rents, and the need for their regular payment, being far beyond the means of the indigent and irregularly waged. As White's book describes, Rothschild Buildings[41] became home to the semi-skilled and skilled artisan — the majority of whom were Jewish. Newly arrived 'greeners'[42] and casual workers were forced to rely on Jewish charities[43] or on the mercies of the unscrupulous Jewish landlords of Spitalfields.

Partly due to the exposure given the area by the Jack the Ripper murders of 1888 and partly to the concerned response of the elite of British Jewry, by the mid-1890s the face of Spitalfields was changing. In place of the small, mean houses and rookeries in Flower and Dean Street, Thrall Street and those contiguous, stood Nathaniel Buildings, Charlotte de Rothschild Buildings, Lolesworth Buildings, Irene House and Ruth House. The area had become respectable, the dangerous classes had been moved on and in their place had come the alien. However, there were those who did not appreciate the changes. They accused the aliens of denying them their pleasures, bemoaning the disappearance of the women of the night from the surrounding streets.

With the exception of the four years between 1888 and 1892, unemployment and recession were the main economic features of the last twenty years of the century. As more immigrants poured into Spitalfields, homes, and work, became harder to find. As demand accelerated, rents increased, in some instances rising by as much as 25 per cent.[44] The rent for a single room in Spitalfields could be anything from four to seven shillings a week, figures which could represent between 25 to 30 per cent of a tailor's income (when he was in work). In return for this the tailor and his family would be provided with accommodation that was invariably cramped and dirty. As Bernard Gainer confirms, 'In the heart of the alien community, the greatest cramming together could be found.'[45] There was a further iniquity. The imposition of 'key money', a practice whereby an incoming tenant was obliged to hand over a specified sum of money, which could be as much as £20, to the outgoing tenant and/or landlord in order to secure tenancy. Yet the alien immigrant was determined in spirit, if not always successful in body, and prepared to pay the higher rents, endure subletting and pay key money, if that was what it took to live and work in the ghetto that was Spitalfields, the starting point of upward mobility for the incomer. For some, the housing crisis proved to be an ill wind. Immigrant Jewish landlords had no qualms about harassing and exploiting their more unfortunate co-religionists and regarded 'House property a favourite form of interest'.[46] It was the economics of scarcity which enabled those who had to profit from those who had not, the latter invariably being the pauper alien.

At the turn of the nineteenth century, the American journalist and author Jack London recorded his journey into the abyss that was the East End. He described the colour and texture of life in Spitalfields as 'grey and drab . . . the people themselves are filthy . . . the rain when it falls is more like grease than water from heaven'.[47] In his revelatory book, *The People of the Abyss*, London represented the East End as analogous with the darkest jungles of Africa. He records the appalling conditions he encountered in a seven-roomed house in Frying Pan Alley, just off Brick Lane. Six of the rooms (rented out at the going rate or more) measured no more than eight feet by eight feet. In these were housed twenty people, who cooked, ate, slept and worked in the same space. In the seventh room, measuring seven feet by eight feet, he found five sweated (male) workers making shoes.[48] London's account confirms the way in which the high level of rents imposed the practice of subletting. Though this style of living may have eased the budgets of the most needy, it did little to improve their quality of life or reduce levels of overcrowding in Spitalfields.

The effects of demolition and displacement and the downside of the building of model dwellings are made clear in this quotation from Russell and Lewis's investigation into the Jews in London, which was published at the beginning of the twentieth century. It explains how and why Spitalfields had managed to achieve such a high density of population and such a high level of rents:

> The two-storied tenement . . . having been often displaced by the model dwellings, which shelter hundreds of families upon a comparatively narrow site . . . (the Jew) overcrowds his home, and therefore can afford to pay a higher price than that previously obtained and therefore gradually displaces the gentile population.[49]

The image of Spitalfields as an overcrowded, unhealthy and exotic ghetto persisted into the early twentieth century. There were still people living in properties with no running water and, in the Jewish-owned Booth Street Buildings, there were just thirty water closets for 600 people. In 1901, Middlesex Street, better known as Petticoat Lane, and its environs was described by S. Gelberg as, a 'howling living pandemonium of cosmopolitan costerism, a curious tangle of humanity'. He goes on to paint a picture of an area of impoverishment and survival, hardship and vibrancy:

> On the weekday, however the scene is transformed . . . you are in a city of endless toil. . . . All day long, and far into the night, the factories make dismal music in the ghetto. . . . Why do the Jews labour so? . . . [they are] alien Dick Whittingtons inside curls and *jupizes* [long coats]

who have put down their bundles a while to peer into the promised land beyond and thereafter rest not till they have retired beaten from the struggle or found social salvation in Maida Vale. . . . And if the ghetto is not wholly poor it is not entirely famished. Kosher restaurants abound in it; kosher butcher shops are clustered in their bunches. . . . Altogether, indeed, a unique little cosmos, this East End Hebrew colony – a poverty stricken, wealthy, hungry, feasting, praying, bargaining fragment of a 'Nation of Priests'.[50]

Spitalfields had indeed become Little Jerusalem. In addition to the Jewish butcher shops, grocery shops, fresh and fried fish shops and dairies, the many hundreds of sweatshops, 900 of which the social investigator Beatrice Potter *supposedly* visited,[51] and in which the English language was rarely, if at all heard, were the other requirements of Jewish settlement: synagogues, schools and charitable institutions. *The Jewish Year Book* for 1896 lists twenty *chevras*[52] in the Spitalfields area alone that were members of the Federation of Synagogues.[53] These were synagogues established by Eastern European immigrants who did not feel at home in the Anglicised, church-like places of worship founded by the elite of British Jewry. In addition to those affiliated to the Federation were other *chevras* considered too poor or unsanitary to be absorbed into the body whose honorary president was Lord Rothschild. Spitalfields also boasted a Jewish Ladies Association for Preventive and Rescue Work, an organisation set up to save single, female migrants from the white-slave trade; a Soup Kitchen for the Jewish Poor (in Fashion Street); a Jewish Working Men's Club and five *mikvahs*.[54] Finally there was the largest voluntary school in London, the Jews' Free School in Bell Lane which, in 1896, recorded a student body of 3,573 of which 1,368 were born overseas.[55]

As Chapter 7 below illustrates, the Jewish immigrant entrepreneurial spirit also left its architectural imprint on the landscape of Spitalfields. In 1905 a Jewish immigrant, Abraham Davis, had a vision. He set out to create what we, in the twenty-first century, call a shopping mall. It was to be a development which would incorporate shops, a reading room and steam baths. Davis took out a lease on land in Fashion Street and erected his Fashion Street Arcade. Though somewhat smaller than the 250 shops he had originally envisaged, the scheme, completed in 1909, held sixty-nine shops which were fronted by a 'Moorish design in pale red brick, dressed with moulded red brick and terracotta and lavishly ornamented with cement'.[56] The concept, almost seventy years before its time, not surprisingly proved to be a failure. Davis was made bankrupt, and the dream building turned into workshops with living accommodation above. At the end of the twentieth century, all that remained of the original building, which survived both the Blitz and the demolitions of the 1950s and 1960s, was its frontage, which Sheppard described as one which 'might have strayed from the amusement quarter of a seedy seaside town'. Fortunately, this view was not one held by the modern-day entrepreneurs who are redeveloping the site and taking great care to preserve that 'seedy' exterior.

The first peacetime immigration legislation, the 1905 Aliens Act, was a direct response to the uncontrolled entry of pauper aliens and the problems they caused, namely unemployment and overcrowding. By 1908 the housing crisis was over. In place of the overcrowded houses and tenements were empty rooms. The movement away from the East End was due to a combination of factors, of which a reduction in immigrant numbers from Eastern Europe was but one. It was the development of the underground railway and trams systems which, together with the extension of cheap fares on the above-ground railways, that encouraged those who could do so to move out to the developing suburbs. The traditional view has been, as put forward by the Jewish historian, Lloyd Gartner that 'It was not the Jews who vacated the houses.'[57] However, more recently the economic historian Andrew Godley has challenged this belief. He suggests that in the years leading to the outbreak of the First World War there was a clearly defined movement out from the East End of London. By '1910–1914 probably over one-quarter of London's East European Jews were living in areas of sec- ondary settlement, enjoying the benefits of larger dwellings and the sense of having escaped from the East End'.[58] The movement of Jewish immigrants out of the East End accelerated after the First World War. While some had accumulated sufficient funds during the hostilities to move out to the emerging suburbs, others were pushed by London County Council's harsh policy towards aliens, adopted in the early 1920s. The decision not to employ aliens, not to provide them with local government housing and not to offer scholarships to their children, was the catalyst for those that could to depart.

For those who remained, life in Spitalfields was a mixture of hardship and hope. There was a desire to move upwards, even if it was only to the 'build- ings' (Rothschild) where, in spite of the bedbugs, which kept you up all night in the summer, and the high rent, you would have a scullery and, if not a bath, then at least your own water closet. Most of all there was a sense of community, indeed of communities within the larger community. For the Jewish East End was Little Jerusalem and within its buildings, alleys and streets developed the communal spirit which made Spitalfields an exotic, dangerous and tantalising place.

At the outbreak of the Second World War, Spitalfields was still seen as a place on the edge. Writing in 1939, Ashley Smith captured the aroma and character of the area as he described:

> The virtual ghetto of Hanbury Street and Old Montague Street where the flavours of unEnglish meals fill the air. Where the clansman of some distant Polish or Russian town occupy whole lengths of a street ... Jewish vitality and Jewish unhappiness and restlessness thrown like some bitter herb into the cooking pot of mighty London.[59]

It took Hitler's bombs and the slum demolitions of the 1950s and 1960s to lay the foundations for the next immigrant invasion and for the arrival of Banglatown.

Mosques, saris and bagels

In the years that followed the Second World War the appearance and character of Spitalfields changed yet again. The desire for socio-economic upward mobility together with the end of empire, resulted in the disintegration of one immigrant community and the emergence of another. Unlike the gradual disappearance of the Huguenots into the mainstream, pre-1939 the Jewish East End, that which Israel Zangwill had once called 'this London ghetto of ours',[60] was a vibrant reality. By the early 1950s it was no longer – the children of the ghetto had moved out to suburbs to the northwest and northeast of London. By the close of the decade, pioneers of the next minority community had begun arriving in Spitalfields. With the exception of the building of the East London Mosque in Whitechapel Road (in reality just beyond the boundaries of Spitalfields), they altered little architecturally. However, the exotic sounds and smells of South Asia soon proclaimed the formation of a new community and the creation of a new ghetto.

The Spitalfields that accommodated the post-Second World War immigrants from the Indian subcontinent was one that was structurally altered in the years immediately preceding their arrival. Bomb damage, slum demolition, rebuilding, conversions and wasteland awaiting private development, created a shortage of decent homes in the ward. This in spite of the fact that the population had declined from its 28,000 high in 1901 to 8,284 in 1961, when immigration from East Pakistan was underway. It was a reduction that continued until the 1980s when family reunions amongst Bangladeshis began to push the graph upwards. At the 2001 Decennial Census, the population was recorded as 10,500, still well under half that of 100 years before.

In spite of London's East End being within the Target Area A bombing zone, Spitalfields suffered less severely than the Docks and Bethnal Green and Stepney.[61] The street map of 'Bombing in Stepney', found in the Tower Hamlets Local History Archives, suggests that Spitalfields was not a target as such and that those bombs that did fall did so more by accident than design. It is almost as if a protective circle had been drawn around the main body of the area, thus enabling the preservation of the Georgian and Victorian architecture of Fournier, Princelet and Hanbury Streets.[62] The bombing was at its heaviest in a line running west to east between Old Montague Street and Whitechapel Road, thus reinforcing the view that the bombers targeted the main roads.[63] The immediate postwar years revealed a Spitalfields which differed little to that of the Victorian era, even in terms of the appalling housing conditions it offered to its poorest tenants and newer arrivals. The 1957 Housing Act did little to alleviate conditions. It was a veritable action replay of what had accompanied the Cross Act, seventy-five years before. Though the worst slum buildings were, by law, demolished, little suitable rebuilding followed. Certainly nothing that would, or could, accommodate the New Commonwealth immigrants who were now arriving. But even the demolitions were sparse. According to Charlie Forman, the 'Spitalfields slums were almost intact long after most of the rest of the East End slums had disappeared.'[64] It was not until after 1969 that the old Victorian buildings – Charlotte de Rothschild Buildings, Ruth House, Irene House, Lolesworth Buildings and others – were demolished. By 1986 the Ordnance Survey maps for the area boasted the rebuilding in Flower and Dean Walk and Nathaniel Close. The maps also confirm the old truism that, in places of poverty and overcrowding, new building produces insufficient homes.

It was on the streets of Brick Lane that the changing ethnic identity of Spitalfields could be best observed. In the late 1950s and early 1960s, single male sojourners from Sylhet could be seen in the three Bengali-owned cafes, *Nazrul, Blue Café* and *Alf's Hideaway.*[65] Some of the Bengali immigrants who settled in Princelet Street and Old Montague Street in the early 1960s had moved north across the Whitechapel Road from Cable Street, when the 'coloured quarter',[66] the focus of Michael Banton's seminal study, was put under order of demolition in 1961. Even if there had been availability, ineligibility meant that council housing was not an option for the new migrant arrivals in Spitalfields. The sole alternative was private housing.

The early male immigrant arrivals, men who at that stage considered themselves as sojourners, initially manifested little concern about the quality of their housing. Solutions to overcrowding and unsanitary conditions were low on the list of priorities, for soon, as rich men of high status, they would return triumphant to Bangladesh. There were also advantages to being crowded into one room with six or seven others of your countrymen. Fraternal closeness facilitated the development of emotional and financial support mechanisms, which acted as charitable substitutes in an environment with no elite-established infrastructure of benevolence, as had been put in place by the Huguenots and Anglo-Jews. In the case of the young Bengali men, 'If one or two of them [male migrants] were working they would help out and lend money to the others until they too had jobs.'[67] Though this nonchalant attitude was adopted by many of the early arrivals, a minority recognised the potential in property ownership and the letting of accommodation to their fellow immigrants. This was almost an action replay of the economic activity carried on by Eastern European Jewish landlords in Spitalfields a century before. The high rents, subletting, sub-subletting and the passing of key money only serving to exacerbate what were, by the early 1970s, conditions of extreme overcrowding and unsanitary living.

The decade between 1971 and 1981 was one in which the pattern of Bangladeshi immigration changed from one of pioneering sojourning males to family reunions. It was a decade during which the structure of the Bangladeshi community was drastically altered; one in which the newly emerging community's housing needs became a political issue; and one in which the community's presence as an increasingly vibrant representative minority group rather than a male enclave, began to make itself visible on the streets of Spitalfields. Gradually Bangladeshi space expanded outwards from Old Montague Street and Princelet Street. Raphael Samuel has portrayed 1960s' Old Montague Street as a conspicuous point of ethnic group interface. Even though the sojourners from Bangladesh were moving in, some having come north from Cable Street and the demolitions, he was still able to detect the Jewish Ghetto. As he recorded, 'it was the nearest thing in the East End to the way I imagined a *shtetl* . . . in the 1960s there were still vats of herrings in front of the extremely modest two storey cottages'.[68] Bengali numbers were increasing as housing stock was reducing following a programme of aggressive demolition, with no accompanying rebuilding. By 1980, 50 of Spitalfields' 250 acres were derelict and much of what had been left standing was uninhabitable. The area was now one of the most overcrowded in London. This situation did little for the newly reunited Bangladeshi families whose needs were not just housing *per se*, but largescale housing which could accommodate families of five or more.

As had the Jews and Huguenots before them, the Bangladeshi community clung to the western part of the borough of Tower Hamlets. It was there that jobs in the clothing workshops and restaurants were to be found. As requests for local government housing fell upon deaf ears, private landlords, often Pakistani or Bangladeshi, were able to extract exorbitant rents from those who wished to live near their place of work. If social housing was offered, it was all too often in the east of the borough, away from the main nexus of community, and always of the poorest quality. Inevitably, it was that vacated by white families who had been moved to better accommodation. Bob Brett, Director of Housing for Tower Hamlets in the 1980s, recalls that, 'Bangladeshis got the worst housing . . . the worst estates were predominantly Bangladeshi.'[69] If Bengalis were moved to council estates, they were invariably those with a 'white barrier' where non-whites were subjected to physical and mental abuse. A few families stuck it out, others chose to return to Spitalfields and rent privately owned properties which, though geographically acceptable, were in every other way totally unacceptable. Infestation was standard and overcrowding equal to that at the end of the nineteenth century. In 1979, in one terrace in Princelet Street, 150 immigrants were herded together in a space which, in 1951, had been home to a maximum of seventy-seven people.[70] The new immigrants adopted a strategy emulated from the white community, that of squatting in condemned properties. It was a tactic which led to an unexpected alliance of desperate immigrants and natives who, on occasions, jointly sat it out in squats in Spitalfields. It was in 1976 that the first large-scale all-Bangladeshi squat was held in Old Montague Street. Twenty-two adults and fifty children displayed their tenacity, and determination to remain in Spitalfields, by sitting it out until an acceptable solution was reached.

As the family reunions got underway, the Bengali population of Spital-fields became an increasingly visible community. One of the most signific-ant pronouncements of their spatial, religious and gendered[71] presence was the opening of the London *Jamme Masjid* mosque on the corner of Fournier Street and Brick Lane in the early 1970s. The building, which had started life as the Huguenots' *La Neuve Église*, had undergone its third religious transition. Having gone from Christianity to Judaism, it now housed members of the local Muslim community. No outward architectural changes marked the arrival of Islam in Brick Lane, but when the building was filled with, and expelled, its worshippers, the streets of Spitalfields took on a new identity.

In qualitative terms, it was the small clothing factories and workshops of Spitalfields which, in the 1950s and 1960s, underwent an ethnic transition, changing workforce from Jews and Cypriots to Pakistanis and Bangladeshis. With time, ownership too would pass on from the old ethnic bosses to those newly arrived from the Indian subcontinent. It was an almost invisible transition: the traditional cellars, attics and backrooms remained; only the ethnicity of the sweated bodies within them changed. The mechanics of sweated labour continued: workers were employed in the worst conditions, for the lowest wages, for the longest hours. Often arriving before dawn and departing after dusk, the immigrant workers were hidden from daylight and the prying eyes of factory and workshop inspectors and other investigators.[72] From the mid-1960s until the early 1980s, the clothing industry was a major provider of employment for immigrant Bangladeshi males in Tower Hamlets. Some estimates have put the number employed in the factories and workshops in the area as 20 per cent of the community or 10,000 persons. Naila Kabeer suggests that the figure was considerably higher than this.[73] However, in the mid-1980s the clothing factories began to close down, their owners having found it economically expedient to give work out to local sweatshops, homeworkers or factories in Eastern Europe or the third world where labour costs were far lower than those in London, even in Spitalfields. The redundancies accompanying the closures were one of the main reasons for Spitalfields featuring at the top of the unemployment tables for London.

The increasing presence and economic activity of Bengalis in Spitalfields can be charted by analysing the entries for Brick Lane in the London Post Office Street Directories between 1951 and 1981.[74] It is evident that in 1951 Brick Lane was still a centre of Jewish economic activity. Using names as a guide to ethnicity, along the length of Brick Lane were listed Jewish tailors, bakers, furriers, kosher butchers, confectioners, egg wholesalers, pro-visions merchants, booksellers and a pharmacist. Kelly's Street Directory for 1951 shows some 134 active Jewish businesses in that one street alone.[75] No Asian outlets or residences are documented. In 1961, though the number of Jewish businesses is barely reduced, the first Asian outlet is recorded. The *Bombay Restaurant* is at no. 118, *Muslim Hallal* butcher at no. 166 and *Mehmet Ali* the greengrocer at no. 181.[76] The opening of two ethnic food outlets suggests that the nascent community had begun to develop a domesticated lifestyle, while the needs of men still living a bachelor existence and unused, or unwilling, to prepare their own food were served by the *Bombay Restaurant*. By 1972 a definite Bengali presence is identifiable, one which contained all the basic elements of community and which denoted the transition from a group of sojourners to a commune of settlers. The Street Directory now listed Pakistani or Bengali clothing manufacturers, leather factories, butchers, cafes and grocers,[77] plus the all-important travel agents needed to organise return visits, family reunifications and, for some, the sending of remittances via 'donkeys'[78] to *Londoni* villages. Brick Lane had shed the carapace of Little Jerusalem but was not yet Banglatown. For the next ten to fifteen years the street was truly multi-cultural, Jewish, Bengali and English activities carried out side by side, the latter most overtly defined by the public houses which would disappear as the decade passed.[79] The metamorphosis was almost complete by 1981, the increasing female presence signalled by the appearance of shops selling saris, baubles, bangles and beads.[80] The Street Directory now listed only twelve Jewish outlets, and it is possible that some of those were in fact owned and run by Pakistani or Bangladeshi entrepreneurs.[81] In 1991, Wolman's Pharmacy, the one remaining Jewish-owned business, finally closed its doors; at the time of writing, the shop is a south Asian music outlet. But the echo of the past has not gone completely. Just to the north of Banglatown is the beigel shop. The Jewish bread ring of life in a variety of flavours, with a variety of fillings, is sought after by consumers from all cultures and all parts of the capital. They patiently lined the pavements of Brick Lane in the early hours of the morning to get their fix. This is not multi-culturalism, this is inter-culturalism.

By the time the twentieth century drew to a close, the local Bangladeshi economy was well rooted. As confirmation of this, and as a display of ethnic self-confidence, in 1997 Shirazul Haque, the owner of *Shampan*, the highly successful restaurant on the corner of Hanbury Street and Brick Lane, together with a group of Bengali entrepreneurs, conceived the idea of transforming the central section of Brick Lane into a mono-cultural enclave to be known as Banglatown. Not everyone approved of a self-ghettoisation project which was at odds with the Englishness of London's East End. A correspondent to the *Daily Telegraph* found the notion 'offensive', stating that

> The attempt to change established place names is an attempt to pervert history, and to create foreign ghettos in the heart of our cities ... [this is] a proposed development that explicitly denies [integration] and puts self-conscious separatism in its place.[82]

The spatial and cultural pronouncement of the Bengali presence in Brick Lane was also ill received by the more religious members of the local Muslim community. As one activist from the East London Mosque explained, 'They [the supporters of Banglatown] promote nationalism and it stops the Muslims to think Islamically ... Muslims start to identify with Bengali rather than Muslim.'[83] Other members of the community considered that Banglatown was merely a marketing ploy to enrich its promoters. It did nothing to improve local housing or education or to combat racism. This was not the view put forward by Jane Jacobs, writing in 1996, she saw it as 'part of a broader plan [by local businessmen] to control redevelopment in their favour: acquire land, ensure social amenity and establish opportunities for Bengali youths to enter the City workforce'.[84]

Banglatown may have started off as a segregated area but it is now something very different. By day and by night it draws to its throbbing pavements outsiders, tourists and young middle-class, predominantly white, professionals eager to taste the exoticism of 'elsewhere'. Some have likened it to 'A Turkish bazaar' which 'throngs with pavement touts, hustling customers towards the cheapest menu'.[85] Yet nothing remains quite the same. Banglatown is transmuting by the minute as the essence of the current immigrant group – the Bengalis – is being replaced by another. Affluent middle-class professionals are moving into the western edge of Spitalfields bringing with them the minimalist and the barista. How long will it be before these replace the balti and sari?

Conclusion

Spitalfields was conceived as a place on the edge – as such it provided a refuge for those escaping religious persecution and economic suffocation, offering hope to those seeking to make their fortunes and either move on or return home. Throughout the past 400 years the district has been perceived as the outsiders' communal space, a self-created ghetto to which those on the margin could retire until ready to move into the mainstream. Not all the residents took, or take, the path of integration and assimilation, there are those who chose, or choose, to maintain their otherness. Over the centuries Spitalfields has facilitated freedom of choice, enabling its inhabitants to come or go, move in or move out, at will. The forces of upward mobility have been powered by the fads and fancies of the receiving society, the clothing industry proving the most favoured of routes. Even before the seventeenth century migrant skills benefited both host and ethnic communities.

And yet, even as this book is being written, Spitalfields and Banglatown[86] is changing. A new group of 'immigrants' is settling on the western edges of the ward. They are affluent and ambitious middle-class professionals and businesspeople[87] who can afford to purchase homes of the past which now change hands at seven-figure sums. But its history remains an indelible part of the landscape – it is there in the bricks and wooden portals of what was Church Street, in the Star of David embossed on the drainpipes of Christ Church School,[88] and in the Islamisation of the building on the corner of Brick Lane and Fournier Street. It is into this space that the new generation of migrants is moving. They too are beginning to make their imprint on the landscape: witness the sophisticated bars, clubs and craft outlets, delis and design studios, and elegantly refurbished properties. Will these newcomers push the extant Bengali community into London's eastern corridor? Or will there be a return to a world in which poverty and affluence, insider and outsider, once again live cheek-by-jowl on the edge?

Notes

1 S. Sassen, 'Rebuilding the Global City: Economy, Ethnicity and Space', in A. King (ed.), *re-Presenting the City: Ethnicity, Capital and Culture in the 21st Century Metropolis*, Basingstoke, Macmillan, 1996, p. 23.
2 It has been suggested that the cockney 'lingo' is a fusion of the old Huguenot patois and 'working man's' English. However, Gareth Stedman Jones suggests that it derives from Middle English *Cokeney*, meaning cock's egg, a misshapen egg. According to Edwin Pugh the word originally meant townee, a Londoner, 'the supreme type of Englishman'; by the early twentieth century the cockney had become associated with the East End, and as such could mean 'jingoistic Londoner'. See G. Stedman Jones, 'The "Cockney" and the Nation', in D. Feldman and G. Stedman Jones (eds), *Metropolis London*, London, Routledge, 1989, pp. 272–324.
3 It was not only the non-English born who settled outside the city's walls, native-born artisans settled in Spitalfields to escape the controls and taxes of the City of London and its guilds.
4 Recent government policies of dispersal and accommodation centres have removed the role of first point of settlement from areas proximate to points of disembarkation. It remains to be seen whether, in time, those immigrants permitted to remain in Britain, migrate back to the traditional ghettoes.
5 L. Wirth, *The Ghetto*, Chicago, University of Chicago Press, 1928, p. 4.
6 It needs to be pointed out that, though the Jews were 'readmitted' to England in 1656, it was not until the last half of the eighteenth century that their 'presence' reached significant numbers, estimated to be between 8,000 and 10,000, and it was not until the nineteenth century that the increase became significant. As has been suggested, the revocation of the Edict of Nantes resulted in between 16,000 and 20,000 Huguenots settling in the Spitalfields area and some further 15,000 settling in and around the area known as Soho.
7 Until the building of the London Docks at the beginning of the nineteenth century, ships would anchor, load and unload at the Pool of London.
8 Quoted in R. Porter, *London: A Social History*, London, Hamish Hamilton, 1994, p. 118.
9 Brick Lane was so named because the land around it was used for brick earth. The bricks were fired locally and either used to build local properties or transported to the river southwards down the track that became known as Brick Lane.
10 It is possible that Wren was referring to the southernmost end of Brick Lane which, in the map of 1686, does appear as nothing more than a narrow lane, whilst further to the north the 'Lane' is more clearly defined as a thoroughfare.
11 See W.J. Fishman, *East End Jewish Radicals 1875–1914*, London, Duckworth, 1975.
12 P. Ackroyd, *London: The Biography*, London, Chatto and Windus, 2000, p. 531.
13 A. Palmer, *The East End: Four Centuries of London Life*, London, John Murray, 1989, p. 7.

14 J. Stow, *Survey of London*, Oxford, Clarendon, 1908 edition, p. 116.
15 Ibid., p. ix.
16 Later Flower and Dean Street.
17 Ackroyd, op. cit., p. 676.
18 F.H.W. Sheppard (ed.), *Survey of London, Vol. XXVII, Spitalfields and Mile End New Town*, London, London County Council, 1957, p. 3.
19 Ibid., p. 4.
20 Tenter land was the area in which milled or printed fabric (cloth or silk) was stretched out to dry on a framework of tenterhooks so that it would not lose its shape.
21 A. Kershen, *Uniting the Tailors*, Ilford, Frank Cass, 1995, p. 102.
22 Ibid.
23 Sheppard, op. cit., p. 238.
24 Ibid., p. 188.
25 From John Noorthouck, *A New History of London,* London, R. Baldwin, 1773, pp. 274, 758–9.
26 See Chapter 7 below.
27 Weinreb and C. Hibbert (eds), *London Encyclopaedia*, Basingstoke, Macmillan, 1983, p. 808.
28 Quoted in Ken Leech, 'The Decay of Spitalfields', *East London Papers*, 7 (2), 1964, p. 58.
29 Porter op. cit., pp. 195–6.
30 J.H. Scott, *Spitalfields*, London, 1894, p. 12.
31 Gareth Stedman Jones, *Outcast London*, London, Penguin, 1983, p. 215.
32 Ibid., p. 198.
33 Ibid., p. 162.
34 *Dwellings of the Poor*, report of the Dwellings Committee of the Charity Organisation Society, London, 1881, pp. 46–7.
35 A description of Spitalfields circa 1900 which appears in Howard Angus Kennedy, 'London's Social Settlements', in George R. Sims, *Living London*, London, Cassell, 1902, p. 267.
36 Quoted in B. Gainer, *The Alien Invasion: The Origins of the 1905 Aliens Act*, London, Heinemann Educational, 1972, p. 38.
37 The Eastern European population expanded from 26,742 in 1891 to 53,537 in 1901, with 48,433 of the 53,537 living in the East End, the majority in Stepney – which at that time included Spitalfields.
38 *Jewish Chronicle*, 27 February 1885.
39 Ibid.
40 Memorandum of Association of the Four Per Cent Industrial Dwellings Co. Ltd. 1885, quoted in J. White, *Rothschild Buildings*, London, Routledge & Kegan Paul, 1980, p. 20.
41 For more detail about the residents, architecture and experience of living in Rothschild Buildings, see White, op. cit.
42 Greener was the name given to someone who was 'green' or unskilled in a trade.
43 See Chapter 5 below.
44 D. Feldman, *Englishmen and Jews: Social Relations and Political Culture 1840–1914*, New Haven and London, Yale University Press, 1994, p. 173.
45 Gainer, op. cit., p. 38.
46 Ibid., p. 42.
47 J. London, *The People of the Abyss*, 1903, London, Journeyman Press, 1977 edition, p. 94.
48 Ibid., p. 30.

49 C. Russell and H. Lewis, *The Jew in London,* London, T. Fisher Unwin, 1900, p. 196.
50 S. Gelberg, 'Living in London', quoted in Peter Marcan, *Down in the East End*, London, Peter Marcan Publications, 1986, pp. 38–40.
51 Kershen, op. cit., p. 108.
52 Small synagogues. See Chapter 4 below.
53 For details of the Federation of Synagogues, its origins, composition etc., see Chapter 4 below.
54 Religious baths.
55 Details from *The Jewish Year Book 1896*, facsimile edition, Ilford, Vallentine Mitchell, 1996, pp. 34–61.
56 Sheppard, op. cit., p. 251.
57 L. Gartner, *The Jewish Immigrant in England 1870–1914*, London, Simons, 1973, p. 148.
58 Godley, 'Leaving the East End', in A. Kershen (ed.), *London the Promised Land? The Migrant Experience in a Capital City*, Aldershot, Avebury, 1997, p. 61.
59 Ashley Smith, *A City Stirs*, London, Chapman and Hall, 1939, p. 144.
60 I. Zangwill, *The Children of the Ghetto*, Woking, Leicester University Press, 1977 edition, p. 1.
61 Amongst the more well-known landmarks to be demolished or badly damaged through enemy bombing was the Jews' Free School in Bell Lane and the elementary school in Old Montague Street.
62 The map shows that some 'stray' bombs did fall on the area but these knocked out single houses rather than great swathes.
63 For details of ruins in the area see Ordnance Survey Maps Plan TQ 3381 NE and Plan TQ 3481 NW 1948, in the Tower Hamlets Local History Library.
64 C. Forman, *Spitalfields: A Battle for Land*, London, Hilary Shipman, 1989, p. 72.
65 The latter, in spite of its name, was a popular haunt of those smoking, or looking to buy, cannabis and, for this reason, subject to regular police raids. Information from the Rev. Ken Leech in a conversation with the author, 18 February 2003.
66 M. Banton, *The Coloured Quarter: Coloured Migrants in an English City*, London, Cape, 1955.
67 Author's conversation with a student whose father had arrived as a male immigrant pioneer in the early 1960s, 12 July 2000.
68 M. Girouard, D. Cruickshank, R. Samuel *et al.*, *The Saving of Spitalfields*, London, 1989, pp. 146–7.
69 Bob Brett in discussion with the author, 12 February 2003.
70 Forman, op. cit., p. 88.
71 Whilst the men attend the mosque, women shop in the sari and retail outlets.
72 In the 1980s the author made a number of attempts to gain access to a leather workshop until finally successful. The workshop master, a Pakistani, ensured that none of his employees, Bengalis, spoke to me. I suspect that, if not illegal migrants, they may well have been unregistered workers and could have been drawing social benefit.
73 N. Kabeer, *The Power to Choose*, London and New York, Verso, 2000, p. 216.
74 After 1981 (and to a lesser extent before) the Directories became increasingly unreliable as those collating the material seem to have taken a somewhat maverick view as to what should and should not be included.
75 *Post Office London Directory 1951*, London, Kelly's Directories, 1951, p. 115.
76 *Post Office London Directory 1961*, London, Kelly's Directories, 1961, p. 371.
77 *Post Office London Directory 1971*, London, Kelly's Directories, 1971, p. 187.
78 The name given to individuals who go back and forth to Bangladesh carrying remittances in cash.

79 At the time of going to press (autumn 2004) there are perhaps two public houses remaining in Brick Lane. However, the situation is fluid and some may open as others may close, dependent on local demand and fluctuations in the make-up of the local population.

80 It should also be noted that the street signs in the area of Spitalfields which is predominantly Bengali are written in both English and Bengali. Interestingly, though the Bangladeshi community has moved further north into the area of Bethnal Green, from a point approximately two turnings north from the railway arches – the traditional demarcation line of native and alien – the street signs are only in English.

81 See Chapter 7 below.

82 *Daily Telegraph*, 10 January 1997.

83 D. Garbin, 'Migration, territories diasporiques et politiques identitaires: Bengalis musulmans entre "Banglatown" (Londres) et Sylhet (Bangladesh)' unpublished Ph.D thesis, University of François Rabelais de Tours, 2004, p. 373.

84 J.M. Jacobs, *Edge of Empire, Postcolonialism and the City*, London, Routledge, 1996, p. 100.

85 *Guardian*, 13 April 2004.

86 In the 2001 Census the ward, previously known as Spitalfields, appeared as Spitalfields and Banglatown.

87 From a variety of ethnic and religious backgrounds.

88 In order for the school to be used as a Sunday religious school for local Jewish children in the nineteenth and early twentieth centuries there had to be some sign of a Jewish identity/presence. The solution was found in the embossing of the *Magen David* (Star of David) on the drainpipes to the left and right of the school's main entrance.

4   Religion

This chapter sets out to explore the way in which the practice of, and adherence to, Calvinism, Judaism and Islam influenced the initial settlement and subsequent integration of Huguenots, Jews and Bangladeshis in Spitalfields. In essence this is not a theological evaluation or a measure of immigrant religiosity. Rather it is an attempt to comprehend how each of the three groups accommodated the prescriptives of their religion in Spitalfields, specifically within the context of space, economic activity and diet. At this point it is perhaps worth reminding the reader that the three are linked by more than just spatial chronology. All were monotheistic and believed that God was omniscient, omnipotent and omnipresent. All three looked back to Abraham and his roots. Christianity followed the crucifixion, whilst Islam emerged in the seventh century as a result of the prophet Muhammad's belief that he had been called upon to 'purify the religion which the Jews and the Christians had distorted'. All three knew marginalisation and persecution.

For the Huguenots, religion was the force that drove them from France and transformed them into refugees.[1] It was because of their conviction in the all-embracing Calvinist 'discipline of life' that they were prepared to convert their Francophilian patriotism into loyalty to England. Faith in their God and his teachings had made Jews wanderers and outsiders for nearly 2,000 years – it was the essence of their ethnicity, transported communities and societal marginalisation. Yet, unlike the Huguenots, the majority of Eastern European Jews who migrated during the latter decades of the nineteenth century did not move as a result of religious persecution but rather in an attempt to secure an economic future in an environment free from political, social and religious constraints. It was this that drew Jews, in common with millions of non-Jews, westward.[2] The ambitious young men who left Bangladesh in the late 1950s and early 1960s crossed the seven seas and thirteen rivers with the hope of making enough money to enable them to return home with the means to buy both material and social status. Religion was an intrinsic part of their background and travelled with them, even though on arrival in London some gave precedence to the baser pleasures of metropolitan life.[3] For those sojourners, although religion did not feature as a constituent in the migratory decision-making process, it would contribute to the structuring of their lives in the *bidesh*.

For each of the three groups under the microscope in this book, religion became a central factor in their migrant experience. It provided a focus, a control centre for the newly emerging community and if not the source, then the conduit, for the welfare and support so needed by impoverished immigrants in Spitalfields. It is religion that is responsible for the spatial and architectural links which enable us to unite semantically three such temporally and ethnically separate minority groups. The commonalities of the three religions have all too often been forgotten, buried under violent attempts at proselytisation or misconceived reactions to the perceived ill treatment. Set against a history of religious conflict and maltreatment, this chapter will illustrate the way in which religion featured in the structuring of immigrant life in Spitalfields, in communal control and as a shield from the harshness of what was, for the incomers, an alien environment. In what follows, we will examine the place of religion in the migrants' lives and explore the way in which each group established and organised their religious base in Spitalfields. We will see that, despite attempts by some to obfuscate the reality, when we start to unpick the tapestry which is the immigrant experience in Spitalfields, amongst its many threads the strongest are those of religion.

To praise him all my days

In his memoirs the Reverend Jacques Fontaine provides graphic and disturbing descriptions of the way in which in France, in the years leading to 1598, men and women were put to death for doing nothing more than praying in a Protestant chapel.[4] Therefore it is not surprising that one of the first acts of the earliest Calvinist arrivals in London was to establish churches in which Calvinism could be freely observed without the fear that its overt practice would result in violent death. Only five years after their first community had been established in France, French Calvinist refugees, 'those strangers banished and cast out from their own country for the sake of the Gospel of the Church',[5] were granted permission by Edward VI to establish their 'Strangers' Church' in London. In October 1550 (three months after the Protestant refugees from the Lowlands had taken over the dissolved monastery, Augustine Friars, as their Dutch Church), the nascent French community took over the lease of the Church of St Anthony's Hospital in Threadneedle Street. Although the lease was initially for twenty-one years, the French church remained there until 1841 when it was transferred to Soho due to the rebuilding of Threadneedle Street.[6] The move to Soho, and the relinquishing of a religious base at the eastern end of London, is evidence of the way the demographic and religious profile of the Huguenot community of London had changed by the middle of the nineteenth century.

The Protestant sympathies of Edward VI provided the strangers with a window of opportunity. Not only were they permitted to establish their own church but, in addition, they were able to 'exercise church discipline in accordance with God's word' and 'to act and organise matters in our own way'. There was one formal requisite, that the appointment of ministers be approved by the English monarch.[7] King Edward's short reign was followed by another equally brief, that of his Catholic sister Mary. Her presence on the throne acted as a deterrent to would-be Protestant arrivals. However, the ascendance of Elizabeth in 1558 relit the beacon of refuge for those suffering increasing persecution across the Channel. Though they discouraged foreign membership of English churches, Elizabeth and her government were prepared to tolerate the establishment of strangers' churches, seeing them as a means of controlling an immigrant population whose economic presence was beneficial to the nation. It is a characteristic of the prevailing policy towards immigrants who were perceived to be of economic benefit to the country that, while England was prepared to welcome French religious dissenters, the same indulgence was not afforded the indigenous population. Presbyterians and other non-conformists were persecuted by the Anglican church and remained marginalised and threatened. Thus, while French men and women could worship in a *different* way, English men and women could not. More than a century later this policy was also followed by James II. He allowed the indigenous population little religious autonomy yet, in his Declaration of Tolerance granted Calvinists 'permission to exercise their ministry amongst their own people according to their own customs, ceremonies and discipline'.

Robin Gwynn has accurately described the difficulties of quantitatively assessing the size of the early foreign Protestant communities.[8] Their numbers peaked just before the Edict of Nantes and then reduced as some Huguenots returned to France. Statistics suggest that, by 1630, the French church's congregation, made up of English- and French-born Calvinists, numbered 1,400.[9] Between 1640 and 1660 emigration from France slowed right down. The reasons were twofold. First, this was the 'golden period' for Calvinists in France and, second, the English Civil War created uncertainty and chaos in the foreign churches and doubts amongst those considering emigration to England. The Restoration put further, and divisive, pressures on the French churches in England. Charles II decreed that he would only license new foreign or strangers' congregations if they agreed to follow the Anglican Book of Common Prayer as translated into French by Dr Jean Durel.[10] This ruling directly affected the recently formed Calvinist congregation in Westminster which, under Cromwell, had been permitted church accommodation. Under Charles's rule, though allowed to take over the chapel at the Savoy, it had to conform to the new edict. Fortunately, the Threadneedle Street church had been established before the ordination was pronounced and therefore was not required, nor did it choose, to adopt the Anglican liturgy. However, the presence of a conformist French church worried members of the Threadneedle Street Consistory, who feared it might weaken their hold on the French immigrant community in London. Accordingly they appealed against the Savoy chapel's continued existence. The appeal was refused.[11]

In 1687, conscious of the growing insecurity of his position, James II attempted to curry favour with the non-conformists by issuing a Declaration of Indulgence, which promised his subjects 'liberty of conscience and the free exercise of religion'.[12] This was a relief for the Huguenot community of Spitalfields, as it had not adopted Durel's prayer book. The combination of James's Declaration of 1687; the Bloodless Revolution of 1688 which brought William of Orange and his wife Mary to the throne; and William's subsequent Toleration Act of 1689, made England, and more specifically London, a favoured place of settlement for Calvinists seeking refuge after 1685.

It is important to define the timing of the large-scale arrival of Huguenot refugees from France. In the same way in which 1881, the year of the assassination of the Tsar of Russia, has been claimed as the turning point for Eastern European mass immigration to Britain,[13] so 1685, the year of the revocation of the Edict of Nantes, has generally been given as the starting point for the large-scale entry of Huguenots to England. To accept this would be to ignore the political context.[14] The year 1685 was when James II succeeded to the throne. Once king, he was eager to re-establish Catholicism in his realm. In an attempt to thwart these ambitions, the Duke of Monmouth, illegitimate son of Charles II, orchestrated a rebellion intended to overthrow his uncle. Monmouth and his Protestant supporters were rapidly put down and subsequently harshly treated by Judge Jeffreys, who sentenced the duke and others to death. Following the attempted rebellion, five members of the French church were arrested, though later released. For Calvinists seeking a religious haven, England at that time did not appear an ideal choice. Huguenots already settled there were tense and uneasy. And it was doubtless fear rather than oversight that led to there being no formal mention of the revocation of the Edict of Nantes, nor the failed rebellion in England, in the Consistory Minutes for that momentous year. Two years later, James, fearful of the growing opposition, changed course. The Declaration of Indulgence was a formal manifestation of his U-turn. However, it proved insufficient. In 1688 William of Orange, together with his wife Mary, took the throne and, by so doing, secured Protestantism in England. It was at this point, as confirmed by the Consistory records, 'the Huguenots began to stream in'.[15]

The Consistory Minutes for the years between 1679 and 1692 reflect the unease and insecurity rippling through the community during the early stages of the settlement process. The constant inflow of new arrivals from France created considerable financial and administrative burdens. The post-1685 Minutes of the Consistory of the French church reflect the anxiety of the congregation. They report the 'increasing arrival of refugees', which was creating 'an extraordinary burden for Threadneedle Street as the number of

French refugees increases daily and the church cannot house them alongside other members'.[16] There were also fears that opponents and enemies in France would be sent across the Channel to spy and report back on those who had transferred their loyalty and their religious affiliation. Accordingly, extreme caution was exercised over the acceptance of refugees. To gain acceptance, incoming refugees had to persuade both the church and community of Threadneedle Street that they were who they said they were and that any previous deviation from Calvinism had been in order to save their and their family's lives. To overcome the first hurdle, refugees had to present a *témoignage*[17] from their former church in France to prove their identity and a *méreaux*[18] to prove that they were not spies. In order to reverse religious deviance, refugees who had become crypto-Calvinists had to make *reconnaissance*, '*à la paix de l'église*' and make abjuration by (re)embracing Protestantism. The making of *reconnaissance*, though a rite which was 'highly prescriptive and judgemental',[19] also facilitated communal bonding, an aid to developing the home away from home.

The Calvinistic theology that man was accountable to God and that the practice of Calvinism was a collective self-discipline, a theology of predestination, was one which gave its adherents certainty in the face of persecution. It was a form of Protestantism that taught 'election by grace', and 'that it was an absolute duty to consider oneself chosen to combat all doubts and temptations in order to continue in God's grace'. Total conviction that this was the only way to run one's life provided the mental and physical backbone for those forced to leave all but their beliefs and skills behind them. From the perspective of the receiving society, a religion which encouraged industriousness and thrift and the use of wealth for the general good was a positive reference for those seeking to find refuge and security in foreign, if not totally alien territory.[20] It is also possible that the more tangible Huguenot traits of frugality, sobriety and honesty, as evident in the architecture of the French churches, facilitated acceptance of the incomers by the receiving society.[21] Huguenot chapels and churches were traditionally simple, analogous in design with English non-conformist chapels. Internally, there were no altars and no statues, the design and location of the pulpit emphasising the important role of the sermon within the service. Painted windows and crosses were not allowed, not even on the exterior of the buildings, which were usually rectangular, though they could be circular or oval.

The primacy of the Old Testament, a facet of puritanical Christianity, is evident in the Calvinist liturgy, while certain of the rituals are more resonant of orthodox Judaism and Islam than of Anglicanism and Catholicism. Men and women were seated apart and the wearing of hats by men during the service was not discouraged. Hats were removed for the reading of commandments, singing of psalms and saying of prayers but replaced for the reading of the scripture and during the sermon, which could last up to four hours. The preacher normally put his hat on for the sermon, a practice which alarmed Englishmen who visited the French churches as they 'could not endure this and having gone to the Huguenot churches threatened never to go back – this led to some preachers not wearing a hat whilst giving the sermon'.[22] This change in practice was a clear acknowledgement by members of the refugee community of the necessity to pacify any xenophobic or anti-Calvinist feelings forthcoming in the receiving society.

Irrespective of size or the social standing of the various members of the congregation, all the temples and pastors were considered equal – though perhaps some more equal than others. Laymen played a significant role in the service and preachers were selected by ballot. Church government was by democratic Consistory with the church's role laid down in the ecclesiastical discipline of the French church of London in 1641. As noted, particular stress was placed upon policing and disciplining, the latter a core element of the Calvinist creed. The governance of the French church was divided between the pastors, elders and deacons, the last two normally emanating from the higher social levels of the refugee community. The role of the pastors was to preach; to watch over the morals of their flock; to govern and to instruct the youth 'in the languages and sciences which are aids to the acquisition of learning'. It was the responsibility of the elders to assemble the congregation and report scandals to the Consistory. The role of the deacons was to carry out the pastoral work, visiting the sick and the poor. It was an organisational structure which underlined the concerns of the church to monitor and govern all the activities of the nascent community. As Bernard Cottret has suggested, the Consistories 'intervened at every stage of refugee life'.[23] However, as numbers increased, the tight control on the community was forced to relax. The newer churches were unable to operate at the same pace as the mother church (Threadneedle Street); tended to be less organised; and, in most instances, were run without the help of the deacons.[24]

Accommodation for worshippers was becoming an obvious problem. East London, incorporating Threadneedle Street, was clearly an economic and religious magnet for many of the incoming refugees and, in June 1687, a decision was taken to build an extension to 'reduce the crush'.[25] It was at this point that Calvinism made its spatial debut in Spitalfields. *L'Hôpital* was opened in Black Eagle Street in 1688, as a chapel of ease and annexe of Threadneedle Street. However, the continuing tide of refugees, including many from Dieppe and Lintot, demanded more than just additional church accommodation. There was an urgent need for financial support, for food, homes and jobs. As will be described in the following chapter, help was forthcoming from a variety of Huguenot and English sources. A suggestion was even put forward by the concerned elders of Threadneedle Street that the more recent refugees be encouraged to migrate onward to the English colony in North America, more particularly to Carolina, an area which welcomed dissenters.[26]

The establishment of new churches in Spitalfields was verification of the effectiveness of the positive policies of James and, subsequently William, towards foreign non-conformists. The years 1687–8 are particularly significant, for not only did *L'Hôpital* open its doors in Black Eagle Street but, in addition, a second place of worship, the Church of St Jean Spitalfields, was founded in St John Street, at the northern end of Brick Lane. That church's location, on the edge of Spitalfields, somewhat removed from the more affluent area of Princes Street, Church Street and Wood Street, together with the composition of the congregation, is reflective of the way in which socioeconomic status influenced the spatial distribution of the fledgling community. The Church of St Jean was, 'a congregation chiefly formed of silk weavers', who 'mostly hailed from Pays de Caux in Haute Normandie and from Picardy'.[27] This information in the church's register confirms the theory that a combination of geographic roots and trade is a persuasive factor in the religious organisation of immigrants and refugees. It is a pattern frequently to be found in the setting up of *chevras* and friendly societies by Eastern European Jews some 200 years later. The building occupied by the congregation of St Jean was one used contemporaneously by English non-conformists. For a while, as the records show, 'the house and conditions suited each'.[28] However, as the English membership dwindled, the Calvinists gradually took over control and ownership of the building which became solely used for Huguenot services. This architectural intersection of minority religious groups is an early example of what became, from the nineteenth century onwards, a more common occurrence in and around Spitalfields, with synagogues occupying buildings that were previously churches or chapels.

By 1739 there were some nine French churches in Spitalfields. The location of the nine is indicative of the spatial distribution of the community. There was a cluster of Calvinist churches in the centre of the ward, with others situated to the northeast (close to Bethnal Green) and on the western boundary (close to the city). There were none in proximity to Whitechapel Road, where few Huguenots had settled. However, not all stayed loyal to Calvinism. For, in spite of still residing in the area, some of the more successful Huguenots, amongst them those who were officers of the parish, demonstrated their upward social mobility and assimilation into mainstream society by transferring their allegiance to Christ Church. This was Hawksmoor's magnificent edifice which stood at the western end of Church (Fournier) Street and was constructed and inaugurated in response to the New Churches Act of 1711.

By the 1730s the Black Eagle Street Church had grown too small for its expanding congregation. A new site was selected at the eastern end of Church Street and a petition submitted to George II requesting permission to build a new church. It was to be 'A monument of the unrelenting cruelty of our common enemy'. The somewhat obsequious wording of the petition is a reminder that, forty-nine years on from the revocation of the Edict of Nantes, with a now established Calvinist community active in commerce and aware of its civic and religious responsibilities, there was still unease and insecurity. It was still felt necessary to reassure the monarch, and possibly remind certain Huguenots, of the loyalty of those for whom the French monarch and government were the enemy. In the words of the petition:

> We humbly hope that your Majesty will be pleased to grant us our petition ... none of your subjects are more zealous for the Protestant religion, nor better affected to your Majesty's sacred person, illustrious family and government than we and our congregation. . . . May the most prosperous successes constantly attend your Majesty's arms and undertaking, may the longest, the happiest and most glorious life end in eternal unalterable felicity.[29]

The petition was approved and letters of patent issued authorising both the building of the church and the establishment of a school for boys and girls. *La Neuve Église* was opened in 1743 on the corner of what is now Fournier Street and Brick Lane. It measured a considerable eighty-six by sixty feet and, in keeping with the Calvinist tradition, had an interior which was 'austere' and an exterior which, with its tall arched windows and triangular pediment with sundial in its tympanum, was 'bold in scale and quietly dignified in expression'.[30] Seemingly at odds with a building that typified sobriety and temperance, below the church were vaults used by beer brewers and wine merchants until the end of the nineteenth century. The building remained a Calvinist church until 1803. In 1809 it was leased to the London Society for Promoting Christianity among Jews and became known as the 'Jews' Chapel'. Ten years later it was transformed into a Methodist chapel, at times accommodating as many as 1,100 worshippers. At the end of the nineteenth century, in 1899, a group of ultra-orthodox Eastern European Jews converted it into the Great Synagogue of the *Mazhike Hadath*.[31] Though the interior was destroyed by fire at the end of the Second World War, the building, suitably restored, remained a synagogue until the end of the 1960s when another religious intersection took place and it became a mosque. At the time of writing, it still straddles Fournier Street and Brick Lane, a constant reminder of the role played by religion in the lives of the immigrant communities of Spitalfields.

While recording the fear and threat that accompanied those troubled times of transition and acclimatisation, a reading of the Threadneedle Street Minutes also refutes the stereotype of the God fearing, law-abiding, temperate Huguenot. The refugees did not always behave as morally or as quietly as may have been desired. Members of the French church were censored for activities which included debauchery, wife-beating, blasphemy, pregnancy whilst unmarried, obtaining money from the church under false pretences, irreverent behaviour and bad temper. However, one must question whether the extracts from the Minutes reveal people who had intentionally left their chosen path or people cracking under the pressures of a hasty and involuntary departure from their homeland, combined with poverty, overcrowding, the absence of all that was familiar and a church unable to cope with the continuing flood of necessitous refugees.[32] Amongst the wrongdoings recorded were:

> 21 August 1681: Jean Baptiste Roger come to confess his fault in having struck his wife.
> 18 September 1681: M. Michel Castel accused of various blasphemes against the Christian religion.
> 21 July 1682: Marie widow of Jean Martin, being pregnant although unmarried.
> 29 April 1683: £10 to be given to cure Matthieu Bonserguet of the venereal disease.[33]

In addition to those quoted above, there were instances of 'innocent' bigamy, when self-assumed widows and widowers, unaware that their partners were still alive, married again. Intemperance was another hazard: on occasions after imbibing excessive alcohol, the refugees became violent. The Minutes record that the tavernkeepers of Spitalfields were regularly admonished for providing drink during the sermon though, if these extended to four hours, such lapses are not surprising. Cottret suggests that the French Protestants 'took pride in being difficult'.[34] But perhaps what we see here is the reaction of people who escaped to freedom from a strictly disciplined (even if of their own making) background, one overshadowed by the threat of persecution which might have ended in imprisonment or death. The expression of that freedom took many forms, ranging from reinforced religiosity to a rejection of the strictures of religion. For it must be borne in mind that Protestant Calvinism was very young and very demanding and that there were those who found its regime excessive, possibly young adults who had accompanied their parents physically, but not religiously.

By the end of the seventeenth century, it had become obvious that there would be no early return to France. Over the next eighty years the tidal waves of immigrant Huguenots reduced to a trickle, although small numbers continued to arrive almost up until the outbreak of the revolution in 1789. Gradually English names replaced French; intermarriage between English and French families increased; and membership of the French churches was replaced by affiliation to English churches such as Christ Church, where the more affluent members of the Huguenot community were buried in the crypt. In contrast to the Jews and the Bangladeshis, 'Burial [or its location] didn't matter to the Huguenots.'[35] By the dawn of the nineteenth century the majority of the Huguenots of Spitalfields had assimilated and moved on. For those who were left, with the exception of a fortunate few, the failing silk industry offered a future of impoverishment and little hope.[36]

'God's peculiar people' in Spitalfields

The spine of Judaism is the belief that God is the sole creator and is 'indivisible, incorporal, eternal and unique', both the 'Grand Designer' and a personal God, with whom each Jew has entered into a covenant. Judaism, in common with the other two religions under discussion, is a prescriptive religion. In common with Islam, orthodox Judaism permeates all of life: diet, marriage and work. It is governed by laws and codes. There is the Oral Law, the *Torah* – based on the five books of Moses – and the Written Law, the *Talmud*, created by the ancient rabbis. The debate over the latter's irrefutability was the cause of internal secessions in the nineteenth and early twentieth centuries, which resulted in the formation of Reform and Progressive communities in London and the provinces.[37]

The rules of conduct which permeate all levels of Jewish life are called the *halachah*. For immigrants arriving in Spitalfields in the last half of the nineteenth century, certain of the *halachic* laws would seem to have been explicitly directed to those who found themselves in an alien society. *Halachic* laws are the outward notification of the obligations of the community and the individual. Jews are required to uphold a number of moral virtues as well as religious rituals. Foremost of the former are the two pillars, *tzedekah* (charity or righteousness) and *rachamunus* (compassion). A Jew must also show respect for parents; offer hospitality to travellers; visit the sick; maintain the essence and nexus of family life; accompany the dead to the grave; and attend synagogue for worship twice a day as well as during the festivals. A Jew might carry on a personal relationship with the Maker in any given place or situation. For example, Aleichem's *Tevye*[38] the milkman was portrayed as having an open line to God. However, religious services and prayers are performed in a synagogue and no less than ten men (*minyan*) are required to be in attendance.[39]

A Jewish place of worship can be as lavish or as simple as its congregants desire or can afford. In its most basic form, the tangible requirements are a container (the Ark) for the Five Books of Moses (the *Torah*). The Ark could be a simple box, to be moved into place at will, in the place of worship. In the late nineteenth-century Jewish East End, the place of worship might also have served as a clothing workshop or the backroom of a domestic dwelling. There is also a need for the prayer desk from which the reader recites the service and, in addition if desired, a central pulpit (*Bimah*). Prayer desk and pulpit can be, and, in Spitalfields, often were, combined. Worshippers can be accommodated as simply or as lavishly as desired – on pews, cushions or chairs.

Within the context of this volume, the synagogues of the East End of London can be categorised as those extant before 1880, and those which were established post-1880 by immigrants living and working in Spitalfields.[40] The first group is subdivisible by social status. On the boundaries of the city and Spitalfields were the three cathedral synagogues of the Ashkenazi community. These formed the basis of the United Synagogue, established by Act of Parliament in 1870.[41] The three were: the Great in Dukes Place (established in 1692, newly built in 1722 and destroyed by bombing in the Second World War); the Hambro (established in 1726 and by the late nineteenth century located in Fenchurch Street); and the New (established in 1760 and relocated to Bishopsgate in 1855). In addition, there was the main synagogue of the much smaller Sephardi community[42] (established in 1657 and newly built in Bevis Marks in 1701 and still, at the beginning of the twenty-first century, used for services). With their dog-collared reverends, emphasis on decorum, Anglicised and socially elevated members and high membership fees (at an annual £3 7s, well beyond the reach of the poorly paid and exploited immigrant worker), these synagogues were eschewed by the immigrants who saw them as tools of Anglicisation rather than places of religious celebration.

The arrival of impoverished Jews from Holland, Central and Eastern Europe in the eighteenth and early nineteenth centuries resulted in the establishment of synagogues closer to the location and likings of the 'working classes'.[43] In Spitalfields there were a number of small synagogues or *chevrot*, including Sandys Row (established in 1851), Princes (Princelet) Street (established in 1870), Fashion Street (established in 1858) and Whites Row (established in 1860). These early synagogues served the specific needs of Dutch, German and Polish migrants who initially chose to worship in *chevrot*[44] either with their *landsleight*[45] or with those in the same trade. A number of the early synagogues had previously been French Calvinist chapels, their neutral appearance, lack of ostentation and internal galleries, making them ideal for conversion. For example, Sandys Row synagogue was a French church until 1801, while the Eye of Jacobs Society's religious base was previously the Artillery Lane chapel.[46] Doubtless conscious of cost, time and the need to retain the religiosity of the immigrants, the Chief Rabbi,[47] commenting on this trend in 1877, stated that, 'It would always be more convenient for a congregation, in want of a synagogue, to purchase for this purpose a disused church or chapel than to erect a fresh structure.'[48] *La Neuve Église* is perhaps the most famous example of this form of religious continuity and change, in 1899 becoming the synagogue of the *Mazhike Hadath* at a conversion cost of some £6,000.[49]

As immigrant arrivals increased, so the number of *chevrot* grew, providing as they did so a bridge with Eastern Europe, their names resonant of the old country even if their location was within the confines of the self-created East End ghetto. Grodno Synagogue was located in Spital Street, Kovno Synagogue in Catherine Wheel Alley and the Warsaw Synagogue in Gun Street.[50] The designation 'synagogue' was somewhat elaborate for the poorly furnished and maintained rooms or small buildings. Trade, geography and, even at times extended family need, spurred the establishment of small, homely places of worship. Harry Blacker recorded that:

Any room large enough to hold ten men or more was established as a synagogue. Uncle Charlie was my great uncle ... like my father he was a cabinet maker.... Because of his large family Charlie rented a complete house. The front room, ground floor was used as a synagogue on the Sabbath. A portable beautifully made wardrobe served as an ark for the solitary scroll it housed. On a shelf beneath it, the prayer books and Pentateuchs were stored, so that the sin of carrying on the Sabbath could be avoided.

Every Saturday without exception at least fourteen men would assemble for the service, Uncle Charlie providing five of them as well as leading the prayers.... The service itself was simple, Uncle Charlie stood on a high desk facing the ark, and in the traditional sing-song voice, led us through the intricacies of the Sabbath prayers.... Before the concluding prayers and following the reading of a weekly portion of the Torah, an impromptu sermon would be delivered by a visiting learned man. This was invariably in Yiddish, besprinkled with Hebrew quotations and English grace notes.[51]

The *chevrot* varied in size and condition. Many were built on the backs of existing buildings or in converted, or operative, workshops. Contemporary descriptions enable us to appreciate the poverty and discomfort those places of worship exuded. *Chevra Kehol Chassidim*, located to the south of Spitalfields, in Fieldgate Street, was

approached through a somewhat dingy passage, and ... built in the same way as many workshops in the locality on what was originally an open space at the back of the house. There are between 80 and 90 seats for males and no provision for females.[52]

Kurland Synagogue in Cannon Street Road had no accommodation for women and was reported as 'not such as to command respect ... it is unsafe from a fire point of view as, if a fire occurred in the house there would be a panic in the synagogue and possibly not a soul could escape unhurt'.[53]

For the male immigrant, both settled and more recently arrived, his *chevra* or *shul*[54] was far more than just a place of worship − it was almost a second home, a club and some-time friendly society which might provide benefits during sickness, unemployment and old age.[55] It was a male meeting place where current political, social and economic issues could be (heatedly) debated, before, after and frequently during, the service. Women were always segregated, hidden from view either by a curtain or in the gallery above. For many male immigrants, the *chevra* became the centre of their transposed lives. It was a space which facilitated self-identification and rooting, enabling the fusing of *der heim* with the here. Beatrice Potter described the phenomenon of the East End *chevrots* as 'Self-creating, self-supporting and self-governing communities'.[56] Initially the small East End

Synagogues or *stiebels*, were independent both of the British Chief Rabbi and of each other. As bridges with lives left behind, members of the *chevrot* looked to Eastern Europe for rulings on matters of community and religion, for 'the religion of the ghetto was supranational and owed little spiritual allegiance to British religious leaders'.[57] However, though initially this transitional stage and its vehicles were viewed sympathetically, by the early 1880s concerns about the 'undesirable features'[58] of the *chevrot* and their impact on the image and structure of the Anglo-Jewish community were being articulated. In an editorial of 1880 the *Jewish Chronicle* voiced the view of many in the Anglicised community:

> To form 'wheels within wheels' or little communities within a great one is to weaken the general body. They have no right, if permanent residents to isolate themselves from their English co-religionists, ... they should assimilate themselves completely, with the community among whom they dwell.[59]

Even at that early stage in the large-scale migration, the need for the immigrants to integrate and assimilate, to iron out their ghetto bends and become acceptable members of *English* society, was a paramount ambition of the more established Jewish community.

By the mid-1880s, certain English politicians and commentators were expressing their concern over the continuing arrival of pauper Eastern European Jews. This, together with the alien nature and self-selected isolation of the *chevrot*, and their apparent unsanitary nature, prompted members of the established London Jewish community to take action. Under the leadership of Samuel Montagu, at that time Liberal MP for Whitechapel and later the first Lord Swaythling, the Federation of Synagogues was founded in 1887. It had an initial sixteen founder members, which included those *chevrot* which pre-dated 1880 but were not members of the United Synagogue, as well as eight which had been more recently formed. Others were admitted as members as the Federation deemed them suitable. Geoffrey Alderman, in his history of the Federation, explains that Montagu's aim was to provide the *chevrot* with a 'communal framework of their own which would leave them a reasonable amount of autonomy in religious affairs, but which would at the same time bring them within the ambit of the already-existing communal organisation'.[60] In 1889 the Federation sealed its independence through the purchase of a burial ground at Edmonton, North London. Having established their own synagogal body and acquired a cemetery, the Eastern European immigrant community in London believed that they had ensured their separation from Anglo-Jewry. In reality, with Lord Rothschild as President and Samuel Montagu as Vice-President and Acting President, they were very much under its control.

The synagogue was at the centre of the (male) immigrants' life. It was a place of worship, a club, a friendly society and even employment exchange.

Irrespective of his level of religiosity, the Eastern European immigrant male would visit the *chevra* as his English counterpart might visit the pub. Within that club, the hierarchies of the secular world were turned on their heads as workshop masters and middlemen became subservient to their more knowledgeable employees who often took the services. The hubbub of sound which greeted the visitor to the *chevra* could be interpreted as the gateway to that which was familiar or, by the outsider, as an indecorous but moving atmosphere. Following a visit to an East End *chevra* for the *The Jew in London*, the book he wrote with Charles Russell, Harry Lewis reported that

> There is no decorum and during parts of the service there is much talking and noisy movement ... a devotion full of self-abandonment. It is indeed difficult to realise how strong is the affection which the Jewish liturgy excites amongst those who have grown up under its influence.[61]

Israel Zangwill's literary skills evoke the passion and alien nature of the style of worship to be found in the houses of prayer of the Eastern European Jews:

> The method of praying at these things was equally complex and uncouth ... here a rising and there a bow, now three steps backwards and now a beating of the breast, this bit for the congregation and that for the minister; variations of a page, a word, a syllable, even a vowel, ready for every possible contingency.[62]

Beatrice Potter, whose attitude to the Jewish immigrant was, at best, ambivalent, provides a sympathetic and evocative description of a *chevra* on a Sabbath morning:

> It is a curious and touching sight to enter one of the poorer and more wretched of these places [*chevrat*] on a Sabbath morning. Probably the one you will choose will be situated in a small alley or narrow court, or it may be built out in a back yard. To reach the entrance you stumble over broken pavement and household debris; possibly you pick your way over the rickety bridge connecting it with the cottage property fronting the street. From the outside it appears a long wooden building surmounted by a skylight, very similar in construction to the ordinary sweater's workshop. You enter; the heat and odour convince you that the skylight is not used for ventilation. From behind the trellis of the 'ladies gallery' you see at the far end of the room the richly curtained Ark of the Covenant, wherein are laid, attired in gorgeous vestments, the sacred scrolls of the law.[63]

If the *chevra* was the male domain, then home was the female realm. In the synagogue a woman was hidden and subsidiary, as Zangwill's description of a young woman's attendance at service conveys:

she crossed the threshold of a large *chevra* she had known in her girl-
hood, mounted the stairs and entered the female compartment without
hostile challenge. . . . This room had no connection with the men's . . . it
was simply a room above theirs and the declaration of the unknown
cantor came but faintly through the flooring. . . . When the weather or
the wills of the more important ladies permitted, the window at the end
was opened; it gave upon a little balcony below which the men's
chamber projected considerably, having been built out into the back
yard. When this window was opened simultaneously with the skylight
in the men's synagogue, the fervid roulades of the cantor were as audible
to the women as to their masters.[64]

In the home the Jewish wife ruled supreme. It was her role to ensure that
the home conformed to religious requirements, that no forbidden foods
(swine, carrion eaters, shellfish, etc.) were served or consumed. It was the
Jewish wife's responsibility to ensure that all that was required for the festivals and the Sabbath was prepared according to *halachah*, and that the children and head of the household were cared for in the Jewish way. For this
reason, 'Jewish women didn't work.' Or at least that was the message that
the elders of the community and established Anglo-Jewry wished to convey.
However, the reality was frequently very different. Jewish women, married
as well as single, did work. They carried out a variety of economic activities
in order to enable families to get through the slack times or to supplement
the meagre earnings of the tailors, pressers, machiners, cabinet makers, etc.
during periods of economic recession. Other wives worked in order that
their studious husbands could continue to study *Torah*.[65]

The *Jewish Year Book* for 1896 lists sixteen of the twenty-five Federation
Synagogues[66] as located in Spitalfields. This provides a clear indication of the
religious spatialisation of the 'alien' immigrant community. However, an
abundance of synagogues should not be read as confirmation of religiosity.
Whilst some immigrants maintained the religious prescriptives, others were
forced, or chose, to abandon them. The main reason for this was the need to
work on the Sabbath in order to satisfy the demands of their employers who,
invariably, were themselves Jews. This practice was not readily accepted. In
1894 orthodox tailors formed a Sabbath Observance branch of the Amalgamated Society of Tailors in order to protest against exploitation by their
employers. In 1899 the *Mazhike Hadath* sponsored a Jewish National Tailors'
Union whose main objective was to secure the acceptance of Saturday as the
day of rest.[67] In spite of these attempts, inevitably, religion was subservient to
work and the unions folded. Non-attendance at the synagogue did not
necessarily mean that dietary and other religious requirements were sacrificed. Men who were forced to toil in order to put bread in the stomachs of
their families could be regarded with leniency. However, the plight of the
sweated worker found little support from the Chief Rabbi, Hermann Adler.
He opposed the proposal put forward by labour leader Lewis Lyons that the

Jewish unemployed should march barefoot through the streets of London and turned down a suggestion that Lyons preach a 'labour sermon' from the pulpit of the Great Synagogue, which bordered on Spitalfields. This, in the eyes of the spiritual leader of Anglo-Jewry, was atheistic.[68] But he was wrong for, as Bill Fishman has said, 'Religion was ingrained in the cultural experience of the *shtetl*, and an inalienable part of his identity as a Jew.'[69]

There were others, though small in number who, having arrived in the promised land, spurned Judaism and subscribed to another belief, that of anarcho-socialism. The anarchists were anti-religion. They held *Yom Kippur* balls on that most sacred of holy days and ate ham (a forbidden food) sandwiches outside the synagogues. In this way they sought to express their dislike of the manacle of religion and of the class system, one which they believed was manifest in the synagogue where the 'rich overdressed and over fed' were to be found in their reserved seating while the poor were 'pressed by the door, hungry and ill clad with no prospects of a sumptuous fast-breaking meal to return to'.[70] In the event their activities drew little support and much contempt for such blasphemous acts.

The prerequisites for the development of a Jewish community are a synagogue and a cemetery – without these a *real* community cannot be said to exist or indeed function in a religious sense. For Jews arriving in Spitalfields in the last quarter of the nineteenth century there was no lack of synagogues in which to pray or Jewish cemeteries in which to be buried. By 1887 the members of the Federation of Synagogues had their own burial ground to the north of the East End, in Edmonton. But a Jewish neighbourhood has temporal as well as spiritual needs, even if the former is a result of the latter, and it is by looking at the growth of Jewish-owned retail food outlets that we can assess the way in which the 'Jewish East End' became a reality. In 1881 the street section of *Kelly's Post Office London Directory* lists just three or four Jewish shops in Middlesex and Wentworth Streets, including one butcher and one grocer. Eight years on, *Kelly's Post Office London Directory* for 1889 provides us with a clear picture of the expansion of the community and the location of its retail heartland. In Brick Lane and the surrounding streets such as Fashion Street, Old Montague Street, Princes Street and Chicksand Street there were a few Jewish outlets. The directory listed a baker (Aaron Levy), greengrocer (Samuel Levy) and butcher (Simon Zyschek), together with several chandlers, and the occasional tobacconist. It was in West Spitalfields, in Wentworth Street and Middlesex Street, that Jewish food shopping took place.

One of the primary delights of the Jewish diet was the Sabbath eve chicken soup[71] (called by some, Jewish Penicillin). It was a food which even the poorest housewife strove to provide. In order to conform with *halachah*, the fowl had to be supplied by a kosher butcher whose produce was approved by the religious board. In 1889, in Wentworth and Middlesex Streets, there were six kosher butcher shops, one female-owned. In addition, there were two fishmongers and two fried fish shops,[72] one run by a Mrs

Polly Nathan.[73] This is evidence that Jewish married women did carry out economic activities, though we do not know whether the lady butcher or Mrs Nathan were married or widowed. Confirmation that the Jewish shops were restricted to the notional boundaries of the Jewish East End ghetto is provided by the fact that, just beyond its border, in Aldgate High Street, though there were numerous meat salesmen and 'carcase' butchers, none of them bore a Jewish-sounding name. By 1894 Middlesex Street and Wentworth Street had become the hub of the local Jewish domestic economy. There were now eight butcher shops, five grocers, two greengrocers, two pickle makers, two bakers, one egg merchant, one provision dealer and Polly Nathan still selling fried fish. *The Jewish Year Book 1896* contains a list of butchers 'Licensed to sell Kosher Meat and Poultry for the year 1896'[74] – within the area embracing Aldgate eastward to Mile End and Bethnal Green southward to Commercial Road there are no less than 126 butchers and poulterers listed. This suggests not only the (increased) size of the community and its members' financial ability to purchase poultry, if not meat, but additionally, in the days before the motor vehicle, the necessity for retail outlets to be close to the points of consumption.

In many instances, levels of religiosity fell as the first decades of the twentieth century, and the assimilation process progressed, though attachment to the traditions of religion and to synagogue membership remained. The reasons for this were complex, embracing self-identity, security, community and welfare. Allied to these was the need, and desire, to be buried in sacred ground. 'The carrot of [synagogue] membership was membership of the Burial Society . . . such facilities on consecrated land were difficult and expensive to provide.'[75] Accordingly, loyalty to the religious institutions remained and, whilst the community survived, the synagogues in and around Spitalfields were secure in their membership. It was with the movement out of the East End which began in the 1920s, accelerated in the 1930s, and was almost completed by the close of the 1950s, that local synagogue membership fell. As Jews moved to the suburbs, they demonstrated their upward social mobility and disloyalty to first-generational roots by transferring their allegiance from the Eastern European-influenced Federation of Synagogues to the more Anglicised, and socially elevated, United Synagogue. A minority made the even more extreme transition to the Reform and Liberal Progressive movements. Many East End *chevrot* fell into disuse, some becoming warehouses or factories. Even the *Mazhike Hadath* grew silent, the fabric of the building adjusting itself in order to accommodate the religious needs of the next immigrant entrants to Spitalfields, Muslims from Bangladesh.

Islam in spitalfields

Islam, which means submission to God, pervades all earthly activities: the social, the domestic, the economic and the political. It embraces the public and private space of its adherents and has five main tenets or pillars:

- *Kalima* or *shahadah* – profession of faith and awareness that God is one (the same God as that of the Jews and the Christians) and that Muhammad is his 'genuine' messenger.
- *Namaj* – daily prayer: whilst the Quran (Koran) states that Muslims be called to prayer at sunset, nightfall and sunrise, in practice the call to prayer (*muezzin*) takes place five times a day, the additional calls being at midday and mid-afternoon. Wherever prayer takes place the worshipper is required to face Mecca. Though preferable, the daily prayer sessions do not have to take place in a mosque, though it is common for general attendance on a Friday.
- *Zahat* – charity in the form of a religious tax, which is formally collected once a year in the period of *hajj* or *sadqua*, the small sums of money Bengalis in Tower Hamlets might give at any time of the year either to the mosque or to be transferred to Sylhet.[76] In the context of Islam, charity refers to welfare and almsgiving to the needy, the poor, debtors, slaves and beggars. Muslims are 'supposed' to give one-fortieth of their wealth to charity though there is no formal collection, the giving being on the conscience of the individual.
- *Roja* – fasting, in order to empathise with the poor. During the month of Ramadan, Muslims, with specified exceptions, take no food or drink and abstain from sex from sunrise to sunset.
- *Hajj* – pilgrimage: all Muslims should make the pilgrimage to Mecca during the twelfth month of the Muslim calendar once in their lives. Having performed this rite, the *haji* is regarded as one to be respected above those who have not made the journey.

The most sacred book for Muslims is the Quran (Koran) which is made up of the divinely inspired speeches of the prophet Muhammad; other sayings and teachings appear in the *Hadith*. In addition to the five pillars, Muslims are required to observe specific dietary laws and are told by the Quran what they may eat: 'The food of those to whom the Book was given [in this instance Jews not Christians] is lawful for you and yours for them', thus it was forbidden to partake of 'carrion, blood and the flesh of swine'.[77] The followers of Islam are also told how the slaughtering of animals should be carried out and to wash at mealtimes, prior to, and during, prayer. In the history of the early settlement of Bangladeshis in Spitalfields, the commonality of the dietary laws for Jews and Muslims created another point of ethnic intersection as initially kosher (Jewish) butchers provided meat for both religions. While this created a domestic meeting place, the need for frequent ablutions created workplace separation as, in a number of factories and workshops, non-Muslim employers refused to provide for, or sympathise with, this aspect of Islamic observance. As explained to Katy Gardner in her recent study, *Age, Narrative and Migration*: 'In the English factories they would not allow us water, not even a bottle to hold the water. They'd tell us off. They would ask why we had it. It was a problem.'[78]

To be a follower of Islam is 'truly to be a follower of a prescriptive religion'.[79] It is a way of life which emphasises purity, hard work and accumulation of capital for the common good, a way of life that would have been familiar to the migrant Calvinists. As is evidenced in the *bari* and in the mosque, Islam clearly separates and gradates the genders. The Quran implies that good women are obedient to their menfolk, as it is written: 'Men have authority over women . . . God has made the one superior to the other.'[80] In the *bari* there are clear gender divisions – the female maintains the domestic sphere and is there for the propagation of children for, as stated in the Quran, 'women are tillage'.[81] If they transgress, they can be beaten if the husband so wishes, and divorced if that is his wish also. Within Islam women are free to attend public worship but not to request divorce. Inside the mosque, women are segregated from men and, in fact, pray mostly at home, though the East London Mosque in Whitechapel, makes provision for women to congregate, to pray and to learn.[82] However, whilst often the hidden other, as in Judaism, the female can be a powerful force within the household.

Bearing in mind the demands of Islam, it is obvious that, particularly in the early period of Bangladeshi settlement in Spitalfields, strict adherence to the Quran was not going to be easy. However, before we explore how religion and integration coalesced in Bangladeshi Spitalfields we need to look briefly at the place and practice of Islam in Bangladesh.

The partition of 1947 created the Islamic Republic of Pakistan. However, Islam had always been the dominant religion in East Pakistan and remained so after it became the independent nation-state of Bangladesh in 1971. The country has an 85 per cent Muslim population which includes a small number of urban Shiites. At the beginning of the twenty-first century, there were an estimated 190,000 mosques in Bangladesh. Although constituted as a democratic republic in 1971, the role of Islam has become increasingly significant and, in 1988, an 'Islamic way of life' was proclaimed in a constitutional amendment. The politicians stopped short of creating an Islamic state, fearful of the political repercussions. In Sylhet, as elsewhere in Bangladesh, Islam permeates all elements of daily life.

Islam in Bangladesh is syncretic, drawing on both Sunni and Sufi, the spiritual element of the latter a powerful factor with rural Muslims. Sufism emphasises love, as opposed to fear, of God and advocates the use of spiritual guides or saints. These are known as *pirs* and are perceived as mediators between God and the individual on earth. Within the villages of rural Bangladesh the mosque has a central role, as much a community centre as a place of prayer. In keeping with the demands of *zahat*, villagers often give up 2.5 per cent of their crop to the mosque to ensure its financial support. In the name of charity, those who are able to afford it provide for their poorer kin and give alms to beggars, in return for the unfortunates' prayers to Allah on their behalf. As Gardner explains, 'The poor in the villages accept their poverty by believing that is what Allah has ordained' and that 'Allah helps those who help themselves.'[83]

The syncretic nature of Islam in the villages of Sylhet where, as one religious (non-Muslim) commentator has explained, 'To be a Muslim in rural Bangladesh is more a statement of which group you belong to than of how you understand the word',[84] is most clearly demonstrated by the Sylhetis' strongly held belief in the spirits and the cult of the *pir*. In Islam a belief in the evil eye is acceptable. The transportation of the belief in *jinns* (spirits and ghosts) to Tower Hamlets is most powerfully manifest in the treatment and diagnosis of mental and physical health disorders. Practising physician Veronica White has noted that 'These spirits are strongly felt to be the cause of psychiatric problems and the afflicted are regarded as possessed.'[85] In his work, John Eade has shown how the health needs of the Muslim immigrants have been met by non-medically qualified religious community leaders – for example, a *mullah* might attempt to treat severe wind pains by recommending the patient place a piece of paper inscribed with Quran verses on the affected part of the body.[86] The mobility of these ancient beliefs, said to predate the arrival of Islam in Sylhet,[87] underlines the need for members of the receiving society to be conscious of, and have some knowledge of, the cultural and religious background of people from Bangladesh.

Even though, prior to the 1960s, the number of Muslims in Spitalfields was small,[88] religious provision for them existed. In 1910 a decision was taken to build a house of prayer for the Muslim community of East London,[89] but it was not until 1940 that the East London Mosque was opened in three converted houses in Commercial Road. In those early years the mosque attracted lascars, restaurant workers and other Northeast Indians to prayer on a Friday night. As its more modern and lavish successor would do from the late 1980s, it provided a focal point for communal meeting, discourse and, of course, debates surrounding politics in the *desh*. The growth of the Bengali community was, as Eade suggests, strongly influential in the establishment of further mosques in and around Spitalfields and other parts of the Borough of Tower Hamlets. However, as there was, and remains, no legal requirement for the registration of mosques, unless they are charitable organisations, it is impossible to quantify them precisely or chart their location. For those wanting to pray communally, all that is necessary is the designation of a room in a flat, a house, or even a shed, for the purpose. Since its reopening in Whitechapel Road in 1985, the expanded East London Mosque, though not geographically within the boundaries of Spitalfields, has exerted considerable influence over the younger members of the local community. In contrast, the Brick Lane *Jamme Masjid*, or London Great Mosque, is perceived as the elders'[90] mosque and as such does not have the same influence and attraction for the younger, more globally engaged Muslims of Spitalfields.

The East London Mosque has strong connections with the Arab world and received £1.1m of the £2m cost of rebuilding from King Fahd of Saudi Arabia. From its impressive location on Whitechapel Road (one of its rear walls being a party with the Fieldgate Street Synagogue, one of the few, or only, places in the world where mosque and synagogue literally conjoin), the mosque can accommodate up to 3,000 male worshippers. It offers 'separate facilities for female worshippers',[91] though not all women wish to avail themselves of the opportunity, some preferring to say their prayers at home. It is a true communal centre, providing educational and recreational facilities for all ages and both genders as well as co-ordinating with publicly funded bodies in the fight against drug-taking by local youngsters. Conscious of the need to educate the local Muslim community while at the same time retaining the Bangladeshi Muslim identity, there are mother tongue classes for children and adults; classes for schoolgirls and housewives; homework classes; Saturday Islamic School; classes in Arabic and Islamic Studies; plus a further selection of adult classes at the weekends. There is a library; an extensive women's section with an under-five nursery; a common room; and a planned large-scale extension to provide improved facilities as well as some housing.[92] In addition to its all-embracing, Muslim centric programme, the mosque purports to be keen to further relations with the local non-Muslim community, some of whom have lodged protests over the broadcast call to prayer and the overcrowded pavement on religious holidays.

The East London Mosque is, in the true sense of Islam, less concerned with national boundaries than with global religious unity. In contrast, the impressively titled London Great Mosque is a child of Bangladesh and its fight for independence, maintaining close connections with the nation-state and its government. For even though the East London Mosque was located close to the Bangladeshi heartland,[93] it was not *sui generis* and is more closely linked with the Middle East than with South Asia. By the end of the 1960s some of the early East Pakistani arrivals were settling in and around Brick Lane, having moved north after the demolition of Cable Street began. As dreams of return were replaced by those of family reunification, religion appeared on the agenda of those who had once been carefree sojourners. It became desirable to have a suitably sized mosque, close to the heart of the community in which the religious fusion of Sunni and Sufi, as practised at home, could be continued. Geographically, architecturally and historically, the building on the corner of Fournier Street and Brick Lane was ideal. There could be no doubt of the suitability of what had traditionally been the extant immigrant community's place of worship. By 1970 the building had been vacated by the Jewish community, the majority of whom had long since departed for the suburbs. Its location, size, internal layout and potential encouraged Bengalis living nearby to raise funds to buy the building with the intention of converting it into a mosque and in September 1974 the building was purchased from the *Mazhike Hadath*. No external alterations were planned but internal changes were proposed in order to accommodate the expanding local Muslim community. However, the intended 'gutting' of the interior was opposed by local conservationists keen to see the building preserved as near as possible to its Georgian origins. The issue became a battle between myopic architectural historians and contemporary religious need. The *East London Advertiser* reported that the 'Pakistanis want[ed] to pull down three inner galleries and Tuscan column to provide the open space needed for their services.'[94] 'A Huguenot refugees' chapel was now defined by the conservationist lobby as a vital expression of an indigenous urban culture and landscape.'[95] The Bangladeshi community defended their intentions by explaining that, by altering the building's interior so as to accommodate the maximum number, worshippers would be removed from the streets outside, thus reducing the congestion which tended to inflame racist emotions. Whether this argument was the one that forced the issue is not clear but, in 1976, the London *Jamme Masjid* mosque was opened. Local Bengalis regarded it as a structural manifestation of the financial and political support of the Bangladeshi government and its High Commission in London. The edifice, and its congregants, gained even further status when, amongst other notables, the President of Bangladesh attended prayers at the mosque and subsequently approved a donation from his government for further improvements. Whilst not providing the extensive range of facilities as the East London Mosque, the *Jamme Masjid* does have a *madrassah* (for religious teaching), in this way continuing the tradition of its predecessor, the *Mazhike Hadath*. In addition, though not itself dispensing welfare, it is linked with the Bangladeshi Welfare Association,[96] which is based in the adjoining property, next door in Fournier Street. As Eade has described,[97] by the end of the 1980s Islam had a defined spatial presence in, and adjacent to, Spitalfields, though it should be noted that, in comparison to the multiplicity of *chevras* at the end of the nineteenth century and French churches in the middle of the eighteenth century, that presence was not overtly excessive.

In contrast to the Huguenots, but in common with the Jews of Spitalfields, Muslim Bangladeshis do care about where they are buried, many of the elders retaining a desire to make their last journey the return home. However, as in the Jewish religion, the *Hadith* requires burial within twenty-four hours. Within the context of wishing to be buried in Bangladesh, this is not always possible. In spite of the irreligious time lapse, at one time it was more general practice for bodies to be sent back for burial in Bangladesh, where the recognised rituals of mourning and bereavement could be carried out. Writing in 1998, Gardner reported that the *Hajji Talseem*, the funeral service run by the East London Mosque, estimated that between 60 and 70 per cent of bodies were sent back to the *desh* for burial.[98] As one Bangladeshi explained to me, in the early days of the Bengali community it was more commonly felt that Britain was 'Not a Muslim country, we don't bury our relatives here.'[99] When possible, the early sojourner's remains would be returned home so that in the years to come, kith and kin could pay regular visits to the grave. Those who are now the elders of the Bangladeshi community in Spitalfields, and who were amongst the earliest settlers, retain an affinity with the *desh*, it is where they feel rooted and thus where they want to be buried.[100] However, for socio-economic as well as religious reasons, the practice of return burials is becoming less frequent. The cost of sending a body back to the *desh* is approximately £2,500. This, plus the cost of relatives' flights and their loss of income, has introduced an economic factor. In addition, as the decades have passed, and the return become an even more distant dream, close relatives who might visit the graves of their departed kin are more likely to be living in London than Sylhet. The following interview carried out by David Garbin highlights the conflicting emotions accompanying the decision whether to be buried in the *desh* or *bidesh*:

> It's important to come back here [Bangladesh] to be buried for some people in bidesh. People [in the mosque in Sylhet town] would say, '*Londoni lash*, a body from London, has come', there would be a coffin, colourful, kept outside [the mosque], people would look at it. People would pray. Relatives and friends would carry it. One of my mama [maternal uncle] died in Canada, in Toronto. Some relatives went to Toronto, those who couldn't go, immediately at the time went later, for example my uncle went, a year later.

> **So he was buried in Canada then?**
> Yes because it's not Islamic to transfer the body. This ceremony of this *Londoni* body being flown here, is more emotional, more cultural than Islamic. You're supposed to be buried wherever you died. Because according to Islamic principles, it's God's earth, so wherever you bury it doesn't matter much ... in my mama case, he was very sick and he said that 'don't fly me back and don't leave me in a coffin for two days, bury me and that's it'. They would say it before, where they want to be buried.[101]

At the dawning of the twenty-first century, more Bangladeshi burials are taking place in the *bidesh*, in the Muslim sections of public cemeteries in Tottenham, Walthamstow or Forest Gate – all some distance to the northeast of Tower Hamlets. Recently a pressure group has called for the provision of a Muslim cemetery that would be more accessible for the bereaved, one within the borough. It is a demand unlikely to meet with approval. First- and second-generation London-born Bangladeshis living in a more Islamicised space than their elders in the 1960s and 1970s, now consider that return to the *desh* is unrealistic. They believe that burial should conform with the doctrine of Islam rather than attempt to fulfil the myth of return.

It is not unusual for those whose religion or ethnicity is under threat to become more observant. The Huguenots and the Eastern European Jews, the former primarily religious refugees, the latter a combination of economic migrant and religious refugee, ensured that, at the very earliest stages of arrival in Spitalfields, there was a house of worship available where they could practise their chosen form of liturgy and ritual. Research over the past twenty years has shown that this was not generally the case with the young sojourners from Bangladesh. The tensions in what became Bangladesh, in the years prior to 1971, were political and secular – religion was never under threat. Both Adams, writing in the 1980s, and Gardner, writing almost two decades later, provide evidence of the (self-confessed) lax religious behaviour of the Bengali immigrants in Spitalfields. They record examples of young men breaking the basic Islamic codes by visiting pubs and betting on horses, practices also noted by Carey and Shukur in their 1985 survey.[102] As one Bengali elder told Gardner in the 1990s, following his arrival he became '[A] broken Muslim. I had a white woman. I never lost my religion but then I never really prayed or anything.'[103] In the 1980s, Adams's interviews with Bengali men revealed little difference: 'Those who came to this country . . . they didn't bother much, about religious faith, only occasionally, at *Eid*, but people never kept the fast. . . . In those days people didn't observe religious things properly.'[104] Whilst another informed

> In the early days we never thought of having halal meat . . . just avoided pork. . . . In the early times the only religious thing was that after *Ramadan* they used to go for the *Eid* prayers to the East London Mosque . . . and not only Muslims, Hindus and everybody used to come to enjoy the feast.[105]

However, religiosity was not far below the surface. Giving evidence to the Home Office Sub-Committee on Race Relations and Immigration in 1986, Councillor Ali stated: 'Religion is the cultural concept they [the Bangladeshi people] cannot give up. Bangladeshi people more or less are very religious people.'[106] It would be an accurate assessment to say that, in the nascent years of their settlement in Spitalfields, for the young male Bangladeshi, community religion, though not abandoned, was put on hold. As it began to dawn on many of the sojourners that their 'return' would be considerably delayed, family reunions started and religious practice began to play a more important role in the life of what was becoming, with the arrival of wives and children, a dynamic family-oriented community. This is not surprising as Sylhetis, who comprise 95 per cent of the Bengali community of Spitalfields are 'more conservative and religious than most Bengalis'. Research in Bangladesh has shown that 59 per cent of Sylhetis pray daily as compared to 35 per cent in the rest of the country.[107] Though it was not always easy, the men increasingly fused religion with their economic activity, movement from indigenous-owned factories and work-shops to those run by Pakistanis or Bengalis facilitating this aspect of London life.

For the newly arriving females, the majority having had to make the transition from the security of the *bari* in an essentially rural environment to the dislocation and isolation of a tower block in the East End of London, it was hard. Not only had they left a familiar landscape for one that was completely alien but, in most cases, they were joining male partners they hardly knew. In her recent book Gardner devotes space to the experiences of some of those women who settled in Spitalfields. She expresses her (academic's) disappointment at the way in which they 'seemed to skip over what *I* thought were the important issues':[108] those which related predominantly to geographic and cultural transition. Gardner suggests that this is because her subjects had spent most of their time in Tower Hamlets confined to trans- ported Bengali space and community. They had not considered what she believed were the positive visual and cultural aspects of their journey, but then perhaps these women did not consider these as in any way 'positive'. It was the traditional 'other' role of the Muslim wife which both helped and hindered the integration process. High-rise living was hard after outdoor village life, as indeed was caring for husbands who became sick or were ageing, physical conditions which were often the reasons for bringing over new, young wives. According to Sarah White, Muslim female otherness is affirmed and reified by *purdah*, an essentialist religious practice which defines the positioning of the genders. Though, as disciples of the 'new Islam' confirm, where women are concerned, this positioning is not immutable but subject to change according to place, space, social context and age. *Purdah*, which is used to enforce the female otherness – modesty and honour – of Muslim women can be physically adopted in a variety of ways, from the wearing of a *burkah* or *hijab*, which covers from head to toe, to the holding of an umbrella which covers the head and face 'when a stranger passes on a village path'.[109] Veiling is more important for the younger, fertile women. With age and the menopause older women, whilst covering their heads for prayer, are less cautious with regard to general 'modest' behaviour.

Purdah is not simply the physical application of a religious tenet, it is more a psychological garment. The form it takes and the reasons for donning it can vary with the individual and does vary with the generations in Spitalfields. Naila Kabeer has shown that, amongst some of the early Bangladeshi female arrivals, those who wore the *burkah* in Bangladesh now consider cardigans, jumpers and anoraks in the same way, believing that these provide the same personal anonymity and physical and psychological coverage. As one informant explained, '*purdah* isn't the clothes you wear but what is inside your head'.[110] For others the wearing of the *burkah* has helped overcome the challenge of undertaking tasks and activities never contem- plated in Bangladesh. Financial need resulting from jobless husbands or widowhood have forced women to become prime earners and activists. Not always able to work at home, they are often forced to go to work in factories and workshops. In other instances, the male head of household's infirmity may necessitate journeys from the private into the public space to visit housing officers, hospitals and general practitioners. For some the cardigan and anorak suffice, for others the *hijab* or *burkah* liberate, conferring a sense of visual invisibility when venturing into alien territory. In this way, female negotiation of religious tenets enables the development of strategies to help cope with geographic and social transition.

Bengali females born in England have not had to face the geographic transition made by their mothers, who even now have linguistic, cultural and physical inhibitions when leaving Bangladeshi space.[111] However, young diasporic Muslim women, and men, though more adept at integrating into the western everyday, have had to address another issue, the function and practice of Islam within their westernised lives. In a survey, mainly carried out before 11 September 2001, Sarah Glynn interviewed a selection of young male and female Bengalis in East London. Noting their return to fundamentalist religious values and the increasing numbers of young Bengali women wearing the black *hijab* or *burkah*,[112] Glynn sought to correlate this trend with improved levels of educational achievement and raised employment ambitions. Many of these women felt liberated by wearing traditional Islamic dress, claiming it enabled them to maintain religious separation while enjoying the benefits of education. One feature of the teaching of the new Islam acknowledges the dominant male status while accepting that, within the context of western economies where the male income is not always secure, women may need to work outside the home.[113] Yet, not all *hijab*-wearing young women should be identified as radical for, as one student told me, 'Just because I wear the veil doesn't mean that I am a fundamentalist or old-fashioned, I just observe the tenets and traditions of my religion.'[114] At the other end of the scale is the young woman who told me that it was only if she wore the *hijab* that her parents would allow her to go outside the home and attend university. However, while some females have used Islam as a means of escape from the extended hold of the village, other English-born Bengalis, particularly young males, have recognised it as a way of life which enables them to come to terms with the rejections and racism they have had to face on the streets of Spitalfields. Sadly, some young Bengalis have chosen another route. One which embraces drugs, alcohol and prostitution as a means of compensating for the failure of western culture and society to facilitate their transition from outsider to insider. This problem is now being addressed by volunteers and clerics at the East London Mosque who are running an outreach programme in at attempt to prevent ruined young lives.

Conclusion

This chapter has provided a limited survey of the way in which the three groups of immigrants under examination in this book used religion as an aid to the often painful process of settlement and integration. Certain points have emerged. In each case, to a greater or lesser extent, the French Calvinists, Eastern European Jews and Muslim Bengalis, spatialised their religion within Spitalfields. The Huguenots initiated this in 1743, when they put down an architectural marker on the landscape as a religious preserve for themselves and those immigrants who would come after. As such, the building on the corner of Fournier Street and Brick Lane has remained a central place of immigrant prayer for more than 260 years.[115] Within the context of religious spatialisation, it is evident that the Huguenots and the Jews exhibited a tendency to establish houses of worship based on the nexus of trade and residence that had existed in their sending societies. In the case of the Bangladeshis, while there are a number of small mosques, no doubt owing a debt to village loyalties and associations, the main places of worship have become the Great London Mosque, which acts as a focal point for Islam within the boundaries of Spitalfields, and the East London Mosque, which has become of increasing importance to young East London Muslims. They, as did young East End Jews in the 1920s and 1930s, have welcomed a religious and ideological base which is in touch with contemporary society. Whether it be transference to the Anglican, the Anglicised or the globalised, it would appear that, in all three cases, the second and third generations have sought to correlate religious practice with their views of modernity.

There are similarities between Judaism and Islam that do not occur in Calvinism. Islam and Judaism are highly prescriptive religions, laying down laws regarding work, diet and marriage. While providing a moral code under which adherents should live their lives in the seventeenth and eighteenth centuries and maintaining 'fierce discipline' for those who broke it,[116] Calvinism does not permeate day-to-day activities in the same way. The parallels between Jews and Muslims meant that, in the early days of Bengali settlement in Spitalfields, the only suitable sources of *halal* meat were Jewish butchers. And, in the days before the differences outweighed the similarities, the relationship between Jewish landlords and Muslim tenants and Jewish employers and Muslim workers was one of tolerance and understanding.

One of the most obvious images drawn in this chapter is the contrast between the patterns of religiosity as reflected by the Calvinists and Jews and those of the Bangladeshi followers of Islam. For the Huguenots and Eastern European Jews, the process of absorption into the mainstream was accompanied by a movement away from membership of essentially foreign churches and synagogues to those which were English or, in the case of the Jews, more 'British'. While the spatial Calvinist transition can be traced within Spitalfields, from *La Neuve Église* at the eastern edge of Fournier Street to Christ Church at its western edge, that of the Eastern European Jews took place as a result of the migration from the East End to the suburbs of London and the transferral of synagogue membership from the essentially Eastern European, East End-based Federation of Synagogues to the Anglicised United Synagogue, a body created by a very British Act of Parliament in 1870.[117] Though statistics are impossible to come by, it has been suggested that these religious transitions were often accompanied by a reduction in religiosity.

For the immigrants from Bangladesh and their children the picture is different. The early arrivals may well have neglected Islam, as confessed by that once 'broken Muslim', but they never left it. The opening of the London *Jamme Masjid* and the refurbishment of the East London Mosque are proof of the need for places of worship. In addition, the behaviour of young 'British' Muslims suggests that marginalisation, racialisation and the teachings of certain *mullahs* has resulted in a reverse movement, from a more relaxed to a more stringent form of religious observance, one which is perceived as globally unifying rather than locally isolating. Education and self-advancement may be the priority but on Islam's terms. Young Bengalis now promote their identity as primarily Muslim, then Bengali or British Bengali – never English. This would be a complete anathema to Jews who, as the assimilation process took hold, increasingly considered themselves to be English men and women of the Mosaic persuasion, or to the Huguenots for whom Calvinism was, for a while at least, the priority, the *raison d'être* for escaping from Louis XIV. For them religion was never in conflict with national loyalty. Once return to *mon pays* became a myth, the Huguenots transferred their allegiance to the English and then, come the eighteenth century, the British, monarchy and state.

In none of the three religions did, or do, women play a clerical role, yet in each case the place of the female within the household is central to the regulation of religion within the domestic domain. Women tend to be responsible for the well-being of the family. They are under constant pressure to provide adequate and healthy food, often on a low budget. In addition, for the Jewish and Muslim housewife, unlike her Huguenot counterpart, the tenets of religion requiring the avoidance of 'forbidden foods' meant that poverty was not the only obstacle to overcome when planning the family diet: food must conform to the rigours of religion. It is also evident that, whatever the myth or stereotype, when financial necessity demanded, the married female would negotiate the public space in search of an economic activity to support the household budget. Ironically, as we will see below, there was little stigma attached to female employment in the pre-industrial, Huguenot period. The dishonour and, arguably, emasculation associated with having a working wife is a feature of the industrial period and, though in the postmodern era a working wife is the norm rather than the exception for religious Muslims, it is still a source of discomfort and embarrassment.

At the outset of this chapter, the question was posed as to how the Huguenots, Jews and Bangladeshis accommodated the requirements of their religion within the spatial, economic and dietary confines of Spitalfields. It is the nature of the place that its evolution has been determined by its inhabitants. Even before the large-scale arrival of the Huguenots, the area had become known as one which provided sanctuary for religious dissidents and employment for the skilled, as well as the semi-skilled and unskilled, who could not find work within the city walls. It was only to be expected that, once the immigrants had established their place of settlement in an alien land, they would find a means to provide for all aspects of their religion, the nutritional as well as the spiritual.

The place of religion within the migrant experience is manifold – it acts as an anchor for those who may feel lost or marginalised; it provides a nexus between the sending and receiving societies and a familiar spatial landmark in an alien landscape. For some, religion is a manacle on a transnational chain, one to be avoided if not totally rejected. For all outsiders, it is a figurative and literal centre of community and welfare and, as such, as the next chapter illustrates, a given for strangers, aliens and Asians in Spitalfields.

Notes

1 We cannot rule out the possibility that some Huguenots would have migrated for economic reasons but there is no way of proving this.

2 The role of religion in the rationalisation of the reasons for emigration needs careful analysis, for it was not Jews alone who were making the trek from east to west in order to secure a better standard of life for themselves and the generations to come.

3 K. Gardner, 'Identity, Age and Masculinity amongst Bengali Elders in East London', in A. Kershen (ed.), *A Question of Identity*, Aldershot, Ashgate, 1998, p. 165.

4 Dianne W. Ressinger, *Memoirs of the Reverend Jacques Fontaine 1658–1728*, London, The Huguenot Society of Great Britain and Ireland, 1992, pp. 27–9.

5 T. Murdoch, *The Quiet Conquest: The Huguenots 1685–1985*, London, Museum of London, 1985, p. 58.

6 E.C. Ouvry, 'Huguenot Societies and Churches, Past, Present and Future', *Proceedings of the Huguenot Society of London*, Vol. XVI, 1937–1941, London, Spotiswoode and Vallentine, 1941, p. 13.

7 Murdoch, op. cit., p. 58.

8 R. Gwynn, *Huguenot Heritage: The History and Contribution of the Huguenots in Britain*, Brighton, Sussex Academic Press, 2001 edition, p. 37.

9 Ibid., pp. 40–2.

10 D. Agnew, *Protestant Exiles from France in the Reign of Louis XIV*, London, Reeves and Turner, 1869, pp. 66–7.

11 Gwynn, op. cit., pp. 121–2.

12 Gwynn, op. cit., p. 29.

13 The year 1881 was not only that of the assassination but also the year in which the Decennial Census would reveal the significant increase in arrivals from Russia and Russia-Poland. Until recently, it had been common practice for some historians to select that year as the starting point for the large-scale immigration of Eastern European Jews. In reality they were arriving in increasing numbers from the mid-1870s onwards, the peak period being from 1882 until the early 1900s. The year 1882 marked the passage of the May Laws which followed the assassination of Alexander II and a renewal of the pogroms. The laws confined Jews in the Pale to urban areas and severely limited their rural economic activities and future economic opportunities.

14 I am very grateful to Robin Gwynn for pointing this out to me in a discussion between us on 30 June 2003.

15 Ibid.

16 *Minutes of the Consistory of the French Church 1679–92*, London, Publications of the Huguenot Society of Great Britain and Ireland, Vol. LVIII, 1994, p. 185.

17 A declaration or testament.
18 A letter.
19 Carolyn Lougee Chappell, 'The Pains I Took to Save My/His Family', *French Historical Studies*, 22 (1), 1999, p. 13.
20 See the discussion of the influence of Calvinism on the economic activities of Huguenots in Spitalfields in Chapter 7 below.
21 This is not to say there were no xenophobic reactions; these will be considered in Chapter 8 below.
22 Agnew, op. cit., p. 70.
23 B. Cottret, *The Huguenots in England: Immigration and Settlement 1550–1700*, Cambridge, Cambridge University Press, 1991, p. 241.
24 Gwynn, op. cit., p. 132.
25 Ibid.
26 There had been a Jewish presence in (South) Carolina since 1654, see Michael A. Meyer, *Response to Modernity*, London and New York, Oxford University Press, 1988, p. 228. It should be remembered that Huguenots were not accepted in the part of North America (Canada) occupied by the French.
27 *Register of the Church of Saint Jean Spitalfields*, London, Huguenot Society of London, Vol. XXXLX, 1928, p. xi.
28 Ibid.
29 *Proceedings of Huguenot Society of Great Britain and Ireland*, 1888–91, Vol. III, London, Spottiswoode & Co., 1892, p. 575.
30 F.H.W. Sheppard (ed.), *Survey of London, Vol. XXVII Spitalfields and Mile End New Town*, London, London County Council, 1957, p. 222.
31 Ibid.
32 See Gwynn, op. cit., p. 132.
33 *Minutes of the Consistory of the French Church in London, 1679–92*, op. cit., pp. 59–61.
34 Cottret, op. cit., p. 241.
35 Meeting with Gwynn, 30 June 2003.
36 See Chapter 7 below for details of the demise of the silk industry in Spitalfields.
37 See A. Kershen and J. Romain, *Tradition and Change: A History of Reform Judaism in Britain 1840–1995*, Ilford, Vallentine Mitchell, 1995 and A. Kershen, *150 Years of History of Progressive Judaism in Britain*, London, London Museum of Jewish Life, 1990.
38 Whilst not everyone is familiar with Aleichem's story, most will recognise *Tevye* as the milkman/father in the stage musical *Fiddler on the Roof*.
39 Whilst the ten males is a prerequisite for the service, prayers can be led either by a synagogue official or a 'knowledgeable male'.
40 The religious prohibition on riding on the Sabbath and festivals, plus the twice daily services resulted in synagogues being constructed in close proximity to the living and working quarters of the immigrants. As will be described below, this religious requirement had a great bearing on synagogue location.
41 For the history of the United Synagogue, see A. Newman, *The United Synagogue 1870–1970*, London, Routledge & Kegan Paul, 1977.
42 Ashkenazi Jews were those who, after the fall of the Second Temple, migrated to Central and Eastern Europe. Sephardi Jews were those who settled in Southern Europe, the Iberian peninsula and North Africa.
43 A working class as such was not identified till the late 1830s onwards.
44 A *chevra* is described both as a club and as a small synagogue, the title of club probably emanating from its role as both community centre and place of worship. However, many of the small East End synagogues were known as *chevras* or *chevrot*.

45 Those from the same *shtetl* or town.

46 Sheppard, op. cit., p. 202.

47 Religious head of the United Synagogue.

48 *Jewish Chronicle*, 7 September 1877.

49 The site on the corner of Fournier Street and Brick Lane was leased to the *Talmud Torah*, a religious school, by the French church, and it was they that sublet the chapel to the *Mazhike Hadath* community, one which in common with others had rejected Anglicised Judaism. In the 1920s the *Mazhike Hadath* purchased the building from the French church. I am grateful for Martin Paisner of Berwin Leighton Paisner for letting me have sight of the file on the deeds of the building.

50 G. Alderman, *The Federation of Synagogues 1887–1987*, London, Federation of Synagogues, 1987, pp. 11–12.

51 H. Blacker, *Just Like It Was: Memoirs of Mittel East*, Ilford, Vallentine Mitchell, 1974, pp. 71–2.

52 Federation of Synagogues Minutes, 19 January 1887.

53 Alderman, op. cit., p. 13.

54 It is an interesting fact that the synagogue is frequently referred to in the first person possessive.

55 See *Jewish Chronicle*, 10 October 1873 and also Chapter 5 below.

56 C. Booth, *Life and Labour*, Vol. 1 London, Macmillan, 1889, p. 172.

57 J. Glasman, 'London Synagogues and the Jewish Community *c.*1870–1900', unpublished M.Sc. thesis, Bartlett School of Architecture, London University, 1981/82, p. 47.

58 *Jewish Chronicle*, 15 June 1883.

59 *Jewish Chronicle*, 6 February 1880.

60 Alderman, op. cit., p. 18.

61 C. Russell and H.S. Lewis, *The Jew in London: A Study of Racial Character and Present-day Conditions*, London, T. Fisher Unwin, 1900, p. 120.

62 Israel Zangwill, *Children of the Ghetto*, Woking, Leicester University Press, 1892 (1977 edition), Vol. 1, p. 256.

63 Booth, op. cit., p. 170.

64 Zangwill, op. cit., Vol. 2, p. 326.

65 The author's grandmother worked as a dressmaker in order that her husband could spend his days learning more about, and debating, Judaism.

66 It should be borne in mind that not all of the extant *chevrot* were, at that time, deemed suitable for membership of the Federation.

67 A. Kershen, *Uniting the Tailors*, Ilford, Frank Cass, 1995, p. 141.

68 Ibid., p. 140.

69 W.J. Fishman, *East End Jewish Radicals*, London, Duckworth, 1995 edition, p. 211.

70 Ibid.

71 If families did not have adequate cooking facilities, then often food for the Sabbath meals was cooked in the local baker's oven and collected before the Sabbath began.

72 The Jewish practice of frying fish was heavily criticised by anti-alienists who even went so far as to refer to it in the anti-alien debate at the Trades Union Congress Conference of 1892.

73 *Kelly's Post Office London Directory, Commercial and Streets for 1889*, London, 1899, p. 61.

74 Ibid., pp. 62–3.

75 Glasman, op. cit., p. 79.

76 I am grateful to David Garbin for pointing this out to me.

77 *The Koran*, London, Penguin Classics, 1999 edition, pp. 79–80.
78 K. Gardner, *Age, Narrative and Migration*, Oxford, Berg, 2002, p. 101.
79 Comment of Immam Shafique Rhahman in conversation with the author, 25 June 2002.
80 *The Koran*, op. cit., p. 64.
81 Ibid., p. 71.
82 As will be shown below, this is unlike the situation in the Brick Lane mosque, the house of prayer of many of the elders of the Bangladeshi community. Those women who attend the East London Mosque tend to be the younger ones who evidence the generational differences that are becoming manifest amongst the Bangladeshis of Spitalfields and Banglatown.
83 K. Gardner, *Global Migrants, Local Lives*, Oxford, Clarendon Press, 1995, p. 234.
84 J. Webber, 'Islam in Bangladesh', Introductory notes for CCBI's Conference, 'Movements in Islam' undated, unpublished paper.
85 V. White, 'Health Advocacy in Medicine', in A. Kershen (ed.), *Language, Labour and Migration*, Aldershot, Ashgate, 2000, p. 83.
86 J. Eade, 'The Power of the Experts: The Plurality of Beliefs and Practices concerning Health and Illness among Bangladeshis', in L. Marks and M. Warboys (eds), *Migrants, Minorities and Medicine*, London, Routledge, 1997, pp. 257–8.
87 Webber, op. cit., p. 2.
88 See Caroline Adams, *Across Seven Seas and Thirteen Rivers*, London, Thap Books, 1987, pp. 39–44.
89 http://www.eastlondon-mosque.org.uk/html/history/htm (accessed 30 June 2002).
90 The term 'elder' when used to describe a member of the Bengali community is not necessarily descriptive of age but rather of status, particularly that of grandparent. A Bengali man may become a grandfather in his forties but is still referred to as an elder.
91 See website in note 89 above.
92 On the local campaign for the extension of the East London Mosque and the way money was collected through donation within the Bengali community in Tower Hamlets, see David Garbin, 'Migration, territories diasporiques et politiques identitaires: Bengalis musulmans entre "Banglatown" (Londres) et Sylhet (Bangladesh)', unpublished Ph.D. thesis. University of François Rabelais de Tours, 2004, pp. 378–87.
93 In 1975 it made a temporary move to Fieldgate Street, just behind Whitechapel Road to the south.
94 *East London Advertiser*, 27 November 1970.
95 J. Eade, 'The Political Articulation of Community and the Islamisation of Space in London', in R. Barot (ed.), *Religion and Ethnicity, Minorities and Social Change in the Metropolis*, Kampon, Netherlands, Kok Pharos, 1993, p. 31.
96 See Chapter 5 below.
97 See Eade, 'The Political', op. cit.
98 K. Gardner, 'Death, Burial and Bereavement amongst Bengali Muslims in Tower Hamlets, East London', *Journal of Ethnic and Migration Studies*, 22 (3), 1998, p. 516.
99 Meeting with Mafijur Rafique, 4 July 2003.
100 Garbin, op. cit., pp. 194–9.
101 Ibid., p. 198.
102 S. Carey and A. Shukur, 'Profile of Bangladeshi Community in East London', in *New Community*, 12 (3), 1985–6, p. 411.
103 K. Gardner, 'Identity, Age and Masculinity amongst Bengali Elders in East

London' in A. Kershen (ed.), *A Question of Identity*, Aldershot, Ashgate, 1998, p. 165.

104 Adams, op. cit., p. 160.

105 Ibid.

106 *Home Affairs Sub-Committee on Race Relations and Immigration*, Vol. II, 1986, London, HMSO, p. 264.

107 N. Kabeer, *The Power to Choose*, London and New York, Verso, 2000, p. 195.

108 Gardner, *Age*, op. cit., p. 120.

109 Ibid., p. 136.

110 Kabeer, op. cit., p. 236.

111 See Chapter 6 below.

112 A trend noticeable over the past five to eight years at the author's university, Queen Mary, University of London.

113 S. Glynn, 'Bengali Muslims: The New East End Radicals?', *Ethnic and Racial Studies*, 23 (6), November 2002, p. 280.

114 Conversation with third-year undergraduate student at Queen Mary, University of London, May 2002.

115 In September 2004 planning permission was granted for a change to the landscape of the corner of Fournier Street and Brick Lane. Following an application on behalf of the *Jamme Masjid*, it was agreed that, in addition to internal changes to the building, which is Grade II listed, there could be some minor external changes. However the most controversial element of the revisions was the proposed (and approved) erection of a minaret, 29 metres in height and 1.2 metres wide, on a bunker, which is the property of the mosque, on the pavement in front of the building. Although not actually a part of the 1743 building, the minaret will undeniably change the nature of the area and reinforce its multi-cultural identity. It should be noted that permission for the erection of the minaret was granted with the proviso that it could not be used for the call to prayer. Information from Tower Hamlets Borough Council Development Committee Report No. DC037/045, 15 September 2004.

116 I am grateful to Peter Catterall for bringing this to my attention.

117 Newman, op. cit., p. 17.

5   Charity and welfare

Irrespective of the temporal divides, the incomers featured in this book fall into the following categories. There are the 'fortunates', those able to support themselves and dependents from monies and goods previously deposited or brought with them, or those with skills and abilities to ensure employment, security and improved quality of life. Then there are the economic migrants, legal and illegal, who have limited economic opportunity or who, in their sending society, are subjected to economic deprivation as a result of the local economy, ethnicity, religion or gender. They come with few, if any, funds but are prepared to work long and hard to achieve upward economic mobility for themselves and their families, either by remaining in Britain or by returning to their country of origin when they have sufficient savings. Finally, there are the refugees and asylum seekers who have come seeking sanctuary from persecution. With the exception of the 'fortunates', the newly arrived immigrant invariably requires assistance, in the form of housing, health care, schooling and, at times, ready money. At the time of writing, attitudes towards economic migrants and asylum seekers[1] are generally unsympathetic, the perception being that these incomers are individuals intent on taking advantage of charities and the welfare state. Both historically, and at the present time, these two support systems differ and it would be helpful at the outset of this chapter to define the way in which they have been understood and applied, since before the birth of the welfare state.[2] Charity is a familiar and at times abused word. For Calvinists, Jews and Muslims, the concept of charity is an essential part of their religion. It implies benevolence to the poor or unfortunate, by deed and/or by donation, as for example through church collections or almsgiving. For the recipient it is a blessing even though it may occasionally, be an embarrassment. Charity is not an individual's right, but results from another's compassionate recognition of need. Welfare is different. In contemporary terms, it can be defined as a means by which the maintenance of persons – in a condition of well-being, health and prosperity – can be effected by statutory procedure or social effort. Within the broader context of the modern welfare state, it is a system whereby the state undertakes to protect the health and well-being of citizens, especially those in financial or social need by means of state-funded bodies, grants, pensions, etc. As defined in this way, it is a citizen's right. Fortunately for those seeking refuge and asylum in Britain, the state does not insist on *all* those in receipt being 'citizens', thus the legitimate refugee or asylum seeker may receive some state benefit. Welfare is intended to help a recipient maintain an acceptable standard of living and is administered and distributed through the state or non-governmental organisations which might, or might not, be attached to a religious body. In contrast, charity is far more arbitrary, dependent on an individual's good nature, goodwill and available finance.

This chapter investigates the need for, and provision of, charity and welfare for the impoverished stranger Huguenots, pauper alien Eastern European Jews and economically necessitous Bangladeshis. It will consider how civic or government support for immigrants has been perceived by the recipients and providers and how great a factor the provision of state-sanctioned welfare has been in increasing – or decreasing – levels of xeno-phobia, anti-alienism and racism.

'La charité est la plus excellente de toutes les vertus Chrétiennes.'[3]

It has already been established that, in spite of the presumption that the French Calvinist refugees brought with them skills and money, in reality many were semi-skilled or unskilled and in possession of few if any funds. Some, including those who had been wealthy in France, escaped with just their and their family's lives. Fortunately for the future infrastructure of the Huguenot community, a minority of perspicacious early refugees (or economic migrants) 'were wealthy and [had] brought a great deal of money with them'.[4] For the less fortunate, help was forthcoming from a variety of English and French sources. These included the Anglican church,[5] the monarchy and the nascent English-Huguenot community.

Though the 'torrent' of Calvinist refugees did not arrive until 1686–7, following the English monarchy's pronouncements of tolerance, the seventeenth-century Huguenot flights from France began to gather pace with the imposition of the Dragonnades in 1681. For reasons of economic benefit, flavoured with perhaps a pinch of altruism, in 1683 Charles II acknowledged the Huguenots' plight by instructing English sea captains to transport refugees across the Channel. They were assured that there would be no border restrictions and that they would be given the freedom to work within the normal restrictions imposed on aliens. Most significantly, the king, as head of the Anglican church, issued Letters Patent authorising charitable collections for the pauper refugees to be held in churches throughout his realm. The proceeds of this Brief were mainly distributed in London, where the majority of the necessitous incomers were assembled. The specified recipients were to be clergymen and their families, unwed noble-women and orphans.[6] In the few remaining years of his reign Charles issued a Royal Brief annually. Following the king's death in November 1685, his successor James II, albeit with extreme reluctance, ordered a further Brief which produced a collection of £40,000. It has been suggested that the issuing of the Briefs by the Stuart monarchs resulted from religious and political pressure and that the sum of £40,000 was more an expression of James's subjects' dislike of his rule than of their sympathy for the refugees.[7]

The 1688 'Bloodless Revolution' and the installation of a true and 'passionate' Protestant monarchy in 1689, enabled the formalisation of state provision for the Huguenots. Under William and Mary, an annual provision for French Protestants, a Royal Bounty in the form of grants from the crown's revenues appropriated to the civil list, was put in place. It survived from the reign of William III until 1876, though at its latter end it had become greatly reduced. William and Mary's support for the French Protestants was evident. In 1689 they issued a Declaration inviting Calvinists to come to England. They supported this pronouncement in deed by making personal donations to the Briefs.[8] As noted in the previous chapter, the volume of refugee arrivals in the closing decades of the seventeenth century was such that Threadneedle Street and the other French churches found it an increasing strain to provide charity. From 1696 the Royal Bounty became a major provider.[9] There being no twentieth-century-type welfare state, the administration and distribution of the Bounty was made through the Threadneedle Street church. This operated as follows: there was a supervisory group of Lords Commissioners, an English committee which laid down criteria for relief and checked accounts and a French committee which oversaw relief. It was the French committee that held the real power, as it made the decisions on how the money was distributed and who the recipients would be.

In order to ensure that those seeking help by way of the Bounty were genuine refugees and not just economic opportunists, certain restrictions were applied. With the exception of church ministers, help was only available for those who had arrived in England before 1685. It was not to be awarded to anyone who had resided in a Protestant country prior to arrival, nor to those who had been in receipt of recent relief, nor to ministers ordained since leaving France.[10] This was in line with the prevailing belief that able-bodied men recently come of age and capable of working or serving in the army should gain assistance only once. As the previous chapter has shown, it was the Threadneedle Street French church which was at the heart of the early Huguenot community. Through it a form of communal government and organisation was set in place and the nascent Huguenot community was able to develop a charitable nexus which, supplemented by the generosity of the English monarchy and public, would prove a means of support for necessitous Huguenots for several centuries to come.

It is clear that though available, even in the seventeenth century, charity and welfare were seen as a means of social control, as a way of keeping the stranger refugees off the streets, of facilitating the assimilation process and of getting the fit and able back to work. In aims and objectives, the philosophy seems little different to that of Samuel Smiles or Margaret Thatcher. However, neither their English hosts nor the earlier Huguenot arrivals had any wish for the Calvinist refugees to suffer more than was necessary. Self-help was part of the Calvinist ethic and there was a determination that the incomers become self-sufficient as rapidly as possible. As a means of pump priming, the French churches acted as banks to the immigrants, providing loans at around 6 per cent interest. Once the immigrants had been given a start, charity was reserved for the 'hopeless cases'.[11]

An examination of the records of the Distribution of the Royal Bounty for 1696 provides us with a profile of the span and value of monies distributed. Necessity crossed social boundaries: the lower-class needy received a total of £604; the middle-class needy £693 19s 3d and necessitous nobility £304 14s.[12] The lower figure is more an indication of fewer numbers than lesser need. Because of their previous privileged position and lifestyle, members of the nobility were less well equipped than others to provide for themselves and their families in a strange and not always welcoming country. Without charity many faced poverty or worse, the debtors' prison. The records also reveal that between 1695 and 1709 female recipients – 12,216 over thirteen years of age – outnumbered their male counterparts.[13] Research has shown that the immigration of the Huguenots followed a pattern of chain migration. In the vanguard were unaccompanied men – between 1686 and 1688 most assistance went to single men. By the early 1700s, family reunifications had begun and the number of destitute refugees grew rapidly.[14] From this time the majority of those receiving help were families.

In the first few years after the revocation of the Edict of Nantes, 41 per cent of payments went to recipients in the top social bracket. Many, particularly the women, had fled with little but what they stood up in, and grants were provided to enable them to purchase clothing.[15] Wealthier, earlier settled Huguenots made their contributions too. But even in a climate of hardship and stress, snobbery and class separation prevailed. Established and influential Huguenots used charity as a means of accelerating the assimilation process of those who might bring discredit upon their nascent community. Reports at the time record that 'Persons of a lesser sort were given a pound to go to the country for his [*sic*] establishment.'[16] In this instance 'establishment' meant acculturation or assimilation.

Initially, the more settled and affluent French Calvinists provided incoming hopeless cases with money with which to purchase the basic necessities, particularly food. However, when it was discovered that this 'charity' was mostly spent on brandy and tobacco, the Huguenot elders decided to distribute vouchers, or 'portions', through *Maisons de Charité*, which were established in Spitalfields and Soho. From these *maisons*, food and vegetables, and even on occasions beer, were distributed. In Spitalfields, the house of charity, that was established sometime between 1689 and 1694[17] and located in 'Flower the Luce' (Fleur de Lys) Street,[18] became known as the Soup(e). There, in return for printed portion tickets allocated by the directors of the Soup, Threadneedle Street or one of the allied French churches, applicants received, 'a pan of good broth mixed with six ounces of good bread and half a pound of meat'.[19] By 1741, reductions in charitable funds, together with increased demand, brought a halt to the provision of meat and soup. From that time on, until the end of the century, only bread was issued to applicants who, even in 1776, still numbered as many as 127 families.

It has been written elsewhere that 'The Calvinist tradition of caring for the needy was well organised and they could call upon the services of a sizeable, well integrated and often affluent membership.'[20] Evidence of this is to be found in the variety of institutions and activities the Huguenots initiated. The French church maintained almshouses and rooms for the storage of clothes and other items and also provided the services of teachers, a doctor and a surgeon. By contrast to the hopeless poor, deserving families in need were given money. For example, a family of two adults and nine children was allowed an initial four shillings a week, which reduced to two shillings a week after four or five months.[21] Though education was a primary objective of the community, records reveal that children at the French Charity School in Corlet's Court, Spitalfields, spent only a portion of the day learning. The rest of the time they worked for themselves and their parents. The Protestant work ethic was inculcated at an early age.

While the children were protected and educated, the elderly were cared for. An old person in need of support was sent to the *hospital* (hospice), commonly known as the 'pest house', which was opened in 1681 to provide sanctuary for sick and old Huguenot refugees.[22] There they would be given 'shoes, breeches, shirts and other items of apparel, a pension and afterwards [be] placed in an old people's home'.[23] In 1708, the pest house was replaced by the French hospital, *La Providence*, founded following a bequeath of £1,000 from Jacques de Gastigny for the establishment of a hospice for distressed Protestants. *La Providence* had its own chapel and was independent of the French churches. It was not located within Spitalfields, but stood to its west, just off City Road, in Islington. As late as 1760, *La Providence* housed 234 poor people. By the mid-nineteenth century, though it still limited its intake to those who could trace their descent from the original refugees, the French nature of the institution had all but disappeared. Writing in 1853, Agnew highlighted the process of assimilation that had taken place over three-quarters of a century:

> The hospital has lost much of its distinctive national character. Sixty years ago a visitor might have heard the inmates chattering away in antiquated French. They speak English now, probably some of them do not know a word of French because the majority of their ancestors in four generations had been English.[24]

In 1862 the French hospital was relocated eastwards on three acres of land in Victoria Park, Hackney. Following the Second World War, the hospital moved again, first to Sussex and then to Kent. By that time it had taken on a completely new role, no longer housing the distressed poor or their descendants, it became a repository for Huguenot records, relics and literature and, as acknowledged by Ouvry, 'The chief centre of all our Huguenot institutions'.[25]

The refugee Calvinists carried with them a religious discipline which counted self-help as one of its guiding principles. It is not surprising, therefore that, as soon as possible, they set about establishing a pragmatic and efficient method of saving and providing for personal and family need in the future. One of the major manifestations of this was the foundation of mutual or friendly societies through which monies could be put aside, literally, in locked strong boxes, available for immediate withdrawal when necessary. The exact origin of the friendly societies is not clear – their possible roots being as offshoots from freemasonry, burial clubs, mediaeval guilds or a combination of all three. Writing at the end of the nineteenth century, Waller suggested that, as an *Association de secours mutuel* was founded in Lille in 1580, 'it seems clear that the refugees from France were familiar with the ideas embodied in them'[26] and that they imported the concept to England. Indeed it does seem likely that the Huguenots were responsible for introducing the notion of friendly societies into England. Records show that, twenty-three years before the foundation of the Amiable Society, the first recorded English society, the *Société des Enfants de Nîmes*, was established in 1683 by refugees from '*Nismes, St. Cezaire, Cayfargues, Bouillargues, Courbessac et terres adjacentes*'.[27] In nearly every instance the Huguenots founded friendly societies based on a territorial or trade nexus. In addition to the above were others that bore the titles of Lintot, Paris, Saint Onge and Angoumois, and yet another from the region of Normandy, while, as early as February 1692, a group of journeymen tailors associated for 'mutual support to succour one another in sickness and need'.[28]

It was common practice for the societies to hold their meetings in local inns or public houses, which were often designated society headquarters.[29] The Society of Lintot was based in Brick Lane and its membership restricted to members of the church of Lintot. The society kept all its funds and documents in a metal box with two separate locks, the box only to be opened in the presence of six of the society's members. The Norman Society – a provincial rather than village or trade association – was founded in 1703. Its rules, as of 1724,[30] provide us with an insight both into the level of individual capital held by the society and the strict moral code imposed upon the membership, one principle of membership being that members did not indulge in gambling. When sick, members were visited by the secretary and treasurer of the society and, provided the member's capital investment in the society remained at £100, given nine shillings a week benefit. Once savings went below the £100 level, relief payment was reduced. It appears to have been a system of allowance in inverse ratio to need. Upon a member's death, burial expenses were covered up to a maximum of £2 10s. As a capital sum of £100 was the suggested median, it is clear that the society's members could not be classified as poor.

The Society of Parisians, established in 1687, provides still further insight into the financial requirements and moral imperatives. Contributions to 'the box' were one shilling a month. Benefits were paid out at eight shillings a week for sickness, for up to fifty-two weeks, and then four shillings a week after that. Funeral money, at £5, was more generous than the Society of Lintot and, for those who were in the French hospital, there was a payout of sixpence per week. The rules required that there be no playing of games at meetings, no swearing and no anti-Protestant sympathies. The printed rules of the society began with the words: '*La Charité est la plus excellénte de toutes les vertus chrétiennes ... c'est dans le dessein de cultiver cette excellente vertu ... que Dieu nous mit au Coeur de former cette Société.*'[31] When Waller was carrying out his research at the end of the nineteenth century, the society's box was still in use and, by this time, had three locks. In spite of the Huguenot community's assimilation into mainstream life, the emergence of the welfare state and trade unions, early eighteenth-century societies such as the *Société de Saint Onge and Angoumois*, the Norman Society and the Society of Lintot, survived into the second half of the twentieth century.

By the end of the first half of the eighteenth century, the Huguenots had constructed a nexus of charitable organisations and societies that would provide for their hopeless poor and those in work who wished to save for the future. The deeply embedded self-help philosophy is visible at every step, as is the didactic element of charity. Pride in self and community was a driving force in the construction of that nexus, though the state's role, small though it may have been, should not be overlooked. When we come to examine the charity and welfare of the next major immigrant community in Spitalfields we find much that is reminiscent of its predecessors. What we do not find is any provision by monarch or state for the alien paupers whose presence created powerful antagonisms even though they provided economic benefits for insider and outsider alike.

Tzedekah and *rachamunus*[32]

By the middle of the nineteenth century, charitable provision available for the indigent Jews of London covered 'the needy, the hungry, the mad, the orphaned, the blind and the sick, not to mention the rituals of life from birth to burial'.[33] This blanket coverage was fully in keeping with the Jewish religious doctrine of *tzedekah* laid down by the rabbis centuries before. They had prescribed that there should be charitable provision for the less fortunate by way of food, clothing, hospitals for the sick and aged infirm, burials, hospice for travellers and, where necessary, monetary relief.

Long before articulated by William Beveridge, it was a 'cradle-to-grave' philosophy. Taking the Bible as the guideline, without specifying an exact sum, it was accepted that regular donations should be made to charity. Ten per cent of income was considered a realistic figure.

Communal provision for their poor was not something new to seventeenth- and eighteenth-century Jewish migrants, particularly those from Eastern Europe. Russian and Russian-Polish immigrants came from autonomous backgrounds and imported a tradition of charitable organisation and distribution through individual synagogues. But altruism was not the only spur; there were other forces at play. Whilst the self-support ethos must not be overlooked, there is another element, one found in the diasporic baggage unpacked at each place of settlement. That of an overriding concern that poor Jews should not be a burden on the receiving society. From the readmission of 1656 through to the second half of the nineteenth century, and on into the welfare state, there is a thread of concern and action which manifests as charitable organisations. There is yet a third aspect of the act of charity, that which relates to hubris and status – the performance of 'giving' – in the political sense, as a means of obtaining communal power and prestige.[34] At varying levels, and within narrow or broader spheres, those donating funds were able to ascend the social ladder. Those nearer the top were not only able to decide on specific beneficiaries and the size and terms of their benefit, but, in addition, were able to play a didactic role in the lives of the poor. This was decades before the English Charity Organisation Society was to do the same amongst the indigenous 'deserving' poor.[35]

As the numbers of alien poor in Spitalfields grew, the main objectives of the Jewish charitable societies can be listed as: the inculcation of the self-help ethos into the immigrant mind-frame; provision for the 'deserving poor' who could not help themselves; and, in common with the Huguenots who had sent the lower-class impoverished refugees into the country for their 'establishment', the ironing out of the ghetto bends.

The beginning of the nineteenth century revealed a paradox in the concept of Jewish charity. Whilst individual synagogues distributed alms to the poor, a spectrum of independent charities provided for schooling, food, clothing and help for (married) pregnant women, widowers, orphans and the elderly. The poor were divided up into the following three categories: those on regular or stipendiary relief; the casual poor; and the strange poor,[36] the latter referring to those who came from outside the locality as opposed to being from overseas. There was a commonly accepted view that, even if some Jews were poor, they were honourable. However, a report by Patrick Colquhoun, appearing in 1800, on *The Police of the Metropolis*, highlighted the disturbing fact that many young Jewish boys and girls had become criminalised due to economic desperation.[37] Colquhoun found that, though Jews were not disposed to crime, the lack of a training system for poor boys and girls had resulted in many turning to crime as a means of survival. It was a condition which would be familiar to those who, 200 years on, argue that youth criminality is a result of nurture, i.e. social exclusion and the failures of the system, rather than of nature.

Colquhoun's report did not fall upon deaf ears. Joshua Van Oven, a surgeon and communal activist, lost no time in proposing that the community, as a whole, take remedial action by setting up a Jewish relief board to provide a Jewish workhouse, hospital, old age home and trade school.[38] The broad sweep of provisions suggests both altruism and concern for the community's public image. However, the concept was far in advance of its time and received insufficient support to enable it to go forward. Opposition came from more than one source. The Sephardim declined to support it because they were concerned that such an association with the Ashkenazim would be socially demeaning and financially iniquitous. For their part, the Ashkenazi community opposed the scheme because they believed, rightly, that it would put excessive power into the hands of the wealthy few.[39]

Following the tradition established in the seventeenth century (the first Sephardi charity, one for the care of the sick and burying the dead, was set up in 1664, eight years after the readmission),[40] the two early nineteenth-century religious branches of London Jewry (the Sephardim and the Ashkenazim) went their own ways in respect of charitable provision. One of the longest surviving Ashkenazi communal charities was the *Meshebat Naphesh* (Bread, Meat and Coal Society), established in 1779[41] to distribute bread, meat and coal to the London Jewish poor during the winter season. The founding of the Bread, Meat and Coal Society, in common with one founded around the same time by the Sephardi community, resulted from the distress caused by the high price of bread and the London bread riots of 1778. As in the case of Huguenot charitable provision, self-help was the Bread, Meat and Coal's guiding principle. A minimum of one penny per week for a specified time had to be paid into the society before benefit could be applied for. The beneficiaries were chosen by lottery. In 1780 the lucky ticket-holder received, over a period of three months, 1 s 9 d of bread, 1 s 9 d of meat and two bushels of coal.[42] Some 160 years later the society was still providing for the poor. In 1940 it paid out at the rate of one shilling per week for bread, meat and coal.[43]

In order to provide poor and hungry Jews with food during the winter months, a number of Jewish soup kitchens were opened in Spitalfields. The first soup kitchen appeared at the end of the eighteenth century. The most enduring opened in 1893, at the height of the Eastern European influx. Its principles were very similar to those practised by William Booth, the founder of the Salvation Army. Feed the hungry first, then investigate or, as in the case of Booth, bring on religion. The soup kitchen operated from the heart of Spitalfields at a time when the combination of an ever-expanding immigrant community and rising levels of local – and national – unemployment meant that in winter and at Passover (when the seasonal charities came into operation), those provided for numbered in the thousands. For example, in April 1898 2,500 families were given food, 1,000 having been beneficiaries during the winter. By 1905 the number of those receiving regular support had risen to 2,000 families.[44] The compassionate policy of the kitchen was under constant pressure from the Jewish establishment and, though it did not feed *all* those who applied for food – no money was ever given out – in 1905 it did agree to provide weekly lists of those relieved.

Orphaned young, and necessitous old, Jews in Spitalfields, found some indoor relief in the Jews Hospital founded in 1795. However, Colquhoun's report suggests it was somewhat ineffectual in disciplining the young that were admitted into its industrial school. Concern about the control and education of the young, particularly the orphaned young, led to the foundation of the *Talmud Torah* school. In 1817 this became the Jews' Free School, a teaching institution which, by the end of the nineteenth century, had become one of the most admired in Europe. At its location in Bell Lane, in the heart of Spitalfields, it accommodated over 3,000 pupils.[45]

With one exception, all the Jewish charitable organisations refused to provide the strange or outsider poor with immediate relief. The exception was one run by the Sephardi community which, as a result of its close links with Dutch Jews, offered benefit to those who had left Holland with good cause. Charitable policy in the late eighteenth century was little different to that of 200 years later. There was a determination not to be perceived as a 'soft touch' by those who were drawn to Britain because of its reputation for tolerance towards migrants. In the eighteenth and nineteenth centuries, Jewish communal leaders were anxious to deter the entry of pauper aliens in order to avoid inciting anti-Jewish and anti-alien sentiments.

By 1820 the multiplicity of Jewish charitable organisations operating in London were mainly focused on Spitalfields and the surrounding area of the East End. They provided for the poor of a community which, in total, numbered between 25,000 to 30,000 souls. The charities included: the Jews' Free School; an infants school; orphans' charities; seven clothing charities; a ladies' benevolent institution (for married women in childbirth); two societies for the indigent blind; two societies for widows; a widows' home; Jewish soup kitchen; Bread, Meat and Coal Society; Jews' Hospital; and a number of almshouses. In spite, or perhaps because, of the multiplicity of organisations, the distribution of charity was haphazard and often inadequate. This was as true of synagogal practices as of that of the secular bodies. The arrangements were confused and, complex and, rather than resolve the problems of pauperism, in reality they exacerbated them.[46]

By the middle of the nineteenth century at least 25 per cent of London's Jewish population was impoverished. The need to rationalise charitable provision was pressing. A plan put forward in 1844 for the centralisation of all charitable institutions failed. However, one which proposed the creation of a Jewish Board of Guardians modelled on the parochial Poor Law Boards was accepted. The Board, which represented the three main London Ashkenazi synagogues, opened in 1859. Initially its role was to provide only for the 'strange' Jewish poor in London. This was not to be an open-door policy but rather one which would control excessive immigration by imposing a self-sufficiency requirement and by refusing relief to anyone who could not prove they had been resident in the country for at least six months.

Although set up to provide for necessitous outsiders, the Jewish Board of Guardians was soon forced to extend its scope in order to provide for all the London Jewish *deserving* poor. The undeserving poor were left to the mercy of the parish Poor Law Boards which made no concessions to religion or marital status. The philosophy of the Board was to 'make every Jewish citizen, as far as possible, a self-supporting and self-respecting unit of population' or, in twenty-first-century terms, 'to get those on benefit back to work as quickly as possible'. The methodology was didactic and invasive. It first examined the past and present circumstances of all those who applied for help and then subjected those selected to domiciliary visits. These were carried out on a regular basis, with the intention of instructing wives and mothers in the correct method of household management, though how many of the middle-class 'visitors' from Maida Vale and Bloomsbury understood the running of a working-class home in Spitalfields, is debatable. The Board also loaned out sewing machines to help those eager to enter the clothing trade. In 1876 this role was handed over to the Singer Sewing Machine Co. on the grounds that the company was better organised to deal with supply and demand. A covert reason for the termination of the practice was that, as an increasing number of Jews were becoming tailors, the Board did not want to be held responsible for them 'taking the jobs of Englishmen'. This sentiment, which would become commonplace by the end of the 1890s,[47] was one anticipated by the *Jewish Chronicle* as early as 1872. In an editorial, the newspaper criticised the Board's actions, commenting that it was providing fuel for the labour pool of 'an already full industry'.[48]

In the years leading up to 1881, the demand from the poor Jews of Spitalfields for relief was steady but not overwhelming. All this changed after the assassination of Tsar Alexander II. From the 1880s onwards, until the outbreak of the First World War, there were peaks and troughs of immigration from Eastern Europe. These coincided with the economic depression in Britain which lasted, with the exception of a small window of economic advancement between 1888 and 1892, from the mid-1870s until shortly before the outbreak of war. In the area of Spitalfields, high levels of immigrant unemployment put pressure on existing Jewish charities and encouraged the formation of others. Concerns over the volume of arrivals, the financial burden they placed on the community, the impact on the native population and the resultant negative reaction, encouraged certain members of British Jewry to take preventive action. They placed advertisements in the Eastern European Yiddish press, and sent word back down the networks to the *shtetls* and cities of the Pale, warning would-be emigrants that, rather than finding the streets of London paved with gold, they would find only hardship and suffering. The message of the despatches, ignored by the majority, was clear: stay at home.

The advertisements and communications had little effect and immigrant numbers increased dramatically. Fortunately for the new arrivals, the philosophy of delayed relief was not one supported by all the Jewish residents of London's East End. There were those such as Simon Cohen, who had compassion for the tired, hungry, scared and bedraggled arrivals. In 1884 he opened a temporary shelter. However, the establishment, concerned that it would act as a magnet to pauper aliens from Eastern Europe, demanded, and achieved, its closure. Fortunately, there were those who manifested *rachamunus*. In 1885, in Leman Street, just to the south of Spitalfields and not far from the Pool of London, a permanent Poor Jews Temporary Shelter was established with the support of Samuel Montagu, Ellis Abraham Frankau and Hermann Landau. The Shelter provided accommodation for immigrants and transmigrants for up to two weeks. The main occupants proved to be transmigrants, a large number of whom, from the mid-1890s onwards, were in transit to South Africa. In Eugene Black's words, the Shelter was 'an accommodation station', which at times even helped the disillusioned find their way back to Russia.[49] Within the Shelter the ethos of self-help ruled. As laid down under the Poor Law Act of 1834, all able-bodied males were made to undertake work in payment for board and lodging. But there was also compassion. The Shelter sent representatives to the Docks to meet every newly arrived ship carrying steerage passengers from Eastern Europe in order to ensure that neither they, nor their belongings, fell into the hands of co-religionist sharks.

The flood of Eastern European immigrants into Spitalfields and Whitechapel put tremendous strains on the Jewish communal charitable network. By the time the 1905 Aliens Act was passed, there were more than forty Jewish philanthropic institutions and almost 100 charities operating in London.[50] In spite of the existence of the Jewish Board of Guardians, there was still duplication and confusion. Twelve societies provided food and fuel handouts and four distributed meals (though to different sections of the deserving poor). All the main synagogues, through their ladies' guilds, provided clothes whilst there was also a selection of old age homes and, just beyond the East End's boundaries at Norwood, an orphanage. Prostitution and the white-slave trade were other issues that the Jewish community was forced to address. Young Jewish girls from Eastern Europe were being brought into London either to remain as prostitutes or to be shipped to the brothels of South Africa, and South America, particularly Buenos Aires, where their services were valued. Some girls were duped by pimps who promised them marriage and riches; others travelled willingly and knowingly, convinced that life in a brothel could offer more than that of the *shtetl*.[51] As part of their programme to prevent the abuse and trafficking of young female migrants, representatives of the Jewish Association for the Protection of Girls and Women met all the incoming ships and escorted the girls to safety.[52] In spite of this some girls got through the net, for it is estimated that there were some 450 Jewish prostitutes active in London's East End.[53]

A multiplicity of organisations manifested *tzedekah* and *rachamunus*. They also acted as political and social stepping stones for communal activists, many of whom enjoyed the status and power their positions gave them. In addition, the charities provided a livelihood for the secretaries, caseworkers, solicitors and collectors employed by them. What developed has been described by Black as a 'tangled rarely pruned thicket of benevolence' in which '[W]ell intentioned amateurs stumbled over one another, visiting, investigating, serving and ordering the unfortunate.'[54]

Irrespective of the aims, objectives and organisational control of the charitable societies, there was one guiding principle – self-help. Nowhere was this more evident than in the creation and maintenance of Jewish friendly societies, the seeds of which were sown in the eighteenth century and which blossomed extensively in the nineteenth. The societies provided overt evidence of the industriousness and providence of the regularly employed Jewish immigrant who followed the philosophy of self-help. Though the Huguenots must be credited with establishing the earliest form of friendly society in England, benevolent and benefit societies to provide burial and mourning funds for Jews can be traced back to just after the readmission.[55] Run through the synagogues, these were a combination of the religious and the secular, with much of their funds contributed by the wealthier members. Initially these societies included in their objectives the establishment of places of worship, the provision of dowries and the supply of coal and bread to the needy.[56] One example of the link between synagogue and society is evidenced by the society founded by a group of Dutch Jews in Spitalfields and based in Sandys Row. This evolved into a synagogue with an eventual membership of 500 souls.

The concept of a society which encouraged self-protection and self-help and which posed no threat to employers was to be welcomed and secured. In 1801 the Friendly Societies Act was passed and, by encouraging societies to register, was a forerunner of the bureaucratic trends of the 1830s. It is through the registrations that we can trace, what appear to be, the earliest established Jewish friendly societies in London. The first recorded, the Pursuers of Peace, was founded in 1797 and included amongst its officers a rabbi and lay synagogue officials. In 1820 the Loyal United Lodge of Sons of Israel was registered, followed three years later by the Lovers of Peace and Justice. The intriguingly named Sephardi society, Charity Escapes an Early Death, first appeared in 1830. The names and the structure of these early societies reflect providence allied to Anglicisation, together with what seems to have been a desire to be recognised by the wider host society.

The societies founded before the second half of the nineteenth century provide evidence that the Jewish community in Spitalfields, and others elsewhere in London and the provinces, had been established for some time. In the second half of the century, with the influx from Eastern Europe, the balance changed. As a consequence, the nature and naming of the friendly societies altered too. The Jewish friendly societies that emerged from the 1860s, as those founded by the Huguenots more than a century earlier, tended to be associations of fellow workers or townspeople. Examples included the Cigarette Makers and Tobacco Cutters Benefit Society, the Cracow Jewish Friendly Society and others established by immigrants from Warsaw, Deneburg, Vitebsk, Zhitomir, Siedletz and Plotsk.[57] There appears to have been no attempt to hide roots or religious identity, though, in not using *Israelite* or *Hebrew*, there seems to have been a move towards Anglicisation.

Friendly societies satisfied more than a financial need amongst the immigrant community. They also had a didactic element, encouraging thrift, self-management and self-discipline. In addition, they provided physical as well as financial support at times of bereavement and sickness and, from their registered headquarters in public houses, were a base for social interaction – the use of an inn or public house as a registered office was common nineteenth-century practice for trade societies, guilds and trade unions. But there were those who sought more, those who looked for ceremony and status. This was to be found in the various friendly society lodges and orders, some such as the Order of *Achei Brith* which, in 1888, had a membership of 2,800 and was expressly Jewish. Others were Jewish lodges of Christian orders such as that of the Ancient Order of Foresters. The advent of Zionism brought a further dimension and division. A number of societies, such as the Hans Herzl Lodge founded in 1905, was open only to those who supported the political Zionist ideal.

By the start of the twentieth-century, Jewish friendly societies could be split into three specific groups: the very basic organisations linked to the *chevras* and small synagogues which provided mainly for death-related expenses; the lodges with their councils, rituals and paraphernalia of office which gave the hard-working artisan, shopkeeper or tradesman a sense of importance and occasion; and, finally, the standard friendly society which provided a spectrum of benefits. In spite of the plethora of societies – in 1910 the *Jewish Year Book* listed 320 extant societies – it is impossible to provide an accurate profile of the percentage of society affiliates. A considerable number of cautious savers took out membership of two or even three societies in a desire to acquire maximum benefits.

As is apparent, friendly societies accommodated the needs of the regularly employed or self-employed. For those who were neither, there was the possibility of trade union membership, if the worker could afford the dues. For example in the clothing trade, between 1872 and 1914 there were some fifty-two trade unions.[58] Many only existed for a short while, briefly offering some security to tailors, machiners and cutters who found work in the busy periods and then had to survive the slack. However, the ephemeral nature of these trade societies and the workers' poor job security, often an unknown from one week to the next, made them a poor man's choice and thus offered little competition to the friendly society. The threat, and beginning of the end for the friendly societies, came with the basket of welfare legislation introduced by the Liberal government between 1906 and 1912. Old age pensions and National Insurance weakened the movement, though the latter was not open to aliens until after the First World War. Self-help took on a new dimension, no longer just a political and social philosophy of choice but a mandatory payment to secure benefits meant to ensure that none went hungry, cold or homeless.

From the earliest time of the readmission, the Jewish community of London sought to create a network of charitable organisations that would keep the poor off the streets and away from the parish Poor Law Boards. The focal point of need was Spitalfields, the traditional home of the poor, marginalised and alien. The self-help principle was the dominant ideology. Rules and regulations were put in place in order to encourage the practice of self-maintenance; to prevent fraudulent appeals; and, in true nineteenth-century style, to discourage strangers and the undeserving poor. At the same time, the communal charitable institutions and societies provided benefactors and organisers with an opportunity to acquire status, upward social mobility and, for some, employment. But there was also compassion for those in need of material and mental support and a manifest personal involvement and commitment from the Cousinhood, the elite of British Jewry. As we will see below, when the earliest of the single, hard-working, male Bangladeshis arrived as sojourners, there was no influential and affluent established community, no charitable networks. All that there was to help them was the anonymous, bureaucratic and soulless welfare state.

'God has promised those that have faith and do good works forgiveness and a rich reward'[59]

Zahat is one of the five pillars of Islam. Its manifestation, both in Bangladesh and in the Bangladeshi diaspora, differs somewhat to the way in which charity and welfare were organised by the Huguenots and Jews in Spitalfields. For Muslims, charity is usually perceived and practiced as alms-giving, either directly to beggars and as such 'an exchange with God',[60] or indirectly through the village or local mosque. The rich providing for the poorer members of their extended family is not seen as a charitable act but rather as a duty. As explained in a memorandum to the Home Affairs Sub-Committee on Race Relations and Immigration in 1986, 'Bangladeshis have tended to look for help to members of their extended family rather than to rely on welfare or other services provided by statutory agencies, or to seek help from statutory sources for funding for community projects.'[61] The informant might well have added that neither did they look to the wealthy and influential unless they were kin. Thus, when the first single, male Bengali sojourners arrived in Britain in the late 1950s and early 1960s, there was neither the existence nor the expectation of a charitable network operated by a wealthy, more established elite, to house, feed and employ them. Those early arrivals expected to fend for themselves and support each other, those in employment subsidising those who were not.[62] As described by Yosuf Choudhury, people from the same villages would live together, pool their earnings, deduct for subsistence and send the residue back to Bangladesh to 'invest in land, property etc.'.[63] In those early years the sending back of remittances was a priority for those who, at that time, did not realise that the pressures imposed by this practice would eventually change their lives forever and their status from sojourner to immigrant. Without the tradition and paradigms, or the presence of an established, affluent elite, the network of charities that existed for the migrants in Spital-fields in the eighteenth, nineteenth and early twentieth centuries, did not, and could not, become a feature of the Bangladeshi process of settlement. As the daughter of one of those early arrivals explained,

> My dad said there were no formal charities (apart from the Bangladeshi/Pakistani Welfare Association ... which was not really a community charity). ... People helped and supported each other, money was lent and borrowed informally based on trust and personal relation-ships ... no interest applied.[64]

Even in the 1980s when a Bangladeshi elite began to emerge, composed of high-status groups attached to the High Commission or state banks (and as such not settlers) and some 150 entrepreneurs who had made money from restaurants and the clothing trade settled in and around London,[65] no attempts were made to set up financial support mechanisms for needy coun-trymen and -women in the overcrowded and deprived areas of Spitalfields and East London. The reality was that the poor and disadvantaged back home in Bangladesh needed help more.

One of the common complaints of the anti-immigrant brigade is that the incomers target Britain because it is perceived as an 'easy touch'. An exami-nation of the concerns raised about the problems facing the evolving Bangladeshi community of the 1960s, 1970s and 1980s, reveals that, by contrast, in that early period, there was a very low up-take of state welfare benefit by Bangladeshis, married or single. There were several reasons for this. First, the new arrivals had not been raised in the tradition of social benefit. As S. Rajul told the House of Commons Committee on Race Rela-tions in 1986, 'We [Bangladeshis] do not have a welfare state.'[66] It was to the family rather than to state institutions that the needy looked. In the *desh*, and by some migrants in the *bidesh*, family is perceived as, 'a big umbrella where you can meet all together and hold you close'.[67] However, this was not the main explanation for the paucity of Bengali applicants for state benefit; the major causes were ignorance (of how to apply and what was available) and illiteracy. The 1986 Sub-Committee Report highlighted the fact that the Bangladeshi unemployed in Tower Hamlets had 'great diffi-culty because ... quite a substantial number among them cannot read or write English. Neither Stepney nor Poplar had interpreters to help claimants for benefits.'[68] It was clearly apparent that Bengali women, even less literate and articulate than their menfolk in the majority language,[69] did not use health facilities such as ante-natal and post-natal services as much as other groups.[70] It was argued by some giving evidence to the House of Commons Sub-Committee that social services did not understand the problems of the Bangladeshi community and did not provide Bengali-speaking social workers.[71] The accusations were not strictly fair as, in the first half of the 1980s, both central and local government had begun to recognise the need to provide 'appropriate services for the Asian population of Tower Hamlets'. In defence of the machinery of government, it was acknowledged that there was a need to 'overcome organisational inertia, racism and entrenched views from internal parties at all levels'.[72] In fact, during 1982–3, Tower Hamlets Social Services had set up a specialist team with the prerequisite that its main expertise must be the Bengali language. This combination of majority-language deficiency, the isolating nature of first-generational immigration and lack of sending-society paradigms, prevented the early settlers improving the quality of their lives in Spitalfields by accessing state benefit or by forming their own communal organisations.

Those arriving in the 1950s and 1960s found community of sorts in the East London Mosque and in the Pakistani Welfare Association (PWA). The latter, founded in 1952 in a café in Cable Street, by a 'close-knit core group of Bengali seamen',[73] did not constitute welfare as the refugee Huguenots and Eastern European Jews had experienced it on arrival, that is as a source of material aid, rather the PWA provided advice and direction. Initially, the PWA, which on independence became the Bangladeshi Welfare Association (BWA), helped East Pakistani workers with 'letter writing, form filling, accommodation etc'.[74] Assuming the mantle of a general trade union, the Association also set out to resolve certain workers' issues, particularly those resulting from the discrimination they suffered at the hands of West Pakistani employers or the High Commission. In the 1960s, as the numbers of East Pakistani immigrants swelled and family reunification was in its earliest stages, the PWA was instrumental in putting in place certain basic community facilities, including the organisation of hospital visits for members of the community and the foundation of the Muslim Burial Society. Wearing its workers' protection hat, the Association also organised the setting up of the Pakistan Caterers' Association in 1964.[75] The following year the PWA took premises at 29 Fournier Street,[76] on the corner of Brick Lane and Fournier Street, to use as a base and communal centre.

During the 1970s, the profile of the Spitalfields' Bangladeshi community changed, as reunification took over from primary migration and families began to outnumber single sojourners. It became essentially a young community and one increasingly riven by internal differences resulting from disputes between first- and second-generation migrants and by the politics of the villages, which were transported across the continents and played out in Spitalfields.[77] All too frequently, and to no one's advantage, community groups either collapsed or weakened themselves by internecine fighting for precious local and national government funds. During this period the BWA, itself undergoing problems due to generational divisions, remained largely inactive. This is not to suggest that there were no communal activists seeking to secure improved conditions for the Bangladeshis in and around Spitalfields. A number of organisations were established but, as indicated above, and very much in the way of the ephemeral Jewish trade unions of almost a 100 years before, they were terminally fractured by political infighting.

The generation that founded the *action* groups of the 1970s was far more proactive and aggressive than its predecessors. Its designations were combative rather than complacent – for example the Spitalfields *Action* Group (1974), the Bengali Housing *Action* Group or BHAG (1976), the Asian Unemployment *Outreach* Project (1979). The major issue of the time was housing. Bangladeshi families were living in some of the worst available housing, both private and council, unable to afford to become home-owners or to rent decent accommodation and discriminated against by those who allocated social housing.[78] In 1975, desperation resulted in twenty-two adults and fifty children, all Bangladeshi, squatting in an empty house in Old Montague Street. The squat, which ended with the squatters being rehoused and the building being demolished, encouraged others to follow the example. BHAG[79] was created to co-ordinate squatting activities. It was a far cry from the passive attempts of the Poor Jews Temporary Shelter, the Jewish Board of Guardians or the French church to improve the domestic situation of newly arrived incomers. BHAG achieved its aim and succeeded in forcing local government to re-evaluate the housing needs of the Bangladeshi community. In spite of this, the council's rehousing schemes continued to treat the Bengalis less than fairly. Equity would take almost two decades to arrive. However, a bridge had been built between Bengali need and state welfare.

By 1985 there was a multiplicity of ethnic action groups in Spitalfields, of which thirty-four were led by Bangladeshis.[80] There were youth groups such as the Federation of Bangladeshi Youth Organisations (1981), initially intended as a vehicle to counteract racism,[81] and the more culturally focused Bengali Youth Movement (1974), whose objective was to organise cultural, social and recreational activities 'of a non political nature'.[82] By 1996, the Movement was playing an active and productive role within the community, running mother-tongue classes and summer projects, providing advice for the unemployed and jobseekers as well as creating links with other (white) community organisations in the borough. Writing at the time, Mohammad Asghar stated that the Movement, one of the leading organisations in the fight against racism in the latter years of the 1970s, was, 'probably the only major Bangladeshi community organisation in the East End that has not so far [in 1996] experienced any leadership crisis or rivalry'.[83]

If housing was the primary issue for the emergent Bangladeshi community, education was not far behind. Once the family reunifications were underway, it became clear that there were a number of problems to be resolved if the children of the immigrants were to integrate into mainstream education. Coming from homes where English was rarely, if at all, spoken, there was an urgent need to bring children 'up to speed' in the English language. In addition, there was a determination to preserve an Islamic/ Bangladeshi identity. Community schools took on the role, not only of providing back-up for the local state schools, but also of teachers and protectors of mother tongue, culture and the Islamic religion. In 1977, the first community school in Tower Hamlets was opened by Nural Huque, a graduate from Dhaka. He and his wife, both teachers, persevered in poor accommodation and, in spite of having no supporting funding, soon had a student body of sixty-three. Huque's example of supplementary education embracing both English educational requirements and Bangladeshi cultural priorities inspired others and, by 1996, there were twenty-six community schools in Tower Hamlets. Not all attempts to ameliorate the educational needs of the community were successful. In 1983 the Bangladeshi Educational Needs in Tower Hamlets (BENTH) organisation was formed, with its main *raison d'être* to enlighten the community as to their education rights. Within two years internal infighting had led to BENTH's collapse.

As will be described below,[84] largely as a result of the local community's activism, Tower Hamlets council incorporated the benefits of bilingualism and biculturalism into its education policy. It established a programme of development of mother tongue alongside the teaching of English. The objective was to 'offer pupils the opportunity to read and enjoy literature in their mother tongue'.[85] At the time of writing, local policy for children between the ages of five and eleven[86] is to instruct Sylheti speakers in Bengali. Teaching is provided by teachers with an 'A' level qualification in Bengali, obtained either in Bangladesh or Britain, plus some experience of teaching.[87] The tuition is carried out in supplementary classes, organised jointly by local community organisations and the LEA, which run for approximately two hours at the end of the school day. A recently published directory listed forty-six separate projects running Bengali mother-tongue classes as well as one offering both Urdu and Bengali, one offering Bengali/Arabic and three others offering Chinese, Cantonese and Vietnamese.[88] This illustrates not only the determination of the Bangladeshi community to ensure their youth are taught the language of their 'home' country but also the diverse nature of the local immigrant population.

As shown by both Eade and Asghar,[89] the history of Bangladeshi community organisations is more one of failure as a result of the transference of village politics to the streets of Tower Hamlets than of the creation of a unifying communal spirit. In 1982 the *Kobi Nazrul* Centre was opened as a family centre for the local Bangladeshi community. In 1984 it was closed down due to internal squabbling and, though reopened in 1987, it was barely functional, having lost virtually all of its 1,000 book library and much of its equipment following the earlier closure. After the reopening, further material was found to have been 'misplaced' and within a short while the organisation disintegrated. Asghar suggests that one reason for this failure was that this form of communal organisation was 'not in the cultural experience' of the Bangladeshi community,[90] and indeed one questions the viability of a library for a substantially illiterate community. Yet another communal organisation, the *Nari Samity* (Women's Association) had a short shelf-life. Founded in 1978 to provide a social centre for reunited wives who found living amongst the squats and racism of late 1970s' Tower Hamlets very hard, the association garnered little support from the men of the community, who proved unwilling to allow their wives to leave home for both traditional reasons and for reasons of safety. Perhaps an additional, covert concern was that the womenfolk might become politicised or too liberated. Thus another society was doomed to fail.

It is clear that the Bengalis, in common with the other two communities that are the subjects of this book, placed, and still place, a very high priority on what they call *zahat*. They look to the mosque to co-ordinate collection and distribution, a role still taken on by the local East End mosques or through the *thana*. Charitable organisations which provide for members of the community are rarely on the agenda, for in the villages and towns of Bangladesh the responsibility of caring for the poorer members of the family lies with the wealthier kin, a function perceived neither as charity nor welfare but as a traditional family responsibility. Bangladeshis entering Britain in the 1950s and 1960s came from a culture which did not have, and still does not have, a welfare state. Neither is there an inherited, independent self-help ethos, nor a long established and/or wealthy *bideshi* elitist infrastructure concerned to support and guide as much to preempt criticism as to manifest altruism. The evolving Bangladeshi diaspora has not found it easy to adjust to the more westernised forms of charitable activity requiring investment in the over here, particularly when poverty at home is so demanding. However, the passage of time has seen some change, perhaps as much an outcome of the acceptance that there will be no return, at least not in this lifetime.

> Recently many organisations have been set up based on Bangladeshi sub-regions or *thana*. Depending on what part of Sylhet he comes from a man can become a member. These organisations or trusts help pay for your funerals or raise money for charities in Bangladesh. Funding is based on membership fees and general contributions.[91]

It is estimated that, at the time of writing, there are some thirty *thana* in East London.[92] According to David Garbin, the *thana* in Tower Hamlets have a multiple role: in addition to co-ordinating the collection of money to be redistributed in Sylhet, they have a political function – politicians from Bangladesh promoting *desh* politics frequently visit Britain to raise funds. In this way the politics of home are transported and supported in the *bidesh*.

Finally, the *thana* operate in the social sphere, organising outings and meetings in an attempt to maintain the traditions and identity of the Sylheti village in the elsewhere. One is tempted to suggest that the streets and buildings of Spitalfields, permeated with the providential habits of previous incumbents, have passed down the concept of self-help and the friendly society to a diasporic group whose geographic and cultural roots are literally and metaphorically continents away from those who first introduced the idea. There is however a difference between the then and the now. In the case of the Huguenots and Jews, monies accrued over here were redistributed over here. In the case of the Bangladeshi societies, monies accrued over here are redistributed over there. In this way the links between Tower Hamlets and Sylhet are reinforced.

Conclusion

Be it *charité, tzedekah* or *zahat*, charity is at the core of the beliefs and practices of the three main immigrant groups who have made their diasporic homes in Spitalfields. In spite of the disparities in time and sending society, religious teaching and need have been at the heart of the practices we have seen described above. However, it is here that the similarities would appear to end and what has become clear is that the factors which determine procedure are indebted to both sending and receiving societies. In the case of the Huguenots and Jews, the presence in England (and then Britain) of a small wealthy, integrated and accepted established society, enabled later impoverished and persecuted incomers to secure some succour on arrival without having to resort to the local Poor Law Board. The religious, cultural and economic acceptability of the Huguenots encouraged monarch, government and the indigenous population to make additional provision. Yet, whilst government laid down certain, pragmatic stipulations, it was co-religionists who sought to ensure that pseudo-refugees or opportunists were not assisted. A residency requirement was laid down and the self-help ethic inculcated. This practice was emulated two centuries later by the established Jewish community, one more concerned than any not to be perceived as creating incentives for potential migrants from Eastern Europe. For late nineteenth-century Jewish incomers there was no monarch eager to ease the economic pains of arrival. All that was available from the state was a Poor House which made no concessions to religious difference or gender. Charity and welfare for incoming pauper Jews was dependent upon established co-religionists who, though altruistic, also enjoyed, indeed thrived on, the political status and control charitable involvement gave them. Politics was also a factor in Bangladeshi communal organisation, but those of Sylheti towns and villages, rather than those of Spitalfields. In this context, politics have proved divisive and destructive and, with very few exceptions, have done little to improve quality of life for those needing help in the diaspora.

In the case of each group, the concerns of the charitable organisations that did survive were concentrated on the everyday, on housing, clothing, feeding, education, and as we have seen in the previous chapter, religion. For Huguenots and Jews assimilation proved an important factor. They established schools which, in addition to their normal functions, would accelerate the integration of their youth into mainstream society. The Bangladeshi community also set up charitably funded (supplementary) schools. However, these projects were as much concerned with the retention of national identity, particularly through language,[93] as with ensuring that Bangladeshi youth was absorbing the national curriculum and culture.

There are a number of lessons to be learned from the way in which the Huguenots, Jews and Bangladeshis organised their charitable activities. First, without the presence of an earlier settled, established, and affluent cohort, it is hard to create a charitable infrastructure to accommodate the requirements of immigrants who are not catered for, either informally by the receiving society or, formally by the state. Second, there must be co-operation, co-ordination and organisation which is apolitical and not power-hungry. Without equity, rationalisation and co-ordination, the fair distribution of charity becomes almost an impossibility. Third, even in the era of the welfare state (for however long that remains a viable entity), without linguistic knowledge and interaction, immigrants entitled to state welfare all too often go without as a result of ignorance and illiteracy. Without linguistic communication, the needy go hungry and homeless. Linguistic interaction between immigrant and host is vital for those who are lost and alone in an alien environment. As the next chapter illustrates, language is not only a bridge to assimilation, it is also a bridge to survival in an alien society.

Notes

1 Currently, 'legal' economic migrants can only enter the country if they have a work permit. Asylum seekers can receive limited benefits whilst awaiting the decision as to whether they can remain but the payment provided is £20 less per week than Income Support and they are not (legally) allowed to work.

2 The welfare state formally came into being in Britain in July 1948 with the introduction of the National Health Service. It was a system which was intended to protect British citizens from the cradle to the grave. However, social legislation dates back to the Liberal government of 1906–14. Between 1906 and 1911 it introduced a basket of welfare legislation including free school meals and medical inspections, health insurance, old age pensions and trade boards.

3 Quoted in W.C. Waller, 'Early Huguenot Friendly Societies', *Huguenot Society Proceedings*, VI, 1898–1901, Aberdeen, Aberdeen University Press, 1902, p. 206.

4 R. Sundstrom, 'Aid and Assimiliation: A Study of Economic Support Given French Protestants in England 1680–1727', unpublished Ph.D. thesis, Kent State University, 1972, p. 27.

5 The Bishop of London, Henry Compton, when referring to the Huguenots, declared in 1686 that 'you have such an object of Charity before you, as it may

be, no case could more deserve your pity'. See S. Nishikawa, 'Henry Compton, Bishop of London and Foreign Protestants', in R. Vigne and C. Littleton (eds), *From Strangers to Citizens*, Brighton, Sussex Academic Press, 2001, p. 359.

6 Sundstrom, op. cit., p. 37.
7 R. Smith, 'Financial Aid to French Protestant Refugees 1681–1727: Briefs and the Royal Bounty', *Proceedings of the Huguenot Society of London*, Vol. XXII, London, Huguenot Society of Great Britain and Ireland, 1976, p. 249.
8 Between 1696 and 1727 the Civil List was weakened and the monarch in debt, thus no supplementary funds were available for the Huguenots.
9 Sundstrom, op. cit., p. 55.
10 M. Escott, 'Royal Bounty Grants to Huguenot Refugees', *Huguenot Society Publications*, Vol. XXV, 1989–93, London, Huguenot Society of Great Britain and Ireland, 1993, p. 258.
11 B. Cottret, *The Huguenots in England: Immigration and Settlement 1550–1700*, Cambridge, Cambridge University Press, 1991, p. 253.
12 Sundstrom, op. cit., p. 61.
13 Escott, op. cit., p. 263.
14 In 1704 there were 1,500 refugees in London living on 8d a day, or less than 5s per week. See Sundstrom, op. cit., p. 75.
15 Ibid.
16 Ibid.
17 Reports vary as to the exact date of its foundation.
18 T. Murdoch, *The Quiet Conquest: The Huguenots 1685–1985*, London, Museum of London, 1985, p. 78.
19 Ibid.
20 Vigne and Littleton op. cit., p. 377.
21 R. Gwynn, *Huguenot Heritage: The History and Contribution of the Huguenots in Britain*, Brighton, Sussex Academic Press, 2001 edition, p. 138.
22 C. Marmoy, 'La Maison de Charité de Spittlefields', *Huguenot Society of Great Britain and Ireland Publications 1977–82*, Vol. XXIII, London, Huguenot Society of Great Britain and Ireland, 1982, p. 138.
23 Gwynn, op. cit., p. 138.
24 D. Agnew, *Protestant Exiles from France in the Reign of Louis XIV*, London, Reeves and Turner, 1869, p. 74.
25 E.C. Ouvry, 'Huguenot Societies and Churches, Past, Present and Future', *Proceedings of the Huguenot Society of London*, Vol. XVI, 1937–41, London, Spottiswoode and Vallentine, 1941, p. 23.
26 Ibid.
27 Gwynn, op. cit., p. 215.
28 Waller, op. cit., p. 203.
29 This a tradition which is followed by the trade societies and unions of the nineteenth and early twentieth centuries.
30 Rule book in the archives of the Huguenot Society, London, NW1.
31 Waller, op. cit., pp. 206–7.
32 Charity and compassion.
33 E. Black, *The Social Politics of Anglo-Jewry 1880–1920*, Oxford, Blackwell, 1988, p. 71.
34 For this point see Black, op. cit., p. 75 and V. Lipman, *A Century of Social Service 1859–1959: The History of the Jewish Board of Guardians*, London, Routledge and Kegan Paul, 1959, p. 10.
35 The Charity Organisation Society (COS) was founded in 1869. Its philosophy was to ensure that charity was distributed to the 'deserving' as opposed to 'undeserving' poor by means of thorough investigation of the applicant's case.

The COS was also concerned that the poor be 'educated' as to the proper use of the funds they received and be visited by those who could direct them.

36 Until well into the nineteenth century, 'strange' was the noun used to differentiate those who were from another part of the mainland to those who had arrived from beyond Britain's shores.

37 See Lipman, op. cit., p. 7 and T. Endelman, *The Jews of Britain 1650 to 2000*, Berkeley, Los Angeles and London, University of California Press, 2002, p. 46.

38 Endelman, op. cit., p. 84.

39 Almost 200 years on the lacuna has not been bridged. In spite of the creation of Jewish Care in 1990, which brought together a number of London-based communal charitable bodies, at the time of writing there is still separation. The Sephardi community maintains its own welfare board and there are a number of both Ashkenazi and Sephardi organisations, including those that care for the Jewish young and disabled, and one of the largest (Jewish) homes for the elderly in Europe, which remain autonomous.

40 A. Hyamson, *The Sephardim of England*, London, Methuen, 1951, p. 39.

41 The organisation maintained its autonomy for over 200 years and then, by the end of the 1980s, was absorbed into the Jewish Welfare Board, which itself was a reorganised Jewish Board of Guardians.

42 Archives of the Jewish Museum, London, No. 145–1988.

43 The Bread Meat and Coal Society retained its autonomy until its merger with the Jewish Welfare Board in the 1960s.

44 Black, op. cit., pp. 180–1.

45 Although relocated twice since the beginning of the twentieth century, the school is still providing an excellent education for boys and girls. For the history of the Jews' Free School, see G. Black, *J.F.S: A History of the Jews' Free School since 1732*, London, Tymsder Publishing, 1998.

46 Lipman, op. cit., p. 16.

47 See A. Kershen, *Uniting the Tailors*, Ilford, Frank Cass, 1995, p. 106.

48 *Jewish Chronicle*, 19 March 1872.

49 E. Black, op. cit., p. 251.

50 Ibid., p. 93.

51 See E. Bristow, *Prostitution and Prejudice: The Jewish Fight against White Slavery 1870–1939*, Oxford, Oxford University Press, 1982.

52 The Association was originally founded as the Jewish Ladies' Society for Preventive and Rescue Work in 1885.

53 Bristow, op. cit., p. 241.

54 E. Black, op. cit., p. 191.

55 R. Kalman, 'The Friendly Societies of London 1793–1911; with particular reference to the East End of London', unpublished MA dissertation, University of London, 1990, p. 45.

56 Ibid.

57 E. Black, op. cit., p. 199.

58 See Kershen, op. cit.

59 *The Koran*, London, Penguin Classics, 1999 edition, p. 80.

60 K. Gardner, *Global Migrants, Local Lives*, Oxford, Clarendon Press, 1995, p. 152.

61 Memoranda submitted by Home Office to Home Affairs Sub-Committee on Race Relations and Immigration, Bangladeshis in Britain, Vol. II, London, HMSO, 1986, p. 206.

62 Information provided by Mafijr Rafique in conversation with author 10 July 2002.

63 Y. Choudhury, *The Roots and Tales of the Bangladeshi Settlers*, Birmingham, Sylhet History Group, 1993, p. 121.

64 Interview with Nazneen Uddin about her father's early experiences in East London, 21 March 2001.
65 See S. Carey and A. Shukur, ' Profile of the Bangladeshi Community in East London', *New Community*, 12 (3), 1985–6, p. 407.
66 Home Affairs Sub-Committee, op. cit., p. 60.
67 www.movinghere.org.uk/stories/story57/htm (accessed 15 February 2004).
68 Home Affairs Sub-Committee, op. cit.
69 See Chapter 6 below.
70 S.E. Curtis and P.E. Ogden, 'Bangladeshis in London: A Challenge to Welfare', *Revue Européenne de Migrations Internationales*, 2 (3), Deember 1986, p. 145.
71 One example of the lack of communication between local government and the immigrant community was the case of the daughter of a Bangladeshi couple put into care by Tower Hamlets Social Services. Social Services were convinced that the bruises on her body were the result of abuse, though her parents said she had had an accident. The Bangladeshi Welfare Association appealed for access after several years on the grounds that, whilst in a foster home, she was missing the cultural and religious elements of her upbringing. The case went on for a number of years.
72 Home Affairs Sub-Committee, op. cit., Vol. II, p. 8.
73 Mohammad Ali Asghar, *Bangladeshi Community Organisations in East London*, London, Bangla Heritage Ltd, 1996, p. 123.
74 Adams, op. cit., p. 55.
75 The Association was intended to help restaurant owners and to facilitate the immigration of restaurant workers rather than to protect workers' rights.
76 Adjacent to the *Mazhike Hadath* synagogue, which at that time was still operating.
77 See John Eade, *The Politics of Community*, Aldershot, Avebury, 1989.
78 Information from Bob Brett, former Director of Housing for Tower Hamlets, 12 February 2003.
79 For a detailed account of BHAG, see Charlie Forman, *Spitalfields: A Battle for Land*, London, Hilary Shipman, 1989, pp. 81–9.
80 Eade, op. cit., p. 33.
81 See *Jubo Barta*, Fifth Issue, May–June 1986, p. 5.
82 Asghar, op. cit., p. 170.
83 Ibid., p. 182.
84 See Chapter 6 below.
85 Draft document: 'Tower Hamlets Policy for Mother Tongue Teaching', undated, unpaginated.
86 Though some classes on offer are for those up to the age of sixteen.
87 Information provided by Ayub Ali in conversation with the author, 7 September 1999.
88 *A Guide to Mother Tongue Classes and Supplementary Education*, London, Tower Hamlets Education, 1997.
89 As referenced above.
90 Asghar, op. cit., p. 162.
91 Interview with Nazneen Uddin, op. cit.
92 David Garbin in conversation with the author, 11 May 2004.
93 As we will see in the following chapter.

6 Mother tongue as a bridge to assimilation?[1]

Language is one of the main pillars of civilised society; a landmark in its evolution. It is the gateway to all levels of day-to-day interaction in the public and private spheres, to intellectual and cultural development and to furthering our understanding of the ways in which humankind functions. As much as it produces union and community, it also separates, creating invisible barriers, alienating outsiders whose otherness is manifested by language. Thus it is not only outward appearance which labels the alien in our midst, so too does speech. As Alladina and Edwards record:

> The outsider, the immigrant and the oppressed have been repeatedly marked and condemned, first for not learning English and second for not learning the right kind of English.[2]

There is no doubt that one of the first priorities of the newly arrived immigrant is the creation of a base which is familiar and safe. Mother tongue is a vital tool. Irrespective of the temporal setting, initially each of the three groups clung to the language of their sending society. However, the Huguenots and the Jews recognised that at some point the language of home would have to become that of the receiving society. By comparison, the Bangladeshi community has shown a reluctance to sacrifice its mother tongue, rather it has sought to retain and encourage its continued usage and general acceptance.

Over the centuries immigrants to London with little or no English have been consigned to linguistic ghettoes. This chapter sets out to examine the way in which Huguenots, Jews and Bangladeshis reacted to the problems of majority-language deficiency. In the early stages of their settlement in Spitalfields, each of our protagonist groups used their mother tongue (or dialect) as a verbal building brick in the construction of a spatial preserve in alien territory. Behind visible and invisible walls they sought to exclude all that was threatening by creating verbal precincts within which they could eliminate the otherness of the receiving society. Using familiar linguistic sounds — songs and 'kitchen' talk — memories of childhood and mothering, tenderness, warmth and security could be conjured up. A fusion of the real and the imagined playing its part in the evolving myth of home. Newly arrived Huguenots, Jews and Bangladeshis in East London clung to their cultural familiars. As the refugees and immigrants from overseas regrouped in Spitalfields, they created enclaves within which the alien mother tongue dominated. For the majority of Huguenots and Jews, desire for merger was an incentive for prioritising the acquisition of English.[3] For Bangladeshis who arrived in the 1950s, 1960s and 1970s, language – most specifically Bengali – had been the catalyst for a war of independence which had been hard fought and hard won. After independence in 1971, language became synonymous with nation. First-generation Bangladeshi immigrants learnt English only if necessary for, as we will see below, within the early domestic/work enclaves Sylheti was often all that was required. Both Bengali and Sylheti were passionately retained as omnipresent manifestations of the new national identity.

In exploring the experiences of linguistic separation and assimilation several questions arise. First, how did each group perceive the role of language? Was it as a means of communication, as a source of national pride, as a weapon for alienists and racists or as a vehicle for assimilation? Second, were the problems of linguistic disability resolved by the adoption of a policy of bilingualism, that is through the retention of mother tongue parallel with the acquisition of the majority language? Or by eschewing the past and eradicating difference, through the exclusive use of majority language and the exclusion of mother tongue? The one a policy of separation yet integration, the other one of total assimilation. In seeking the answers, this chapter exposes linguistic social divisions, illustrates changing attitudes to multilingualism and locates the place of language on the political agenda of local community groups.

Before proceeding, it is important to identify certain linguistic terms and their correlation to the status of the groups under discussion. First, what do we understand by the term *mother tongue*? In most situations the expression is interchangeable with *vernacular* and describes the everyday speech of a group, community or nation. By the sixteenth century, French had become both the vernacular and the language of officialdom in most parts of France. As confirmation, in August 1539, an Edict was laid down requiring that all court proceedings, deeds and judgements were to be written *en langage maternel françois*.[4] Mother tongue had been of special importance to the Calvinists, particularly in Southern France, where they had been active in spreading the language as a means of replacing Latin, the tongue of Roman Catholicism.[5] By comparison, Yiddish has never achieved 'national' status. Even so, it was the 'language' of Jews (excluding the minority bourgeoisie) in nineteenth-century Eastern Europe. It was the written and spoken medium of their daily interaction at home and at work, though not of their prayer, which was in classical Hebrew. Yiddish was both mother tongue and vernacular. However, as will be explained below, the same cannot be said of Sylheti, the medium of conversation used by the majority of Bangladeshis living in the region of Sylhet and of 95 per cent of those living in the London Borough of Tower Hamlets. Sylheti may well be the vernacular, the spoken everyday tongue, but it is Bengali that is now considered the Sylheti people's mother tongue: the national taught, and official, language of Bangladesh. In any discussion of Bangladeshis in Spitalfields and the place of mother tongue we have to be aware of the parallel usage of the informal spoken tongue (Sylheti) and that which is the formal spoken and written language (Bengali).

In spite of the remarks made by some Gallophobics about the 'damned sound of French', and the 'croaking of frogs',[6] an ability to speak French was perceived as a manifestation of gentility. In contrast, Yiddish and Sylheti speakers have frequently been stigmatised as of low social class. At the end of the nineteenth century, Eastern European intellectuals and members of the Anglo-Jewish establishment regarded Yiddish in pejorative terms, as a *jargon*, not a language. In 1883 the *Jewish Chronicle*, the organ of British Jewry, highlighted the need for teachers in the Jews' Free School to 'understand the Jargon'.[7] British government colonial officials and, post-1947 and then post-1971, their Pakistani and Bangladeshi successors, devalued Sylheti, giving it the status of a 'dialect', a distinction which some linguists argue does not exist.[8] Whilst the intricacies of these linguistic debates must be left to the experts, it is important to note the social perceptions of those with the power and influence to determine the role of mother tongue/vernacular in the immigrant experience.

French

The French language evolved from a combination of classical and vulgar Latin, and a sprinkling of Gaulish. By the eighth century a French language had begun to emerge and by 813, in order to be understood, clerics were instructed to preach in *rustica romana lingua*. Latin was retained for the written word, but the new romance vernacular, Old French, 'was now spoken by the masses and understood'.[9] At the time of the Norman Conquest a French language had been fully formed. The arrival of William I brought French to England, where it rapidly became the language of the court while Latin remained the language of officialdom. A socio-linguistic divide was put in place and 'French came to be associated with social aspiration',[10] whilst English was the vernacular of the yeomanry. In his patriotic and anti-gaulist novel *Ivanhoe*, written in 1815, after the successful conclusion to the war with France, Sir Walter Scott expressed his sentiments as follows: 'In short French was the language of honour, of chivalry; and even of justice, while the far more manly and expressive Anglo-Saxon [Old English] was abandoned to the use of rustics and hinds [farm-servants], who knew no other.'[11] There was some two-way traffic. Norman words were absorbed into English whilst Anglo-Saxon terms and words were, by necessity, used even by those whose preference was French. The church frequently acted as the conduit and bilingualism was a requirement for clerics who served a French-speaking hierarchy but cared for an English-speaking flock. French remained the language of the court until the end of the fourteenth century when Henry IV became the first monarch to use English as a first language. By the fifteenth century, 'English had replaced French and Latin in official documents and as a medium of teaching.'[12] What survived was the combined legacy of language status and a more covert linguistic xenophobia,[13] one which would re-emerge when the next French 'invasion' took place.

From the mid-fifteenth to mid-sixteenth centuries, English was used increasingly as the language of science and government, whilst French was 'zealously cultivated by a cultural minority'.[14] In 1530 an Englishman, John Palsgrave, published *Esclarcissment de la lorue françoyse,* which was written in English as an aid to teaching French to English speakers. Not surprisingly there was also a demand for French teachers: both Edward VI and Elizabeth I were taught French by John Belmain, a French Protestant. Teaching was a form of employment well suited to Huguenot refugees who, though poor, were well educated. In the 1560s there were no fewer than eight refugee teachers listed as members of the Threadneedle Street church.[15] One of the most notable amongst the early arrivals was Claude de Sainliens who anglicised his name to Claudius Holyband and, in 1580, published a French–English dictionary.

Even before the revocation of the Edict of Nantes and the large-scale influx of refugees from over the Channel, French loanwords such as faux pas, metier and denim (derived from *serge de Nîmes*) began to appear more frequently in the English language. It became increasingly fashionable for members of the English upper classes to insert French words and phrases into their everyday conversation. It was an affectation which during, and after, the Restoration, writers such as Dryden and Etheridge satirised. According to Terttu Nevalainen, French 'continued to cause concern in the eighteenth century'.[16] Dr Johnson was critical of the practice of translating French into English. This he believed could not be done without 'imparting something of its native idiom . . . if it be suffered to proceed, [it] will reduce us to babble a dialect of *France*'.[17] In spite of both indirect and direct criticisms, until the French revolution, French words such as casserole (1706), police (1730), liqueur (1742), dentist (1759), brochure (1765) and bouquet (1776) continued to find their way into everyday English usage. It was not the protests of the intellectual elite but the vibrations that followed the French revolution, the French wars and the rise of an English middle class that had little time for linguistic snobbery, that were responsible for the decline in popularity of the French language.

Communication and integration

Huguenot refugees, in common with other refugees, both before and after, experienced a conflict of emotions. Though there was a desire to retain the culture and identity of home, French Calvinists, particularly in the periods before a supportive and established ghetto existed, recognised the even more urgent need to communicate with the receiving society. Language being a main tool of communication, the learning of English was seen as a strategy of survival,[18] and therefore something to be undertaken immediately on arrival. In some instances Latin, a heritage from religion and bureaucracy, facilitated initial communication between incomers who spoke no English and natives who spoke no French.[19] Others who arrived later in the history of Huguenot settlement saw no urgency in the acquisition of the language of the receiving society, one such being the noteworthy Charles de Everemond who never spoke English and learnt to understand it 'only after a lengthy stay in Stuart England'.[20] Many of the desperate Calvinist refugees who arrived in the period just preceding, or following, the revocation perceived their stay merely as a sojourn to be endured until the return. For those who arrived in the middle of the sixteenth century that myth did indeed become a reality, but for those who arrived 100 years later, the possibility of a reversal of Louis XIV's policy of intolerance became increasingly unlikely and return a myth which gradually faded into oblivion.

Initially French was the working and domestic language of the refugees. Those at the upper social levels rapidly acknowledged the need to learn English in order to integrate commercially and socially. However, for the semi-skilled and unskilled, and for artisans whose interaction with the receiving society was limited, due to their being employed by Huguenot masters, French remained the language of work as well as of home. As a result, in the first decades of the eighteenth century, it was considered preferable for the clerk of the Weavers' Company, to speak French.[21] Records suggest that the Huguenots were the first to construct a linguistic ghetto in Spitalfields. In 1710 we find reference to their 'persisting in using their own language and tending to live together rather than disperse'.[22] It was said at the time that, 'the stubbornly insular could learn colloquial French there without setting foot outside'.[23] Yet there is also evidence of a more rapid adoption of English. By the early eighteenth century, in the register of *La Patente* Church in Spitalfields, the English word 'weaver' is seen to have replaced the French *Ouvrier en Soye*.[24] Within three generations – the passage of time considered the average for the assimilation of an 'outsider' group – English was beginning to replace French as the main language of communication for Huguenots in Spitalfields. Evidence to the Handloom Weavers Commission presented in 1840 suggests the transition may have been undertaken reluctantly by some. One witness told how, in the 1780s, 'conversation in the street [in Spitalfields] was often French'.[25] The passing of the language of *mon pays* was mourned and, in the decades to follow, there was criticism from those who felt that the French language had become neglected. Some suggested that the descendants of the original refugees were ashamed of their ancestors. Further confirmation of the linguistic transformation can be found in comments made in 1894 by W.M. Beaufort who, when looking back at the records of the French Protestant School noted that, for a number of decades, many of the children attending had 'never been taught French previously'.[26] Yet the many was not all, for until the middle of the nineteenth century the Huguenot patois could still be heard in Spitalfields.

Unlike Yiddish and Sylheti, the French tongue carried with it no social stigma,[27] rather it was the language of the elite and one perceived as manifesting education, even nobility. However, this does not mean that its speakers were eagerly embraced into the arms of the Spitalfields natives. The teachers of French gained entrée to society as employed professionals, as educators, but not automatically as equals. This upwardly mobile step required the acquisition of wealth and social status. Although the ability of an Englishman to converse in, and read, French was evidence of educational and social superiority, those who were French and spoke their mother tongue were subject to criticism and linguistic xenophobia from all levels of society. However, unlike the Irish in centuries to come, the 'Frenchies' did not adopt a strategy of silence, rather those that could took the route of education and assimilation. Gradually, in keeping with their Protestant teaching and background, and using the medium of the church, they integrated into Spitalfields society. Upon the acquisition of wealth, the leaders of the Huguenot community adopted the role of local, even national, philanthropists, becoming respected and productive members of society. Eventually when the assimilation process had been completed – fluency in English a prerequisite – they became the most English of English men and women.

Yiddish

Yiddish is the language of the deracinated, synonymous with diaspora and fusion, representing a synthesis of the distant and recent past. It is a language without a national base or an official role,[28] arguably a language of weakness.[29] It is a language which, through its dynamism, reflects the geographic dispersal of its speakers. Yiddish is more than 1,000 years old, originating between the ninth and twelfth centuries[30] along the banks of the Rhine, in the region of Loter,[31] an area which incorporated Cologne, Maine and Metz. In its earliest form it was a combination of Hebrew, Loez[32] and German, written in Hebrew characters.[33] From the thirteenth century onwards, as Western European persecutions took a hold, Jews migrated eastwards, Yiddish absorbing elements of other languages as they progressed. In what is known as the period of 'middle yiddish' (between 1500 and 1750), a flourishing literature emerged, laying the foundations of a tradition of prose and poetry which commands respect to this day.

By the nineteenth century, the majority of European Jews were to be found in Russia and Russia-Poland, within the Pale of Settlement.[34] 'Modern' or 'new' Yiddish had taken on a different, more lowly mantle. The Jewish orthodoxy considered it inferior to Hebrew, the 'high language' of religion. For the Jewish intellectual and politicised elite, Yiddish was the language of the uneducated and socially subordinate Jews of the ghetto and one they themselves would not use – it was no more than a 'jargon destined to disappear ... a dead language',[35] a language of function, one used by women and unlearned men. But that function had to be acknowledged, for it was the route to the acquisition of the majority language and, in the eyes of Jewish socialists, to fellowship with all the oppressed and exploited Eastern Europeans under tsarist rule. As would be recognised more generally by educationalists in the late twentieth century, literacy in mother tongue was considered by the radicals to be the first step towards articulation and literacy in the majority (in this instance Russian) language. As early as the 1880s, a British government schools inspector working in Spitalfields revealed that: 'It is found that the children whose language is foreign often attain finally a higher standard of English speech than the children handicapped from birth by learning a vulgar and slovenly English.'[36] However, it took almost 100 years before this educational truth was translated into pedagogic application. Currently, bilingualism is accepted as being 'beneficial in general cognitive development'[37] and, as we will see below, within the London Borough of Tower Hamlets, mother-tongue classes are now available for children for whom English is a second language. Though, in the last quarter of the nineteenth century, socialist activists in Russia were most unlikely to have been aware of the findings of British schools inspectors, they were forced to acknowledge that, in spite of their own disregard for Yiddish and their preference for Russian, 'mother tongue' was a more effective vehicle with which to launch a propaganda campaign. They had no option but to 'avail themselves of so powerful a tool as the living tongue [Yiddish] of the folk masses in order to penetrate the very depths of their life and emotions'.[38] Thus, even in the region in which, in reality, Yiddish was the majority language, moves were underway to bridge the gap, to eschew the language of the *shtetl* and substitute the language of the state in the cause of politics and ideology.

With the exception of intellectual refugees escaping the restrictive Russian regime, Eastern European immigrants arriving in London from the 1870s onwards cared little for politics and ideology, their priorities being domestic and economic security. Arriving at the Port of London they carried with them the visible and mental baggage of the diaspora. The stench of steerage travel; poverty; a preparedness to work as long and as hard as was necessary for survival; a language which both identified them as other and separated them from the native workforce and the hopes and dreams which had been a part of the Jewish diaspora since biblical times.[39] These new arrivals were mainly 'greeners' who fuelled the swelling pool of semi- and unskilled exploited labour in London's East End and provided ammunition for anti-alienists keen to control the entry into Britain of pauper aliens.

Bridge building or social control?

The very 'alien' nature of the Eastern European immigrant presence wrought similar reactions from sections of Jewish society, particularly the Anglo-Jewish establishment and Jewish refugee intellectuals, which in all other ways were polarised. The visible concentration of a large number of impoverished aliens in close proximity to the heart of the metropolis and their perceived, if not always real, demands on the labour and housing markets, unnerved a recently emancipated[40] Anglo-Jewish establishment which considered its constituents to be 'Englishmen of the Mosaic persuasion'. They were embarrassed, if not ashamed, of their newly arrived indigent and foreign-looking co-religionists who, by their concentrated visibility, were furthering the cause of anti-alienism. There were some English Jews, such as Morris Joseph, senior minister of the West London Synagogue of British Jews, who considered it no less than the 'Russo-Jewish immigrants' . . . duty to leave behind them the ideas and habits that were tolerated in Russia'.[41] Others, amongst them members of the Cousinhood (the leading families of Anglo-Jewry), reacted in a more positive vein by developing different methods to iron out the ghetto bends as rapidly as possible.[42] A major objective was the eradication of the language of the Pale. Evidence of the low regard in which British Jewry held Yiddish became increasingly overt. In 1880, the 'organ' of British Jewry, the *Jewish Chronicle*, reviewed Yiddish plays with an obvious disdain. The reviewer noted that they were 'performed in the *Judisch Deutsch* dialect, a language which we [British Jewry] should be the last to encourage any efforts to preserve'.[43] At this early stage there was even a reluctance to use the more commonly descriptive title Yiddish as the means of identifying the mother tongue language.

The 1891 Decennial Census figures confirmed what had become visibly obvious – there had been a significant increase in the number of Eastern Europeans resident in England and Wales, the reported total having risen from 14,549 in 1881 to 45,808 in 1891.[44] Eastern Europeans now represented one-sixth of the alien population of Britain. With the British economy in decline and unemployment on the rise support for anti-alienism strengthened. There was little encouragement to be found in the words of J.H. Scott who, writing about the Jews of Spitalfields, described them as, 'Very poor and unlearned, living in overcrowded conditions, general educational status amongst the adults is almost nil and the majority understand no language but some dialect of Yiddish . . . many become atheist and freethinkers.'[45] As part of British Jewry's response to the growing tide of criticism, the Russo-Jewish Committee[46] sponsored a series of free English evening classes. The aim of the classes was to 'impart a knowledge of the English language, habits and usages, to adult Russian Jews and Jewesses'.[47] Nightly attendance was at times as high as 500, though the same persons did not attend regularly. Significantly students were 'five-eighths male and mostly under thirty'.[48] Anglo-Jewry urged immigrants of all ages to eschew Yiddish, 'that miserable jargon which is not a language at all' and learn English. Both young and old were targets for change and, if the task was too arduous or impossible for the older generation, then they were instructed to ensure that their children grew up 'to be identified as English',[49] by speech as well as behaviour. As current evidence has shown, it is much harder to re-educate adults, particularly if their entry level of literacy in the mother tongue is poor. Therefore it was towards the children of the immigrants that the most powerful thrust of Anglicisation through the teaching and learning of English was directed. The policy of schools established by the Jewish establishment[50] to educate their poorer, and often foreign, co-religionists was one which would ensure that students would graduate (aged twelve to thirteen) thinking and speaking as if English. Yiddish, the language Moses Angel, headmaster of the Jews' Free School in the East End of London, considered 'unintelligible', was discouraged from the day a child started school. In some instances children who spoke Yiddish were made to stand on a stool in the centre of the classroom as a punishment, an approach reminiscent of the 'Welsh Not'. This was the sign Welsh children were made to hang around their necks at school if they committed the misdemeanour of using the 'old [Celtic] language'.[51] For the children of the Eastern European immigrants their first day at school often coincided with the first time they heard English spoken. The vernacular of the Eastern European household at the end of the nineteenth century was Yiddish and its continued domestic use was viewed as a major obstacle to proficiency in the majority language. Samuel Montagu went so far as to ask pupils at Jews' Free School to 'refuse to learn Yiddish from their parents'.[52]

In spite of the desire to eradicate Yiddish from the immigrant world, for practical reasons, both at schools and in the home, Yiddish was to be a vehicle for Anglicisation. Teachers in Jewish primary, and English board, schools had to use Yiddish as the initial means of communicating with their pupils, some of whom may only have arrived in the country just days before starting school. For teachers at Christ Church School in Brick Lane this meant learning Yiddish. How else would they interact with their Jewish pupils who, by the late 1880s, made up almost 95 per cent of the student population of the board school? (At the end of the twentieth century, teachers at the same school had to learn Bengali and Sylheti in order to communicate with the children of the latest immigrant community.) Within a short while the children of the immigrants had learnt English, and learnt it well. It became their main language, used to converse with parents in the home, to interact with English children in the streets and, as they grew older, in the workplace and at leisure. Parents accepted that learning English was a necessary, and willing, step their children took on the road to becoming accepted as English men and English women even if they themselves continued to use the 'jargon', on occasions much to the displeasure of their offspring as the following quotation illustrates:

Imagine, even when we go with our father to buy something in a store
... he insists on speaking Yiddish. We are not ashamed of our parents
... but they ought to know where it's proper and where it's not. If they
talk Yiddish among themselves at home, or to us, it's bad enough, but
among strangers and Christians?[53]

The above quotation appeared in an American/Yiddish newspaper in the
early 1930s. However, it expresses only too well the sentiments of the children of (persistently) Yiddish-speaking parents in England, as is confirmed
by the memories of a child growing up in Manchester during the first
decade of the twentieth century: 'Yiddish was frowned upon ... it was kind
of degrading to speak Yiddish.'[54]

The other impetus for Anglicisation came from the radical Jewish intelli-
gentsia and trade unionists (Jewish and English). If the future was to be one
in which workers stood shoulder to shoulder against the forces of capitalism
and exploitation, then there would have to be brotherhood not separation. A
prerequisite for worker unity was vocal communication, if not for all, then
for the majority. However, for all but 'the gifted minority [that] went on to
the *Yeshiva*[55] for intensive Talmudic study',[56] standards of education for Jews
in the towns and villages of Eastern Europe were low. Overall levels of literacy in the Russian Empire were poor – by 1897 only 21 per cent of the
population of the Empire was literate.[57] Therefore we should not be sur-
prised at the poor educational standards of the immigrants, some of whom
could neither read nor write in Yiddish let alone Polish or Russian. Boys
received religious education (in classic Hebrew),[58] at least until the age of
thirteen, the age of *barmitzvah*,[59] and some basic secular education was provided by inadequate teachers in poor conditions. Women received little or
no secular or religious teaching. One explanation for their poor attendance at
the free English classes was that, as they were illiterate in their mother
tongue, it was very hard for them to learn to read and write in English. A
universal problem of teaching a second language to those illiterate in their
mother tongue.

With little education and few, if any, skills, the immigrant arrivals of the
last decades of the nineteenth century had little choice but to take whatever
work was on offer. In an economic environment which had seen a huge
expansion in consumer spending amongst the skilled working and lower
middle classes during the second half of the century, it was the industries
which had grown in response to the new markets which supported, and
exploited, immigrant labour. For Eastern Europeans, not renowned for their
physical strength,[60] those industries included clothing,[61] cabinet making
and other small-scale trades. The willingness of the alien to work for the
lowest of wages, in the worst conditions, for the longest hours i.e. to
conform to the definition of sweated labour,[62] led refugee socialist intellectuals and leaders of English tailoring trade unions to recognise that, if change
was to be brought about, the exploited Jewish workers would have to learn

the language of the majority society and develop basic literacy skills. If illiterate in their mother tongue then that inadequacy too would have to be addressed. It was a recognition which preceded by some fifteen years the establishment of the free English classes.

One of the earliest pioneers of trade union organisation amongst the Jewish tailors of the East End of London, was the 'founding father of Jewish socialism', Aaron Liberman. An intellectual who regarded Yiddish as an inferior medium of communication, in 1876 he founded the Hebrew Socialist Union in Spitalfields. The title of the organisation, and its stated intention to 'spread Socialism among Jews as well as non-Jews ... to unite all workers in the fight against their oppressors'[63] is indicative of the man's linguistic bias and his ideological direction. In spite of the concession made by writing the rules of both unions in Yiddish as well as Hebrew, Liberman's inability to appreciate the immediate economic and cultural needs and preferences of the workers in the East End resulted in the collapse of the main Socialist Union and its tailoring offshoot. Three years later another organisation, the Jewish Workers' Union was established in East London with an impressive pedagogic programme: to set up a library and teach its members to read and write in English and Yiddish. Within a few months, however, the combination of worker disinterest and an inability to pay the weekly fees resulted in the union's collapse.[64]

It was concern about the immigrants' presence and their impact on wage rates that finally persuaded the exclusivist English, Amalgamated Society of Tailors (AST) that it was in the best interests of its members to organise the sub-divisional East End Jewish tailors and admit them to the union via a specifically designated 'Jewish' branch. It was hoped that through organisation the deleterious effect on incomes that resulted from deskilling and undercutting might be reversed. Standing in the way of organisational fellowship was the illiteracy of the tailors in both Yiddish and English. In 1884 the AST reported that the secretary of its newly established Jewish branch was providing lessons in Yiddish speech and accounting.[65] As the trade unionist and journalist Joseph Finn recorded, somewhat despondently, in the first socialist Yiddish newspaper to be published in Britain, the *Polishe Yidel*, 'few [of the immigrant workers] can read an English newspaper, they know no English nor do they want to learn to read or write in Yiddish'.[66] Twenty-two years later, little had changed. In 1906, Moses Sclare, secretary of the Leeds Jewish Tailors', Machiners' and Pressers' Trade Union, giving evidence to the Truck Committee, revealed that, not only were the 'majority of the members unable to read ... but many of the masters were illiterate'.[67] Indeed, fluency in Yiddish was to prove of vital importance to trade union leader Jacob Fine in his dealings with employers as late as the 1930s.[68] In fact, it was the trade union of which Jacob Fine was secretary, the United Ladies' Tailors' Trade Union, based in the East End of London which, until its amalgamation with the National Union of Tailors and Garment Workers in 1939, always published its annual report in

Yiddish and English. This was a clear indication that those early arrivals clung to the *mammaluschen* (mother tongue) for as long as possible.

It was obvious to those who supported its usage, as well as to those who did not, that Yiddish was the vital medium through which to build bridges between alien and English workers and the means to facilitate and accelerate the assimilation of the aliens in their new homeland. The Yiddish press, anarchist and moderate, operated on a variety of agendas and both encouraged and cajoled. The *Polishe Yidel*, published for a short period during 1884 and its successor, the *Arbeiter Fraint* (Workers' Friend), an anarchist newspaper which appeared intermittently between 1885 and 1910, kept their readers informed as to current political events in Britain. They propagated an extremist bias and regularly called upon their readers to, 'unite internationally and with the Christian workers fight the general enemy'.[69] Other journals avoided radical politics: the *Yidisher Telefon* provided local and national news and gossip, the *Yidisher Velt* offered literary excellence whilst seeking to Anglicise its readership through its Yiddish pages; and the long-lived *Yidisher Zhurnal* played its role in building the bridges that brought the immigrant closer to the English way of life. So too did Yiddish theatre. The first performance in London took place in 1886. Yiddish theatre reached its peak in the first decades of the twentieth century and then faded along with the Yiddish-speaking generation. Yiddish theatre embraced a spectrum which covered traditional Eastern European drama through to the equivalent of rowdy and low-humoured East End music hall. Somewhere in between were Yiddish translations of classics by Shakespeare and Ibsen, specially written plays portraying the immigrant experience in England, even opera. Performances of these were not always as sophisticated as might have been hoped – a 1912 production of Rigoletto, though considered by the *Jewish Chronicle* to have been 'A notable operatic triumph', suffered by nature of a translation into Yiddish that was 'less than eloquent' and 'an orchestra that was a tad too small'.[70]

Gradually the Eastern European immigrants of the 1870s, 1880s and 1890s became Anglicised. Their Yiddish conversations, journals, theatre, trade union reports and posters, began to incorporate the language of the receiving society. Announcements of trade union activities, strikes and meetings, whilst still appearing in Hebrew, now carried transliterations of words such as 'strike' and 'secretary' as well as of the names of institutions, organisations and streets which played important roles in the life of the immigrant community. The Anglicisation of words such as 'trade union', spelt out in Hebrew characters rather than the Yiddish/German equivalent *vereingt*, signalled a determination to use mother-tongue characters to help create the bridge between the two cultures and the means of narrowing the linguistic lacuna between groups with common interests. English usage at times becomes confused, as in the example given by Sholem Aleichem whose mother went to the 'chicken to salt the kitchen'.[71] One hundred years on Bangladeshis are following a similar pattern, as will be illustrated below.

Though at times their use of English might be somewhat muddled, they too, like their Eastern European predecessors, have recognised that language is a vital link between communities, particularly those which are ethnically separate yet geographically close. How rapidly that link is forged and how securely those bridges are built depends on both native and newcomer.

Sylheti

Sylheti is a 'language' of place, its eponymity ensuring it is associated as much with the land as with the people of that land.[72] Unlike Yiddish, which immediately calls to mind diaspora and deracination, Sylheti is governed by tangible boundaries and a positive spatial history.[73] Sylheti is the dialect, Sylhet is the homeland.

For almost 200 years, from 1765 until 1947, Sylhet was part of India, thus part of the British Empire. Linguistic and physical links were set in place over the centuries. As Rosina Visram and Caroline Adams have both described,[74] in spite of Sylhet's distance from the coast, the tradition of Sylheti men finding employment as lascars on board British ships sailing from Calcutta predates colonisation. Subsequent interaction between British government officials, local landowners and peasants resulted in the gradual, almost imperceptible, absorption of English words into the Sylheti vocabulary. 'Chair' and 'table' became as much a part of the everyday lives of those who remained in the villages of Sylhet as of those in England. After partition in 1947, when the region became part of East Pakistan, language played an increasingly important role in the destiny of the people. It was an issue which was to spread, as the Sylhetis themselves spread, 'across seven seas and thirteen rivers' to Britain and to the area of highest concentration of Sylheti-speaking Bangladeshis in Britain, the Spitalfields district of Tower Hamlets.

Though the Sylheti presence in East London dates back to the eighteenth century, it was not until the 1950s and 1960s that it became visibly significant. In spite of the difficulties experienced by East Pakistanis in obtaining passports for the United Kingdom, during the 1950s young men began to find their way to Britain. They were making for a destination which they believed would, after a short period of very hard work in the sweatshops of London's East End, enable them to return home as 'rich men of high status'.[75] Their arrival coincided with, and enabled, a transition in the labour and production practices of the Jewish tailoring and furriery workshops of Spitalfields. Jewish sons and daughters no longer saw their future in the rag trade: the route to upward socio-economic mobility was now through the professions, those most favoured being medicine, law and accountancy. However, by the late 1950s, a new source of employers (exploiters) and unskilled and semi-skilled labour was set to take over garment manufacture, now geared more to the production of leather garments than tailored clothes. Mainly non-Sylheti-speaking entrepreneurs took over the running of the workshops whilst Sylheti labour carried out the various sub-divisional processes. The integration of Pakistani immigrants into the traditional economy of the immigrant East End provides a late twentieth-century example of the transitional interaction of two ethnic minority groups, Jews and Asians, within the mainstream economy. The manufacture of clothing was not the only trade which benefited from, and attracted, the young men of Sylhet. Indian curry houses, so much a feature of British life at the end of the twentieth century, were just beginning to become familiar faces on the high street. These too provided employment, however harsh and poorly paid, for the illiterate and non-English-speaking new arrivals.

Whilst there was a level of native – immigrant economic integration, significantly between workshop masters and their wholesale and retail customers,[76] there was little need for linguistic intercourse between the workshop hands and non-Pakistanis. Very few of the men from East Pakistan who came over in the 1960s 'bothered with English', particularly 'if they worked in the London sweatshops or restaurants'.[77] It was not a necessary prerequisite of employment, in fact quite the reverse. Within the workshop, or in the restaurant kitchens, the linguistic interaction that did take place was between Bengali-speaking employers and their Sylheti-speaking sweated labour. Then as now, deficiency in the language of the majority community facilitated the exploitation of labour.

The recession of the late 1960s and early 1970s, allied to the Immigration Act of 1971, slowed down, almost to a halt, the immigration of young men from Sylhet. In London, financial inadequacy and the regular demand for remittances to Bangladesh destroyed the myth of return. Sojourners became settlers and young men's ghettoes were gradually transformed into family-based communities. Some men decided to maintain one family in the *desh* (home) and raise another in the *bidesh* (the foreign land), bringing over new, younger and stronger wives to London. It hardly needs stating that very few of the women, and only a tiny minority of the children, who made the journey from east to west spoke, read or understood English. Levels of literacy in Bengali were little better, with no more than 35 per cent of the population in Bangladesh estimated to be literate.

The Bangladeshi community of Spitalfields gradually spread out from the spine of Brick Lane to the surrounding areas, overspilling into Mile End, Poplar and even Bow.[78] By 1981, there were some 10,000 Bangladeshis resident in Tower Hamlets; by the close of the twentieth century, that number was expected to have risen to between 50,000 and 60,000 but the Decennial Census for 2001 shows that these 'guestimates' were exceeded, the recorded figure being 65,553.[79] As the community expanded so did their problems. Shortages of housing and employment, the eternals of the diasporic condition, were aggravated by language problems. The need for the old, but more especially for the young, to communicate with the majority society at school, at work and for their medical needs, was becoming an increasing problem. For Jews 100 years before it had been a relatively simple matter, or at least was perceived as such by those co-religionists and political and labour activists eager for the aliens to become English men and women. Yiddish had to be eschewed in favour of the majority language. For Bangladeshis it was not that easy as neither mother tongue nor vernacular could be eschewed. Thus the debates had to centre around trilingualism rather than bilingualism: those outside the community had to remember that, for Bangladeshis, language was equated with politics, cultural independence, identity and nationhood.

For Bangladeshis, language was a core issue in their fight for nationhood and an independent identity. The battle began in 1952[80] when the Pakistani government announced its intention to make Urdu, not Bengali, the official language of *all* (including East) Pakistan. The bloody civil war that followed culminated in the creation, in 1971, of Bangladesh, a state whose official language was designated to be Bengali.[81] A language which had gained its formal status by the shedding of blood should have been regarded as inviolable and yet, only a few years after the civil war ended, a further tussle over language emerged. This time the demands were for Sylheti to be given the status of 'a language in its own right'.[82] Some went so far as to call for devolution and independence for the region of Sylhet. Once more, language was at the heart of debates on identity and sovereignty. The reaction of the Bangladesh government and educated elite was reminiscent of that of the Anglo-Jewish establishment the century before. Sylheti was no more than a regional dialect, one associated with poverty and illiteracy, a language common to 'low-class Mohammadans'.[83] Its speakers became the recipients of negative stereotyping. The Bangladesh government adopted a policy of language suppression.[84] Any elevation of the Sylheti language was deemed politically unacceptable. Sylheti was given the stamp of the vernacular, perceived as a means of conversation which had no accompanying literature. Ignorance about the existence of a written form of Sylheti – Sylheti/Nagari – is not uncommon amongst those living within the region as well as those beyond it. Rod Chalmers has traced the written history back to the fifteenth century, its main use being to record religious poetry. A rich language with an alphabet of thirty-four letters as opposed to the fifty of Bengali, Sylheti/Nagari is judged easy to learn. The written history came to a halt in 1971 when, following the civil war with West Pakistan, all the Sylheti/Nagari printing presses were destroyed.[85] Even those reporting to the British government's Home Affairs Committee for the *Report on Bangaldeshis in Britain*, released in 1986, were under the impression that Sylheti had always been a spoken dialect.[86] Thus when, during the 1970s, the problems of language communication in Tower Hamlets became a local issue, it was not just a question of the role of mother tongue in the migrant experience but rather a politicised debate about which of the two mother tongues should take priority.

A bridge, but to where?

Whereas the Jewish community of Tower Hamlets had been encouraged to learn English at the expense of Yiddish, the Bangladeshi community and its leaders were determined to retain their cultural, and newly acquired national, identity. One means of transmitting this to their children, some of whom were British-born, was through the Bengali language. The first mother-tongue classes for Bangladeshis in Tower Hamlets were organised by a non-Sylheti-speaking immigrant, Nurul Huque, in the mid-1970s.[87] The classes given were in Bengali not Sylheti. This decision not only acknow-ledged the superior status of Bengali, but also pragmatically recognised that there would be little mileage in promoting the teaching of a low-grade ver-nacular for which there appeared to be no available literature. Logically, Bengali was the only 'mother tongue' that could be taught. At the same time, it was obvious that Tower Hamlets education services would not be able to cope with an expanding young Bangladeshi community unfamiliar with the English language. What was denied by the Anglo-Jewish establish-ment of the 1880s was now accepted by communal activists and local government officials in the 1980s. Mother tongue was an essential element of the education process for children from minority backgrounds, both as a mean of retaining their ethnic cultural identity and as the vehicle for fluency in the language of the majority society.

During the first half of the 1980s, language came to play an increasingly important role in the communal politics of Tower Hamlets' Bangladeshi population. In 1983, the council put in place an initiative to improve local educational resources, including support for mother-tongue classes in local community schools such as Huque's. At the same time, the battle to achieve recognition for Sylheti as a 'language', which was taking place in Bangladesh, found its way onto the streets of Spitalfields. Demands were made for local Sylheti-speaking people, irrespective of their academic quali-fications or ability, to be given preference over Bengali-speaking teachers from beyond the community when mother-tongue teachers were being selected. The protagonists believed that in this way Sylheti would be upgraded. A local forum for debate was BENTH (Bangladeshis' Educational Needs in Tower Hamlets), one of a number of communal organisations[88] which sought to represent the demands of the Bangladeshis to government bodies such as ILEA. However, in common with other community groups, BENTH was far from a homogenous entity. Supported mainly by young activists, it was riddled with acrimonious internal political divisions. The battle lines became clearly drawn. On the one side was the professional Bengali-speaking elite, on the other, local Sylheti-speaking workers. As 100 years before, the intra-ethnic divide was one of socio-economic class and status. For a while it looked as though the pro-Sylhetis would be victorious. A report produced at the time by Greg Smith suggested that they had the upper hand.[89] However, true to local tradition,[90] internal divisions led to the collapse of BENTH in 1985 and with it the death of the pro-Sylheti campaign, one which never again took centre stage. Shortly afterwards it was decided that *the* mother tongue taught to local Bangladeshi children would be Bengali, in fact there was 'a strong level of demand amongst parents for tuition in mother tongue to be available in the mainstream school curriculum'.[91] For diaspora Bangladeshis in the 1970s and 1980s a national language which had cost the blood of their kinfolk, and which was the source national identity, was one which demanded acceptance beyond the narrow confines of the immigrant ghetto.

What is the current state of play? A draft report prepared by Tower Hamlets council in 1998 acknowledged that nearly 80 per cent of those living in the borough with a 'home language' other than English spoke Bengali/Sylheti (the difference even now not clearly defined). In the document the council emphasised the benefit of bilingualism and biculturalism for the local community as a whole and the importance of developing mother tongue alongside English, a policy now supported by national government. In addition, the council stated its intention to 'offer pupils the opportunity to read and enjoy literature in their mother tongue'.[92] As described in the previous chapter, current policy for children between the ages of five and eleven[93] is to instruct Sylheti speakers in Bengali.

According to Ayub Ali, Head of Mother Tongue Teaching for Tower Hamlets council, the role of Sylheti in the mother-tongue war is no longer a political issue. Bengali is now the accepted mother tongue, viewed by parents not simply as a pathway to education but, more importantly, as a mean of 'inducting a new generation to their own culture'.[94] This was confirmed by interviews carried out by the author with a number of Bangladeshi graduates and undergraduates at the end of the 1990s, all of whom said that their parents had encouraged them to learn 'proper Bengali', in order to 'understand their culture and not forget their roots'.[95] All those questioned insisted on being known as Bengali as opposed to Bangladeshi, thus highlighting language as the heart and soul of their identity. The young people believed that the need to respect their roots was directly linked to the issues of the 1960s'–1970s' civil war, one which was fought on the language issue, 'as kids [we] feel it is our duty to learn Bengali and grow up appreciating why'.[96] They also admitted that there were pragmatic reasons for learning Bengali, ones which emphasised the illiteracy of their parents, most of whom 'could neither read nor write standard Bengali'.[97] These included learning Bengali in order to communicate in writing with officials and family in the *desh*. However, it is significant that, particularly since 11 September 2001, the allegiance of young Bangladeshis to language and nation as the bedrock of identity formation has changed. The language movement and the recently introduced celebration of Bengali Language Day on 21 February each year still remain important for the first-generation immigrants, who continue to define their identity under these terms. However, for their children in the twenty-first-century Bangladeshi diaspora, it is of less significance. As illustrated in Chapter 4, for an increasing number of young Bangladeshis in Britain, identity is tied, not to nation or language, but to Islam. Those who support Bengali Language Day are harshly categorised by young radical Bengali Muslims as 'atheists who don't like Islam'.[98]

In spite of parental determination that their children become fluently bi- or trilingual, knowledge of English being deemed essential for social and economic mobility on the threshold of the twenty-first century, some forty years after the cohorts of young men arrived, Sylheti remains the domestic vernacular of the Bangladeshi community of Tower Hamlets. Many of those early male arrivals 'lacked any interest in learning English', and failed to attend what English classes were on offer. Even if there had been a willingness to learn, paucity, or total lack, of education back in Bangladesh would have made it very difficult for them to 'know how to learn'.[99] A survey in 1985 revealed that, in Spitalfields, 50 per cent of Bangladeshi men and 76 per cent of women spoke English slightly or not at all.[100] And though some men have absorbed English through interaction with the native community at work, socially and in the hospitals,[101] doctors' surgeries and local welfare offices, few of their womenfolk have followed suit. One young interviewee revealed that, though her mother had lived in England for thirty years, she spoke no English. As she explained, there had been no need, as her father and the other male members of the family had always acted as interpreters.[102] This evidence highlights another facet of Bangladeshi culture, the role of women within its society. As James Lloyd Williams, an English teacher and resident of Bangladesh for twenty-five years sees it, Bangladeshi men have shown a reluctance to permit their women the 'freedom to absorb western culture'.[103] Women play a subservient role, their needs secondary to those of their menfolk. All too frequently when wives attended English classes, their husbands had 'put a stop to it', for fear their wives might become bad.[104]

Amongst the current elders of the Bangladeshi community, within the extended nuclear family, in the sweatshops of Brick Lane and thousands of Indian curry houses, Sylheti remains dominant. In spite of this, English has found its way in, as it did under colonial rule, often through the kitchen and workshop door. As the young generation import English into the home, parents are overheard using English, sometimes unconsciously: 'I often hear my mother on the phone and though she is speaking Sylheti, she uses English words such as "shops", "road" or "friend", without realising it.'[105] In a multi-cultural society, even without imposed pressures from an elite, language transference and leakage takes place, both by the code-switching of occasional words and by the prolonged use of the majority language for purposes of communication outside the home environment. This reality leads one to question whether the English language will absorb Sylheti words as it has done Yiddish. For example, in a report which appeared in *The Times* in 1999, the word chutzpah (cheek) was used to describe someone's audacious behaviour without any accompanying translation or italicisation.[106] In the multilingual environment in which today's schoolchildren are growing up, the 'playing' with, and adoption of, words from minority languages is an established fact.[107] Perhaps in years to come Sylheti and Bengali words, as well as Yiddish ones, will have an accepted place within the English language.

The three subject groups of this book recognised in Spitalfields a place of economic opportunity and religious freedom. In their own time each believed that their prospects for advancement lay on the gold-paved streets of East London. All were outsiders whose otherness was identifiable as much by speech as by appearance.[108] As such, one questions what forces determined the way in which their deficiency in the majority language was to be overcome and what part mother tongue played in the process? Was it that of a clearly defined bridge to assimilation, acculturation and Anglicisation or was it as the guardian of a specific ethno-cultural identity? Its role was determined by the importance placed upon the acquisition of the majority language, an attribute not all deemed necessary in the *bidesh*.

Though attitudes towards the place and function of mother tongue have been very different, it should not automatically be assumed that there are no common denominators linking the subjects of this study. Not only were Eastern European Jews and Bangladeshis alienated from the host community by language difference but, in both cases, their ability to acquire the basics of that majority language was hindered by its being written in Roman characters, unlike those of their own which were in Hebrew and Indic. Religious differences too separated and reinforced the use of the minority tongue, both written and spoken. Working conditions provide further examples of shared experience: Huguenots, Jews and Bangladeshis found employment in the silk and clothing workshops of the East End. Whilst we do not have the same primary evidence of sweating amongst the Huguenots as for the two other groups, we do know that the weavers, many unskilled and semi-skilled, retained their native language for a number of decades. In all cases, labour exploitation was carried out by fellow countrymen, though the reactions of one group to the sweating system was very different to that of the others. Finally, it is usually assumed that, within the immigrant communities, the lowest levels of mother-tongue literacy and majority-language literacy and articulacy were to be found amongst members of the older female population who were commonly perceived as having a purely domestic role. This was not true of the Huguenot women. Research has shown that many who came on their own, or only with their children, were forced to learn English in order to survive. Unlike the other two groups, these women were educated and, with the benefit of literacy in their native tongue, found it easier to speak, read and write the language of their place of sanctuary.[109] Recent research has proved that in the case of the Jewish community this was sometimes the case too. Jewish women carried out a diversity of economic activities, some of which necessitated their interaction with the majority community and required, at the very least, a basic knowledge of English.[110] This suggests that, in some ways, the bridge between mother tongue and English may have been an easier one for women to cross in the sixteenth, seventeenth and late nineteenth centuries than it has been for their ethnic-minority sisters of the twentieth century. Finally, if we are to reach any conclusions as to the linguistic policies that have operated in Spitalfields, it is necessary to consider the socio-economic and political imperatives that determined actions and reactions in the past centuries.

Mother tongue and education

It has been established that those who have not enjoyed the benefits of education as children do not 'know how to learn' as adults. Thus any use of mother tongue as a means of achieving bilingualism has to be dependent on some basic learning when young, the primary place of education in the Protestant faith proving of immense value when the practice of that faith was denied. For the male Eastern European Jewish immigrants the foundations were laid in childhood; religious requirements ensured basic literacy in classic Hebrew.[111] That learning could subsequently be put to work when it came to reading Yiddish. The bridge to English was thus negotiable, though exhaustion from the long working day in the sweatshop sometimes made the journey less attractive. For the untutored Jewish female, whose worth was judged by her ability to act as helpmate for her spouse, education was of only minor worth: 'A Jewish woman who is Talmud trained is not a good commodity.'[112] Literacy was the exception rather than the rule, many being denied the opportunity to read – 'For the most part women are barely literate in Yiddish.'[113] Though in the case of the female immigrant bilingual conversation improved with length of settlement.[114] For Muslim Sylhetis religion neither played, nor plays, a necessary part in developing literary abilities. The Quran is written in Arabic, although Bengali versions for the educated minority are available. However, the teaching of the Book is by rote[115] and thus literacy is not a prerequisite. Neither has there been an established Bangladeshi elite insistent upon the eschewing of mother tongue and its replacement by English. Minority-group, political, pedagogic pressures now operate in the reverse direction, concerned with the promotion of the official language of Bangladesh and the reinforcement of a Bengali ethnic identity rather than its denial.

Mother tongue and labour

What part has the workforce played in strengthening or weakening the linguistic bridge? The creation of a French silk-weaving ghetto in the first half of the eighteenth century meant that for those who did not want to, there was no need to learn the native language. Socio-economic mobility was not always a perceived option for the poorest and most exploited who ended up as Parish scavengers, clinging to their patois for comfort and a link to the past, whilst the silk merchants and masters accelerated their integration into 'English' society. The international spread of socialism and the belief in the benefits of worker unity to resolve the problems of exploitation and capitalism acted as the incentive for Jewish refugee intellectuals and Jewish socialists both to tolerate Yiddish and to encourage those for whom it was mother tongue to learn English. At the same time, English trade unionists and political radicals recognised that the bond formed by a common language could only have a positive effect in the struggle to end the evils of sweating. The emergence of new unionism at the end of the 1880s was evidence that those previously considered unorganisable, unskilled, seasonal and casual workers, including Jewish tailors, cabinet makers and shoe makers, could play a constructive role in redressing the status quo. It is difficult to gauge the exact level of success in terms of increased labour literacy in relation to their union organisation but where interaction took place, at trade union assemblies, strike meetings and political rallies,[116] union advancement occurred and language absorption and increased fellow feeling followed.

By comparison to the indictments placed at the thresholds of the Eastern European workforce, Bangladeshis suffer little. They are rarely criticised for taking the jobs of English people. Racist accusations are directed at domestic targets, at Bangladeshi families being awarded larger and more up-to-date council housing. As one critic accusingly said during the 1993 local council by-election, 'Why should they [the Bangladeshis] get all the best flats with all the new showers?'[117] Many Indian subcontinent employers ensure that their labour force has little contact beyond the local working community. On the side of labour, there is little evidence of older workers aspiring to learn English or of any incentives to self-organise. A survey carried out in 1985 revealed that Bangladeshi workers in the clothing trade believed fluency in English was not essential, even a knowledge of Bengali was deemed no more than 'helpful'.[118] Even for those who were keen to learn the pressure of work often provided a disincentive, as one Bengali man explained:

> When I came here, I learnt to speak English through trial and error. After my arrival, I started to attend English as a Second Language classes, but I had to stop shortly after. I could not work and study at the same time. Instead I learnt by listening to other people and trying to reply when spoken to.[119]

The 1985 report also exposed the total disinterest shown by the exploited Sylheti workers in trade union membership.[120] More than a decade later, in a climate of falling membership and disillusionment with trade unionism, the clothing section of the GMB had made virtually no inroads into the Sylheti-speaking sweatshops of Spitalfields.[121] Neither had the Bangladeshi clothing workers established ethnic trade unions as had their Eastern European counterparts 100 years before. The difficulties of trade union organisation amongst a semi- and unskilled casual labour force are reinforced by illiteracy. 'There is no point in distributing trade union literature to workers who cannot read in their own, or any other, language ... we do not have any Sylheti speaking officials to make verbal contact.'[122] This statement was made in 1995 but nine years on, little has changed. At the time of writing (autumn 2004), there are still no Bengali- or Sylheti-speaking GMB officers in the East London area and there are no plans to appoint any. Trade union recruitment amongst Bangladeshis is low, if not non-existent.[123] Yet, without organised representation, the low levels of wages and poor conditions of employment are sustained, with little protest forthcoming from the workers, many of whom are illegal immigrants or dependent upon welfare benefit to supplement a less than minimum wage. There is no portal through which external forces can gain entry and promote the cause of majority-language literacy and articulacy as a means of alleviating labour exploitation.

Mother tongue and the media

The main avenues of mass communication for the immigrant population of Spitalfields at the end of the nineteenth century were the Yiddish press and the Yiddish theatre. Those male members of the community who could read Hebrew fluently, could read Yiddish, and thus be kept informed of events taking place on the broader local and national political canvas. Though few of their readers were directly affected by it, contributors to the shortlived *Polishe Yidel* made sure that they were kept informed of the passage of the 1884 Reform Bill.[124] Twenty-eight years later, the *Arbeiter Fraint* encouraged Jewish tailors to retain their membership of English trade unions as well as providing regular, if somewhat tendentious, reports of the wave of strikes that crossed Britain and of syndicalist activities in America and France. In the theatre, positive steps were taken to enable Yiddish speakers to come to terms with the life and culture of western society through dramatic representation.

At the portal of the twenty-first century, the ethnic media has a far wider span. In East London alone there are eight or nine Bengali and Bengali/English newspapers, a range of available Bengali and Bollywood videos and films, as well as Bangladeshi radio programmes and Bangla TV channels. This volume is not all it might seem. None of the above are in the Sylheti language, thus only a minority of the elders are able to take full advantage of what is on offer. The 'Bollywood' films are most often in Hindi, a language with which the younger members of the community are now becoming conversant. Thus in many ways, for those with little or no Bengali, the ethnic media offers less today for the non-English-, non-Bengali-speaking immigrants of Spitalfields than it did yesterday. Even so, multi-culturalism and multilingualism dominate. More than seventy-five languages are currently spoken in Tower Hamlets, of which English and Bengali/Sylheti are the major tongues. Bangladeshis are able, and encouraged, to remain close to the music, art and food which forms part of their perceived identity. There are even attempts to restore regional identity by bringing back Sylheti/Nagari. James Lloyd Williams is working at reproducing poetry and prose in order that the 'present generation of Sylhetis will want to rediscover their own heritage, culture, history and written language'. He has produced a small volume of poetry in Sylheti/Nagari, Bengali and English, the latter so that those in the *bidesh* might 'have at least a small taste of the rich heritage of Sylhet'.[125] This is not as simple as it might appear, for those unable to read, be it Bengali, Sylheti/Nagari or English, are dependent on the literate minority for a taste of that heritage.

Mother tongue and politics

As Chapter 8 will illustrate, throughout the period under examination in this book, refugees, immigrants and sojourners in Spitalfields were subjected to xenophobia, anti-alienism and racism. The earlier Huguenot arrivals responded by recommending caution and the avoidance of scandal,[126] a dual process of keeping a low profile and assimilating, with part of this strategy being the adoption of the English language. The pace at which this occurred varied from individual to individual and family to family, some, 'like Paul Girardot . . . were determined to master English quickly', others took their time.[127] However, lack of majority-language proficiency did not automatically exclude political activism as two non-English-speaking Huguenots were elected as Spitalfields parish officers. Was their election, as that of some Bangladeshis, some 300 years later, due to regional or trade loyalties back 'home' allied to the desire to have their outsider views represented in the local forum? Or was it merely an acknowledgement by the receiving society that persistent use of the French tongue mattered not?

For Eastern European Jews entering Britain at the end of the nineteenth century, a time of increasing anti-alienism and jingoism, the acquisition of English was deemed politically, as well as socially, vital by the Anglo-Jewish establishment. They interpreted the continued usage of Yiddish as an amplifier which broadcast their alien presence to the streets of East London. Even Samuel Montagu, the Jewish Member of Parliament for Whitechapel and a frequent champion of the immigrant cause, was determined that the language of the aliens be erased as rapidly as possible. Trade unionists, socialists and anarchists were all convinced that a common language (English) was an important weapon in the fight to eliminate worker exploitation and the power of capital over labour. Those were the exogenous forces. However the immigrants' ambition to establish home in a society which offered the possibility of future economic security, for their children if not themselves, should not be ignored. For those with the tenacity and will to survive the hardships, Spitalfields offered an opportunity to establish roots in a nation which, in the late nineteenth century, appeared one of liberal tolerance.[128]

For Bangladeshis the situation was, and remains, different again. The arrivals of the 1950s and 1960s came as sojourners, yet even in the ghetto of temporary residence external forces were at play. The politics of the village were often played out in Brick Lane and Hanbury Street, and contemporary economic and social conditions transformed sojourners into settlers for whom English and Bengali were both foreign tongues. There was no long-established community either to provide a nexus of charitable support or to insist that the recent arrivals become 'English men' and 'English women'. The Bangladeshi community was left to come to terms with the complexities of understanding self-identity through a miasma of language difference and alienation operating in a supposedly multi-cultural society. In the 1982 election campaign linguistic deficiency was proved a useful political tool, enabling public speakers to promote different issues and apply disparate emphases for different audiences, an election address in Bengali being very different to that given in English. Indeed, most Bangladeshi voters of the first generation spoke only Sylheti, being able neither to read nor write in standard Bengali.[129]

In addition to accommodating the impact of spatial transition was the need to absorb the politics of Spitalfields. These issues became complex for, added to the problems of communication, the subtext of Sylheti village politics undermined local Tower Hamlets issues. This situation, which has been dealt with admirably elsewhere by John Eade,[130] was of particular relevance within the context of the battle for language status. Even though the young activists failed to hold the day, they displayed an uncommon vitality. Generally, members of the Bangladeshi community manifested political apathy, but how much of this was the outcome of an inability to comprehend local and national political literature as opposed to general disinterest is hard to assess. The local Labour party attempted to overcome the problem by orally translating party business and minutes into Sylheti prior to the commencement of meetings. Unlike the Jewish experience, total reliance had to be placed upon oral communication. Local ethnic associations and organisations were faced, and in a number of cases still face, the same problem. Here, Sylheti leapfrogs Bengali, as English is the medium used for recording organisational business.[131]

Spitalfields now has a vital and politically active Bangladeshi community with significant representation on the local council and a Bengali mayor. However, it is a point of interest that in the general election of 1997, though a number of Bangladeshi candidates were fielded by, amongst others, the Conservative and Liberal Democrat parties, the elected (Labour party) member was Oona King, who though of ethnic-minority background,[132] had no Bangladeshi connection but was deemed the most acceptable candidate. This proved that electoral voting patterns are determined more by political expediency than by ethnic empathy.[133]

Mother tongue and identity

For Huguenots, Eastern European Jews and Bangladeshis, the issue of the acquisition of majority language is one closely allied to perceptions of identity. French Calvinists clinging to the hope of return sought to preserve their familiarity with, and use of, the French language as a reassurance of who they really were and where their loyalties lay. At the turn of the seventeenth century, a French religious minister was reported as being unwilling to learn English as he reserved himself 'for the first opportunity of returning into his own country . . . as soon as ever he sees an abatement of this present persecution'.[134] Others were more realistic, prepared to undergo a nationality transplant and to eschew mother tongue. They adopted the use of English and with it an allegiance to all things English/British, thus incorporating monarchy and territory. Self-identity was one thing, external perception another. The French, in common with the Irish, were linguistically identifiable as strangers when they spoke. Thus for those Huguenots who wished to 'become English' and be accepted as such, proficiency in the English language was a priority.

For the British Jewish establishment the language of the alien acted as a beacon of difference, for the Bangladeshis it radiates nationhood. For Jews in the diaspora there have always been conflicts of identity, most particularly between religion and citizenship. For the majority of Jews in Britain at the end of the nineteenth century there was no discord, both immigrant-born and English-born observed Judaism whilst being, or striving to become, English. For a minority, the arrival of political Zionism[135] in 1897 posed a challenge which some have still not resolved. In this friction language plays no part – the official language of the state of Israel is *Ivrit*, or modern Hebrew. With the creation of the state in 1948 came the naming of the language, one which set out to 'separate from the Diaspora the language of the Diaspora'.[136] Yiddish acted as a bridge to *Ivrit* in the newly created political homeland of the Jews, by so doing playing the same role as it had for others in the diaspora for hundreds of years.

For Bangladeshis language was, and is, synonymous with identity. The noun 'Bengali'[137] is used today by the young to describe both their mother tongue and what they are, irrespective of where they are. However, as referred to above, an increasing number of young Bengalis are identifying themselves as Bengali Muslim, or Muslim Bengali, thus ensuring that their religious identity is clearly signalled.

Conclusion

For hundreds of years, for diaspora travellers arriving in Spitalfields, mother tongue has been, and still is, a gateway to the future. Educated Huguenots, literate and familiar with learning, were well advanced on the road to assimilation. They eventually became the most English of English men and women. The centuries-old association of French and English acted as an aid for those who wished to accelerate their transformation. Of the three groups highlighted in this book, for the Huguenots, the assimilation process was the least onerous. Religious practice and language facilitated their integration. Many slid easily from the pews of the French church, where English gradually superseded French, into those of Christ Church in Spitalfields.

For the Eastern European Jews language was most definitely a bridge to Anglicisation, acculturation and assimilation, a stepping stone to citizenship and a secular, national pride they had never previously possessed and one which they eagerly grasped.[138] For literate Bangladeshis the bridge has a duality of purpose. It provides a gateway to the acquisition of the English language, something many of the older members of the community illiterate in, their now acknowledged, 'mother tongue' have been unable, and/or unwilling, to access. For the educated younger generation it provides both the mechanism for socio-economic upward mobility and a medium for the reinforcement of national identity through learning and culture. Does this mean that the illiterate are totally excluded? Many of the male elders have had to find their way, building fragile linguistic bridges from Sylheti, using spoken rather than written words to form a basis of communication with the majority society. Their female counterparts, often far more restricted than their Jewish sisters of 100 years ago, may not make the crossing. For although there is some evidence of women carrying out economic activity in the home,[139] there is none illustrating interaction with the majority society and thus little need to use any language but Sylheti. As one young Bengali girl explained: 'My mother used to speak English but she doesn't bother with it any more.'[140] Mother tongue has been, and remains, a necessary bridge in the immigrant journey. As this chapter has demonstrated, it is up to the migrant to determine where it should lead.

The foregoing chapter has looked at the experience of the three groups occupying the same space at different periods on the time-scale, and their attitudes to, and use of, mother tongue. The French patois that was the everyday language of the Spitalfields ghetto is heard no more. But as a language of place and of nation, French has been around since the ninth century, over the centuries providing the world with some of the finest literature and drama it has known. Yiddish was eschewed and had all but died out by the late 1950s. Recently it has enjoyed a renaissance, brought back to life by intellectuals and academics who value its poetry, prose and drama. Courses held in the language are attended by as many non-Jews as Jews. Sylheti is the dominant vernacular of the people of that region both at home and in the diaspora. The children of that diaspora are convinced that the language will survive. Can a language which is degraded in its country of origin as well as by many in the diaspora, is not taught at home or abroad and which has a barely accessible literary past, have a future? As standards of education in Bangladesh, Sylhet included, gradually improve and the children of the villages become literate and articulate in Bengali whilst their counterparts in Britain are brought up on English and Bengali, will Sylheti die? Or will it survive as a spoken dialect, as has Swiss-German in relation to High German, being a language of ease and casualness? It has been said that 'The death of a language equals the death of a culture',[141] thus if Sylheti dies then so does its culture, its history, myths and the Sylheti identity. James Lloyd Williams is attempting to keep the Sylheti culture and identity alive. It remains to be seen whether the young Bengalis will follow suit and incorporate it into their bridge to the future.

Language is not only a vital tool in the assimilation process, it is also a major factor in the creation and duration of nations. Benedict Anderson states that 'Nations are made possible in and through print languages ... therefore anyone can learn a language, become naturalized and become a citizen.'[142] It could also be said that when the language dies, the nation dies. One of the most important aspects of the current (*c.* 2004) debate on Englishness and citizenship is the primacy of host-society language. To quote Sir Bernard Crick, 'Use of the English language itself is possibly the most important means by which diverse communities participate in a common culture – that is why it is so important that new citizens should have a sufficient knowledge of English, Welsh or Scottish Gaelic.'[143] David Blunkett, Home Secretary of the time, is convinced that the acquisition of British citizenship can only be awarded to those who can communicate in the language of the majority society.[144] How would our French Calvinist parish officers and Eastern European illiterate yet economically productive immigrants have reacted to the way in which British citizenship is currently being constructed? How do the Bengali wives who have lived in this country more than twenty years yet, as a result of culture and their husband's innate fears, remain unable to speak more than a few English words, feel about being denied the opportunity to become citizens of the country in which they live and in which they will no doubt die? Mother tongue is undoubtedly a bridge to assimilation but should lack of English fluency be a dam of exclusion?

Notes

1 A version of this chapter first appeared in A.J. Kershen (ed.), *Language, Labour and Migration*, Aldershot, Ashgate, 2000.
2 S. Alladina and V. Edwards, *Multilingualism in the British Isles*, Vol. 1, London, Longman, 1991, p. viii.
3 R. Gwynn, *Huguenot Heritage: The History and Contribution of the Huguenots in Britain*, Brighton, Sussex Academic Press, 2001 edition, p. 113.
4 P. Rickard, *A History of the French Language*, London, Unwin Hyman, second edition, 1989, p. 83.
5 Gwynn, op. cit., p. 211.
6 D. Statt, *Foreigners and Englishmen: The Controversy over Immigration and Population 1600–1760*, London and Toronto, Associated University Press, 1995, p. 48.
7 *Jewish Chronicle*, 4 May 1883.

8 See G. Smith, *Language, Ethnicity, Employment, Education and Research: The Struggle of Sylheti-speaking People in London*, CLE/LMP Working paper No. 13, Community Languages and Education Project, London, University of London Institute of Education, 1985, p. 14.

9 See Rickard, op. cit., pp. 1–19.

10 David Graddol, Dick Leith and Joan Swann, *English: History, Diversity and Change*, London, Routledge, 1996, p. 122.

11 Quotation appears in ibid., p. 120.

12 Ibid., pp. 126–7.

13 See Chapter 8 below.

14 Rickard, op. cit., p. 83.

15 Gwynn, op. cit., p. 103.

16 T. Nevalainen, 'Early Modern English Lexis and Semantics', in *The Cambridge History of the English Language*, Vol. III, 1476–1776, Cambridge, Cambridge University Press, 2001 edition, pp. 360–1.

17 Quoted in ibid.

18 See C. Lougee Chappell, '"The Pains I Took to Save My/His Family", Escape Accounts by a Huguenot Mother and Daughter after the Revocation of the Edict of Nantes', *French Historical Studies*, 22 (1) (Winter 1999), p. 57.

19 Ibid., p. 59.

20 Gwynn, op. cit., p. 211.

21 Ibid., p. 157.

22 Ibid., p. 161, taken from 'a Letter to the French Refugees Concerning Their Behaviour to the Government'.

23 Statt, op. cit., p. 31.

24 Gwynn, op. cit., p. 212.

25 *Report of the Select Commission on the State of the Handloom Weavers II*, 1840, London, Vol. XXIII, pp. 283–4.

26 W.M. Beaufort, *Records of the French Protestant School*, Lymington, (publisher unknown), 1894, p. 2.

27 Though there was, as in every language, high French, for formal use and low French, the everyday vernacular. In addition there were dialects but none carried the stigma associated with Yiddish and Sylheti.

28 Although never a 'national' language, in 1906 the South African Parliament voted Yiddish a European language, but it was not until 1910 that the *Bund* (the Jewish socialist party) held an all-Yiddish-speaking conference. E.S. Goldsmith, *Architects of Yiddish at the Beginning of the Twentieth Century*, Cranbury, Associated University Press, 1976, pp. 96 and 83.

29 See J. Fishman, *Yiddish: Turning to Life*, Philadelphia, John Benjamins Publishing Co., 1991, p. 83.

30 'There was no one-time act of birth'. M. Weinreich, *History of the Yiddish Language*, Chicago and London, University of Chicago Press, 1973, p. 6.

31 The region of Loter is an internal Jewish designation, but can be equated with the region of Lorraine. Weinreich, op. cit., p. 332.

32 The Jewish correlates of Old French and Old Italian. Weinreich, op. cit., p. 100.

33 Ibid.

34 The Pale of Settlement was an area of some 362,000 square miles within which all but the bourgeois minority of the Jewish population of Russia and Russia-Poland were required to live.

35 Goldsmith, op. cit., p. 72.

36 Quoted in G. Black, *J.F.S.: A History of the Jews' Free School since 1732*, London, Tymsder Publishing, 1992, p. 127.

37 G. Smith, op. cit., p. 75.
38 Goldsmith, op. cit., p. 74.
39 For a late twentieth-century approach to the diasporic experience, see R. Cohen, *Global Diasporas*, London, University College Press, 1997.
40 Whilst the entry of a Rothschild into the House of Commons in 1858 marks a major step in the emancipation of the Jews in Britain, their *total* emancipation cannot be said to have taken place until 1871 with the passage of the Promissory Oaths Act.
41 A.J. Kershen and J. Romain, *Tradition and Change: A History of Reform Judaism in Britain 1840–1995*, Ilford, Vallentine Mitchell, 1995, p. 98.
42 Whilst organisations such as the Jewish Board of Guardians and the Russo-Jewish Committee attempted to help the indigent arrivals, they also developed programmes of repatriation. At the same time clubs and organisations such as the Jewish Lads' Brigade were set up by the Anglo-Jewish establishment to facilitate the Anglicisation process.
43 *Jewish Chronicle*, 12 March 1880.
44 Decennial Census 1891, PP 1893–4, CVI.
45 J.H. Scott, *Spitalfields*, London, (no publisher), 1894, p. 9.
46 The Russo-Jewish Committee was established in 1881 in response to the pogroms that followed the assassination of Tsar Alexander II in that same year.
47 Quoted in L. Gartner, *The Jewish Immigrant in England 1870–1914*, London, George Allen & Unwin, 1960, p. 239.
48 Ibid., p. 240.
49 *Jewish Chronicle*, 7 July 1905.
50 The Jews' Free School was founded in the East End in 1732 and between 1880 and 1900 educated one-third of London's Jewish children. In 1900 it had 4,000 pupils. See Black, op. cit. Other Jewish schools included the Westminster Jews' Free School, the Stepney Jewish Schools, the Metropolitan Jewish School and the Jewish Girls' High School.
51 See D.W. Parsons, 'Being Born Lost? The Cultural and Institutional Dimensions of Welsh Identity' in A. Kershen (ed.), *A Question of Identity*, Aldershot, Ashgate, 1998, pp. 25–59.
52 Black, op. cit., p. 126.
53 Quotation appears in N. Green (ed.), *Jewish Workers in the Modern Diaspora*, Berkeley, Los Angeles and London, University of California Press, 1998, p. 194.
54 R. Livshin, 'The Acculturation of the Children of Immigrant Jews in Manchester: 1890–1930' in D. Cesarani (ed.), *The Making of Anglo-Jewry*, Oxford, Blackwell, 1990, p. 82.
55 Rabbinical training colleges of higher education which were also hotbeds of radicalism.
56 A. Kershen, *Uniting the Tailors*, Ilford, Frank Cass, 1995, p. 6.
57 J. Klier, *Imperial Russia's Jewish Question: 1855–81*, Cambridge, Cambridge University Press, 1995, p. xiii.
58 However, whilst the boys would be taught to read the Hebrew alphabet and language, few had any idea of the literal meaning of what they read.
59 Thirteen is the age at which a Jewish male is considered a man.
60 Whereas the Irish immigrants, more used to employment as labourers, found work in the docks and building industries.
61 In London's East End and in cities such as Leeds and Manchester, the clothing industry included tailoring, cap making, slipper and shoe making – the wholesale manufacture of dresses was a sector of industry developed after the First World War.

62 For detailed description of the system of sub-divisional labour as experienced by Eastern European immigrants in London's East End in the years between 1870 and 1939, see Kershen, *Uniting*, op. cit., Chapter 4.

63 Ibid., p. 128.

64 Ibid., p. 11.

65 *Polishe Yidel*, 17 October 1884.

66 Ibid., 1 August 1884.

67 Quoted in Kershen, *Uniting*, op. cit., p. 11.

68 Ibid., p. 145.

69 *Arbeiter Fraint*, 18 March 1905.

70 *Jewish Chronicle,*, 12 April 1912.

71 Green, op. cit., p. 193.

72 It is perhaps necessary to indicate at this point that I have chosen to use the noun 'language' in this instance because of the importance of 'language' in the context of the fight for Bangladeshi independence and the subsequent issues surrounding the role and place of Sylheti within the newly created state. I will revert back to using the nouns 'dialect' and 'vernacular' below in order to retain thematic continuity.

73 For histories see R. Visram, *Ayars, Lascars and Princes*, London, Pluto Press, 1986 and C. Adams, *Across Seven Seas and Thirteen Rivers*, London, Thap Books, 1987.

74 See Visram, op. cit., and Adams, op. cit.

75 See A.J. Kershen, 'Huguenots, Jews and Bangladeshis in Spitalfields and the Spirit of Capitalism', in A.J. Kershen (ed.), *London the Promised Land? The Migrant Experience in a Capital City*, Aldershot, Ashgate, 1997, pp. 66–90.

76 When the author visited a leather garment workshop in the early 1980s, the workshop master ensured that she did not have any verbal contact with the workshop hands.

77 Author's interview with James Lloyd Williams, twenty-five years a resident of Bangladesh and now running a Sylheti translation service in Bethnal Green, 15 July 1999.

78 For the problems of housing within the Bangladeshi community of East London, see Charlie Foreman, *Spitalfields: A Battle for Land*, London, Hilary Shipman, 1989.

79 Statistic supplied by the Census Customer Services department of the ONS: Table Population: All People, Geographical Level England and Wales to Ward; Table S101 Sex and Age of all ethnic minorities in Tower Hamlets. Supplied 20 November 2003.

80 In November 1999 a group of Canadian Bangladeshi students appealed to UNESCO to make 21 February – the day Bangladeshis the world over remember those who died as 'Language Martyrs' – World Wide Language Day. UNESCO has subsequently agreed.

81 Although spoken by one-sixth of the world's population, Bengali is the official language of only one country, Bangladesh.

82 See Smith, op. cit., p. 37.

83 Ibid., p. 20.

84 Ibid., p. 69.

85 For history and explanation of Sylheti/Nagari, see R. Chalmers, 'Paths and Pitfalls in the Exploration of British Bengali Identity', in A. Kershen, *A Question*, op. cit., pp. 120–35 and R. Chalmers, *Learning Sylheti*, London, Centre for Bangladeshi Studies, 1996, pp. 4–11.

86 Chalmers, 'Paths', op. cit., p. 133.

87 Information from the author's meeting with Ayub Ali, Head of Mother

Tongue and Study Support, London Borough of Tower Hamlets, 7 September 1999.

88 For a detailed account of the internal politics of the Bangladeshi community of Tower Hamlets, see J. Eade, *The Politics of Community*, Aldershot, Averbury, 1989.

89 Smith, op. cit., pp. 39–40.

90 A number of the early East End Jewish trade unions and societies collapsed due to internal differences – see W.J. Fishman, *East End Jewish Radicals 1875–1914*, London, Duckworth, 1975 and Kershen, *Uniting*, op. cit.

91 Smith, op. cit., p. 75. This ambition was achieved with the introduction of the new school curriculum in the 1990s when Bengali was listed as a national language which could be taught in secondary schools.

92 Draft Document: Tower Hamlets Policy for Mother Tongue Teaching, undated, unpaginated.

93 Though some classes are on offer to those up to the age of sixteen.

94 Meeting with Ayub Ali, 7 September 1999.

95 Author's meeting with ten Bangladeshi graduates and two undergraduates, 3 June 1999.

96 Ibid.

97 J. Eade, 'The Bangladeshi Community in East London', in C. Clarke, C. Peach and S. Vertovec, *South Asians Overseas*, Cambridge, Cambridge University Press, 1990, p. 328.

98 Sarah Glynn, 'Bengali Muslims: The New East End Radicals?', *Ethnic and Racial Studies*, 23 (6), November 2002, p. 983.

99 James Lloyd Williams, meeting, 15 July 1999.

100 N. Kabeer, *The Power to Choose*, London and New York, Verso, 2000, p. 424.

101 See Chapter 5.

102 Author's meeting, 3 June 1999.

103 James Lloyd Williams, 15 July 1999.

104 See Kabeer, op. cit., p. 245.

105 Author's meeting with young Bangladeshis, 3 June 1999.

106 *The Times*, 5 November 1999.

107 I am grateful to my colleague Professor Jenny Cheshire for pointing this out to me.

108 The French were criticised for their dress and appearance whilst the Eastern Europeans arriving in England were instantly recognisable by their dirty appearance and foreign clothes. Jews generally were caricatured as having hooked noses and dark swarthy looks. See below and C. Holmes, *Anti-Semitism in British Society 1876–1939*, London, Edward Arnold, 1979, pp. 114–15.

109 See Chappell, op. cit.

110 See R. Burman, 'Jewish Women in Manchester, c.1890–1920', in D. Cesarani, op. cit., pp. 55–75.

111 In order to be recognised as having reached maturity, Jewish boys aged thirteen have to undergo *barmitzvah*. This requires reading passages of the *Torah* and *Talmud* in Hebrew from the scroll and prayer book.

112 M. Zborowski and E. Herzog, *Life Is with People: The Culture of the Shtetl*, New York, Schocken, 1970, p. 83.

113 Ibid.

114 The author's grandmother could not read or write, having come to England as a young bride. After many years in London, however, she was able to converse freely and thus enjoy the benefits of radio and television.

115 In common with so much of secular teaching in Bangladesh.

116 See Kershen, *Uniting*, op. cit., for details of these forms of interaction.

117 Derek Beackon, the only BNP candidate ever to be elected to the local council was elected by as a Poplar councillor in the 1993 by-election by disenchanted members of the native community who believed that Bangladeshis were being given the local government accommodation that was by rights theirs. See Chapter 8 below for further detail.

118 Smith, op. cit., p. 36.

119 Kabeer, op. cit., p. 234.

120 Author's conversation with member of clothing division of the GMB, 20 February, 1995.

121 See Kershen, *Uniting*, op. cit., p. 190.

122 Member of the GMB clothing division to the author, 20 February 1995.

123 Author's conversation with London officer of the GMB, 18 October 2004.

124 *Polishe Yidel*, July and August 1884.

125 James Lloyd Williams and Matiar Rahman Chowdhury, *Ten Sylheti Poems*, London, Sylheti Translation and Research, 1998, (unpaginated).

126 B. Cottret, *The Huguenots in England: Immigration and Settlement 1550–1700*, Cambridge, Cambridge University Press, 1991, p. 242.

127 R.Gwynn, *Huguenot Heritage*, Brighton, Sussex Academic Press, 2001 edition, p. 212.

128 Official tolerance endured as long as the alien presented no threat to the indigenous population. Once a threat was perceived; a less tolerant attitude was manifest in the form of the 1905 Aliens Act, passed as a direct response to concerns over the growing alien presence (more detail in Chapter 8 below). Until that point, Britain had operated no peacetime immigration controls. Nor had there been any formal restrictions on where Jews, as Jews, could live, worship or carry out their business. Those restrictions that did operate were imposed on foreigners or non-Christians. That is not to suggest that there were no informal examples of anti-Jewishness or anti-Semitism. The Aliens Act, passed by a Conservative government in 1905 and implemented from January 1906 under the incoming Liberal government, was criticised by some for its ineffectiveness. Whilst it did impose controls on entry, it did not inhibit freedom of speech, economic activity or place of settlement. However, informal forces ensured that immigrants did not find employment in certain sectors, one example being the Civil Service, or settle (comfortably) in certain areas. The Aliens Acts of 1919/20, passed in an atmosphere of post-First World War xenophobia and tensions following the successful 1917 Bolshevik revolution, introduced tighter restraints on 'alien' activity. Once again the alien (Eastern European Jew) was the target, an additional fear being that these aliens might now be Bolshevik agents. Under the new legislation, steerage-passenger immigrants could only gain entry if they had a work permit whilst resident alien immigrants could be deported if found guilty of creating, or being involved in, industrial, military or civilian unrest. The tightening up of controls on outsiders filtered through to the LCC which, for a large part of the 1920s, refused aliens council accommodation, employment and scholarships for them or their children. It is noticeable that, whilst landlords and employers might post notices reading 'no Jews need apply', it was actually the alien who was unacceptable.

129 J. Eade in C. Clarke, C. Peach and S. Vertovec, op. cit., p. 328.

130 See Eade, *The Politics*, op. cit.

131 Meeting with James Lloyd Williams, 15 July 1999.

132 Oona King comes of mixed – African-American and Jewish – parentage.

133 See S. Saggar, *The 1997 General Election: Ethnic Minorities and Electoral Politics*, London, CRE, 1998.

134 Gwynn, op. cit., p. 212.
135 Geoffrey Alderman suggests that the majority of working-class Jews, 'if not anti-Zionist . . . were non-Zionist'. See G. Alderman, *London Jewry and London Politics*, London, Routledge, 1989, p. 74.
136 Weinreich, op. cit., pp. 311–12.
137 This in itself is confusing as there are many people from the Indian subcontinent, particularly from the region of West Bengal, who consider themselves Bengali yet have no association with Bangladesh.
138 Even though some of those early arrivals spoke little or no English they took a pride in being English – in the early 1900s naturalisation could be purchased for the princely sum of £7. Some Jewish residents of Leeds prided themselves on being Yorkshire men first and foremost!
139 Information from third-year Bangladeshi students, 16 October 1999.
140 Meeting with young Banlgadeshis, 3 June 1999.
141 Prof. David Crystal, quoted in *Calabash*, London, Black Literature Development Project, (12), autumn 1999, p. 3.
142 Quoted in Paul Gilroy, *There Ain't No Black in the Union Jack: The Cultural Politics of Race and Nation*, London, Hutchinson, 1987, p. 45.
143 English and Citizenship to Help Integration and Make People Proud to Be British, Inside the Home Office, Ref: 234/2003 3 Sep 2003, http://www.homeoffice.gov.uk/n_story.asp?item_id-587 (accessed 3 September 2003).
144 Unlike government policy at the end of the nineteenth century, Welsh and Scottish Gaelic are permitted, and seemingly given, the same status as English as opposed to being denied legality.

7 Huguenots, Jews and Bangladeshis and the spirit of capitalism[1]

The causal factors behind the movements of people have been referred to in the first two chapters. There is no one theory which satisfactorily explains why an individual or a group moves from one place to another and then follows a variety of patterns: settlement, re-migration or, after an intervening period, movement onwards. For some the initial migration might be a life-or-death decision, for others a test of religious beliefs. For many it has been, and continues to be, a process of carefully weighing up the economic pluses and minuses of what, so often, proves to be a voluntary, yet emotionally, psychologically and physically testing experience. Whatever the motivation, upon arrival in the receiving society the migrant is faced with the necessity of securing a means of survival. All too frequently, and sometimes unfairly, immigrant groups are judged by their perceived ability to succeed commercially in their new environment. The graph of success is often based on past example, as evidenced by Ceri Peach's categorisation of post-Second World War ethnic groups according to the 'Jewish' or 'Irish' model.[2] Success in Britain has been, and continues to be, measured through the eye of western capitalism; the visible creation of profitable and expanding businesses accompanied by social status and a high standard of living.

In order to test the validity of this approach, this chapter sets out to explore the economic experiences of our chosen three immigrant groups in Spitalfields. It seeks to determine how they rationalised their economic activities and whether each – or indeed any – of the three can be categorised under the definitions of Weber's spirit of capitalism. In addition, it considers whether such categorisation can provide an accurate assessment of a specific group's *real* success or failure. Weber's thesis that Protestantism was the pollinator of modern capitalism is open to debate and controversy.[3] Without doubt religion alone cannot be accepted as the spur to the accumulation and investment, commercially or philanthropically, of capital. Temporal factors must be included in the equation. Even if the religious theory were to be adopted, the myopic Weberian adhesion to Protestantism, and more specifically to Calvinism, is hardly acceptable in an era in which western religion in Britain no longer reigns supreme.

Each of the three groups under the microscope is acknowledged as having a collective, if not individual, loyalty to their religion and its teachings: Protestant Calvinism, Old Testament Judaism and Islam. Within the limitations of this chapter, I seek to consider how powerful a stimulus religion has been in the accumulation of wealth and the investment of capital. The Judaeo-Christian tradition is one that encourages and honours commercial success, providing this is of benefit to the wider society. In his writing, Weber suggests that this is not true of the teachings of Islam, which he considered to be the 'polar opposite of Puritanism'.[4] Within Islam, Weber deems, 'rational capitalism is impossible', it being an occidental phenomenon.[5] However, Gardner's research in Bangladesh has shown that this has not been the case and that there are definite grounds for comparison with the other two groups. A number of returned Bangladeshi migrants who accumulated capital in London and invested it in business and splendid houses in Bangladesh, look upon their material success as an opportunity provided by Allah not only to raise their status but also to 'redistribute alms'. For them poverty was the outcome of 'laziness and stupidity'.[6] With these sentiments, which echo mid-Victorian and 1980s, western economic philosophy as well as the voice of Islam, the returned migrants demonstrate a reconciliation of east and west.

In order to answer the questions posed above, the framework of examination has to be sufficiently broad to incorporate both poles of the migrant experience: home (as in over there) and receiving society (as in over here). The forces which led to emigration, the so-called 'push' factors, and the migrants' perception of those forces, cannot be overlooked. External perceptions have tended to view the 350 years of immigration into Spitalfields as lineal. This suggests that the Bangladeshis manifested the same allegiance to the Protestant work ethic as the Huguenots, and the same entrepreneurial ambitions as the Jews. One must question whether this is an accurate assumption, or were the early arrivals, as one observer has suggested, satisfied to rely on welfare benefit and occasional employment, thus bypassing opportunities for capital investment and entrepreneurial activity?[7] Or were they, as suggested in the previous chapter, reluctant to apply for welfare due to a combination of illiteracy and ignorance added to a fear of stigmatisation? Two further issues central to this discourse emerge from this. First, are the Jewish and Huguenot models based more on myth than on reality; and second, has recent analysis erased the records of hardship and failure from the database?

In examining the economic history of the three groups in Spitalfields, a number of factors must be taken into account. These are:

- The socio-economic structure of the native environment.
- The push and pull factors of migration.
- The nature of the immigrant community in terms of race, religion and culture.
- The prevailing economic and industrial structure of the host society.

- The immigrants' ambitions and desires in the context of their self-perception and experience (these may not always coincide with those identified by the onlooker).
- The power and influence of external forces of commerce and government which, in the case of Spitalfields, have always been only a stone's throw away.

It is the geographic and historical uniqueness of Spitalfields, as shown throughout this volume, which provides the starting point for this survey.

The profitable strangers

The Huguenots were the first major immigrant group to settle in Spitalfields. It was not only religious freedom which beckoned, London also offered an opportunity to develop entrepreneurial and technical activities. The majority of those early arrivals were silk-weavers from Northern France, Bas Poitou, Nîmes and Lyons, who brought to the established, but basic,[8] English silk-weaving trade new ideas and techniques for the manufacture of broad silk, figuring of flowered silk and the lustring of taffeta. They were dyers, throwsters, silkmen, brokers, satin dressers, waterers and designers.[9] In Spitalfields, if not engaged in the silk industry, Huguenots also found employment as naval personnel, doctors and religious ministers. Other examples of Huguenot expertise could be found to the west of the City of London, in and around the Soho area, where a number of goldsmiths and silversmiths, clock and instrument makers, sculptors and gun makers settled. It is a directory of talents which, on initial reading, implies that all Huguenots were middle class, skilled and, within a relatively short while of settlement, affluent.

The Huguenot myth is one of the 'profitable strangers'. Their Calvinistic beliefs and practices encouraged industriousness, thrift and the use of wealth for the general good, either through reinvestment in business or through acts of philanthropy. The Huguenots were perceived as refugees from the middle ranks who 'founded middle class families of good standing . . . [and] shone as merchants or financiers among the luminaries of the City'.[10] However, not all the Huguenot refugees were affluent or successful – as we have seen in earlier chapters, there is adequate evidence of pauperism. Whatever the myth, not all the Huguenots 'made it'. For example, the 1753–4 Spitalfields Rate Books record that the parish scavengers spoke only French.[11] Almost seventy years after the revocation, the more successful Huguenots remained concerned that itinerant incomers should not become burdensome nor present a negative image of the immigrant community. Leading charities required proof of six months' residence in England before benefits were provided. This manifestation of 'alien' unease and concern for the image being projected to the native society is a characteristic more associated with late nineteenth-century Anglo-Jewry than with seventeenth-century and early eighteenth-century French Calvinists.

The Huguenots offer an ideal Weberian paradigm, their traits being summarised as 'reverence, chastity, sobriety, frugality, industry and honesty'. Arthur Marshall considered the Protestant refugees to be the 'ablest, most inventive and most steadfast', whose 'instructions gave England the right lines along which to work'.[12] And it is largely to their credit that the English silk industry, although subject to the vagaries of trade cycles and tariff controls, enjoyed more than a century of expansion. It was Huguenot silk merchants and masters who, by taking full advantage of the availability of cheap imported raw Italian and Chinese silk, developed the London industry. In the eighteenth century, government-imposed controls on French silk imports enabled the Huguenots to use Britain's foreign and fiscal policies as tools for the creation of wealth.

In spite of illegal imports from France and the whimsicalities of fashion, those early Huguenot silk merchants and masters prospered. Evidence of this is to be found in the building of fine houses, in Church Street, Spital Square and Princes Street, at the northern end of Spitalfields, between 1718 and 1728, and in the fact that they were also able to purchase 'country houses, books, silver and good furnishings'.[13] Ownership of a 'clean and solid, comfortable middle class home' was a religiously sanctioned ideal.[14] A continuum of success can be traced through the generations. The Ogiers family came from Chassais-l'Église in Bas Poitou, the first refugees arriving in Spitalfields in 1700. Successive generations immigrated throughout the eighteenth century. Five of Peter Ogier II's[15] sons became master weavers, whilst one of his daughters, Louisa Perina, married Samuel Courtauld, whose family were refugees from La Rochelle. Originally a goldsmith, Courtauld[16] moved into the silk industry upon marriage to Louisa. Tessa Murdoch states that is 'impossible to overestimate the importance of the Ogiers in the London silk industry'.[17] They continued to be involved with all branches of the silk industry throughout the eighteenth century. Staunch in their support of the Protestant monarchy, Ogiers and their employees eagerly volunteered to fight the Young Pretender in 1745. The family retained a powerful Huguenot identity by marriage and industry,[18] maintaining residency in Spitalfields until the early nineteenth century. In contrast, other 'silk families' manifested a preference for assimilation and geographic departure from the first point of settlement. By the end of the eighteenth century, the Ouvry family had moved from silk to the professions and had become fully integrated into mainstream society. Some families used intermarriage as a vehicle for accelerating their transfer from outsider to insider. In the first half of the eighteenth century, two of James Ouvry's sons married English girls, as did Captain Peter Lekeux, founder of the Royal Lustring Company.

The Bresson family links with Spitalfields and the silk-weaving industry were amongst the longest lasting of the Huguenot community. William Bresson's great grandfather, Raymond, became a naturalised British subject in 1710. Some 130 years later, in 1840, when the silk-weaving industry was in its final death throes, William owned 200 looms, each worth £1, which he rented out on a weekly basis.[19] He owned 'a house with a garden' and was 'in receipt of work when others were not'.[20] For Bresson and others like him, the spirit of capitalism was gradually being eroded by forces beyond their control. In his evidence to the Handloom Weavers Commission of 1840,[21] Bresson described the appalling conditions endured by those silk-weavers who had fallen on hard times. They lived in overcrowded, small, unsanitary rooms, airless so that the silk would not lose weight, their wage rates not having increased since 1761. As the Huguenot myth of success was fading, so was purity of line, as intermarriage and assimilation added to the mosaic population of London.

To appreciate how, in the eighteenth and nineteenth centuries, Huguenot affluence and poverty developed side-by-side, it is necessary to briefly outline the structure of the silk-weaving industry as it operated in Spitalfields. It is a structure of exploitation of migrant by migrant which persists in Spitalfields to this day. The first link in the silk-weaving trade's chain of production was the importer or merchant. Next came the throwster who threw or twisted the raw silk for the weaver; the throwing often given out to homeworkers classified as the 'poorest of the poor' due to their pathetic rates of pay.[22] A master weaver purchased the thrown and dyed silk and gave it out to the journeyman weaver. When the weaving was completed the master weaver sold the silk to a mercer, who was allowed up to twelve months' credit. Small- and large-scale masters operated in close proximity, 'small' being between forty and 100 looms in operation, 'large' as many as 800.[23] It was the merchants and mercers who outwardly manifested the signs of success and who enjoyed the fruits of the industry when it thrived. In the slack periods, they could limit their losses by the instant cessation of yarn purchases.

Poverty and misery were all too often the companions of the journeymen and working weavers who, with the exception of the most highly skilled, struggled to survive on wages frequently below necessity level. Their plight was not helped by a metropolitan labour pool bloated by the inclusion of child and female labour. As early as 1675, ten years before the revocation of the Edict of Nantes, the 'Frenchies'' practice of undercutting wage rates resulted in xenophobic pronouncements and riots. Following the revocation, the Rector of the Whitechapel Parish Church, Dr Welton, said of the new arrivals, 'This set of rabble are the very offal of the earth, who cannot be content to be safe here from that justice and beggary from which they fled, and to be fattened on what belongs to the poor of our own land and to grow rich at our expense, but must needs rob us of our religion too.'[24] A somewhat contaminated interpretation of the work ethic.

Conditions in the silk-weaving industry began to deteriorate following the end of the Seven Years War in 1763. The period of the war had seen an expansion of trade, but the peace brought with it the renewal of imports from France and hardship. The incomes of the Spitalfields weavers, 50 per cent or more of whom were of Huguenot descent,[25] fell to as little as twelve shillings a week net.[26] Low wages, underemployment and unemployment equalled poverty and riots; and the correspondent of the *London Chronicle* recorded on 18 May 1765 that 'it ... be felt in Spitalfields very seriously'. The government's response to the riots was the passage of the Spitalfields Act of 1773.[27] The Act set out to regulate the wages of journeymen weavers specifically, and only within the boundaries of Spitalfields. Prices for weaving were to be fixed by quarter sessions, entry to the trade was to be limited to two apprentices per weaver and combination was forbidden. In spite of controlling the numbers of those entering the trade, the Act did little to help those whose incomes already depended upon it. In 1785 the desperate Spitalfields weavers revealed that their trade 'was declining ... for want of employment, poverty and distress are deluging like a torrent', whilst in the depression of 1795 the weavers and their families were said to be 'without fire, without raiment, without food'.[28] 'Poor weavers and their families crowded together in vile, filthy and unwholesome chambers, destitute of the most common comforts, and even of the common necessaries of life.'[29] Small-scale masters pawned goods and equipment in order to survive.

Though the silk trade expanded between 1800 and 1826, the condition of the Spitalfields weavers continued to decline. A number of factors accounted for this. Industrialisation through the use of water as a means of driving the power loom initiated the deskilling process and the accompanying use of cheap, female labour. Women were 'employed constantly while the men stood idle'.[30] Some masters moved production out of Spitalfields to where labour could be employed at cheaper rates. By 1808, three-quarters of the Spitalfields poor were unemployed.[31] Following the submission of evidence by the Ribbon Weavers in 1818, it was generally concluded that the Spitalfields Act had been 'detrimental' and had served only to depress trade. Though those journeymen remaining in Spitalfields fought hard against it, in 1826 the Act was repealed and French imports freely entered the country.

The death warrant of the silk-weaving industry was signed in 1860 under the Cobden Free Trade Agreement with France. However, the terminal decline had begun decades earlier. In his evidence to the Select Commission on Handloom Weavers in 1834, William Hale described how the repeal of the Spitalfields Act had resulted in 'deep distress and lamentable destitution', with the poor going about in rags. Houses, built in the belief that trade would improve, lost almost all their value as wages dropped by over 50 per cent.[32] Hale, a silk manufacturer, explained that free competition with overseas had been ruinous. One-third of the looms in Spitalfields were standing idle. The condition of the working people had been degraded, and 'the poor rate had increased and those persons who supply them with provisions had been bankrupted'. In all 'a great deal of misery and disease ... destroys the morals of the people'.[33]

By this time, the more successful of the Huguenot immigrants had long gone from East London to enjoy the fruits of their labour in more salubrious surroundings. Of the less successful migrant dynasties remaining, some silk-weavers moved northeast from Spitalfields to the adjacent, but cheaper, district of Bethnal Green, others turned to dock labour. Some even became part-time street people, such as the tailor/telescope exhibitor Tregent interviewed by Mayhew for his *London Labour and the London Poor*.[34] Others who remained in Spitalfields had merged into the mainstream, now recognisable as Huguenots only by name. They found employment in the variety of seasonal and casual trades that marked the industrial structure of the district. A minority clung to the silk trade as prices fell by more than 30 per cent. Masters who had enjoyed the separation of home and workshop were forced to move the latter into the former, thus reversing the capitalist process. The descendants of those who had brought their industry from France to England and pioneered its expansion now saw free trade with the land of their ancestors put the brakes on their economic future. For those Huguenots remaining in the silk industry, the economic activity which, in the seventeenth and eighteenth centuries, had promised so much now offered very little.

Jewish Economic Man

The Irish followed the Huguenots as the next large-scale immigrant wave into the capital. By 1851 there were an estimated 150,000 in London. However, we are not concerned with them here as very few settled within the small area of Spitalfields. In geographic terms the successors to the Huguenots were the Jews from Eastern Europe. Though pogroms and enforced military service were a part of the migratory push factor, as we have seen, it was the bleak economic horizon of the latter half of the nineteenth century which exerted the most force. For those who could make it, the only hope for material independence and economic security lay westward, for the majority in the *golde medineh*. For a minority, Britain was the promised (silver) land. The exhausted immigrants who landed in London needed to travel no more than half a mile to their first point of settlement. They headed for Spitalfields which, by the close of the 1880s, was considered by certain commentators to have assumed the mantle of a Little Jerusalem.[35] By the century's end, estimates of the number of Eastern Europeans living in Spitalfields and the surrounding area ranged from a conservative 56,000 to as many as 120,000.

On the surface the immigrants from Russia and Russia-Poland bore little resemblance to the Huguenots. Foreign in religion, culture and appearance, they arrived at the docks armed with few skills and little or no money. What they did bring with them was a willingness to work long and hard for the lowest of wages, in the worst of conditions for the longest of hours. In other words a preparedness to become sweated labour if that was the sole avenue to economic advancement. The Jew carried with him the Old Testament philosophy of earthly reward for labour and the right to make a profit, combined with the diasporic tradition of entrepreneurship. Economic activity was perceived as 'part of the totality of man's religious experience in Jewish life'.[36] Hard work was the threshold to financial security, for Jews in the diaspora it was the only form of security. What chances were there for those late nineteenth-century immigrants to translate their dreams into reality?

By the late 1870s the industrial structure of East London, with the exception of the docks, was small-scale and seasonal, concentrating on the finishing trades or the manufacture of clothing, furniture and a range of small items. Jews rarely sought, or found, employment in the docks, they became shoe and slipper makers, cabinet makers, cap makers and stick makers. However, the most popular occupation for the Jewish immigrant was tailoring, an association which can be traced back to biblical times.[37] It was a trade which fitted well into the changing pattern of consumption marking the second half of the nineteenth century. The growth of Empire, industry and bureaucracy had improved the earning capacity of the artisan and white-collar classes. The working man in regular employment was able to enjoy a new phenomenon, surplus income. As clothes were the barometer of status, one way of demonstrating economic mobility was by the purchase of new, as opposed to secondhand, garments. The result was an unprecedented expansion of the London clothing industry.

In East London the tailoring trade was run along pre-industrial, sub-divisional lines. It had grown out of the tradition of old clothes-dealing and clobbering in the area around Spitalfields. Production was carried out in unhealthy workshops, often converted from the old Huguenot houses. Workshops were small-scale, the average containing five or six hands employed by a middleman or master. The structure of the East End tailoring trade bears comparison with that of the Huguenot silk-weaving industry. At the top of the chain was the wholesale house, invariably an established English company based within the City of London's boundaries,[38] which gave work out to the middleman or master. Bundles of cloth ready for making up were then put through the sub-divisional system, a process of production broken down as far as it was economically and physically viable. Within the workshop there existed an hierarchical structure. The machiner was the aristocrat, beneath him came the tailor and the presser, the latter by his deft use of irons weighing as much as twenty-five pounds, able to turn a disaster into a success. These men in turn subcontracted to plain machiners and underpressers.[39] It was an industry that thrived on the lowest levels of wages and skills, on the hunger pangs of the workers and on their dreams of moving out of the overcrowded, unsanitary ghetto to that promised land.

It was not difficult for an immigrant worker to set up as a master. Beatrice Potter (later Webb) described the process:

The ease with which a man may become a master is proverbial in the East End. His living-room becomes his workshop, his landlord or his butcher his security; round the corner he finds a brother Israelite, whose trade is to supply pattern garments, to take a sample of his work to the wholesale house; with a small deposit he secures on the hire-system both sewing machine and presser's table. Altogether it is estimated that with £1 in his pocket any man may rise to the dignity of a 'sweater' ... if he is successful, day by day, year by year, his profit increases and his labour diminishes relatively to the wage and labour of his hands.[40]

As Potter revealed, £1 purchased the status of employer. However, with depressing regularity the employer of one season became employee the next. Seasonality, recessions, depressions and industrial strife ensured that in the 1880s and 1890s, economic security and success were like water in the desert and the immigrants from Eastern Europe the children of Moses; many glimpsed the future, few partook of the fruits.

Unrest amongst the Huguenot journeymen weavers in the eighteenth century led to the Spitalfields Act. The discontent of the Jewish tailors in the late nineteenth century fuelled many a strike and the creation of a multiplicity of shortlived, Jewish tailors' trade unions, whose membership rarely rose above 10 per cent of the workforce. While the labour pool was constantly refilling with greeners there was little chance of improved working conditions. The entrepreneurial spirit was there but, in the years leading up to the First World War, only the ruthless, or fortunate, few made it out of the ghetto.

One of those who did, who had the perspicacity and vision to turn the dream into reality was Morris Cohen, an immigrant from Russia who arrived in England in 1877, with a 'slight knowledge of ladies' tailoring'. In his evidence to the Aliens Commission in 1903, Cohen explained that, when he arrived in England, there were hardly any English ladies' tailors. Female tailored garments were imported from Germany. Three years after his arrival Cohen took his first entrepreneurial steps. Conscious of the growing demand for women's tailored outer garments and aware of the paucity of English ladies' tailors, Cohen made up some samples and showed them to a selection of tailoring masters and wholesalers who were keen to take advantage of the new market opening up. At that time 'All the ladies' tailoring ... was then done abroad, principally in Germany and France.'[41] Within ten years Cohen had opened his, and the country's, first custom-built mantle-making factory in Spital Square, Spitalfields. He employed 180 workers indoors as well as giving work out to other workshop masters. As a result of his initiative, the mantle-making industry in the East End of London provided employment for over 1,000 workers.

Morris Cohen provides an ideal example of the realisation of the spirit of capitalism, fulfilling both economic and religious requirements. He was very successful and, by the outbreak of the First World War, was able to retire to Brighton and enjoy the fruits of his labour. These included a chauffeur-driven car, an elegant home and holidays in Madeira.[42] Additionally, he benefited others far beyond the boundaries of Spitalfields. In 1898 the managing director of Hitchcock Williams, one of the largest wholesalers in London, wrote a letter to the *Jewish Chronicle* which succinctly summed up Cohen's achievements to date. The letter explained that, prior to 1889, the importation of women's mantles into Britain had cost the country an annual £150,000. Cohen's perspicacity had enabled British material and labour to be used for the home and export markets, the latter improving the country's balance of trade by no less than £150,000.[43]

Cohen's entrepreneurial activities did not end with the women's clothing industry. In the early 1900s he bought a number of properties in the East End onto which he built workshop additions. These he rented out to other ladies' tailors. From those acorns the oaks of the clothing industry grew.[44] Amongst those who began their mantle-making days in Cohen's workshops were Alexander Steinberg who founded Alexon, Shyer Green, whose sons created Windsmoor, and Solomon Goldstein, co-founder of Ellis and Goldstein, companies which became the giants of the clothing industry in the post-Second World War years. Morris Cohen died in 1927 and the company he founded survived just ten more years until the death of his eldest son. As a descendant somewhat romantically described it, 'we went from rags to rags in three generations'.[45] The spirit of capitalism burned bright with Morris Cohen and then, as with some of his Huguenot predecessors, gradually faded as other individuals and events took control.

Amongst the immigrant arrivals of the late 1870s and 1880s Cohen's accelerated success story is rare. For most of the closing decades of the nineteenth century, the country's economy was in recession. Life was harsh for the unskilled and semi-skilled who suffered irregular wages and underemployment if not unemployment. It was left to wives and mothers to 'help out'. Whilst the common view was that 'Jewish women didn't work', the reality was that they did and frequently demonstrated more entrepreneurial skills than their menfolk. As dressmakers, small shopowners (some in their kitchens or front rooms), matchmakers, midwifes, stall holders and, as we have seen, owners of fried fish shops, Jewish women ran their own businesses and demonstrated their worth as penny capitalists. Others, with less opportunity, or less inclination, worked for their husbands either in the workshops or at home. One way or another when incomes were low, wives helped out.

However by the first decade of the twentieth century, a minority of Jewish tailoring workers were earning 'a reasonable wage', whilst a fortunate few were earning 'high wages'.[46] By the close of the first decade of the twentieth century the movement away from Spitalfields had begun. The Jewish exit from the East End accelerated during the interwar years. Some left due to the tough anti-alien controls imposed by London County Council, which cut back on the provision of housing and jobs to aliens in the wake of the xenophobia and anti-Bolshevism that came with the peace. Others responded to the call of the suburbs now sprouting up to the northwest and east of London. Willesden, Golders Green, Edgware and Ilford had become the promised land.

Though evidence suggests that Jewish Economic Man was essentially an entrepreneur, and as such assumed by many to be invariably successful, this was not always the case. As Chapter 5 reveals, there were demands on communal charitable organisations throughout the nineteenth and well into the twentieth centuries. Life as a master was precarious, in reality an autonomous occupation but one very much in the control of wholesalers who continually forced prices downwards, thus creating a chain of hardship descending from the workshop boss to the lowliest employee. Recent research has questioned the pace and direction of Jewish immigrant worker advancement in London's East End. Andrew Godley, in his comparative study of Jewish immigrant entrepreneurs in London and New York between 1880 and 1914, puts forward the view that successful entrepreneurship during this period can be correlated with 'an advantaged parental background', in the sending society. He suggests that in both London and New York, 'The assimilated immigrants who had arrived without an advantaged background, and were unable to marry into one, were more likely to become journeymen. Those who were both unassimilated and disadvantaged were more likely to be blue-collar workers.'[47] Thus entrepreneurship was not just the outcome of hard work, but a combination of industriousness and advantaged familial background – nature and nurture. Godley goes even further by suggesting that an explanation for the self-description of a proportion of young Jewish East London males at the end of the nineteenth century as 'journeymen'[48] tailors was not an admission of non-achievement but rather an example of the anti-entrepreneurial snobbery which existed in Britain until very recently. To be ascribed the status of entrepreneur in Britain at that time was, says Godley, 'a dubious compliment', one which bore the lingering odour of anti-alienism. Conversely, to be regarded as a skilled craftsman was to command respect. By comparison, in New York during this same period, entrepreneurship stood for self-help, initiative and individuality, all highly respected traits. Entrepreneurship, as perceived by the anti-alienists in Spitalfields before the outbreak of the First World War, was not a manifestation or glorification of the hard-work ethic. Rather it was the personification of the coldblooded exploiter of underpaid, overworked labour.

Rich and of high status

Out-migration in the 1920s and 1930s coupled with the Blitz resulted in the demise of the Jewish East End. By the 1960s only a few elderly Jewish residents remained. In Spitalfields, economic transition accompanied domestic change. Type of garment, production method and location all underwent changes during the 1950s. By the late 1960s much of the tailoring and dress trade had departed from Spitalfields and the unsanitary sweatshops had become unhealthy leatherwear workshops. The transitional period coincided with the arrival of the third major wave of Spitalfields immigrants. There had long been a tradition of men from the region of Sylhet, in the northeastern corner of India, working as *lascars* on British merchant vessels and jumping ship to find short-term employment in London's East End. A seamen's hostel for Indian sailors existed there in the eighteenth century.[49] In the 1920s a Sylheti opened one of the first Indian restaurants in the capital, whilst a fellow countryman opened a café in Sandys Row, East London in 1938.[50] Before the outbreak of the Second World War, Sylheti seamen seeking work ashore often found jobs, and sometimes lodgings, in Jewish tailoring workshops in Spitalfields. At that time of heightened anti-Semitism, Jewish employers and their families were sympathetic to others who, like themselves, were subjected to fascist threats and violence.[51] Did those pioneers anticipate that, within fifty years, Sylhetis would have formed the largest ethnic community in the area?

During the 1950s and early 1960s the combination of limited economic opportunity at home and perceived job availability in Britain encouraged young men from Sylhet to travel west across those seven seas and thirteen rivers. As we know, the intention was not long-term emigration but short-term residence with employment opportunities for young, single male sojourners, enabling then to send money home as well as accumulate capital to support them and their families on their return.[52] Those who made the journey were not from the poorest families, but from those who could afford to lose a breadwinner for the benefit of future rewards. It was quite common for families, or even sometimes a small village community, to pool their economic resources in order to send one or more young males to the *bidesh*. It was a chance to acquire a job, save money and return home 'as rich men of high status'. Along with that opportunity came a long-term commitment to one's kin and one's village. Close contact is maintained between the Sylheti village and the Spitalfields community, the politics of one at times indivisible from the other. Landownership in the northeastern corner of Pakistan, which became Bangladesh in 1971 after a bloody and bitter civil war, was, and continues to be, the determinant of status; to 'labour on another man's land is humiliating and associated with low social position'.[53] In one of the most overcrowded and impoverished countries in the modern world, migration was, and to a large extent still is, perceived as the only route to upward mobility.[54]

In the decade following the end of the Second World War, the British government followed a policy of encouraging and at times overtly recruiting, overseas labour. It was not easy for East Pakistanis (Sylhetis) to obtain passports for the UK. The Pakistani government reserved that privilege for those from the west of its country. However, during the 1950s a small number of Sylhetis found their way to London's East End as well as to the textile factories of the midlands and the north. The young men were poorly educated, had few skills and little experience of the harshness of urban industrial life. On arrival in London they found themselves living in over-crowded male ghettoes taking up employment in a variety of previously unknown trades. Life in the *bidesh* did not bring comfort and immediate riches, but, initially, it did bring a regular income and the ability to send home the remittances which 'play a vital part in the macro-economic viability of Bangladesh'.[55] Remittances soon became a central part of the native household budget,[56] an income which those left behind came to depend upon. Money or gifts enabled kin back home to demonstrate their, and the sojourner's, raised status through house improvements, land purchase, the opening of a business or a more generous marriage dowry. Those villages which were enjoying the benefits of their émigré kin soon became known as *Londoni* to distinguish them from the less fortunate.

The conditions which enabled some of the earliest migrants to return home within a few years were shortlived. By the early 1960s, Britain's socio-economic climate was changing. The influx of New Commonwealth citizens in the years following 1948 led to heightened racial sensitivity and tensions as the job market contracted.[57] The outcome was the passage of the Commonwealth Immigrants Act of 1962, stipulating that only Commonwealth citizens with Ministry of Labour employment vouchers could enter the country as primary migrants. Ironically, what was intended as a mechanism for control created the impetus for a rush of Sylheti migrants who wanted to get into Britain before it was too late. For a short period of time, labour vouchers were readily forthcoming from relatives and fellow villagers already working in London and the provinces, from prospective employers and from Bangladeshi brokers, in both home and host countries, who promoted and organised migration.[58] At no time was the movement westwards perceived as a permanent departure from the Indian subcontinent. It was a journey overseas that would enable the sojourners to transform their part of Sylhet into the promised land. The reality was far from the dream. As the 1960s sank into recession, men who had arrived with no experience of an urban economy struggled to survive on the residue of the small sums of money being sent home, as job prospects, particularly in industry, declined and employment narrowed. Hopes of early return faded and the process of reuniting families began. It proved a long, as yet still incomplete, drawn-out affair aggravated by the cost of transporting wives and children, providing the documentation required for family authentication, shortage of family accommodation in the male ghettoes, and always the need either to visit wives and children in, or to send money back to, Sylhet.

As in the eighteenth and nineteenth centuries, the face of Spitalfields began to change as the new immigrants moved in, some having come directly from Bangladesh, others moving south after suffering redundancy in the midlands. All sought homes and employment, as so many had done before, at the eastern edge of the capital city. What economic opportunities awaited the Bangladeshi arrivals, untutored in the ways of urban entrepreneurial activity? As the Huguenots and Jews before them, many found work in the clothing industry, in the late 1950s and early 1960s, in the clothing factories and workshops owned by Jews and Cypriots. In that early period the interphasing of two diasporic groups, Jews and Bangladeshis, was marked by mutual respect and support. As one Bangaldeshi man remembered,

> I liked those Jewish people, they took really good care of us. They made you work yes, but they had great respect for people. . . . They made their money and, after a while, from when I came to work they began to go back to their countries.[59]

Some of the earliest Bangladeshi entrepreneurs in Spitalfields opened travel agencies, anticipating their fellow migrants' need for regular returns to the *desh* and for the safe carriage of remittances. Others ventured into the running of food emporiums and clothes shops. Not all have been successful or endured, their survival determined not only by the ability and initiative of their Sylheti owners but also by the vagaries of the national and local economy.

By the 1970s the rag trade, which at that time provided 20 per cent of jobs available in Tower Hamlets, had become the major source of employment for Bangladeshi men in the borough. They had gradually replaced female machinists, who themselves had taken over from Jewish males, in local Jewish- or Cypriot-owned clothing factories and workshops. According to a report presented in 1979,[60] the labour was casual. This can be taken as a euphemism for piecework, paid for by 'clear money', so allowing both employer and employee to avoid tax and national insurance and, in certain instances, enabled the employee to apply for, and receive, state benefit.[61] The organisational structure of the clothing factories was reminiscent of that of the 1930s,[62] Bangladeshi casual workers employed by Bangladeshi or Pakistani subcontractors in small-scale production units which, in all but location, were workshops. However, there was a subtle difference, beyond giving out the work and determining the rates for piecework, the subcontractor/employer had no responsibility for his workers. If there was no work it was not his problem. The exploitation experienced by the semi-skilled and unskilled Bengali men echoes that of earlier groups, and suggests that, in the migrant experience, pioneers that 'suffer' in order to gain an economic foothold in the receiving society demonstrate little compassion or concern for the working conditions of co-patriots or co-religionists who arrive down the chain. Significantly, the new clothing-trade workers and employers had not only taken over the businesses and locations of their Jewish predecessors, but they also maintained their style of operation.

Furriery was another branch of the clothing trade pursued by Jewish immigrants in Spitalfields. As the trade began to decline in the early 1960s, middle-aged furriers turned to leather manufacture, the current fashion rage. As the traditional pattern of business transfer from father to son no longer pertained, there was a need for new blood. Medicine, law and accountancy were now favoured above the rag trade. Initially successors were found from amongst the small Pakistani community whose roots lay, not in Sylhet, but in the region of Mirpur. Many had lost their land in the partition of 1947 and, encouraged by the Pakistani government of the 1950s, travelled to Britain. Those early arrivals displayed an eagerness to accept the challenge and train in the skills of cutting and machining which would enable them to take over existing companies and establish new ones. The first Pakistani-owned leather business in Spitalfields dates from 1957.[63] The Pakistanis soon exhibited entrepreneurial keenness, becoming masters instead of workers, and the leather trade enjoyed a rapid expansion. In the burgeoning Spitalfields leather garment workshops, Bangladeshi immigrants found poorly paid and unskilled employment in an industrial structure mirroring that of the tailoring trade 100 years ago.

The leather industry operates along the age-old sub-divisional lines: wholesalers and middlemen, in this instance, mainly Pakistanis, give work out to small-scale workshops (cut, make and trim, known as CMT) run by Bangladeshis who employ their fellow countrymen as sweated labour. Rates of pay are low – when the Wages Council existed they were usually below the poverty line, today they are either at the minimum wage or undisclosed 'casual money'. Unlike in the Jewish experience,[64] trade union membership is negligible and organised opposition to exploitative fellow Bangladeshis rare. As in the times of the Huguenots and the Jews, the clothing industry is ever susceptible to the peaks and troughs of the economy. The recession of 1988 affected the leather trade severely and significantly increased the number of unemployed Bangladeshis. At this point the mirror image hazes over. Unlike in earlier times, the modern welfare state subsidises the poorly paid or unemployed worker. There is a tacit acceptance of the current pattern of economic activity; welfare, bolstered from time to time by work-shop employment. As this tends to operate in the informal economy, using both legal and illegal immigrant labour, there has been little overt opposition to low wages and poor conditions and a low level of trade union membership.[65] In spite, or perhaps because, of this, the leather trade survives and, at the beginning of the twenty-first century, in Spitalfields and Banglatown, there are overt and dominant reminders of the leather-trade entrepreneurs. Although the majority are Pakistani, there are also a small number of large leather emporiums in Brick Lane and Bethnal Green Road run by Bangladeshi entrepreneurs who cut their teeth in the urban economy of Dhaka and Chittagong as opposed to the rural outback of the villages. These are Spitalfields manifestations of capitalist success. However, for the majority of Bangladeshis in the clothing trade, the dream of success remains a dream.

The changing pattern of the British way of life, the popularity of ethnic food and of eating out that began in the 1960s, impacted on Bangladeshi immigrants looking for work. In response to the growing demand for ethnic food some found employment in, or opened, eating places. As Chapter 3 revealed, by the end of the 1960s there were a few Indian-run cafés and restaurants in Spitalfields. By the 1980s these had been transformed into Indian[66] restaurants 'where the décor, cuisine, availability of alcohol and prices were specifically aimed at members of the white middle-class'.[67] The restaurants provided jobs for those made redundant from the closure of clothing factories and workshops which had transmigrated to third-world countries where the labour was cheap. Spitalfields' appeal to the middle class was enhanced by the inauguration, in 1997, of Banglatown. In part promoted as an opportunity to essentialise and identify the Bengali culture in a positive light, in reality it is largely a commercial enterprise conceived by several Bengali entrepreneurs as part of the local regeneration scheme. The intention was to facilitate the development and diversification of the local economy, create links with the city and break down the negative Bangladeshi stereotypes.[68] Within this example of cultural commodification 'Indian' restaurants play a significant role in attracting diners from the city, the West End and the affluent suburbs. They arrive at dusk to enjoy what Yasmin Alibhai-Brown has called 'boutique multi-culturalism'.[69] And it is in the food and restaurant business that we find the largest number of Bangladeshi entrepreneurs. In a recently produced report, Sean Carey revealed that, in 2002, the area around Brick Lane and Hanbury Street contained no less than forty-one Bangladeshi-owned and -run cafés and restaurants – more than twenty having been opened since 2000. One of the oldest, *Shampan*, which stands on the corner of Hanbury Street and Brick Lane, is reputed to have made its owner, Shirazul Haque, a millionaire. Haque was one of those behind the concept of Banglatown. Carey suggests[70] that the reason for the impressive expansion is to be found in a combination of the success of Banglatown and the Bangladeshi pool of labour which can provide chefs as well as legal and illegal kitchen staff and waiters.[71] However, though the catering trade has attracted school-leavers and those prepared to work after the school-day has ended,[72] and while a number of Spitalfields-trained Bangladeshi (male) chefs have found employment in some of the capital's five star hotels,[73] there is concern that, in the tradition of the Jewish community before them, ambitious young Bangladeshis are now looking to enter the professions rather than work in the trades of their fathers. Others, while remaining in the restaurant trade, are now moving out to the suburbs and managing curry houses in more salubrious surroundings. At the same time the nature of Banglatown is undergoing a transformation. Though young Bengalis consider Brick Lane to be 'theirs',[74] its ethnic singularity is beginning to change. Indian restaurants are making way for trendy, minimalist bars and clubs, sari shops are closing and properties in the west of Spitalfields are being sold to successful professional and business people at prices in excess of £1 million.

The economic recession of the 1980s and increased vigilance by the Inland Revenue resulted in the closure of a number of clothing factories and, as previously noted, a substantial rise in Bangladeshi male unemployment. In order to compensate, some Bangladeshi women began to subsidise the family income by machining garments in the home. Much of this homework came from 'Asian factory owners who employed people from their own communities and exploited them through various "feudal" practices, such as paying a single wage for husband and wife, or by using unpaid family labour.'[75] Whilst some women undertook, and continue to undertake, homework as a means of compensating for their husbands' misfortunes, others are now working at home in order to acquire independent spending power or to send money back to the *desh* to their, rather than their husband's, families. This development goes against one commentator's belief that, though there were sewing machines in the homes, they were not being used.[76] One of the women interviewed by Kabeer explained the anomalies of homeworking:

> Some women are able to benefit from homework, some aren't. Some women's husbands take their money and spend it, some women spend it how they want. Women are benefiting because they are able to buy more food or buy land, but they don't have more confidence when they work at home. It is up to the individual of course but if they went out to work, they would meet ten other people and learn useful things.[77]

In the main, Bangladeshi married women work at home. The reasons are cultural, religious and linguistic. Working married women do not occupy the public space, both religion and language deficiency mediating against this. And it is their cultural heritage which prevents Bengali women taking jobs as waitresses in the local Indian restaurants. By working at home married women can retain their invisibility and, at the same time, combine machining – making jeans or other types of trousers and skirts – with child-care, housework and cooking. In addition, though helping out with the family budget, they are not publicly demeaning their husbands. This is reminiscent of the experience of Jewish wives in Spitalfields more than 100 years ago. However, in contrast with previous female immigrant residents, there is little evidence of the Bangladeshi female entrepreneur, except perhaps for the occasional moneylender.

As a result of the general 'invisibility' of Bangladeshi wives, it is impossible to quantify the Bangladeshi female homeworker workforce, one which has traditionally veered more towards the illegal than the legal. Research carried out in the mid-1990s revealed that only 20 per cent of Bangladeshi women of working age, as compared to 70 per cent of white and Afro-Caribbean women, were officially employed.[78] The 2001 Decennial Census reveals that in the Spitalfields and Banglatown ward, 40 per cent of Bengali females aged between sixteen and twenty-four (205 out of 505) were economically active. Of those over the age of twenty-five, only 148 out of a total of 1,024 declared themselves to be working. The pattern is reflected in the borough as a whole, with only one-third of the Bangladeshi sixteen to twenty-four female cohort being economically active, while only 1,611 of the total of 12,867 over the age of twenty-five were 'in work'.[79] If other accounts are to be believed, it would seem that in Spitalfields, and in the borough as a whole, the majority of married working Bangladeshi women are part of the silent and invisible homeworker army that has long existed in Spitalfields.

The past decade has seen a significant change in the size, activities and economic ambitions of the Bangladeshi community in the London Borough of Tower Hamlets. The size of the resident community has increased by almost 100 per cent, from 36,000 in 1991 to 65,553[80] in 2001, a figure which now represents one-third of the borough's population.[81] In Spitalfields and Banglatown, of the 8,374-strong population, 4,872 are Bangladeshi; two-thirds of that number aged under thirty. At the other end of the scale, only 7 per cent of the ward's Bangladeshi community is of pensionable age. These statistics have significant implications for the economic future of the Bangladeshi community, some of which are beginning to filter through. Perhaps the most important is the apparent reduction in what was a very high level of male Bangladeshi unemployment – in 1995 it was recorded as 43 per cent.[82] The 2001 Census showed a significant drop down to 12 per cent, yet even at that low level, the figure was almost four times the national average. The profile of the ward, and borough, is of a Bengali community dominated by youth. In Spitalfields and the borough as a whole almost three-quarters of Bangladeshis are aged under thirty, as compared to the national figure of one-third.[83] Optimism can be derived from the fact that local Bangladeshi schoolchildren are now, by the age of sixteen, pulling dramatically ahead of their African-Caribbean, African, Pakistani and, at times, their English/Scottish/Welsh peers,[84] with girls achieving at a faster rate than boys. At Queen Mary, University of London, situated just one and one half miles to the east of Spitalfields, 462 British Bangladeshi students are currently registered as undergraduates,[85] studying vocational subjects including law, business studies, economics and medicine. There have also been signs of small-scale entrepreneurial activity amongst the younger, first- or second-generation British-born members of the community. They are now setting up shops, opening restaurants and running CMT, tailoring and leather units.[86] Unlike their fathers, and in a few cases their grandfathers, who originated from a rural background, enjoyed little or no education and still look to Sylhet as home, these young people show less attachment to the old village ways and to the ideal of returning home as rich men of high status. Yousuf Choudhury, one of the earliest Bangladeshi arrivals in Britain, noted some years ago that there was now a 'strong entrepreneurial spirit amongst the Bangladeshis in Spitalfields'.[87] With little desire to return to the *desh*, a small number of young Bangladeshis are now investing their energies and money locally, starting small businesses or entering the professions.

As in all things, there is also a downside. Drug-taking is now rife amongst young male and female Bangladeshis. A recent report estimated that between 'Fifty to 70 per cent of Bangladeshi male youths have experimented with heroin . . . a sizeable minority have become habitual users.'[88] In general the habitual users come from some of the poorer housing estates where social deprivation and marginalisation are the norm. Drug-taking amongst Bangladeshi youths is acting as a disincentive to employment. If more young entrepreneurs are to emerge from the community then further support in terms of improved housing, youth facilities and incentive-related job opportunities[89] are a necessary part of the process.

Conclusion

This examination of the entrepreneurial spirit of Huguenots, Jews and Bangladeshis has perforce been brief. However, there is sufficient evidence to draw certain conclusions regarding the fashioning of their early economic profiles. In spite of the differences in time there are common threads. Each group was perceived as 'alien' upon arrival, spoke a different language and worshipped God in varying degrees of difference. All have occupied the same space, Spitalfields, an area which remains constantly under threat from incursion by the city, the immigrant, poverty and deprivation. The pre-industrial economic structure survives and still acts as a magnet to unskilled aliens. It is a starting point for some and a graveyard for others.

How do we summarise the economic experience of the three groups in Spitalfields? The Huguenot refugees brought with them the sophisticated expertise and labour which facilitated the expansion of the fundamental British silk industry at a time when it was politically viable and economically beneficial for the host society. The Calvinist work ethic encouraged, indeed, advocated, rational economic activity, capital investment and reinvestment using formally free labour. The end goal was not a vulgar expression of wealth but glorification of God through good works and achievements. Yet, interwoven with the Huguenot success story and the advantages enjoyed by those who brought with them a skilled, disciplined, educated and financially secure background are the tragedies of failure, poverty and hunger suffered by exiles who carried little baggage, and who were forced to survive on charity and the lowest wages. In the Huguenot story, the successful and the perspicacious moved on from the first point of settlement. Those who remained, through choice or need, fared less well. All, in spite of their supposed Protestant work ethic, were at the mercy of the more powerful forces of war and peace and the policies that accompanied those two societal conditions. It should not be forgotten that the Huguenot refugees were just that, individuals and families seeking refuge with little or no thought of return. Denied the opportunity to worship as they chose, they cut themselves off from the past. When, following the French revolution almost 100 years later, freedom to worship in the land of their forebears was reinstituted, few if any chose to return. They had found their promised land.

The Eastern European Jews who settled in Spitalfields at the end of the nineteenth century were poor immigrants who sought an economic future and independence far away from a tsardom which offered them nothing but alienation and diminishing economic opportunity. In spite of having left families in the *shtetls* and towns, few had return on the agenda.[90] There was no going back, for what was there to return to in a land in which they would be forever alien, denied freedom of speech, landownership and capital acquisition? The *Talmud*, which elevated a trade and business above agricultural labour, taught that there would be adequate rewards for hard work and that profit was a means of honouring the Lord. This directive was to be put to the test in the promised land which, for many was New York but which, for between 100,000 and 150,000, was London.[91] The migrant Jew carried the experience of thousands of years in a diaspora where material acquisition was the only form of security. Weber acknowledged this when he wrote: 'National or religious minorities which are in a position of subordination . . . are likely through voluntary or involuntary exclusions of political influence to be driven with peculiar force into economic activity and seek recognition in this field'[92]

Whatever the illusion, the reality of that early Eastern European Spitalfields experience was for most hardship and exploitation. A graphic description of life in 1907, which appeared in the Yiddish newspaper, *Arbeiter Fraint*, tells all:

> It is heartbreaking to see how people, fathers of children, workers, good craftsmen work, so hard, such long hours with heads bent, tremble for their bosses, the majority caterers, shoe makers or drivers and all for what, for a slice of bitter bread in the busy time barely just to keep alive and, in the slack time so little.[93]

The Morris Cohens were indeed rare.

The Bangladeshi arrivals of the late 1950s, 1960s and 1970s, followed a religion that was eastern, submissive, prescriptive and supposedly lacking the directive of a work ethic. This belief, as suggested above, is open to debate and dispute. The Islamic insistence that 'Allah helps them that help themselves' provides an incentive to capital acquisition as a means of benefiting self and community. And that is what the sojourners came to do. They did not see themselves as either immigrants or refugees. Except for those seeking political asylum, their stay was to be short, followed by a return home as rich men. Perhaps this explains why the opportunity to take over the running of Spitalfields leather businesses was rejected. The plan was to save and send remittances home to facilitate that return. Economic and social reality moved the goalposts and it is the children, in some cases grandchildren, of those early immigrants who are now caught in a vacuum between two cultures. Children who are growing up in one of the most deprived areas of Britain, children whose parents still look to Sylhet as their home and, though now manifesting respect for an English education and vocational studies, still create educational lacunae by taking their children back on extended visits which can last for a year or more. But the children do not want to return to a land which is foreign in culture and climate – they see their future in global terms, in London and other capital cities, and because of this, their route to, and measure of, success will be of a very different nature to those of their parents.

The myth of success has been ascribed to the Huguenots and the Jews but, as we have seen, this was not always the case. It is still too early to tell what myth will be laid at the door of the Bangladeshis though, according to evidence, some are already following the Jewish path out to the suburbs via 'Newham, Redbridge and even Golders Green'.[94] It is an emergent pattern which contradicts the projected image of failure and lethargy and too soon to identify as an economic role model. And, when choosing that model, caution should be exercised in pinpointing the calendar position. We have seen that in reality not each and every Huguenot and Jew 'made it'. External factors such as trade barriers, economic recessions, wars and immigration controls, possibly even welfare benefit, have been the arbiters of what a capitalist society deems 'success'. Within these limitations religion has played, and continues to play, an influential role. The rise of capitalism was not simply an outcome of the Old Testament and Protestantism, nor were the outward displays of status seen in Sylhet achieved solely as a result of dedication to the teachings of Allah. The other factors identified at the outset of this chapter must be included in the analysis. The economic structure and history of their native environments clearly advantaged Huguenots and Jews while the rural economy in Sylhet did little to prepare its young men for an urban existence. In spite of their being the 'Spitalfields greeners' of the twentieth century, the early arrivals knuckled under and found work in whichever trades offered employment, the fruits of their labour on view in the *Londoni* villages not the London streets. It is only recently that, in streets such as Brick Lane, the successful local Bangladeshi entrepreneurs can be identified. Though, in the tradition of those that came before them, success at times can be shortlived. The host economy which benefited migrant Huguenot silk merchants and weavers upon their arrival also provided an incentive for a minority of late nineteenth-century aliens, including Morris Cohen, though it ravaged others. In more recent times, the late twentieth-century decades of boom and bust did little to help those Bangladeshis who sought a direct route to status, riches and a return to Sylhet. The jury is still out about the long-term success of Banglatown.

It is not only the debate surrounding the Weberian Protestant work ethic which comes over in the story of the Huguenots, Jews and Bangladeshis of Spitalfields. The thoughts of an earlier thinker, Niccolo Machiavelli, should be allowed an airing. In his sixteenth-century treatise, *The Prince*, he wrote 'Fortune, as it were, provided the matter but *they* gave it its form.'[95] The successful Huguenots of the eighteenth century and Jews of the late nineteenth and early twentieth centuries recognised fortune and gave it form in Spitalfields. However, for the early Bangladeshi sojourners, perhaps fortune was not perceived as a leather factory in Brick Lane, but a house and land in Sylhet. For the reality and the myth of the twentieth-century Bangladeshi economic experience we must still bide our time.

When we come to assess the economic achievements of migrant groups, our analysis must be sufficiently broad-based. Currently, it is visits to the *Londoni* villages of Bangladesh, and to the cities of Chittagong and Dhaka, as well as the streets of Spitalfields that provide the markers of success, of nettle-grasping, which enable comparison with centuries past. If the evidence is weighed, it would appear that the Huguenots, Jews and Bangladeshis have each rationalised their economic activities. Their rationales are imbued with more than just religious idealism. They have accommodated material and cultural realities and by so doing, redefined the promised land.

Notes

1 This chapter, in a different form, first appeared in A.J. Kershen (ed.), *London the Promised Land? The Migrant Experience in a Capital City*, Aldershot, Ashgate, 1997.
2 C. Peach, *Ethnicity in the 1991 Census*, Vol. 2, London, HMSO, 1996, pp. 15–16.
3 For different disciplinary approaches to the Protestant work ethic, see H. Lehmann and G. Roth (eds), *Weber's Protestant Work Ethic: Origins, Evidence and Contexts*, Cambridge, Cambridge University Press, 1995.
4 B. Turner, *Weber and Islam*, 1974, quoted in K. Gardner, *Global Migrants, Local Lives*, Oxford, Clarendon Press, 1995, p. 234.
5 M. Weber, *The Protestant Work Ethic and the Spirit of Capitalism*, London, Unwin, 1938, p. 171.
6 Gardner, op. cit., p. 235.
7 The person who made this remark to the author on 23 April 1996 asked to remain anonymous.
8 The origins of the silk-weaving trade are attributed to the Flemings, who introduced the simple process of ribbon making.
9 M. Dorothy George, *London Life in the Eighteenth Century*, London, Penguin, 1992 edition, p. 178 and N. Rothstein, 'Huguenots in the English Silk Industry in the Eighteenth Century, in I. Scouloudi (ed.), *Huguenots in Britain and Their French Background, 1550–1800*, Basingstoke, Macmillan, 1987, p. 132.
10 Quoted in C. Holmes, *John Bull's Island*, London, Macmillan, 1988, p. 7.
11 F.H.W. Sheppard (ed.), *Survey of London*, Vol. XXVII, *Spitalfields and Mile End New Town*, London, Athlone Press, 1975, p. 4.
12 A. Marshall, *Elements of Economics*, London, Macmillan, 1946 edition, p. 11.
13 Rothstein, op. cit., p. 130.
14 According to Weber such property ownership was 'not an ostentation'. See Weber, op. cit., p. 171.
15 Peter Ogier II arrived in Spitalfields in 1730.
16 Courtauld's entry into the silk industry resulted in the foundation of Samuel Courtauld and Co. which became a giant in the textile industry, by 1901 the largest manufacturer of black crepe in the world.
17 T. Murdoch, *The Quiet Conquest: The Huguenots 1685–1985*, London, Museum of London, 1985, p. 296.
18 Ibid.

19 Report of the Select Commission on the State of the Handloom Weavers II, 1840, Vol. XXIII, London, p. 715.

20 Ibid.

21 Ibid.

22 George, op. cit., p. 185.

23 Ibid.

24 H.L. Smith, *The History of East London from the Earliest Times to the End of the Eighteenth Century*, London, Macmillan, 1939, p. 92.

25 L.D. Schwarz, 'Conditions of Life and Work in East London, 1770–1815', unpublished D.Phil. thesis, University of Oxford, 1976, p. 31.

26 Minutes of Evidence of the Petition of the Ribbon Weavers, 1818, (134) IX. p. 147.

27 This was extended in 1792 to include those working in the manufacture of silk mixture and again in 1801 to include women.

28 George, op. cit., p. 187.

29 Quoted in E.P. Thompson, *The Making of the English Working Class*, London, Penguin, 1968 edition, p. 157.

30 Select Committee on Handloom Weavers 1834–5, Analysis of Evidence, 1835 (492)XIII.343, p. 4.

31 Committee on Lotteries 1808, (182)II, 147, p. 205.

32 Select Committee on Handloom Weavers 1834–5, op. cit., p. 4.

33 Ibid.

34 H. Mayhew, *London Labour and the London Poor*, Vol. III, New York, Dover Publications, 1968 edition, p. 79.

35 One of those was Charles Booth, whose revelatory first volume of *Life and Labour of the People of London*, devoted to East London, appeared in 1889.

36 E. Zipperstein, *Business Ethics in Jewish Law*, New York, Ktav, 1993, p. 22.

37 The *Torah* stated that the product of a plant and an animal must not be mixed. Therefore an orthodox Jew went to a clothing maker/tailor who understood the religious requirements of *shatnes*.

38 For example the company of Hitchcock Williams, based in St Paul's Church-yard, which remained in business until the mid-1980s.

39 A. Kershen, *Uniting the Tailors*, Ilford, Frank Cass, 1995, Chapter 3.

40 C. Booth, *Life and Labour of the People of London*, First Series, Poverty, Vol. IV, London, Williams & Norgate 1890–2, pp. 60–1.

41 Royal Commission on Aliens 1903, PP 1903, X, q 18968.

42 The author is grateful to Morris Cohen's family, particularly Clive Moss, for providing this biographical detail.

43 *Jewish Chronicle*, 22 April 1898.

44 Kershen, *Uniting*, op.cit., pp. 102–4.

45 Clive Moss in conversation with the author, 13 December 1994.

46 See A. Godley, 'Leaving the East End: Regional Mobility among East European Jews in London, 1880–1914', in Kershen, *London the Promised Land?*, op. cit., pp. 50–65.

47 A. Godley, *Jewish Immigrant Entrepreneurship in London and New York 1890–1914*, Basingstoke, Palgrave, 2001, p. 123.

48 The nomenclature 'journeyman' can be interpreted in different ways. There are those, such as Godley, who consider it represented an acknowledgeable level of skill and thus was used as a means of denoting status value whilst others, including some of those who worked in the trade in the 1920s and 1930s, considered that it described the way in which tailors found work travelling from one workshop to another rather than referring to their level of skill.

49 R. Visram, *Ayahs, Lascars and Princes*, London, Pluto Press, 1986, p. 39.

50 Y. Choudhury, *The Roots and Tales of Bangladeshi Settlers*, Birmingham, Sylhet Social History Group, 1993, pp. 70 and 77.

51 Ibid., p. 70.

52 First Report from the Home Affairs Committee, *Bangladeshis in Britain*, Session 1986–7, Vol. 1, London, HMSO, 1986, p. 9.

53 Gardner, op. cit., p. 39.

54 The population of Bangladesh in 1994 was estimated to stand at 116 million, life expectancy was forty-seven years, with 100 women dying every day in child-birth. Adult literacy was less than 25 per cent and 70 per cent of the population were aged under thirty. See http://lcweb2.loc.gov/frd/cs/bangladesh/bd_appen. html (accessed 17 June 1994).

55 M. Islam, 'Bangladeshi Migration: An Impact Study', in R. Cohen, *Cambridge Survey of World Migration*, Cambridge, Cambridge University Press, 1995, p. 362.

56 Figures which cover the periods 1991–2 and 1992–3 estimate the overall inflow of remittances to Bangladesh to be approximately $800 million. These figures take account of migrants all over the world, not just from the UK from which, in the past few years, the remittance figure has been reducing. Islam, ibid.

57 Between 1951 and 1961 the number of New Commonwealth immigrants in London rose from 256,000 to 541,000. M. Anwar, *The Myth of Return: Pakistanis in Britain*, London, Heinemann Educational, 1979, p. 4.

58 Gardner, op. cit., pp. 39–48.

59 K. Gardner, *Age, Narrative and Migration*, Oxford, Berg, 2002, p. 102. It should be noted that in fact the movement of those Jewish employers was to the suburbs not 'to their countries'.

60 P. Duffy, 'Bengali Action Research Project, Tower Hamlets, unpublished report for the CRE, 1979', quoted in N. Kabeer, *The Power to Choose*, London and New York, Verso, 2000.

61 Quoted in Kabeer, op. cit., p. 213.

62 Research by the author revealed that in the mid-1930s the company of Ellis and Goldstein began bringing outworkers into their factory though retaining the same subcontracting structure. Ellis and Goldstein Ledger, 1927–56, currently in the possession of the author.

63 Conversation with M. Goodmaker, Clothing Industries Co-ordinator, City Challenge, 13 March 1996.

64 For details of organisation amongst the Jewish tailoring workers of East London, see Kershen, *Uniting*, op. cit., Chapter 5.

65 Conversation with M. Goodmaker, 13 March 1996 and with Peter Corbishley, Clothing Industries Association of East London, 18 March 1996.

66 Though the 'Indian' restaurants in Britain have tended to have been owned by Bangladeshis – a few by Pakistanis – they have been traditionally known as Indian. However, this characteristic is beginning to change as Bangladeshi and Sylheti are now appearing in the names of a number of restaurants.

67 Unpublished report by Sean Carey, 'Brick Lane, Banglatown: A Study of the Catering Sector: Final Report' May 2002, p. 17.

68 See David Garbin, 'Migration, territoires diasporiques et politiques identitaires: Bengalis musulmans entre "Banglatown" (Londres) et Sylhet (Bangladesh),' unpublished Ph.D. thesis, University of François Rabelais de Tours, 2004, p. 351.

69 Yasmin Alibhai-Brown, *After Multiculuralism*, London, The Foreign Policy Centre, 2000, p. 42.

70 Carey, op. cit.

71 The point about illegals is the author's belief, not one put forward by Sean Carey.

72 Conversation with the Rev. John Webber, 14 June 1996.

73 Carey, op. cit., p. 18.

74 Garbin, op. cit., p. 357.
75 Kabeer, op. cit., p. 217.
76 A survey carried out in 1986 suggests that as few as 10 per cent of females engaged in homework whilst ten years later, Peter Corbishley told the author that, despite sewing machines being in the homes, there was little evidence of their being used. Others, members of the Bengali community, suggest that in fact an increasing number of women are working at home.
77 Kabeer, op. cit., p. 303.
78 Ibid., p. 225.
79 Statistics supplied by the Census, Customer Service, 13 November 2003, from ONS, Table Population: All People, Geographical Level England and Wales to Ward; Tables S108 Sex and Age and Economic Activity by Ethnic Group.
80 Seventy per cent of this number aged under thirty.
81 Statistics supplied by the Census, Customer Service, 13 November 2003, from ONS, Table Population: All People, Geographical Level England and Wales to Ward; Table S101 Sex and Age by Ethnic Group. The Decennial Census for 1991 (http://www.statistics.gov.uk/census 2001_1991 accessed 16 February 2004) revealed that there were 36,000 Bangladeshis living in Spitalfields, representing either 60.7 per cent of the area's total population, or 95 per cent according to the London Borough of Tower Hamlets. It should also be noted that there are also a number of illegal immigrants as well as legal migrants who were unwilling to reveal themselves on the Census, particularly as the poll tax was then still in operation.
82 *Living in Bethnal Green: A Survey of Residents in the Bethnal Green City Challenge Area*, issued by LEPU, London, South Bank University, May 1995, p. vii.
83 Statistics supplied by the Census, Customer Services on 13 November 2003, from ONS statistics table, op. cit., and ONS neighbourhood statistics on Spitalfields and Banglatown.
84 *Guardian Education*, 10 September 1996. For more recent statistics on Bangladeshi levels of educational achievement, see the Department of Education and Skills consultation document, 'Aiming High: Raising the Achievement of Minority Ethnic Pupils', March 2003, ref: DfES/0183/2003.
85 Figures from Philip Davis, Statistician, Registry, Queen Mary, University of London, 4 November 2003.
86 Information from Rev. John Webber in conversation with the author, 1 June 1996.
87 Conversation with the author, 20 June 1996.
88 See Sean Carey, 'Looking for the Buzz: Heroin – The Drug of Choice: Drug Use amongst Bangladeshi Youths on the Ocean Estate', unpublished report, produced for the London Borough of Tower Hamlets, October 2000, p. 1.
89 Ibid., pp. 56–61.
90 Up to 50,000 Eastern European Jews did return in the years leading to the First World War. Some could not endure the harsh conditions in the ghettoes of London and the major provincial cities, others were sent back by the Jewish Board of Guardians because they did not fulfil the requirements of settlement.
91 In spite of this, the Passover service still includes a toast to 'next year in Jerusalem' – the promised land.
92 Weber, op. cit., p. 39.
93 Quotation from *Arbeiter Fraint*, 19 March 1907, translated by and taken from Kershen, *Uniting*, op. cit., p. 113.
94 Conversation with John Webber as above.
95 N. Machiavelli, *The Prince*, London, Penguin, 1975 edition, p. 50. The italics in the quote are the author's.

8 Xenophobia, anti-alienism and racism

Before exploring the ways in which the three immigrant groups at the heart of this study were received by the 'natives'[1] of Spitalfields, it is necessary to consider the terms under which their reception is described. In common with the fact that good news rarely gets into the media, so it is generally only the hostile reactions to refugees, immigrants and sojourners, that attract attention. In spite of an inherent human suspicion of things foreign and different, in the very earliest stages of settlement Huguenots, Jews and Bangladeshis rarely met with hostility. However, as their numbers increased and their impact upon local and national socio-economic conditions became visibly and physically significant, the attitudes of many members of the receiving societies[2] changed from a cautious welcome to overt antipathy. A 350-year overview of the issues creating the tensions and the terms in which these were expressed confirms continuity. Throughout the centuries the prime concerns of the native residents of Spitalfields have been the immigrants' impact on local housing and jobs, cultural traditions and health. These are the basic pillars of everyday life and, should they appear endangered, the outsider will always be scapegoated. Yet, whilst the themes have remained constant, the terms of reference have not: group behaviour has been branded by the tensions of the times and, as the centuries passed, the terminology has undergone change.

As victims of (Catholic) religious persecution in the seventeenth century, French Calvinists were welcomed to Protestant England. However, once the industrious and necessitous French refugees began to pose an economic threat to the labour market and their strangeness became manifestly identifiable through language, dress and diet, a xenophobic vocabulary was adopted by those who felt threatened or uneasy. Xenophobia is most commonly defined as a 'fear or hatred of strangers, people from other countries or of anything that is strange or foreign'.[3] In its purest form, it implies a natural, and understandable, antipathy to something or someone foreign or alien. Xenophobia increases when there is a fear that the physical presence, cultural traditions and practices of strangers from another region or nation, might infiltrate those of the majority society. When members of the receiving society are convinced of their own superiority and resort to abusive and/or violent actions towards a minority group, then the individuals from the majority society can be defined as racist and their form of behaviour as racism. In this instance, racism is defined as the doctrine of racial supremacy.[4] As the Bangladeshi community in Spitalfields gained visible significance and made demands on housing and other local amenities, the racist sentiments of a small section of the native community developed into sporadic violent, and on occasions lethal,[5] acts of racism. In these instances the 'locals' were egged on by members of a number of extreme right-wing organisations, most particularly the National Front and subsequently the British National Party (BNP).

The terms 'racist' and 'racism' to describe the behaviour of one group towards another acquired common usage in the postwar years, more particularly from the 1960s onwards. This is not to suggest that discrimination and abuse based on a belief in race superiority was a phenomenon of the second half of the twentieth century. In reality the roots lay in debates that emerged in the second half of the nineteenth century, when discourses on racial science and racial and cultural superiority began in earnest in Central Europe, Britain and America. At the height of the British Empire the discussions incorporated considerations of colour as well as intellect. The imperialist white man was perceived as morally and intellectually superior to his black or brown 'brother'.[6] Victorian racial scientists highlighted the significance of variations in physiognomy, head shape and size. Amongst those who explored the issues of racial difference and discrimination was Joseph Jacobs, a Jew,[7] who used science and statistics to counter what today is known as anti-Semitism. The term, intended to imply 'Jew hatred', was coined by a German, Wilhelm Marr, and first used in 1873. It was a combination of the centuries' old anti-Jewishness, based on the belief that Jews were the Christ-killers, and the new emphasis on racial purity and eugenics. The term anti-Semitism was rarely heard in Britain in the 1880s. The pejorative designation selected to describe Eastern European Jewish immigrants at that time was 'alien'; the protagonists calling for restraints on alien entry became known as anti-alienists and their system of discrimination, anti-alienism.

Though there had been expressions of secular anti-Jewishness from the mid-eighteenth century onwards,[8] it was only during the 1860s and 1870s that the debates began to concentrate on the racial, rather than religious, characteristics of the Jew.[9] During this period the number of Jewish immigrants settling in Spitalfields began to increase significantly. In the eyes of the local community, and to many beyond its boundaries, these (Jewish) aliens from Russia, Russia-Poland and Rumania, were seen as a threat. The term 'alien' found favour with men such as Major William Evans-Gordon, MP for Stepney and an opponent of unrestricted alien immigrant entry. His antipathy was heightened by the gradual incursion into his parliamentary constituency of Eastern European Jews from the neighbouring Spitalfields and Whitechapel wards. The word 'alien' conveyed the very distinct nature of pauper immigrants who were foreign in character and out of harmony with all that was English. Reference to these people as alien was a way of differentiating between the established and *tolerated* Jews, and those who were foreign. The negative reaction to the presence of these outsiders was founded, not in religious differences, but in concerns about jobs and homes. On the surface religion was taken out of the equation.

The strident antipathy directed towards pauper immigrants in the closing decades of the nineteenth and the first decade of the twentieth centuries was a combination of the legacy of anti-Jewishness that predates Christianity, the emerging racial prejudice that would come to be known as anti-Semitism and the local and national concerns raised about the impact of pauper aliens on the staple issues of housing and jobs. All debates centred around the alien, a noun that was increasingly used instead of 'Jew'.[10] It was the recognition that poverty was a problem to be resolved rather than a condition to be endured which put the 'alien question' on the political agenda in the mid-1880s. For just at the time when social scientists were beginning to explore the jungles of the East End of London, so the numbers of immigrants from Eastern Europe were rising. And whilst the occasional Chinaman or 'Mediterranean' Italian might be caught up in the debate, for all intents and purposes it was Eastern European Jews who were the prime targets of the anti-alienists.[11] Men such as Evans-Gordon sought to restrict the entry of pauper aliens into Britain. And it is alien-alienism that provides the third point of the triangle of intolerance that is part of the heritage of Spitalfields.

Wooden shoes

The decades during which French Calvinists migrated to England coincided with a period of significant change in English history. The years leading up to the revocation of the Edict of Nantes were coloured by the political unease accompanying the Restoration. Strangers became objects of suspicion and rumours were rife that the French 'scattering fireballs' had caused the Great Fire of London.[12] The events leading up to, and following, the Bloodless Revolution of 1688 had others suggesting that the French Protestants were in fact agents of Catholicism. In the first half of the eighteenth century, the twice-failed Jacobite invasions served to fuel the fires still further, whilst the series of wars with France created fears of a French fifth column. Between 1689 and the French revolution in 1789, thirty-six years were ones of combat. According to Linda Colley,[13] this tapestry of events provided the landscape upon which a British identity was being forged. Following the Act of Union in 1707, native inhabitants on the British mainland began to define a 'national' identity which had Protestantism at its heart.[14] Though in some ways this was an aid to Huguenot integration, it also encouraged native English men and women to recognise who and what they were, by who and what they were not.

As the Huguenot migrants were, with a few economic exceptions, religious refugees, it is through the lens of religion that we should first explore the xenophobic reactions of the people of Spitalfields to their presence. There is a paradox within the context of religious antagonisms. At the same time as High Anglicans were voicing their unease over the Geneva-looking non-conformity of Calvinism, others, particularly in the run-up to 1688, spread rumours that the refugees were crypto-Catholics. Fear of popery was a powerful force and more than once led to violence, riots and, in Norwich in 1683, death.[15] These passions re-emerged even more forcefully in the eighteenth century. In 1744, as the fear of a Jacobite invasion heightened, a pamphlet was issued which sought to undermine the Calvinist sense of security. It was headed, 'The Swarms of Frenchmen in the Service of the Families of Great Britain are Inconsistent with the Love of Your Religion and Country'.[16] By these terms, not only were the strangers a threat but, in addition, those who employed them ran the risk of being deemed traitors. A further clash of attitudes can be detected from the fact that, at the same time as the Huguenot presence was interpreted by some as an aid to the cause of Protestantism, others feared that such overt support would serve to empower native religious dissenters. It becomes apparent that, in the years leading up to 1750, the expressions of religious xenophobia directed towards the Calvinists were as much a reflection of the debates going on within the Anglican church as they were of reactions to the dissenting refugees' presence.

Robin Gwynn has suggested that, in reality, the arrival of the Calvinists did not engender that much *religious* antagonism.[17] What fired orthodox Anglicans was the spectre of Catholicism and the fear of what a Catholic monarchy and oligarchy might mean for the country. In this sense it was fear of Catholicism rather than of the strangers that brought forth xenophobic reactions from the Anglican church. As early as 1632, Archbishop William Laud pronounced his belief that the foreign churches disturbed the 'unity in the Church of Christ' and posed a threat to his congregants and the realm.[18] In contrast, fifty years later, it was the antipathy to all things Catholic that contributed to the expressions of sympathy and charity accompanying reports of the sufferings undergone by the Huguenots during the the Dragonnades. The tensions did not go unnoticed by the French churches in London. In 1682 the French church in Savoy, which conformed to the Anglican liturgy, issued a pamphlet which advocated general naturalisation and pronounced the loyalty of the French refugees to their new homeland. Eight years on, Huguenot refugees were further cautioned by the Threadneedle Street Consistory to avoid scandalising and to put aside '*tous ces airs fiers et hautierès qui alienent de nous l'espirit de la nation*',[19] referring also to 'The English nation which it is in our interests not to offend'.[20]

The issues that really fired the violent xenophobic reactions of the people of Spitalfields were those relating to the craft skills of the strangers and their impact on employment prospects for the lower-grade workmen. As early as the 1570s, complaints had been raised about the alien threat to the jobs of the indigenous community. The settlement of strangers with craft skills was perceived as endangering the 'poorer elements'. The arrival of Huguenot silk-weavers was met with unease and varying levels of opposition.[21] One hundred years later, in an environment of economic recession, unemployment was becoming a reality for English workers in Spitalfields who saw their jobs being taken by the higher-skilled and wage-undercutting 'strangers' from France. The contemporary rhyme, 'English weavers all may curse their fates, because the French work under-rates', which was circulated in the neighbourhood, said it all. New technology imported from across the Channel put indigenous jobs further in peril. Looms, known as the French invention, which could work ribbon, lace and thread, put thousands of English workers out of work. In 1675 the English weavers of Spitalfields resorted to violence and the King's Guard was called out to prevent a massacre.[22] Whilst no one was injured, those early Luddites savaged Huguenot looms and damaged the homes of the French weavers, in some instances stealing their possessions. Eight years later, native apprentice weavers in Spitalfields warned the king that, if he did not oppose the French weavers, they would resort to violence and 'knock on the head' their foreign counterparts who were undercutting their rates.[23] George Rudé has suggested that it was the local shopkeepers, craftsmen, masters and journeymen, the *menu people*,[24] who protested most vehemently about the Huguenots in Spitalfields. Yet it was the semi-skilled and unskilled refugee silk workers, as opposed to their co-patriot masters and middlemen, who suffered most from the xenophobic words and actions of the local native community.

It was not only French refugee silk workers who were targeted. The City of London's concerns about the threat the French incomers posed to industrious English families encouraged other trades and guilds to impose controls or take aggressive action. French cabinet makers, bakers and glaziers came under attack physically and verbally during the mid-1670s. At the end of the 1680s, French dancing masters were being accused of keeping 'rude and disorderly schools', whilst the Company of Barbers placed a £100 bond on one Louis Saunier, payable if he worked more than four years in London.[25] The City of London jealously guarded its territory, seeking to contain the numbers of those who might receive the privileges of a freeman. As a means of limiting the number of 'Frenchies' entering the trade, the Weavers' Company ordained that French masters had to employ as many English weavers as foreign. Increasingly the Huguenots were perceived as 'taking the bread from out of our mouths'. As late as 1744, English footmen were convinced that French and Swiss immigrants were taking their jobs, whilst others were critical of the fact that Huguenots dominated the fashion trade as wigmakers, hatters, glove and shoe makers.[26] It was not only recent arrivals who came under attack. In the years leading to the revocation, a number of French long-time immigrants were subjected to persecution by their English co-workers. For example, in 1677 a French button-seller, married to an English woman and a resident of twenty years, complained of harassment by his native counterparts, as did a Spitalfields' Huguenot fringe and twist maker who had been in business for ten years and employed two English apprentices.[27] The persistence of persecution in, and adjacent to, the City of London, encouraged some Huguenots to migrate westward. In this way they could avoid the guild controls, including the seven-year apprenticeship requirement, as well as the violence of their Spitalfields' natives. Clusters of French Calvinists soon developed in the villages of Wandsworth, Battersea and Lambeth as well as, of course, in Soho.

The issue which aroused the most forceful xenophobic response, at times well beyond the boundaries of Spitalfields, was the ease with which aliens could achieve denization and naturalisation. These were the means by which strangers could, through Parliament or by the granting of a Crown Letter Patent, acquire the right to obtain all, or some, of the rights of a native-born English man (or after 1707, British subject). To become naturalised required the passage of a Private Bill through Parliament, the taking of an oath in the House of Lords and the provision of proof that the petitioner had taken the sacrament within one month of the Bill's introduction. Naturalisation enabled the successful applicant to acquire almost all the rights – and duties – of a native-born Englishman. These included ownership of land and property, exemption from aliens' customs duties, political and voting rights, access to public office, freedom to trade in the plantations and the right to own an English ship. The cost of such a procedure was somewhere between £63 and £100, and as such, out of reach of all but the wealthiest merchants. It should be noted that, whilst naturalisation would also have benefited the small number of Jewish merchants in England, the religious requirement kept this status out of reach of practising Jews until the end of the 1820s, when it was removed. Denization was the cheaper, and for Jews in the eighteenth century, only alternative. Though providing fewer of the privileges, the cost was far less and, in most instances, satisfied the needs of the majority of the Huguenot merchants. However, the desirability of encouraging wealthy and successful Huguenot businessmen to become naturalised was recognised and, from the 1670s onwards, Parliamentary Bills were put forward to reduce the cost of naturalisation. These were generally favoured by the Lords but, until 1709, failed to get through the Commons. The debates evoked by the Bills reveal the deep-rooted xenophobia that existed amongst certain sections of the Anglican establishment as well as amongst some parliamentarians, civic authorities and trading companies. This was not a grass-roots response to the semi-skilled and unskilled stranger workforce. What was being heard were the voices of those who feared the power the strangers might wield, and the danger they could pose, to the nature of Englishness at a time when the identity of the nation was being sculpted. These emotions were clearly articulated by Sir John Knight, Member of Parliament for Bristol who, in 1693, spoke against an intended Bill as follows:

> should this Bill pass, it will bring as great afflictions on this nation as ever fell upon the Egyptians, and one of their plagues we have at this

time may serve upon us; I mean, that of the land bringing forth Frogs in abundance ... for there is no entering ... the Palaces of our heredity Kings, for the great noise and croaking of the Froglanders ... the serjeant be commanded to open the doors and let us first kick this Bill out of the house then the foreigners out of the Kingdom.[28]

Though the majority of the House condemned Sir John's words and ordered the speech to be burned, the Naturalisation Bill was put aside and not passed until 1709. The General Naturalisation Act remained on the statute book for only three years. In 1712 it was repealed. The reasons were twofold. First, there were growing concerns that the Huguenot industrialists would come to dominate English industry and second, there had been a furore following the arrival of some 13,000 immigrants from the Rheinish Palatinate.[29] In reality, even during the three years when naturalisation had been cheap and generally available, the numbers of those who applied for it represented a small proportion of the Huguenot population – some 600 out of 40,000 to 50,000.[30] The implications are clear: virtually all the French Calvinists came to England in order to practise their religion in freedom and carry out an economic activity that would enable them to live their lives securely in a manner of their choosing. Transfer from the status of stranger to that of a British subject was low on the list of priorities. However, in the eyes of the native society, whatever legal status the 'wooden shoe' or 'frog' might acquire, until all stranger practices were eschewed, the total transformation from outsider to insider could not take place.

Unlike members of the other two groups in this study, the Huguenot refugee's physical characteristics did not immediately identify him or her as other. However, there were the obvious attributes that did. Style of dress, diet and voice were all the subject of xenophobic comment. The French immigrants were stereotyped as dandies and as beggars. French men were 'perfumed, imbroidered, patched and curled'.[31] In their excessively fashionable attire, they were idolised by some of the indigenous society as leaders of fashion and loathed by others for this and for their airs and graces. In his painting, *Noon* (1738) the artist Hogarth, who 150 years later would have answered to the description of Jingoist, caricatured the fashion-conscious foppishness of those attending the French church in Hog Lane, Soho. Gwynn suggests that the figures in the foreground of the painting are 'English mimics of French fashion'.[32] Decades before the painting appeared, the Threadneedle Street church had cautioned its congregants to eschew their 'proud and haughty airs'.[33] Two centuries later, as the tide of anti-alienism grew, the Rev. Morris Joseph of the West London Synagogue of British Jews, urged his congregants to keep a low profile and to encourage the newly arrived immigrants to assimilate as rapidly as possible.[34] If not being subjected to ridicule for their high-fashion style of dress, French Calvinists at the other end of the scale were criticised for their poverty, manifested by their clattering clogs and rags which compensated for clothes.

Comments such as '[the foreigners are] of the meanest rank and not much qualified above common beggars', were not uncommon.[35] In the outbreak of anti-Jewishness and xenophobia that accompanied the Naturalisation Bill of 1753, the slogan 'No Jews, No Wooden Shoes', was the oft-heard chant of those who protested at any easing of the passage from outsider into English-man.[36]

Poverty required that the poorest of the Huguenots existed on a diet of garlic, onions, cabbages and roots, with meat a rare luxury. The effect of this pattern of consumption was to make both consumer and adjacent open drains more than usually foul-smelling. This was a sure recipe for xenophobic sentiments. The association with food was not lost on a xenophobe who described the refugees as being 'the very offal of the earth'.[37] There are two more ingredients in the recipe of xenophobia. These are the threat the incomers pose to the health of the nation and their role as sexual predators. Huguenots who entered England were accused of both. At the opening of the eighteenth century, the French immigrants were considered by xenophobes as 'of an ill conversation and full of many loathsome diseases'. Concerns were voiced about their 'overcrowding London'.[38] At the other end of the scale, French men were portrayed as sexual philanderers who sought to attract women with their exotic dress and exaggerated manners.

Gwynn has rightly suggested that, in spite of the general dislike of the French, the refugees from France enjoyed the 'best reception of those seeking refuge in England over the centuries'.[39] The experience of the Huguenots is one of contradictions. They were objects of sympathy, having suffered the ill treatment meted out by the Catholic monarch and his ministers. However, at the same time they were perceived as strangers who threatened the receiving society with their industrial skills. The French language was seen as elitist, and indicative of a superior education, yet it also threatened the purity of English. The French immigrants combined style with vulgarity, education with ignorance and Protestant dissent with an underlying threat of popery. The deeds and words of Samuel Pepys perhaps best sum up these anomalies. For whilst he wrote, 'we do naturally all . . . hate the French',[40] he also donated money to the Huguenot cause.[41]

'Refuse of the world'[42]

The responses to the growing, and highly visible, concentration of Eastern European Jews in and around Spitalfields during the closing decades of the nineteenth and early decades of the twentieth centuries, have to be examined within the framework of the wider socio-economic landscape and the rise of anti-Semitism. The latter had been on the horizon since the mid-1870s. It followed on Benjamin Disraeli's support for the Turks after the large-scale massacre of the Bulgarian Christians and the debates taking place in Central Europe centring on Jews being perceived as a separate race, as opposed to a distinct religious group. In discussion and in print, members of the British establishment began to question whether a Jew could be a patriot.[43] In other words, could the Jew ever be sufficiently integrated and assimilated into British society that he, or she, would put nation above all else? There was no simple response to this assertion, as the paradoxical events of the First World War would demonstrate. For, whilst at the outbreak of hostilities British Jews rushed to volunteer, Eastern European Jews in Britain did all they could to avoid military service and the prospect of fighting alongside tsarist soldiers who had frequently been party to the horrors of the pogroms. As more and more aliens arrived, British Jews, who so recently had celebrated the acquisition of full emancipation, worried that their new-found status would be threatened by the presence of thousands of poor, unkempt, ill-educated, unskilled and semi-skilled 'foreign' co-religionist immigrants. There were even those members of the Jewish establishment whose uncertainties over the impact of the aliens on general attitudes to Jews in Britain, encouraged them to join forces with English anti-alienists in demanding controls on pauper alien immigration.

As was the case at the time of the Huguenot settlement, so too, in the period during which alien immigration was at its height, British politics and the economy were in flux. From the mid-1870s until almost the end of the 1900s, with a brief respite between 1888 and 1892, the economy was either in stagnation or in recession. During the 1880s levels of unemployment rose dramatically, the years between 1882 and 1886 being the peak period. It is significant that it was in 1882 that a definition of the noun unemployed, as describing someone not in work, first appeared in the *Oxford English Dictionary*.[44] Workers in the seasonal, casual and sweated industries, including clothing and shoe making, were amongst the worst affected. These were the trades in which the newly arrived semi-skilled and unskilled aliens most frequently sought, and found, work. Parallel with this was the emergence of a new approach to poverty. Certain intellectuals, social scientists and philanthropists were coming round to the view that poverty was not simply an acceptable condition of a *laissez-faire* society or market-based economy. Nor was it a state that the poor brought upon themselves. Men and women such as Charles Booth, William Morris, George Sims, Annie Besant and Clare Collett, now believed poverty to be a social *problem* and as such, one that required investigating and resolving by government. These liberal Victorians were concerned, not just with effect, but also with cause. At the same time new political ideologies were being promoted. By the mid-1880s, socialism was manifest in the form of the Social Democratic Federation and Socialist League – within a decade the Independent Labour Party would be founded. The attentions of the investigators, commentators, social scientists and socialists turned to East London, more specifically to the area by that time known as the East End. It was here that some of the worst examples of exploitation, overcrowding and poverty were to be found, and it was here, by no coincidence, that the alien hordes from Eastern Europe settled.

By the second half of the 1880s, the aliens were being held responsible for the combined evils of unsanitary working conditions, sweating, wage undercutting and blacklegging. The focal point of concerns and complaints was the sub-divisional tailoring trade in which up to five-sevenths of the male alien workforce found employment.[45] Following rumours of the transmission of diseases in garments made by workers employed in the East End tailoring workshops to their wearers, in 1884 the journal of the British Medical Council, the *Lancet*, carried out a special investigation into the 'Polish Colony of Jew Tailors' in East London. The reporter found conditions in the Jewish sweatshops to be appalling breeding places for disease. Levels of sanitation were terrible. The journal reported instances where water closets overflowed into the workshops. The environment was still further soured by the common practice of glazing poor quality fabrics with urine.[46] The published findings did little to help the reputation of the immigrants. Three years later, as the first, formal, government response to the, by then, growing furore over the alien (for alien read Jew) and the sweating system, the Board of Trade sent its labour correspondent, John Burnett, to investigate. He described the 'filthy and unsanitary' conditions he had seen in one alien workshop in Spitalfields:

> In small rooms not more than nine or ten feet square, heated by a coke fire for the pressers irons, and at night lighted by flaring gas jets, six, eight, ten and even a dozen workers may be crowded. The conditions of the Public Health Acts, and of the Factory and Workshop Regulation Acts, are utterly disregarded. . . . At a moderate computation there must be at least 2,000 sweaters in the East End of London. . . . A tour of inspection of a few of these places and of the people therein employed gives some idea of the misery and extent of the system.[47]

Having painted the picture of the workshop, Burnett went on to examine the implications for the native workforce. He concluded,

> In this way has grown up in our midst a system so bad in itself and so surrounded by adherent evils as to have caused, not only among the workers themselves, great suffering and misery, but in the minds of others grave apprehensions of public danger.[48]

This was a public reinforcement of the eugenicists' feared correlation of disease and the sweating system and the resultant threat this posed to the nation. According to some commentators at the time, the pauper aliens that settled in England were of inferior stock – 'The best go to America and we keep the refuse.'[49] The superior nature of the English working man was in danger of contamination by interaction and intermarriage with the alien, a feared outcome being 'the extermination of the British workingman in the East End of London'.[50] Even if the native working men did not altogether disappear, there was a danger that they might become weak and 'non-English in character'.[51] The dangers were not only posed by the immigrant tailoring workforce and the garments they produced, nor were they solely affecting the English male workers. As eugenicists saw it, there were far broader implications. The future well-being of the nation was in peril. Karl Pearson, who was concerned with the eugenic implications of Russian immigration, stressed, 'You cannot get a strong and effective nation if many of its stomachs are half fed.'[52] Pearson and others promoted the belief that, whilst alien immigrants took the jobs of English men and employed English females in exploitative and unclean conditions, the end result would doubtless be the birth of weakly children who either would not survive or, if they did, would become a burden on society.

The follow-up to Burnett's report was a succession of public articulations of concern and criticism directed towards the alien worker and his[53] impact on the labour market and methods of production. Most vitriol was directed at the sweaters and sweating. Even though the sweating of unskilled and necessitous labour pre-dated the so-called 'alien invasion', by the mid-1880s, both the origin and perpetuation of the system were being blamed on the economic greed of the alien sweater and the willingness of those sweated to accept the inequities of sweatshop employment. In April 1887, Arnold White, by trade a writer, by inclination a devout patriot and restrictionist, held a public meeting in Mile End, on the borders of the alien ghetto, to rally support for opposition to alien immigration. One month later in a letter to *The Times*, he used evocative imagery to register his disquiet over the 'foreign paupers replacing English workers and driving to despair men, women and children of our blood'. The theme was taken up by the East London press. On 6 August 1887 the *Eastern Argus* published the following:

> A number of men and women land on our wave-beaten shores in a destitute condition and offer to do work at any price . . . [this] drives English labour out of the labour market. All the 'Sweating system' in the East of London is carried on by cheap foreign labour.[54]

The *East London Advertiser* put the responsibility for the evils of the sweating system directly on the doorsteps of the alien Jews:

> Competition is at the bottom of all this evil – foreign competition for the most part. The swarms of foreign Jews who have invaded the East End labour market are chiefly responsible for the sweating system and the grave evils which are flowing from it. . . . If this foreign immigration can be checked half the battle against the sweating system will be over.[55]

The pressure was maintained by the Member of Parliament for Bow and Bromley, Captain Colomb, who was quoted in the *East End News* as saying that he objected, 'to England with its overcrowded population being made a human ash pit for the refuse population of the world!'.[56] Others, including the Rev. S.G. Reaney, were openly critical of what they believed was the immigrants' and their children's non-negotiable otherness. Using less sympathetic terms than one might expect from a member of the clergy, he stated that

> those who live and labour in the great East End feel hot and angry at the sight of the faces so un-English and the sound of the speech so utterly foreign. . . . In face, instinct, language and character their children are aliens, and still exiles. They seldom really become citizens.[57]

Pressure was such that the government was forced to take action and, early in 1888, it established a House of Lords Committee to investigate the sweating system. Originally intended to concentrate solely on sweating in the East End of London, and most particularly in the clothing industry, an outbreak of smallpox in the Leylands district of Leeds, another area of concentrated Eastern European settlement,[58] resulted in the Committee's remit being extended. It was to be a nationwide investigation and to incorporate other sweated trades including dock labour, lace making and chain making. The Committee sat well into 1889. Its findings and recommendations did little to redress the problem. The Committee found that the evils of sweating had been grossly exaggerated and, accordingly, there should be no immediate restrictions imposed on alien entry. However, though the alien had not been deemed culpable, no attempt had been made to attack the root cause of the sweating problem which, to paraphrase the words of Beatrice Potter, lay in the hands of the nation, not the alien. In essence, the outcome of eighteen months of evidence and analysis was that the sweating system continued unabated and would do for many decades to come. In addition, though found innocent of some of the more extreme charges, the pressure on the semi-skilled and unskilled Eastern European Jews of Spitalfields remained.

Even when the economy was in remission, calls for controls on the entry of alien labour persisted. The Liberal Unionist politician Joseph Chamberlain forcefully voiced his concern over the 'tens of thousands of foreigners who come to our shores every year who are destitute of all apparent means of subsistence and who are accustomed workmen'. Using words that seem little different to those being used 100 years on, Chamberlain articulated his fear that England was fast becoming 'the dumping ground of Europe'.[59] In an essay in his anti-alien/anti-Semitic volume, *The Destitute Alien in Great Britain*, published in 1892, Arnold White employed the metaphor of usury to highlight the way in which the alien was ousting the native worker. He declared that 'the Polish Jew drives the British Workman out of the Labour Market just as *base* currency drives a *pure* currency out of existence'.[60] Though this was a clear assault on the alien workman, was this also a suggestion that Polish Jews passed debased coins into the economy?[61] Another strident, anti-alien voice came from the Trades Union Congress, many of whose members took an extremely negative view of the alien presence. Annually, from 1890 until 1895, resolutions were laid down at Conference demanding an end to pauper alien immigration. At the 1892 Trades Union Congress Conference, representative John Hodge complained about 'The enormous immigration of destitute aliens [who] take work at any price such that the tailoring and kindred trades have been practically ruined.'[62] This was a total distortion of the truth. Hodge then went on to reinforce Burnett's findings by referring to the, 'aliens' preparedness to accept sub-standards in return for employment at rates no Englishman would accept'.[63] At the 1895 Conference, Ben Tillett, champion of the recently founded dockers' union and an organiser of unskilled labour, complained that the sweating system enabled certain aliens to 'enjoy a life of ease'.[64] In this he was no doubt alluding to middlemen and masters. Another unionist at the conference called for controls to prohibit 'the refuse of the world' from entering the country. Polish Jews, he said, were 'a blighted blister on the shoe of industry'. It was at that 1895 Conference that a resolution to stop the immigration of pauper aliens was finally passed.

All the words, findings, recommendations and resolutions did little to resolve the sweating system or put an end to the embattlement of the alien. Whilst some anti-aliens demanded immigration restrictions, others looked to the Jewish workers themselves to put an end to wage undercutting and, by so doing, enable English men to compete for work at a living wage. They were convinced that in this way native unemployment would reduce. English females could be released from the workforce and their husbands earn enough to provide for the family. As a consequence migrants would be discouraged from coming to Britain. Or at least that was the theory; in reality research has shown that the Jewish immigrants frequently did 'the jobs that Englishmen would not do'.[65] The alien worker was at the base of a chain of production, controlled by English wholesalers, whose demands for reductions in the cost of manufacture served only to reinforce the sweating system. The Jewish trade unionist Joseph Finn[66] explained this in his pamphlet, *A Voice from the Alien*, which was published in response to the Trades Union Congress Conference resolution of 1895. He argued that, rather than reduce employment opportunities, the Eastern European Jewish immigrants had increased them and thus production and the export trade. The letter written to the *Jewish Chronicle* in 1898 by the managing director of Hitchcock Williams confirmed Finn's assertion. The letter read:

> Foreign Jewish tailors introduced new methods of manufacture and created a trade which has become a distinct gain to the country's commerce. We [Hitchcock Williams] were the first wholesale mantle manufacturers to employ foreign Jewish tailors in a factory. Prior to 1889 women's mantles imported amounted to the sum of £150,000 per

annum as English female factory workers were unable to produce them. British instead of German material was used and money previously exported went to British firms. Other English firms followed the example and Germany admits loss of trade to Britain. These foreign Jews do a class of work which our workers cannot undertake with success and they earn a high rate of pay.[67]

By the time the letter was published the heat of the alien labour issue had begun to cool. It was replaced by one which would burn as fiercely and even more effectively. The issue was that of housing.

As described in Chapter 3, by the 1880s housing conditions in and around Spitalfields could be summed up as overcrowded and unsanitary. The increasing number of Eastern European Jews settling in the area served only to aggravate an already severe situation. The alien Jew, tenant and landlord alike, became the scapegoat for all inequities. This was in an era when the provision of accommodation for the poorest members of society rested in the hands of a few philanthropists and a plethora of rack-renting Jewish land-lords. The latter were to be found mostly in and around Spitalfields. Even before the census figures of 1891 and 1901 revealed the high concentration of aliens in and around the district, Jews were being criticised for their unhygienic domestic habits and their 'horrible smells'.[68] In the same year (1884) as the *Lancet* exposed the abominable conditions under which many alien tailoring workshops operated, the *East London Observer* reported on the appalling state of the immigrants' homes. In a somewhat unsavoury article, which appeared in the usually sympathetic and liberally minded newspaper, it was recorded that:

> Foreign Jews ... either do not know how to use the latrine, water and other sanitary accommodation provided, or prefer their own semi-barbarous habits and use the floor of their rooms and passages to deposit their filth. Even in places where caretakers see that yards and closets are cleared away every morning, dirt and destruction follow the same day.[69]

No doubt some of the more recently arrived immigrants from the backward *shtetls* of Russia and Poland were, initially, ignorant of the workings of the latrine. The Medical Officer for Health for Stepney reported that Jewish tenants, 'not used to sophisticated sanitary equipment', put refuse down the latrines.[70] However, the offensive conditions were not always the fault of the incomers. Jewish landlords such as Gershon Harris, the owner of Booth Street Buildings, considered amongst the worst dwellings in Spitalfields, did little to maintain their properties in a sanitary condition. It is not surprising there-fore that Charles Booth summed up the situation in the following terms:

> No Gentile could live in the same house with these poor foreign Jews and even as neighbours they are unpleasant; and since people of this

race, though sometimes quarrelsome amongst themselves are gregarious and sociable, each small street or group of houses tend to become entirely Jewish. The crowding that results is very great, and the dirt reported as indescribable. House and land values rise, however.[71]

It was not only the fear of dirt and disease that aroused disquiet amongst the native community. There was also the powerful image of the alien as invader. From the late 1880s onwards in the press and in public speeches, foreign Jews were increasingly being accused of forcing native East Enders out of their houses and streets, 'day after day, and filling up all the place. . . . There is no chance of the Christian people getting in.'[72] The indigenous Spitalfields residents were (supposedly) in constant fear of eviction due to the alien's willingness to pay the exorbitant rents demanded by their co-religionist landlords. Speaking at a meeting in his constituency in 1903, Major William Evans-Gordon graphically described the way he saw the situation:

> There is hardly an Englishman in this room who does not live under the constant danger of being driven from his home, pushed out into the streets, not by the natural increase of our own population, but by the off-scum of Europe.[73]

In both the heartland of Spitalfields, and on its periphery, English men were being forced out of their own districts by the 'scrapings of Russia and Poland'.[74]

The creation of the London County Council in 1889, and the subsequent provision of local government housing, was an attempt by the state to improve conditions in the worst parts of the capital. At the end of the 1890s, the 'Old Nicol' rookery was demolished and model dwellings, to be known as the Boundary Street Estate, the first of their kind to be provided by public funds, were built on the north side of Bethnal Green Road. In spite of the location being a traditional stronghold of the native East Ender, a number of those housed in the new flats were Jews. Estimates as to how many varied from between 27 per cent to 50 per cent.[75] The presence of the alien was not welcome, and Jews living on what became known as 'Jew's Island' became subject to sporadic violent attacks.

It was the high rents and the resultant subletting accompanying them that pushed the more unfortunate and impecunious English residents of Spitalfields outwards. Unsympathetic anti-alienists ignored the fact that for many immigrants, proximity to place of work was a prerequisite for employment. Most tailoring workshop masters and middlemen demanded that their workers live no more than half a mile from the place of manufacture. It was a vicious circle of exploitation. The only way to get a job was to live near the place of employment, which meant paying high rents. The solution to this was subletting, the outcome, extremes of overcrowding. In some instances families of nine and ten were discovered living in one room; in other situations, two families crammed onto one floor. It was not only the

Jewish landlords who benefited from the misfortunes of their less fortunate co-religionist brethren. A number of local English landlords jumped on the bandwagon, ironically putting out signs which read, 'To let, no Christians need apply',[76] rather than the usual 'Rooms to Let, every convenience, quiet house, Jews and children objected to'.[77] As the nineteenth century drew to its close, the alien landlord was being held culpable for some of the worst examples of overcrowding and unsanitary living. The following paragraph from the anti-alien *East London Advertiser* illustrates how, by 1903, the year in which the Royal Commission on Aliens was established, the Jewish landlord was coming under attack from the local press:

> The evils of housing in London are always intensified in districts where alien landlords rule. . . . The alien on his arrival knows no sanitary laws and fall an easy prey to the rack-rent landlord, who in these districts is frequently an alien Jew. It is the Jew alien landlord who sets the pace in the East End; he imposes excessive demands and goes one or more worse than the British landlord. He is merciless and unscrupulous, has elastic ideas of what constitutes a habitable dwelling and, while ostensibly more respectful of the laws and authorities than the British householder, nevertheless manages to get round both. . . . The Jewish landlord would not succeed in his methods were not his chief victims the alien tenants, for he is able with these people to raise the rents above the market rate. Aliens will insist on crowding together in certain quarters. They are more helpless than the British tenant, who migrates more easily and is more persistent in resisting oppressive demands.[78]

The article, whilst pointing the finger at the alien landlord, did at least offer some sympathy to the alien tenant. Evans-Gordon and the British Brothers League[79] did not. They sought to demonstrate that the Eastern European immigrants were indeed outsiders, emanating from a different culture and showing few signs of assimilating in the way of their English and German counterparts. In his evidence to the Royal Commission on Aliens the Stepney MP was adamant:

> The aliens will not conform to our ideas, and, above all, they have no sort of neighbourly feeling. English Jews will associate far more, and Germans will, but these Russian Poles do not appear to be able to budge an inch. A foreign Jew will take a house, and he moves in on a Sunday morning, which rather, of course, upsets all the British people there. [. . .] You will see houses with sand put down in the passages instead of oilcloth or carpet. Most extraordinary sights are seen. In one place last summer there was a kind of leads to a house with other houses backing on to it, and two alien families put out their beds on the leads and two married couples slept out on the leads, much to the amusement of all the surrounding neighbourhood.[80,81]

Evans-Gordon's statement underlines the myopic character of xenophobes and anti-alienists who either refused to accept, or did not appreciate, the fact that it takes approximately three generations for outsiders to merge with mainstream society. That is always assuming they wish to do so. Twenty-two years before his evidence to the Commission, the 'organ of British Jewry', the *Jewish Chronicle*, had expressed an equally pessimistic opinion of the alien immigrant's ability to integrate. In a censorious editorial it stated that 'They [the aliens] retain all the habits of their former home and display no desire to assimilate with the people among whom they dwell.'[82] With the passage of time both prognostications would be proven to have been ill founded.

In addition to accusations stemming from the repercussions of a depressed economy and the poor housing stock were those which had their roots in the myths and fears of old. The Whitechapel (Jack the Ripper) murders, which horrified the population, were considered by the *East London Observer* as 'such a horrible crime ... that it must have been done by a JEW',[83] and indeed for a short while a Polish Jew from Hanbury Street came under suspicion.[84] Even when the suspect was found innocent and released, the alien remained the scapegoat and rumours persisted that the Ripper must be a Jew. All six of the Whitechapel murders were perpetrated upon prostitutes in, or very close to, Spitalfields and the alien Jew's involvement with prostitution, as in the roles of pimp, white-slave trader and even prostitute, provided another weapon for the anti-alienists. Sexual antagonism and envy are regular features of xenophobic vocabulary, and the castigations of Jews emanating from those sources[85] were no more than those launched at Negro and Chinese immigrants during the same period.

The threat the alien invaders posed to the health of the nation, particularly during a period when there was widening concern over the physical efficiency of the population following the revelations of the poor condition of many of the native East Enders who had volunteered to fight the Boers, was yet another string to the bow of the anti-alienists. A number sought to expose the Eastern European Jews as foul-smelling carriers of disease and there were constant references to the fact that the foreign Jews rarely washed. Charles Booth, in his 1887 paper to the Royal Statistical Society, remarked that the Jews 'take several years to get washed', and Joseph Bannister, writing in *England under the Jews*, at the turn of the nineteenth century stated that: 'They [the Jews] may have bathed in the Jordan a couple of thousand years ago, but very few of them appear to have bathed in anything else.'[86] Furthermore, a doctor giving evidence to the Royal Commission explained that the Jew was a carrier of disease and, as a result, Britain received the 'scabby headed, the sore-eyed, the vermin infested'.[87] As he viewed it, Jews were the importers of lupus, trachoma, favus, eczema and scurvy.

If all that was said about them was true then economically, morally, socially and physically the nation would do well to impose some controls on the arrival of the pauper aliens. In an attempt to get to the truth, and in response to the increasing tensions, in 1903 the government established a Royal Commission on Aliens to investigate the impact of the alien on the British economy and society. The outcome was the 1905 Aliens Act. Paradoxically it was passed under a Tory government but entered the statute book under Liberal rule. Though less harsh[88] than some had hoped for, the Act marks a distinct watershed in British immigration history. Resulting from internal social and economic pressures rather than from the threat of war, it was the first of its kind to control immigrant entry during peacetime.

Undeniably the heritage of anti-Jewishness was the burden of all diasporic Jews in Christendom. When combined with emergent late nineteenth-century intellectual anti-Semitism, the cocktail became quite potent. In the case of the Eastern European Jews in Spitalfields, it is not always easy to draw a demarcation line between racial anti-Semitism and animosities directed at the alien because he, or she, posed a threat to native jobs and homes.[89] In certain instances, particularly in the case of men such as White, Bannister and Evans-Gordon, there was a definite fusion of the two. At times anti-Semitic sentiments were echoed at the grass roots. For example, a Stepney member of the British Brothers League demanded that 'no more Jews be brought into the country'.[90] Colin Holmes underlines the dichotomy when he writes that:

> The whole debate surrounding the Royal Commission and alien immigration which finally resulted in the 1905 legislation makes no sense unless it is understood that a discussion was taking place primarily about *Jewish* immigration. But whatever was implicit in the situation, the fact remains that the legislation was aimed at aliens rather than specifically at Jews as Jews. In the circumstances of the time 'alien' was widely interpreted as 'Jew' and, whether implicitly or explicitly, they were discussed as if they were synonymous. Nevertheless, in its form, it is more appropriate to categorize the 1905 legislation as anti-alien rather than anti-Semitic. There was nothing specifically in the legislation which discriminated against Jews as such.[91]

'Nothing specifically in the legislation which discriminated against Jews as such', maybe, but amongst those who argued for the legislation, not only was there a powerful resonance of anti-Semitism but also hints of the racism that was to follow in the years ahead.

Anti-alienism did not end with the Aliens Act or even the First World War. With the exception of the Irish, who occupied an uneasy middle place,[92] Eastern European Jews represented the largest minority ethnic group in Britain until after the Second World War. As such they remained scapegoats for the inequities of society. In the 1930s, once again against a landscape of economic depression, East End Jews were targeted by Oswald Mosley and the British Union of Fascists. Jews, many of whom now British-

born, were once again accused of taking the jobs of English men, of perpetu-
ating the sweating system and of changing the nature of the East End from
an essentially English one to that of a Jewish ghetto. Costly, inadequate and
unsanitary housing provided further food for the fascists who saw the root of
the problem stemming from 'Jew landlords with the money bags'.[93]

Whether the descriptive term is anti-alienism or anti-Semitism, at the
end of the nineteenth century and in the interwar years of the twentieth, it
was the threat to native housing and employment and the very 'peculiarness'
of the Jew that brought forth abuse and violence. Even though more than
thirty years had passed, a World War had been fought and won and the
horrors of the Holocaust revealed, the Bengali settlers in Spitalfields found,
to their cost, that once their presence impacted visually, socially and
economically, the issues and the actions of the receiving society would
hardly have changed.

'Doing a Paki'[94]

As with the other two groups, the arrival and settlement of Bangladeshis in
Britain in the second half of the twentieth century, has to be viewed within
the broader socio-economic landscape, this time one of a Britain that was
shedding its colonial dependencies and coming to terms with the local and
global repercussions. The period of the early 1950s through to the late
1960s is one during which the mother country went from eagerly recruiting
Commonwealth labour for industry and the civic infrastructures to one that
subsequently shed and then marginalized that self-same labour. At the same
time the indigenous population in areas such as Spitalfields were experienc-
ing poor housing and unemployment in conditions which, even without the
immigrant presence, would have created discontent and tension.

It was in the late 1950s that numbers of young men from what was then
East Pakistan set out for Britain looking for short-term employment that
would enable them to return home rich. Many were drawn to the midlands
and industrial north by thriving textile and industrial companies eager to
employ workers who did not mind taking the unsocial nightshifts and doing
the more unpleasant jobs. Even after the passage of the 1962 Commonwealth Immigration Act,[95] vouchers were eagerly supplied to maintain the
workforce. However, the oil crisis and recession of the early 1970s brought
redundancies and a movement south to the capital by those who believed
they would find work in the restaurants and sweatshops of the East End.
Immigration to the metropolis, combined with the start of family reunifications, served only to increase the tensions that had started to emerge in
Spitalfields.

The earliest Bangladeshi arrivals to Spitalfields did not meet with the
antipathy and violence that was to invade the lives of many immigrant
families in the 1970s, 1980s and early 1990s. Lascars had been part of East
London life since the eighteenth century and the presence of single Asian

(Bengali) males initially generated no threat. After all, they were temporary residents who intended to stay only until they had sufficient money to return to their families and villages as rich *Londoni*. It was the crossing from Cable Street to the north side of Whitechapel Road, which began in the 1960s,[96] that heralded the transition from sojourner to immigrant. From this point return became a myth. The male sojourners began to realise that their future lay not in an impressive stone-built house in a *Londoni* village, but in London's overcrowded and intensely urban East End. That short metropolitan migration marked the end of the carefree, if hard-working, bachelorhood and the beginning of family life with all its responsibilities. Having accepted that return was to be delayed, the men became keen to construct a home in the *bidesh*. This could be achieved either by reuniting with wives and children from Bangladesh or by importing new, young brides. The evolution of a community of Bangladeshis and its visible concentration in and around Spitafields began to ring alarm bells. Community equalled families and signalled permanency. Permanent settlement meant not only the proximity of an alien culture but also outsider need for housing, schooling and medical support. There was a, not unfounded, fear that further financial strain would be put on a borough which was one of the poorest in the capital – one ill served by decent social housing and jobs. Locals considered the provision of social housing to be their, not the immigrants', right. Even though during the 1970s and early 1980s Tower Hamlets Borough Council Housing Department treated the Bengalis less than fairly,[97] there were still objections to their presence on 'white' estates. In Spitalfields, in the decades that followed, reaction to that presence ranged from verbal abuse and physical assault to murder.

Unlike the past, it was not the alien threat to jobs that was most incendiary. In truth, Bengali men were doing jobs that 'English men' could not (cooking and working in the Indian restaurants) or would not (sweated labour in the leather workshops) do. The two areas of tension were housing and racial nationalism; both echoes of the past. The problems surrounding the housing of Bengali families were covered in Chapter 3. As had been the case with the Eastern European Jews in the late nineteenth century so it proved in the late twentieth century; impoverished immigrants living in overcrowded conditions created local tensions. These were further aggravated by the fear that the outsiders would seep out of their 'ghetto' into native territory. Members of the local community were apprehensive that their homes might be at risk. There was however, a significant difference between the nineteenth and twentieth centuries. In the former, there was no social housing, only privately owned dwellings, some run by philanthropic organisations, all looking for a profitable return on their investment. Thus, until 1901 and the opening of the Boundary Estate, there were no accusations of bias being shown by the local borough towards one group.[98] This was not the case in the second half of the twentieth century. Tensions rapidly developed. Long-time East Enders, intolerant of a 'mass' of outsiders, were concerned to ensure the continuing provision of decent social housing for themselves and their children (the latter known as sons and daughters allocation). In an ideal world the distribution of housing within the borough of Tower Hamlets would have been a rational and, as far as possible, an unbiased process. It was not an ideal world. As noted above, as a result of mismanagement, ignorance of the cultural and domestic needs of the immigrants and the institutionalised racism that existed in the housing offices, Bengalis were allotted some of the worst accommodation on the oldest and most rundown estates in the borough. In addition, council officials often failed to provide the information that would have enabled Bengalis to be included on the list for the better housing estates and for the correct grading qualifications.[99] In spite of this, there were those native East Enders who considered the iniquitous treatment to be justified. In a letter to the *East London Advertiser* one woman argued that, 'These people [the Bengalis] seem to be quite happy living in their own environment: after all, it's what they have made it.'[100] Others voiced their concern that the children of 'white' council tenants were being forced out of the area in order to make way for the 'coloured people'. In July 1984, a public meeting was held to discuss violence against Bengali tenants on an estate just beyond the boundaries of Spitalfields. At the meeting a racist-inspired local recommended that 'you should put all these people [the Bengalis] in Fairfoot Road – and I'll drop a petrol bomb on them'.[101] Petrol bombing of Bangladeshi homes was not just an idle threat. It soon became a practice employed by racists objecting to a minority ethnic community living in their midst.

One solution to the housing of the Bangladeshi community was suggested by the then Director of Housing for the Greater London Council in 1978. He requested that he be authorised 'to set aside a few blocks of flats in or near Spitalfields specifically for the occupation of people from Bangladesh'.[102] What *may* have been put forward as a practical solution to a current problem was interpreted as a racist attempt to create a ghetto. According to the Rev. Kenneth Leech,[103] the pronouncement forged an impressive unity between whites and Bengalis, hundreds of whom attended a meeting to protest at the possibility of a state- (or local government-) created ghetto. Less than two weeks after the plan had been mooted, it was buried following a recommendation by the Minister for the Environment, Peter Shore.[104] In a statement, Shore told the GLC that: 'It would be wrong to earmark particular blocks or estates for the explicit occupation of particular ethnic minorities.'[105] The GLC responded by confirming that housing stock would in future be allocated solely on the basis of housing need, and not on a racially segregated basis. However, as Charlie Forman has shown, this did not mean that Bangladeshis would instantly be provided with decent housing on the newer estates or that they would be treated on a totally fair basis. Gradually the older estates around Spitalfields filled up with Bengalis and, in spite of the lack of modern facilities, were in demand. Though formalised ghettoisation had been unacceptable, self-created

Bangladeshi ghettoes began to appear on the Spitalfields landscape. The knock-on effect was that, with a limited amount of housing stock available in and around Spitalfields, the GLC, and then Tower Hamlets council when it took over housing provision, had little option but to *offer* Bengalis housing on estates beyond the boundaries of Spitalfields, where they were a minority. Their arrival on the all-white estates was instantly perceived as a threat. The radius of violence now spread from core to periphery. When the immigrants were moved to better quality housing on outlying all-white estates, they were met by 'reception committees' whose sole intent was to intimidate the incomers with the hope of scaring them away. Some did move away; others, in spite of continued physical and verbal abuse, stood their ground.

In the 1890s and early 1900s, there were only the occasional violent physical attacks on aliens. In the 1970s and 1980s these became an almost weekly occurrence in and around Brick Lane. According to Richard Thurlow, it was no coincidence that the violent assaults on South Asians in Spitalfields corresponded with the rise of the National Front and its propagandising amongst teenage skinheads and football hooligans.[106] Some eighteen months after the Front's inception, in December 1969, the first racial attack by whites on 'black' people in Spitalfields took place. It is relevant to note that, until the spring of 1970, the Bengali community in Spitalfields was referred to pejoratively as 'black' – local bus drivers were reported as calling Bengalis 'bloody blacks'. It was the spring/summer 1970 edition of the journal of the Institute of Race Relations that singled out the fact that a new term had been introduced to describe assaults on Asians. It reported that 'Tower Hamlets was one of the first areas to suffer a disturbing and ugly phenomenon labelled by newspapers Paki-bashing.'[107] Though the term did not appear in the press until 1970, it was first used just beyond the border of Spitalfields, on the Collingwood Estate in Bethnal Green, in 1968. This corresponds to the time when aggressive young male whites, with razored heads, became known as 'skinheads'.[108] In April of 1970 an incident in which two Asian workers at the London Chest Hospital, in Bethnal Green, just to the east of Spitalfields, were physically assaulted, catapulted the issue and the area into the national press. The *Sunday Times* devoted an entire page to the racist persecution which was afflicting the 4,000 to 7,000 Pakistanis[109] living 'near Spitalfields Market in indescribable housing conditions'. The article revealed that in January and February of that year there had been regular attacks by skinheads on Pakistanis in Spitalfields. The writer of the article believed that the main reasons for 'Paki-bashing' were theft or 'just crude beatings up'. Some young, white, teenage attackers were even being egged on by their parents.[110] Pragmatically, the *Observer* advised that, 'Any Asian careless enough to be walking the streets alone at night is a fool.'[111] On 3 April 1970, Tosir Ali, a kitchen porter, was murdered in Bow, East London, a district of Tower Hamlets approximately one mile from Spitalfields. In Spitalfields itself, violence continued throughout the month of

April, reaching a climax when 150 young whites rampaged through Brick Lane, injuring five Bengalis. It is indicative of the nature of the racial activities of that time that the most vicious attacks on Bengalis were perpetrated by one, two or at most three attackers, in the shadows away from concentrated settlement and outside the precinct of Spitalfields. In contrast, the rampaging and racist propagandising was carried out by large groups, often in excess of 100, in and around Brick Lane, along the spine of Spitalfields.

The cycle of individual and group attacks persisted throughout the 1970s, the focal point increasingly being Spitalfields, the area which by that time held the largest proportion of Asian (Bangladeshi) immigrants. It was not by chance that during this period the National Front was a major presence in the area. The junction at which the immigrant quarter of Spitalfields met the native environs of Bethnal Green has long been a stronghold of nationalism and fascism. The extreme right-wing National Labour Party formed its East London branch in the Carpenters Arms public house in Cheshire Street (just at the top of Brick Lane) and, in the 1960s, the first incarnation of the British National Party (BNP)[112] sold their newspaper *Combat* close by the Carpenters Arms. The East London successor to the BNP was the National Front, founded in 1966–7. By the 1970s it was focusing on the newly emerging Bengali community in Spitalfields. Its leaders and their supporters set up their stalls to sell literature and make speeches in and around the northern area of Brick Lane. Their favoured pitches were under the railway arches and along Bethnal Green Road. From these pitches they would swear and spit at any Bengalis that walked past.[113] Two public houses, the Blade Bone and the Salmon and Ball, stood as guardians of white supremacy at the west and east ends of Bethnal Green Road, playing host, as they had done in the 1930s, to the advocates of fascism and racial nationalism.

Brick Lane became a centre of racist violence and, as the number of incidents mounted, the frustration of the Bangladeshi community at the inadequacy (and at times racism) of the police rose too. Young Asians, frustrated not only by police inaction but also by their elders' reluctance to respond to verbal and physical abuse, became politically activated and mobilised. These were young men who had been reunited with their fathers in the very early 1970s, just after the war of independence, at the age of fifteen or sixteen. Their experiences in Bangladesh had schooled them in political activism, as one of the founders of the Bangladeshi Youth Movement explained to David Garbin:

> My family was from a prestigious background, with a lot of land, and they were involved in anti-Pakistan politics.... So I grew up in this, political activism ... I got interested in secular politics [. . .] All these have influenced the way I was thinking in Bangladesh, but also the way I was thinking in London. Because I had a political culture. . . . So when I came to London, I was familiar with activism, and with other young

people, same as me, we did first this cultural programme, we had a drama group. And lots of racism, discriminations in Tower Hamlets, we reacted against that, it was another oppression . . . for me it was natural to get involved. Because I had this double frustration in Bangladesh and in London. . . . Anger in Bangladesh and anger in London. . . . In Bangladesh I saw the war . . . and in London, no jobs, no housing, and racial attacks every day, it was a real struggle for us.[114]

Not prepared to accept the constant harassment, the young men saw the solution in the creation of their own defence organisations. In 1976, the Anti-Racist Committee of Asians in East London, and a number of smaller Bangladeshi vigilante groups were formed. Even though in their infancy, the groups successfully organised a mass meeting in Brick Lane. This was followed by a protest march to Leman Street Police Station fronted by banners declaiming 'keep blood off the streets'. The aftermath, the arrest of a number of young Bangladeshi vigilantes yet not one white activist, served to emphasise the institutionalised racism that existed at local police level. Tensions were at their peak between March and May 1976 when thirty cases of assaults on Asians were recorded in Brick Lane. In total five Bengalis died in racial violence in London's East End in 1976.[115] The next year brought no relaxation in tension and, in June 1977, the *East London Advertiser* reported that:

Racial violence has recently centred around the Brick Lane area. The presence of National Front supporters at Sunday markets in the Lane has prompted claims and counter claims of violent attacks. The National Front has been concentrating on utilising bands of white youths to give verbal support to Front members selling newspapers in the Lane. An *Advertiser* reporter recently saw NF supporters swearing and spitting at Asians who walked past members selling papers near Bethnal Green.[116]

Street violence was accompanied by attacks on families in their homes, particularly on predominantly white council estates where Bangladeshis were in a minority. Stones were thrown through windows, excrement and petrol bombs were posted through letterboxes. In the common parts of the estates young Asian men were stabbed, beaten and kicked to the ground. However, it was the female members of the Bangladeshi community, those least likely to fight back, who were the most frequent targets. Eggs and tomatoes were thrown at them and children and young girls were kicked in the street by youths who would then run away laughing.[117] Women and young children were terrified to go out and became prisoners in their own homes. Though some families did take self-defence lessons, fear of further attack inhibited individuals and families from reporting incidents to the police. If they did the advice given was often 'Go sleep in the bathroom'.[118] Bangladeshis pleaded with the council to be rehoused. However, their cries for help rarely received a positive response.[119] The attacks continued and Spitalfields remained a centre of racist activity. A report issued by the Council for Racial Equality (CRE) in 1979 highlighted the gravity of the situation when it revealed the level of serious to fatal racist attacks. In 1976, 25 per cent of all attacks were recorded as serious to fatal. In 1977, though there was a drop in the level of 'serious', there was an overall increase in the number of attacks. Then 1978 saw a reversal of the downward trend plus a rise to 50 per cent of those assaults that were serious to fatal.[120] Kenneth Leech disputes the assumption made by the CRE that Brick Lane was the focal point for racial violence. He refers to a report by the local Trades Council which shows that most attacks on Bangladeshis in the mid-1970s took place outside the perimeter of the area and that its reputation for safety was one of the reasons the Bengalis chose to live there.[121] The organised racists chose Brick Lane and its environs for their sporadic rampages because it was the heart of the alien community, because they had safety in numbers and because these occasions provided them with headline coverage. The brutal, and often fatal, attacks on individuals took place away from the limelight in secluded and peripheral locations. That is why, from time to time, until the early 1990s, Brick Lane was the chosen location for large-scale racist demonstrations and racial assaults.

In 1978, it was one of those fatal attacks that put racism in Spitalfields back on the front pages of the national press. This time support for the besieged Bangladeshis of Spitalfields came from beyond, as well as within, its boundaries. On 4 May 1978, a twenty-five-year-old Bangladeshi machinist, Altab Ali, was murdered in Adler Street, just to the south of Spitalfields, by one black and two white youths. After the initial shock, 'a massive wave of protest' swept through East London.[122] On 14 May, 7,000 Bengalis marched behind the murdered man's coffin from Brick Lane to Downing Street. With passions high further demonstrations followed and, on 11 June, 'a major eruption of violence'. Yet again, white youths rampaged through Brick Lane, breaking shop windows, throwing bottles and lumps of concrete and damaging shops and cars. Throughout that summer there were a number of violent incidents and follow-up anti-racist marches. In spite of the cause of the demonstrations, according to Leech, police action was directed most frequently at those opposing the brutality of racism rather than at those inciting anti-Bangladeshi activity.[123]

The CRE report of events of 1978, *Brick Lane and Beyond*, was criticised by Leech for its factual omissions[124] and by the *Guardian* newspaper for its attempt at whitewashing.[125] The report referred to the area in and around Spitalfields as a 'Touchstone of deepening racial conflict and violence'.[126] The *Evening Standard* referred to Spitalfields as 'A source of almost national shame' warning that, 'A crisis is developing among the Bengali community.'[127] Throughout the 1980s the saga of violence continued, as skinheads and young hooligans were encouraged by organisations such as the National Front, British Movement, BNP, Column 88 and Combat 18.

Young thugs relished the opportunity to injure innocents such as a Bengali doctor[128] or children at Morpeth School.[129] They vandalised restaurants and Bangladeshi sweatshops and threw bricks at mosques.[130] By the end of the 1980s there had been a significant increase in brutal attacks and more fatalities, some now within the boundaries of Spitalfields. Amongst these were the murder of Ishmot Ali in a block of flats immediately behind Brick Lane Police Station and the kidnapping of Sao Miah from the Chicksand housing estate. Miah's burnt remains were discovered some time later, his murderers were not. Brick Lane may have been a popular place for Bengalis to live, but evidence shows that it was not *that* secure.

Racial violence in Tower Hamlets continued. Bangladeshis were now being rehoused beyond the boundaries of Spitalfields. Though there was a lessening of attacks within its confines, there were a number of vicious assaults beyond its boundaries. The most infamous was that perpetrated on seventeen-year-old Quddus Ali. He was left in a coma after being beaten by a gang of eight racists at the eastern edge of Whitechapel Road, almost outside the London Hospital. The attack took place in September 1993. Shortly afterwards Derek Beackon was elected a BNP[131] councillor on the Isle of Dogs, a ward of the borough of Tower Hamlets within which a number of Bangladeshis had been decanted. Beackon's election was the result of a number of factors. Primarily the local (white) residents had become disillusioned with all three mainstream political parties. Neither Labour nor the Liberal Democrats had done much for them while in control of the local council, and the Tories had not held a seat on the council for more than a decade.[132] The main gripe was housing, and what the 'Islanders' believed, erroneously,[133] was its iniquitous distribution. Locals believed the myths that had been spread around the borough claiming that Bengalis on the island were being awarded, 'All the best flats with showers'.[134] The BNP took this up and made it their campaign weapon. Beackon's success was the local community's cry for help. Initially the accession of a member of the BNP to a position of power resulted in a 300 per cent increase in racist attacks in the borough.[135] This level was drastically reduced when Beackon, who proved to be an incompetent councillor, lost his seat the following year. For a brief period, however, local racists had been spurred on by what they mistakenly interpreted as popular support.

Levels of racial violence in and around Spitalfields continued to decline throughout the 1990s and into the twenty-first century. The high profile and popularity of Banglatown with its constant inflow of visitors has acted as a deterrent against the old-style racist rampages. The most recent, if questionable, racist outbreak was the fire-bombing of the white enclave public house, The Pride of Spitalfields, in April 2003.[136] This time,[137] in a significant role reversal, young Bengalis, believing that Brick Lane was theirs,[138] threatened the 'white outsiders'.

Though one source of violence might be on the decline, another has taken its place. Now the murder and mayhem is all too often the result of internecine Bangladeshi gang warfare. Disillusioned and jobless Bengali youth on the more deprived estates have become criminalised and engaged in drug wars whilst an, albeit small, number of Bengali girls have become prostitutes in order to feed their, or their partners'/pimps' drug habits.[139] In the early years of the twenty-first century, racist rampages, abuse and violence directed at Bangladeshis and Pakistanis occurs rarely in Spitalfields, and only infrequently in the Shadwell region of London's Docklands.[140] It has moved north to the depressed, desolate and marginalised areas of Oldham, Bradford and Burnley.

Conclusion

Though the syntax and semantics underwent changes over the centuries, the verbal expressions of xenophobia, anti-alienism and racism resulting from immigrant settlement in Spitalfields display an impressive continuity. Irrespective of outward bravado, all were rooted in fear, a fear that gained potency as outsider numbers increased. The native poor feared for their jobs, and vented their irrational, and rational, anger on the wage-undercutting Huguenot silk-weavers and Jewish sub-divisional tailors. The sounds of French, Yiddish and Sylheti and the odours of stewed vegetables, of fried fish and of curry, whilst acknowledged as exotic, were nevertheless perceived as threats to the traditional East End way of life. In an area in which the tradition of sub-standard and overcrowded housing can be traced back to the writings of Stow and Strype, the supply, quality and distribution of housing has been a traditional weapon in the anti-alien battle. Housing, health and national efficiency as political issues did not reach maturity until the late nineteenth century and thus it was the Eastern European Jews who became the focus of criticism, analysis, debate and, eventually, the catalyst for immigration legislation. The association of immigrants and poor housing continued throughout the twentieth century. For the immigrants in Spitalfields poor quality housing was not their choice but their 'award', and the Bengalis, to a far greater extent than the Jews before them, became political pawns and victims in the iniquitous housing battles of Spitalfields and its surrounding wards.

It was during the period of Huguenot settlement that the British population was formulating its identity. By the 1890s the nation had been forged. The arrival of 'hordes' of pauper alien Jews, almost 120,000 settling in and around Spitalfields, threatened that identity. Those in power grew uneasy at the prospect of the dilution of British culture and purity. An articulate and literate few, obsessed by ideological racism, set out to arrest this assault on nation and nationhood. The Aliens Act of 1905 was a much watered-down outcome of what they had intended. In the decades following the end of the Second World War, the transition from a mono-cultural to a multi-cultural Britain began. As with other non-European groups, the Bangladeshis of Spitalfields suffered physically and emotionally from the nationalists' resistance to social fusion. The fascist far right, as it had done in the 1930s, once again identified, and attempted to mobilise, local and national fears. Using skinheads and poorly educated, unemployed teenagers as the agents of racism, they set out to terrorise the newest wave of Spitalfield's settlers with levels of violence the earlier arrivals had not experienced. The Bangladeshis neither fled nor weakened; they held fast and, by the end of the twentieth century, were making their contribution to the economic and cultural landscape of Spitalfields.

The one constant in the history of xenophobia in Spitalfields is the fear of strangers. The variables are the prime causes. In the case of the Huguenots it was jobs, with lesser issues including religious non-conformity, the possibility of crypto-Catholicism, diet, language, dress and, on occasions, possible fifth column activists. Being 'God's peculiar people' had made Jews outsiders and subjects of anti-Jewishness for centuries. The Eastern European Jewish immigrants' experience in Spitalfields could hardly have been expected to differ. However, it was as aliens, and their impact on jobs, homes and the threatened encroachment of territory, rather than their religious practice and the myths that accompanied it, that ignited opposition. Whether this was anti-Semitism, anti-alienism, or a combination of both, can only be determined by analysis of specific circumstances and the individuals involved. If religion set the Jews apart, then colour was what identified and separated the immigrants from Bangladesh. Until 11 September 2001 and the consequent Islamophobia, negative responses to the followers of Islam came, not from theology and practice, but rather as a result of perceived spatial and audio abuse, when those attending prayers spilled out onto the streets, or when the broadcast call to prayer threatened an intrusion into the daily lives of the local East Enders.

In the case of the Bengalis, in the 1970s, 1980s and 1990s, the grounds for racism were clearly defined as housing, 'abuse of the welfare state' and inferior otherness. 'Taking the jobs of Englishmen' was not the theme chanted by the racists, rather it was 'taking the welfare'. It was obvious to all that Bangladeshis were 'doing jobs English men would not, or could not, do'. Perhaps surprisingly, as yet there has been no attempt to use the health of the Bengali community as a racist weapon[141] in the way it was by those who sought to stigmatise Huguenots and Eastern European Jews. However, the BNP is now conforming with past traditions by endeavouring to portray Muslim men as sexual predators.[142]

Spitalfields is unique, its location and landscape having acted as a magnet for those seeking economic opportunity, religious and personal freedom and upward mobility. Yet once the number of new arrivals has reached critical mass, it is those precious liberties which have drawn forth the receiving society's negative responses. In each case, in the early stages of settlement, there have been few examples of native backlash. It is only when the host community believes its jobs, homes and culture are threatened that, with encouragement from those who manipulate fears into ammunition for their own xenophobic purposes, there has been, in the case of each of the three groups under examination in this book, literally and metaphorically, 'blood on the streets'.

The history of xenophobia, anti-alienism and racism in Spitalfields provides important lessons. These, and those elicited from the earlier chapters, are examined in the following, concluding, chapter.

Notes

1   Some of these 'natives' themselves being the descendants of earlier immigrants.
2   The plural 'societies' is used here in the temporal as opposed to spatial sense.
3   The word, which came into the English language in the early twentieth century, evolved from the Greek *xenos* meaning guest, stranger or foreigner and *phobos* meaning fear. See *Shorter Oxford English Dictionary*, Oxford, Oxford University Press, 2002 edition, p. 3688.
4   See *Shorter*, op. cit., p. 2446. For a discussion on the ideology and application of the word racism, see E. Cashmore, *Dictionary of Race and Ethnic Relations*, Routledge, 4th edition, 1996, pp. 308–11.
5   One of the most tragic and well remembered was that which occurred in May 1978 when a twenty-five-year-old Bangladeshi, Altab Ali, was murdered just south of Spitalfields in the area now known as Altab Ali Park.
6   See Douglas A. Lorimer, *Colour, Class and the Victorians*, London, Leicester University Press, 1978.
7   For more about Jacobs, see J. Efron, *Defenders of Race*, New Haven, Yale University Press, 1994, Chapter 4.
8   See T. Endelman, *The Jews of Britain 1656 to 2000*, Berkeley, Los Angeles and London, University of California Press, 2002, p. 165.
9   In 1905 rich Jews became targeted when the *Protocols of the Elders of Zion* appeared in Russia. It was a document purported to contain details of an international Jewish conspiracy to take control of the world. Although an obvious forgery, it has been reissued with regularity and even in the twenty-first century can be found on sale in certain outlets around the world.
10 C. Holmes, *John Bull's Island*, London, Macmillan, 1988, p. 296.
11 For a detailed account of the debates surrounding the alien issue, see B. Gainer, *The Alien Invasion: The Origins of the 1905 Aliens Act*, London, Heinemann Educational, 1972; J. Garrard, *The English and Immigration 1880–1910*, London, Oxford University Press, 1971; and D. Feldman, *Englishmen and Jews: Social Relations and Political Culture 1840–1914*, New Haven and London, Yale University Press, 1994, Chapter 2.
12 Robin Gwynn, unpublished Ph.D. thesis, University of London, 'The Ecclesiastical Organisation of French Protestants in England in the Later Seventeenth Century, with Special Reference to London', 1976, p. 240.
13 See Linda Colley, *Britons: Forging the Nation 1707–1837*, London, Vintage, 1996, Chapter 1.
14 Ibid.
15 D. Statt, *Foreigners and Englishmen: The Controversy over Immigration and Population 1600–1760*, London and Toronto, Associated University Press, 1995, p. 171.
16 Ibid., p. 172.
17 Gwynn thesis, op. cit., p. 262.
18 Ibid., p. 54.
19 Ibid., p. 261.

20 B. Cottret, *The Huguenots in England: Immigration and Settlement 1550–1700*, Cambridge, Cambridge University Press, 1991, p. 242.
21 Ibid., p. 110.
22 Statt, op. cit., p. 183.
23 Gwynn thesis, op. cit., p. 117.
24 See G. Rudé, *Paris and London in the Eighteenth Century: Studies in Popular Protest*, New York, Viking, 1971, p. 50.
25 Gwynn thesis, op. cit., p. 121.
26 Tessa Murdoch, *The Quiet Conquest: The Huguenots 1685–1985*, London, Museum of London, 1985, p. 308.
27 Ibid., pp. 177–8.
28 R. Gwynn, *Huguenot Heritage: The History and Contribution of the Huguenots in Britain*, Brighton, Sussex Academic Press, 2001 edition, pp. 151–2.
29 Statt, op. cit., p. 20.
30 Ibid., p. 37.
31 Ibid., p. 189.
32 Gwynn, *Huguenot*, op. cit., facing p. 111.
33 Gwynn thesis, op. cit., p. 261.
34 A.J. Kershen and J. Romain, *Tradition and Change: A History of Reform Judaism in Britain 1840–1995*, Ilford, Vallentine Mitchell, 1995, p. 96.
35 Statt, op. cit., p. 138.
36 The riots which followed the passage of the Bill, which became known as the Jew Bill, were in the main directed against the Jews, who as a result of the Bill would have been able to become naturalised British subjects through an Act of Parliament without taking the Sacrament.
37 H.L. Smith, *The History of East London from the Earliest Times to the End of the Eighteenth Century*, London, Macmillan, 1939, p. 92.
38 B. Coward, *The Stuart Age 1603–1714*, London, Longman, 1980, quoted in Gwynn, thesis, op. cit., p. 113.
39 Gwynn thesis, op. cit., p. 124.
40 *Diary Pepys 11*, p. 188 quoted in Statt, op. cit., p. 191.
41 C. Tomalin, *Samuel Pepys: The Unequalled Self*, London, Penguin, 2002, p. 343.
42 This was the way one trade unionist referred to the Eastern European immigrants during a debate on pauper aliens at the Trades Union Congress Conference of September 1895 which was reported in the *Jewish Chronicle*, 13 September 1895.
43 G. Smith, 'Can Jews Be Patriots?' *Nineteenth Century*, London, May 1878, pp. 878–97. For a detailed account of Disraeli and attitudes during the Balkan Crisis, see Feldman, op. cit., Chapter 4.
44 See W.J. Fishman, *East End 1888*, 2nd edition, London, Hanbury, 2001, p. 49.
45 For a full account of the alien involvement in the tailoring trade in Spitalfields, see A. Kershen, *Uniting the Tailors*, Ilford, Frank Cass, 1995.
46 See the *Lancet*, 5 March 1884 and Kershen, *Uniting*, op. cit., p. 110.
47 *Report to the Board of Trade on the Sweating System at the East End of London*, 1887, PP LXXXIX, London, pp. 4–7.
48 Ibid.
49 Quoted in Gainer, op. cit., p. 113.
50 Ibid.
51 Ibid.
52 See Karl Pearson and Margaret Moul, 'The Problem of Alien Immigration into Great Britain; Illustrated by an Examination of Russian and Polish Jewish Children', *Annals of Eugenics*, Vol. I, October 1925, pp. 5–127.

53 Jewish women never featured in the surveys or castigations. Jewish women 'did not work' (see Chapter 7). However, irrespective of the reality, they were not referred to in the debates and criticisms.
54 *Eastern Argos*, 6 August 1887.
55 *East London Advertiser*, 3 March 1888.
56 *East End News*, 21 February 1888.
57 A. White (ed.), *The Destitute Alien in Great Britain*, London, Sonnenschein & Co., 1892, p. 20.
58 For detail on the Eastern European Jewish community in Leeds during the late nineteenth and early twentieth centuries and their engagement in the sweated trades, see Kershen, *Uniting*, op. cit., Chapters 2 and 3.
59 Quoted in G. Drage, 'Alien Immigration', *Fortnightly Review*, Vol. LVII (1895), pp. 37–46.
60 White, op. cit., p. 59.
61 I am grateful to Todd Endelman for suggesting the possibility of this additional accusation.
62 Gainer, op. cit., p. 136.
63 White, op. cit., p. 110.
64 Gainer, op. cit., p. 56.
65 Kershen, *Uniting*, op. cit., p. 28.
66 For details of Finn; see Kershen, *Uniting*, op. cit., pp. 63–8.
67 *Jewish Chronicle*, 22 April 1898.
68 Feldman, op. cit., p. 183.
69 *East London Observer*, 22 November 1884.
70 White, op. cit., p. 63.
71 Charles Booth, *Life and Labour, of the People of London*, Vol. I, 3rd series, London, Williams & Norgate, 1889, pp. 1–2.
72 Gainer, op. cit., p. 42.
73 Ibid., p. 36.
74 *Eastern Post*, 31 August 1901.
75 See London County Council, *Minutes of Proceedings*, Report of the Housing of the Working Classes Committee, 17 March 1903.
76 Gainer, op. cit., p. 43.
77 *East London Observer*, 21 April 1906.
78 C. Holmes, *Anti-Semitism in British Society 1876–1939*, London, Edward Arnold, 1979, pp. 15–16.
79 The British Brothers League was founded in the East End of London in 1901 and actively agitated against the pauper aliens and Jewish alien immigration between 1901 and 1905. See Holmes, ibid., pp. 89–97.
80 A 'lead' was in fact a lead roof, and it was common practice in the very hot weather to put beds out on the roof.
81 Ibid., p. 29.
82 *Jewish Chronicle*, 12 August 1881.
83 Quoted in Fishman, *East End 1888*, London, Hanbury, 2001, p. 217, from *East London Observer*, 15 September 1888.
84 Fishman, *1888*, op. cit., p. 217. For an account of the Whitechapel murders, see ibid., pp. 209–23.
85 See E. Bristow, *Prostitution and Prejudice: The Jewish Fight against White Slavery 1870–1939*, Oxford, Oxford University Press, 1982, pp. 236–43.
86 Bannister quoted in Holmes, *Anti-Semitism*, op. cit., p. 40.
87 Quoted in ibid., p. 38.
88 The Act did not put an end to the entry of aliens, rather it imposed some controls in order to ensure that those allowed entry were to some extent self-sufficient and

healthy. The right of asylum for those escaping political and religious persecution was maintained.

89 Colin Holmes considers this issue with clarity and depth in *Anti-Semitism*, op. cit., pp. 89–103.

90 Ibid., p. 96.

91 Ibid., p. 101.

92 See Roger Swift and Sheridan Gilley (eds), *The Irish in Britain*, London, Pinter Publishers, 1988, Chapter 1.

93 R. Skidelsky, *Oswald Mosley*, Basingstoke, Macmillan, 1981 edition, p. 395.

94 'Doing a Paki' was a term used by racist thugs to describe a violent attack on a Bangladeshi youth. See Submission to Part 2 of Sir William Macpherson's Inquiry into the matters arising from the death of Stephen Lawrence, http://www.file:C:\SUBMISSION.htm (accessed 12 January 2004).

95 The 1962 Act introduced vouchers for Commonwealth citizens wishing to work in the UK. There were three types: those given to employers in the UK to bring in workers; those issued to skilled applicants; and those issued to 'others'. The workers from Bangladesh fell into the first and third categories.

96 See Chapter 3 above.

97 See C. Forman, *Spitalfields: A Battle for Land*, London, Hilary Shipman, 1989.

98 The Boundary Estate was the first to be built, distributed and maintained by local government. Thus by the beginning of the twentieth century the criticisms of preference began to be heard.

99 Forman, op. cit., p. 212.

100 Letter written in August 1982, quoted in Forman, op. cit., p. 187.

101 Ibid., p.188.

102 Leech, op. cit., p. 16.

103 Ken Leech lived and worked in the East End from 1958 until 2004. For most of that period he was the priest of St Botolph's Church, Aldgate and very much involved with issues surrounding the local community, native and immigrant.

104 *Guardian*, 14 June 1978.

105 Ken Leech, *Brick Lane 1978*, Birmingham, AFFOR, 1980, p. 16.

106 See Richard Thurlow, *Fascism in Britain: A History 1918–1985*, Oxford, Blackwell, 1987, p. 282.

107 *Race Relations*, Spring/Summer 1970 (no place of publication nor publisher).

108 Kenneth Leech in conversation with the author, 2 February 2004.

109 It has to be remembered that until the establishment of the independent state of Bangladesh, the people living in Spitalfields – who were predominantly from Sylhet – were classified as Pakistani. Even after the establishment of Bangladesh, attacks on its nationals in Britain remained known as Paki-bashing.

110 *Sunday Times*, 19 April 1970.

111 *Observer*, 5 April 1970.

112 The BNP was formed in 1960 by the merging of the White Defence League and the National Labour Party; another group was based in Leeds and flourished in the 1970s. At the end of the 1970s the National Front went into terminal decline and splintered, one sector, the New National Front, metamorphosing into the BNP in 1982. In the decade that followed other splinter groups aligned with it and a third group emerged in the 1990s.

113 *East London Advertiser*, 3 June 1977.

114 David Garbin, 'Migration, territoires diasporiques et politiques identitaires: Bengalis musulmans entre "Banglatown" (Londres) et Sylhet (Bangladesh)', unpublished Ph.D. thesis, University of François Rabelais de Tours, 2004, p. 303.

115 *Guardian*, 6 June 1977.
116 *East London Advertiser*, 3 June 1977.
117 See *The Times*, 23 December 1977.
118 *The Next Step*, No. 9, (no publication details) November–December 1980.
119 *Morning Star*, 30 April 1975.
120 *Brick Lane and Beyond*, London, CRE, 1979, p. 28.
121 Leech, op. cit., p. 20.
122 *East London Advertiser*, 12 May 1978.
123 Leech, op. cit., p. 11.
124 Ibid., pp. 18–23.
125 *Guardian*, 7 April 1979.
126 Leech, op. cit., p. 4.
127 *Evening Standard*, 25 July 1979.
128 See *Sunday Times*, 8 February 1981.
129 *East London Advertiser*, 17 January 1986.
130 *East London Advertiser*, 7 November 1986.
131 This was the first time a member of the BNP, or any such right-wing extremist party, was elected to any local or national government position.
132 It is only very recently that the Tories gained their first seat on Tower Hamlets council for some twenty years.
133 Bob Brett, at the time Housing Director for the Isle of Dogs, told the author that, though it was true that some Bengalis in the west of the borough were being awarded good quality housing, this was certainly not true of those living in the eastern parts of the borough. The accusations being made were based on nothing more than rumour which had spread from west to east. Bob Brett in discussion with the author, 18 February 2004.
134 Bob Brett, one-time Director of Housing in Tower Hamlets, in conversation with the author, 18 February 2004.
135 <SUBMISSIONCL>, op. cit.
136 Though no proof exists, Kenneth Leech believes that the fire-bombing was carried out by young Bengalis; to author, 2 February 2004.
137 The information comes from the Rev. Kenneth Leech in conversation with the author on 2 February 2004.
138 See previous chapter.
139 In an attempt to combat drug-taking by young Bengalis, the local mosque and local social services have joined together in an outreach group.
140 However, in April 2001, Shiblur Rahman, a middle-aged Bengali restaurant worker was stabbed to death in Bow by a group of white thugs shouting racist slogans when he returned from work late at night.
141 Research carried out by Dr Veronica White, now a consultant at Barts and the Royal London Hospitals, has shown a marked rise in cases of tuberculosis in Tower Hamlets over the past decade. Information given to the author by Dr White, 14 November 2003.
142 On the BBC 1 television programme, *The Secret Agent*, shown on 15 July 2004 at 9 pm, the Chairman of the BNP, Nick Griffin, was shown making a speech in which he accused Muslim men of using white women for sex in a casual and disrespectful way.

Conclusion

The foregoing chapters have provided an opportunity to explore the immigrant experience at grass-roots level and, in the words of the introduction, examine some of 'the dynamics which drive the processes of settlement and assimilation'. The intention has been to discover whether those dynamics are solely determined by the time and the place(s) of settlement; whether they are the perennial rites of passage that any migrant, anywhere, must undergo; or whether they are an amalgam of both. In this book, I have highlighted specific aspects of the migratory and assimilative experiences of seventeenth- and eighteenth-century Huguenots, late nineteenth-century Eastern European Jews and twentieth-century Bangladeshis in Spitalfields. The cultural, religious, geographic and temporal disparities identified at the outset suggested that, for each group, the process would be very different. However, as has become apparent, there were, in fact, distinct similarities in their experience and it is only by comparing and contrasting the patterns of settlement that a fully informed response to the question which lies at the heart of this book can be made.

It was only in the last decades of the nineteenth century that geographers began to think about the implications of, and forces behind, the local, regional and national movement of people. It was Ravenstein who put forward a series of laws which subsequently became condensed into the 'push and pull' theory. For hundreds of years people had been moving voluntarily or as a result of coercion; singly or in groups; as pioneers or as components of a 'chain'. They were pushed and pulled by the effects of mercantilism, Empire-building, globalisation or simply by human need and desire. Yet it was only from the 1970s onwards that more advanced theories were forthcoming. The outcome has been a multiplicity of theories, some of which completely dismiss 'push and pull', while others accept it as a starting point. No single theory can satisfactorily account for the phenomenon and effect of migration. It has become increasingly apparent that, in the complex world of the twenty-first century, a flexible approach is essential when selecting theoretical and typological tools.

I believe that, except in the case of removal by force, there exists, in varying proportions, a push and pull factor in all migrations. This was certainly the case with the migrant groups featured in this book, a common denominator being the magnetism of the eastern environs of London. Even so, there were variations. The economic structure of Spitalfields, its location in close proximity to the City and West End of London, and the prospects this offered immigrants with energy and initiative, was a powerful attraction. Yet the reputation of Spitalfields as a sanctuary for religious and political dissidents is not to be underestimated. Whilst, for some, the pull was a definable single factor, there were many for whom the coalition of human rights[1] and job opportunities in a capital city made Spitalfields the perfect choice as a first point of settlement. The same was true of the forces that drew the migrants away from their homes. In certain instances, the reasons for departure were separately identifiable as religious persecution, diminishing economic opportunity or denial of political freedom. At other times, it was a fusion of all three. For while some Eastern European Jews and most Huguenots left their homelands because of religious discrimination, a minority of Huguenots, most Eastern European Jews and nearly all the Bengali males,[2] immigrated to Spitalfields in the belief that it offered economic potential in the form of jobs or entrepreneurial prospects. At the same time, some Huguenots, whose primary reason for emigration was the search for religious freedom, chose London because of the nascent silk trade, similarly, some Jews, escaping the pogroms, headed for Spitalfields because of its burgeoning tailoring trade. An appreciation of the balance of these factors is important when evaluating specific migrant experiences.

Even more important is an awareness of a circumstance rarely considered when the big picture of migration is under the microscope, namely, that of the heterogenous nature of what, too frequently, are portrayed as homogenous, diasporic communities. Both historically, and at the time of writing, commentators and critics have been predisposed to ignore diversity within outsider groups. As with all communities, beneath the carapace of all-embracing religion or ethnicity are to be found varying levels of skill, intellect, education, economic status, religiosity, politics and personal ambition, playing their parts in the migrant decision-making process and in the pattern of immigrant settlement. Rarely is there reference to the diverse cultural and geographic backgrounds of peoples who are simplistically categorised under the collective description of either Muslim or Jew. In the current climate of concern over the movement and settlement of migrants, an awareness and appreciation of internal group diversity would make the analysis and resolution of immigrant needs and expectations less stressful and more rewarding.

Though the physical boundaries of Spitalfields have altered little since the seventeenth century, and though some of the buildings that were home to Huguenot silk-weavers, Jewish tailors and Bengali squatters still stand (although now inhabited by affluent professionals), the landscape of today is not that of yesterday. It is encrusted with layers of personal and group experience, built on the physical and emotional outcome of the inhabitants' desires and needs, their hopes and sorrows, their successes and failures. Central to all of these, at different stages of the assimilation process, is the place of religion and its structural manifestation. Although the Huguenots could not have foreseen it, and the latest inhabitants might be reluctant to acknowledge it, the three groups are inextricably linked by one historic building that stands on the corner of Brick Lane and Fournier Street. Whether church, synagogue or mosque, it is, and has always been, a visual reminder of the presence of God – the one and same God of Calvinists, Jews and Muslims – in the lives of the migrants of Spitalfields. As described in Chapter 4, the level and pace of absorption into the mainstream proved influential in determining the subsequent pattern of observance and practice. For Huguenots and Jews, part of the transition from outsider to insider was the Anglicisation of ritual and liturgy. As Claude Montefiore, co-founder of the Liberal Jewish movement remarked, 'I am an Englishman of the Mosaic persuasion.' For him being a Jew and being an English man were not mutually exclusive. One served to enrich the other.[3]

However, if the migrant experience was one of real, or even perceived, rejection and marginalisation, then the adoption of an essentially Anglicised form of worship had no appeal. Some marginalised incomers reacted by adhering to a mode of religious practice which did not conform to the ways of the majority society. Rather, the immigrant selected a place of worship which provided a refuge from that which alienated and within which the outsider could become the insider. It may be in the style of one that is reminiscent of home and cultural background, as was true of the *shtetl* Jews in the early years of settlement in Spitalfields and Hasidic Jews more recently. Alternatively, others remained loyal to a supra-national branch of Christianity, as was the case of many Roman Catholic Irish immigrants in nineteenth-century London. Whilst occupying that middle place between insider and alien, within 'their' church which looked beyond the nation-state to Rome for leadership, the Irish migrants could put aside alienation and marginalisation. As Chapter 4 and Chapter 8 illustrate, this has also been true for many young Muslims. Islam unites. It has restored pride and confidence to those disillusioned in the diaspora and has enabled young Bengalis, female as well as male, to make academic and career inroads in what many had considered hostile territory.[4] In the world of the migrant, religion is a multi-purpose tool. It can be an aid to integration, a link between over here and over there, as well as a sanctuary from the inhospitality of the receiving society.

The time-span over which the migrant prioritises religion does vary. It might just be for the period of transition from outsider to insider or it might continue on throughout the diasporic journey. However, not all new arrivals from the three subject groups examined turned to religion for support during the integration process. There were those who considered it an unnecessary and unwanted mechanism of control, one to be temporarily ignored or completely rejected. At times, the reception provided by the host society often influenced the migrant's future religious route. As illustrated above, on arrival some young male Muslims put their religion to one side whilst tasting the secular pleasures on offer. However, once the family had been reunited and the pressures of marginalisation and discrimination had become hard to bear, a return to Islam became a distinct option.

Chapter 5 highlights that one pillar of religion that remained common to the three protagonist groups of this book was charity, the provision of a means of support by co-religionists and/or co-patriots for incomers unable to support themselves. The presence of an established diasporic community ensured that needy seventeenth- and eighteenth-century French Calvinists and nineteenth-century Eastern European Jews were provided for without their having to apply to the local Poor Law Board, always a last resort for those unable to fend for themselves. The absence of an earlier settled and affluent Bangladeshi community resulted in pioneer Bengali arrivals having to rely on their own, informal, support systems. Charity collected in the *bidesh* was distributed where it was needed most, in Bangladesh. However, as we have seen, contrary to the view promoted by anti-immigrationists, in the early period of settlement, few of the single male Bengali arrivals applied for, or received, welfare benefit. Those who needed it most tended to be the uninformed or ill informed who suffered unnecessary hardship through not having claimed for what, at the time, was theirs by right.

There are certain lessons to be learnt from the experience of all three groups. First, the presence of an established, affluent, co-diasporic community does ensure that, initially at least, indigent arrivals will be monitored and cared for. Second, the existence of a welfare state does not automatically guarantee that the needy will receive designated state benefits; ignorance and embarrassment often stand in the way. Finally, it should be noted that both co-diasporics and the receiving society operate on the mistaken perception that the provision of welfare (whether state or charitable) is the most powerful force in attracting economic migrants and asylum seekers. As a result, in order to prevent a flood of immigrants, governments impose residency, age and ability restrictions on those who may, or may not, receive support. Even the Huguenots and Jews imposed a six months residency qualification on the distribution of charity, concerned that their co-religionists 'over there' might emigrate for the wrong reasons. This approach flies in the face of history, which shows that immigrants, and those refugees who have the freedom to do so, select a first point of settlement principally because it offers an opportunity to satisfy the *raison d'être* of migration, namely the creation of a future for themselves and their families. Migrants migrate because they wish to lead a productive existence.

In order to pursue that productive existence, the basic needs have to be satisfied. The migrant's ideal shopping list would be: decent accommodation, a job, an ability to interact with mainstream society and a non-hostile environment. How successful were the members of our three protagonist groups in achieving these goals? For the Eastern European Jews and the

Bangladeshis, housing proved a major problem in terms of both availability and suitability. In contrast, there was no such problem for the Huguenots, who either lived in the poor, mean houses of Stow's description,[5] or in newly built, elegant homes which, as a result of material success, enabled them to glorify God.

The language barrier was one that all had to cross. Some did so successfully, others never attempted the journey. However, as far as jobs were concerned, deficiency in the majority language was not necessarily an inhibiting factor. Those Huguenots, Jews and Bangladeshis who were inarticulate in the majority language still found employment with co-patriots or co-religionists, many of whom lost no opportunity to exploit the more recent arrivals.

From the seventeenth century through to the twenty-first, immigrants have been accused of wage-undercutting and the experience of the Huguenots, Eastern European Jews and Bengalis was no different. Despite some immigrants being employed in jobs that English men would just not do,[6] xenophobes, anti-aliens and racists still sought to convey the impression that immigrants were taking employment away from native workers. And while that myth portrayed Huguenots and Eastern European Jews as successful entrepreneurs and ideal examples of economic man,[7] the reality was that, particularly in the case of the Jews in late nineteenth-century Spitalfields, there were actually few success stories. Immigrant achievement takes a long time, often generations, and that is why it is difficult to measure the level of success of the Bengali settlers at this early stage. The signs are that this group is indeed breeding its own entrepreneurs, their success now becoming visible, not only in the *Londoni* villages and in Sylhet town, but also on the streets of Spitalfields.

The migrant's dream is that assimilation and integration can take place within a peaceful, non-aggressive environment. Whilst this is often the case when immigrant numbers are small, as the concentration of a specific stranger group becomes larger and more visible, tensions emerge. As the outsiders' position changes, when claims are made on territory and when the alien appears to be seeking legitimation by establishing local rootedness and, by so doing, threatens the power and position of the established community, receiving-society affability all too often turns to hostility. The status quo is transformed from one of peaceful co-existence to one of outright aggression. As the French language increasingly echoed through the streets, as the smell of their 'roots' pervaded the air and French weavers became 'profitable strangers', sympathy and compassion were replaced by xenophobia and, at times, violence. When increasing numbers of foreign Jews settled in and around Spitalfields, working all hours in unhygienic workshops and exacerbating the existing housing problem, it would have been surprising if their presence and difference had not brought forth a negative response. Speech, diet, dress and physiognomy became objects for stigmatisation. The Eastern European Jews, even if not different in skin colour to the majority of the population in Britain, were physiognomically stereotyped and as such were still racialised; a precursor perhaps to the more recent perception of the Irish as the 'white blacks'.[8]

Although skin colour is a key factor, it is not, and has not been, the sole stimulus for a racialised response to the outsider presence. However, by the time of the large-scale Bengali arrival in the late 1950s and early 1960s, racism related to colour was firmly on the xenophobe agenda and a focal point for political and grass-root activists. Having identified Bangldeshis as 'black', the response to their presence was indicative of the racist mentality that existed in Britain at the time. The South Asians were not white, ergo they were black and, even though after 1971 they were Bangladeshis not 'Pakis', the racists continued with what was for them a pejorative coding.

Having presented the evidence, what are the findings? It has become obvious that there are principal rites of passage all immigrants must go through, namely: a) the acquisition of suitable accommodation and employment in a non-hostile environment which offers future prospects; and b) once the first roots are laid down, through family reunification or by marriage with a partner from either the sending or receiving society, the process of (re)constructing home in the elsewhere. These are the constants of settlement and form part of the immigrant experience irrespective of whether it is taking place in the seventeenth or the twenty-first century. There is one contemporary exception to this rule. This relates to the transnational migrants whose rootedness lies within themselves and for whom territoriality is unimportant.[9]

From the moment of departure and throughout the diasporic journey, the migrant changes, from the person that existed over there to the one that will live over here. Whether the journey from *mon pays*, *der heim* or the *desh*, took two days, two weeks or two months, whether it was by train, boat, plane or on foot, migrants, some of whom may never before have travelled more than a few miles from home, saw different landscapes,[10] met with other nationalities, heard other languages, smelt (if not ate) other foods, and experienced separation from home and family. Their lives were enriched by the experience of migration. They would never be the same again. They had gone through the first rite of passage and now identified themselves differently and were identified differently by others. No longer insiders and one of us, they had become outsiders and one of them. As such, on arrival in the place of settlement they remained close to the ghetto, the familiar and the welcoming. However, change is not one-sided. The presence of each group made its own unique impact on the landscape of Spitalfields, overlaying what had stood before with Petty France, Little Jerusalem and Banglatown. They changed not only place, but people. Over the centuries the indigenous population was surrounded by new religions, foreign dress and new foods. Though doubtless many indigenes would automatically reject the notion, in truth their lives too were altered and 'enriched'.

As well as the similarities in the experience of the three migrant groups, there are also differences, and not all of a positive nature. Whilst the Huguenots and Jews were subjected to vocal and, at times, physical xenophobia and anti-alienism, the Bengali experience of such attitudes has been more virulent. As Chapter 8 revealed, a number of Bangladeshis have been murdered for these reasons, one death occurring as recently as 2003. Even in the 1930s and 1940s, during the years when Oswald Mosley and his Blackshirts paraded on the periphery of Spitalfields, no Jews were actually killed. So how is this increase in the degree of violence to be explained? Does the answer lie specifically in the changing nature of racism over the centuries or in the general trend towards social malaise and lack of discipline and respect that has become a part of twenty-first-century Britain? This must remain an open question until all the evidence is at hand, though the socio-economic marginalisation of certain diasporic groups; the influence of drugs on perceptions of right and wrong; the portrayal of violence by the media as something glamorous; and the incidence of institutionalised racism do little to ease tensions in deprived areas where there is a significant ethnic-minority presence. Other differences referred to in earlier chapters can be identified in the light of the established history of the Huguenot and Eastern European Jewish settlement in Spitalfields. The full history of the Bengali community is still to be written. Accordingly, a complete analysis cannot be made until one, or even two, more generations have been allowed to pass.

Spitalfields provides a perfect laboratory for an exploration of the different stages of migration and settlement. It, and its inhabitants, demonstrate both the permanent and the transitory states. The former is a canvas upon which strangers in a foreign land can paint their preferred landscape. The latter is merely part of the permanency for a brief moment in time. For hundreds of years in Spitalfields, insiders and outsiders have come face to face with each other. Some have come to terms with difference and have interacted at work and at play. Others have remained separate and remote from the mainstream. Unequivocally, as the incomer and host societies come together, it is in the hands of both of them to decide to what extent they are prepared to adapt and thus determine the success or failure of the migrant's rites of passage.

Notes

1 Particularly compared to life in Catholic France or the Pale of Settlement.
2 A very small, unquantifiable number, left Bangladesh as asylum seekers, having opposed the governing regime.
3 A.J. Kershen and J. Romain, *Tradition and Change: A History of Reform Judaism 1840–1995*, Ilford, Vallentine Mitchell, 1995, p. 116.
4 This issue was one discussed by four young women on the BBC 1 *Panorama* programme, shown on 13 June 2004, at 10.15 pm. All wearers of the veil, they believed that this should be of no hindrance in their academic and professional careers.
5 J. Stow, *Survey of London*, Oxford, Clarendon, 1908 edition, p. 116.
6 See for example, A. Kershen, *Uniting the Tailors*, Ilford, Frank Cass, 1995, p. 28.
7 See before, Chapters 7 and 8.

8 See B. Walter, '"Shamrocks Growing out of Their Mouths": Language and the Racialisation of the Irish in Britain', in A. Kershen (ed.), *Language, Labour and Migration*, Aldershot, Ashgate, 2000, pp. 57–73.

9 For a discussion on this, see D. Kaplan, 'Territorial Identities and Geographic Scale', in G. Herb and D. Kaplan (eds), *Nested Identities: Nationalism, Territory and Scale*, Oxford and Maryland, Rowan and Littlefield, 1999, pp. 31–52.

10 Some Eastern European Jews had never seen the sea before they embarked to sail to Britain.

Bibliography

Abramsky, C., Jachimczk, M. and Polonsky, A. (eds), *The Jews in Poland*, Oxford, Blackwell, 1986.

Ackroyd, P., *London: The Biography*, London, Chatto and Windus, 2000.

Adams, C., *Across Seven Seas and Thirteen Rivers*, London, Thap Books, 1987.

Adams, G., *The Huguenots and French Opinion 1685–1787*, Waterloo, Ontario, Wilfred Laurier University Press, 1991.

Agnew, D., *Protestant Exiles from France in the Reign of Louis XIV*, London, Reeves and Turner, 1869.

Aiming High: Raising the Achievement of Minority Ethnic Pupils, Department of Education and Skills consultation document, ref: DfES/0183/2003, March 2003.

Alderman, G., *London Jewry and London Politics 1889–1986*, London, Routledge, 1989.

—— *The Federation of Synagogues 1887–1987*, London, Federation of Synagogues, 1987.

Ali, M., *Brick Lane*, London, Doubleday, 2003.

Alibhai-Brown, Y., *After Multiculuralism*, London, The Foreign Policy Centre, 2000.

Alladina, S. and Edwards, V., *Multilingualism in the British Isles*, Vol. 1, London, Longman, 1991.

Anwar, M., *The Myth of Return: Pakistanis in Britain*, London, Heinemann Educational, 1979.

Asghar, M.A., *Bangladeshi Community Organisations in East London*, London, Bangla Heritage Ltd, 1996.

Banton, M., *The Coloured Quarter: Coloured Migrants in an English City*, London, Cape, 1955.

Beaufort, W.M., *Records of the French Protestant School*, Lymington, (publisher unknown), 1894.

Black, E., *The Social Politics of Anglo-Jewry 1880–1920*, Oxford, Blackwell, 1988.

Black, G., *J.F.S: A History of the Jews' Free School since 1732*, London, Tymsder Publishing, 1998.

Blacker, H., *Just Like It Was: Memoirs of Mittel East*, Ilford, Vallentine Mitchell, 1974.

Bloch, A., 'It's Not Working: Refugee Employment and Urban Regeneration', in A. Kershen (ed.), *Language, Labour and Migration*, Aldershot, Ashgate, 2000.

Booth, C., *Life and Labour of the People of London*, 1st series, Poverty, Vol. IV, London, Williams & Norgate, 1890–2.

—— *Life and Labour of the People of London*, Vol. I, 3rd series, London, Williams & Norgate, 1889; London, Macmillan, 1889.

Borjas, G., 'Economic Theory and International Migration', *International Migration Review*, 23 (3), 1989.

Brick Lane and Beyond, London, CRE, 1979.

Bristow, E., *Prostitution and Prejudice: The Jewish Fight against White Slavery 1870–1939*, Oxford, Oxford University Press, 1982.

Burman, R., 'Jewish Women in Manchester, c. 1890–1920', in D. Cesarani (ed.), *The Making of Modern Anglo Jewry*, Oxford, Blackwell, 1992.

Calabash, London, Black Literature Development Project, autumn 1999.

Carey, S. and Shukur, A., 'Profile of Bangladeshi Community in East London', *New Community*, 12 (3), 1985–6.

Cashmore, E., *Dictionary of Race and Ethnic Relations*, 4th edition, London, Routledge, 1996.

Castles, S. and Miller, M., *The Age of Migration*, New York and Basingstoke, Palgrave Macmillan, 2003 edition.

Chalmers, R., 'Paths and Pitfalls in the Exploration of British Bengali Identity', in A. Kershen (ed.), *A Question of Identity*, Aldershot, Ashgate, 1998.

—— *Learning Sylheti*, London, Centre for Bangladeshi Studies, 1996.

Choudhury, Y., *The Roots and Tales of the Bangladeshi Settlers*, Birmingham, Sylhet History Group, 1993.

Cohen, R., *Global Diasporas*, London, University College Press, 1997.

—— *Theories of Migration*, Cheltenham, Edward Elgar, 1996.

—— *Cambridge Survey of World Migration*, Cambridge, Cambridge University Press, 1995.

Colley, L., *Britons: Forging the Nation 1707–1837*, London, Vintage, 1996.

Cottret, B., *The Huguenots in England: Immigration and Settlement 1550–1700*, Cambridge, Cambridge University Press, 1991.

Curtis, S.E. and Ogden, P.E., 'Bangladeshis in London: A Challenge to Welfare', *Revue Européenne de Migrations Internationales*, 2 (3), December 1986.

Dijur, J., 'Jews in the Russian Economy', in J. Frumkin, G. Aronson and A. Goldenweiser (eds), *Russian Jewry 1860–1917*, New York and London, Thomas Yoseloff, 1966.

Drage, G., 'Alien Immigration', *Fortnightly Review*, Vol. LVII, 1895.

Durkheim, E., *The Elementary Forms of Religious Life*, London, Allen and Unwin, 1976 edition.

Eade, J., 'The Power of the Experts: The Plurality of Beliefs and Practices concerning Health and Illness among Bangladeshis', in L. Marks and M. Worboys (eds), *Migrants, Minorities and Medicine*, London, Routledge, 1997.

—— 'The Political Articulation of Community and the Islamisation of Space in London', in R. Barot (ed.), *Religion and Ethnicity, Minorities and Social Change in the Metropolis*, Kampen Netherlands, Kok Pharos, 1993.

—— 'The Bangladeshi Community in East London', in C. Clarke, C. Peach and S. Vertovec, *South Asians Overseas*, Cambridge, Cambridge University Press, 1990.

—— *The Politics of Community*, Aldershot, Avebury, 1989.

Efron, J., *Defenders of Race*, New Haven, Yale University Press, 1994.

Endelman, T., *The Jews of Britain 1650 to 2000*, Berkeley, Los Angeles and London, University of California Press, 2002.

—— *The Jews of Georgian England*, Philadelphia, Jewish Publication Society of America, 1979.

Escott, M., 'Royal Bounty Grants to Huguenot Refugees', *Huguenot Society*

Publications, Vol. XXV, 1989–93, London, Huguenot Society of Great Britain and Ireland, 1993.

Feldman, D., *Englishmen and Jews: Social Relations and Political Culture 1840–1914*, New Haven and London, Yale University Press, 1994.

Feldman, D., and Stedman Jones, G. (eds), *Metropolis London*, London, Routledge, 1989.

Fishman, J., *Yiddish: Turning to Life*, Philadelphia, John Benjamins Publishing Co., 1991.

Fishman, W.J., *East End 1888*, London, Hanbury, 2001.

—— *East End Jewish Radicals 1875–1914*, London, Duckworth, 1975.

Forman, C., *Spitalfields: A Battle for Land*, London, Hilary Shipman, 1989.

Frumkin, J., Aronson, G. and Goldenweiser, A. (eds), *Russian Jewry 1860–1917*, New York and London, Thomas Yoseloff, 1966.

Gainer, B., *The Alien Invasion: The Origins of the 1905 Aliens Act*, London, Heinemann Educational, 1972.

Gardner, K., *Age, Narrative and Migration*, Oxford, Berg, 2002.

—— 'Death, Burial and Bereavement amongst Bengali Muslims in Tower Hamlets, East London', *Journal of Ethnic and Migration Studies*, 22 (3), 1998.

—— 'Identity, Age and Masculinity amongst Bengali Elders in East London', in A. Kershen (ed.), *A Question of Identity*, Aldershot, Ashgate, 1998.

—— *Global Migrants, Local Lives*, Oxford, Clarendon Press, 1995.

Gardner, K. and Shukur, A., 'I'm Bengali, I'm Asian and I'm Living Here: The Changing Identity of British Bengalis', in R. Ballard (ed.), *Desh Pardesh: The South Asian Presence in Britain*, London, Hurst, 1994.

Garrard, J., *The English and Immigration 1880–1910*, London, Oxford University Press, 1971.

Gartner, L., *The Jewish Immigrant in England 1870–1914*, London, George Allen and Unwin, 1960; London, Simons, 1973.

George, M. Dorothy, *London Life in the Eighteenth Century*, London, Penguin, 1992.

Gilroy, P., *There Ain't No Black in the Union Jack: The Cultural Politics of Race and Nation*, London, Hutchinson, 1987.

Girouard, M., Cruickshank, D., Samuel R. *et al.*, *The Saving of Spitalfields*, London, 1989.

Glynn, S., 'Bengali Muslims: The New East End Radicals?', in *Ethnic and Racial Studies*, 23 (6), November 2002.

Godley, A., *Jewish Immigrant Entrepreneurship in London and New York 1890–1914*, Basingstoke, Palgrave, 2001.

—— 'Leaving the East End: Regional Mobility among East European Jews in London, 1880–1914', in A. Kershen, (ed.), *London the Promised Land? The Migrant Experience in a Capital City*, Aldershot, Avebury, 1997.

Goldsmith, E.S., *Architects of Yiddish at the Beginning of the Twentieth Century*, Cranbury, Associated University Press, 1976.

Graddol, D., Leith, D. and Swann, J., *English: History, Diversity and Change*, London, Routledge, 1996.

Green, N. (ed.), *Jewish Workers in the Modern Diaspora*, Berkeley, Los Angeles and London, University of California Press, 1998.

A Guide to Mother Tongue Classes and Supplementary Education, London, Tower Hamlets Education, 1997.

Gwynn, R., *Huguenot Heritage: The History and Contribution of the Huguenots in Britain*, Brighton, Sussex Academic Press, 2001.

Hobsbawm, E., 'Introduction', in A. Mack (ed.), 'Home a Place in the World', *Social Research*, 58 (1), 1991.

Hoerder, D., 'Segmented Macrosystems and Networking Individuals', in J. and L. Lucassen (eds), *Migration, Migration History, History*, Bern, Peter Lang, 1997.

Holmes, C., *John Bull's Island*, London, Macmillan, 1988.

—— *Anti-Semitism in British Society 1876–1939*, London, Edward Arnold, 1979.

Hyamson, A., *The Sephardim of England*, London, Methuen, 1951.

Islam, M., 'Bangladeshi Migration: An Impact Study', in R. Cohen, *Cambridge Survey of World Migration*, Cambridge, Cambridge University Press, 1995.

Jacobs, J.M., *Edge of Empire, Postcolonialism and the City*, London, Routledge, 1996.

Joly, D. and Cohen, R., *Reluctant Host*, Aldershot, Avebury, 1989.

Kabeer, N., *The Power to Choose*, London and New York, Verso, 2000.

Kaplan, D., 'Territorial Identities and Geographic Scale', in G. Herb and D. Kaplan (eds), *Nested Identities: Nationalism, Territory and Scale*, Oxford and Maryland, Rowan and Littlefield, 1999.

Kelly's Post Office London Directory, Commercial and Streets for 1889, London, Kelly's Directories, 1899.

Kershen, A. J. (ed.), *Food in the Migrant Experience*, Aldershot, Ashgate, 2002.

—— (ed.), *Language, Labour and Migration*, Aldershot, Ashgate, 2000.

—— (ed.), *A Question of Identity*, Aldershot, Ashgate, 1998.

—— 'Huguenots, Jews and Bangladeshis in Spitalfields and the Spirit of Captitalism', (ed.), *London the Promised Land? The Migrant Experience in a Capital City*, Aldershot, Ashgate, 1997.

——*Uniting the Tailors*, Ilford, Frank Cass, 1995.

—— *150 Years of History of Progressive Judaism in Britain*, London, London Museum of Jewish Life, 1990.

Kershen, A. J. and Romain, J., *Tradition and Change: A History of Reform Judaism in Britain 1840–1995*, Ilford, Vallentine Mitchell, 1995.

King, A. (ed.), *re-Presenting the City: Ethnicity, Capital and Culture in the 21st Century Metropolis*, Basingstoke, Macmillan, 1996.

Klier, J., 'What Exactly Was the *shtetl?*', in G. Estraikh and M. Krutikov (eds), *The Shtetl: Image and Reality*, Oxford, Legenda: published by the European Humanities Research Centre, 2000.

—— *Imperial Russia's Jewish Question: 1855–81*, Cambridge, Cambridge University Press, 1995.

The Koran, London, Penguin Classics, 1999 edition.

Kosak, H., *Cultures of Opposition: Jewish Immigrant Workers*, New York, State University of New York Press, 2000.

Labrousse, E., 'Great Britain as Envisaged by the Huguenots', in I. Scouloudi (ed.), *Huguenots in Britain and Their French Background 1550–1880*, Basingstoke, Macmillan, 1987.

Lahiri, S., 'Patterns of Resistance: Indian Seamen in Imperial Britain', in A. Kershen, (ed.), *Language, Labour and Migration*, Aldershot, Ashgate, 2000.

Leech, K., *Brick Lane 1978*, Birmingham, AFFOR, 1980.

—— 'The Decay of Spitalfields', *East London Papers*, 7 (2), 1964.

Lehmann, H. and Roth, G. (eds), *Weber's Protestant Work Ethic: Origins, Evidence and Contexts*, Cambridge, Cambridge University Press, 1995.

Lipman, V., *A History of the Jews of Britain since 1858*, Leicester, Leicester University Press, 1990.

—— A Century of Social Service 1859–1959: The History of the Jewish Board of Guardians, London, Routledge and Kegan Paul, 1959.

Living in Bethnal Green: A Survey of Residents in the Bethnal Green City Challenge Area, issued by LEPU, London, South Bank University, May 1995.

Livshin, R., 'The Acculturation of the Children of Immigrant Jews in Manchester: 1890–1930' in D. Cesarani (ed.), The Making of Anglo-Jewry, Oxford, Blackwell, 1992.

London, J., The People of the Abyss, 1903, London, Journeyman Press, 1977 edition.

Lorimer, D.A., Colour, Class and the Victorians, London, Leicester University Press, 1978.

Lougee Chappell, C., 'The Pains I Took to Save My/His Family', French Historical Studies, 22 (1), 1999.

Lucassen, J. and L., 'Migration, Migration History, History; Old Paradigms and New Persepectives', in J. and L. Lucassen (eds), Migration, Migration History, History, Bern, Peter Lang, 1997.

Machiavelli, N., The Prince, London, Penguin, 1975 edition.

Marcan, P., Down in the East End, London, Peter Marcan Publications, 1986.

Marmoy, C., 'La Maison de Charité de Spittlefields', Huguenot Society of Great Britain and Ireland Publications 1977–82, Vol. XXIII, London, Huguenot Society of Great Britain and Ireland, 1982.

Marshall, A., Elements of Economics, London, Macmillan, 1946 edition.

Massil, S., The Jewish Year Book 1896, facsimile edition, Ilford, Vallentine Mitchell, 1996 edition.

Mayhew, H., London Labour and the London Poor, Vol. III, New York, Dover Publications, 1968 edition.

Mendelsohn, E., Class Struggles in the Pale, Cambridge, Cambridge University Press, 1970.

Mettam, R., 'Louis XIV and the Persecution of the Huguenots' in I. Scouloudi (ed.), Huguenots in Britain and Their French Background 1550–1880, Basingstoke, Macmillan, 1987.

Meyer, M.A., Response to Modernity, London and New York, Oxford University Press, 1988.

Minutes of the Consistory of the French Church 1679–92, London, Publications of the Huguenot Society of Great Britain and Ireland, Vol. LVIII, 1994.

Murdoch, T., The Quiet Conquest: The Huguenots 1685–1985, London, Museum of London, 1985.

Nevalainen, T., 'Early Modern English Lexis and Semantics', in The Cambridge History of the English Language, Vol. III, 1476–1776, Cambridge, Cambridge University Press, 2001 edition.

The New English Bible, Swindon, Bible Society, 1995 edition.

Newman, A., The United Synagogue 1870–1970, London, Routledge & Kegan Paul, 1977.

The Next Step, No. 9, (no publication details) November–December 1980.

Nikolinokas, M., 'Notes towards a General Theory of Migration in Late Capitalism', Race and Class, XVII (1), 1975.

Nishikawa, S., 'Henry Compton, Bishop of London and Foreign Protestants', in R. Vigne and C. Littleton (eds), From Strangers to Citizens, Brighton, Sussex Academic Press, 2001.

Noorthouck, J., A New History of London, London, R. Baldwin, 1773.

Ouvry, E.C., 'Huguenot Societies and Churches, Past, Present and Future', *Proceedings of the Huguenot Society of London*, Vol. XVI, 1937–1941, London, Spotiswoode and Vallentine, 1941.

Palmer, A., *The East End: Four Centuries of London Life*, London, John Murray, 1989.

Parsons, D.W., 'Being Born Lost? The Cultural and Institutional Dimensions of Welsh Identity' in A. Kershen (ed.), *A Question of Identity*, Aldershot, Ashgate, 1998.

Peach, C., *Ethnicity in the 1991 Census*, Vol. 2, London, HMSO, 1996.

Pearson, K. and Moul, M., 'The Problem of Alien Immigration into Great Britain; Illustrated by an Examination of Russian and Polish Jewish Children', *Annals of Eugenics*, Vol. I, October 1925, pp. 5–127.

Porter, R., *London: A Social History*, London, Hamish Hamilton, 1994.

Portes, A., 'Conclusion: Towards a New World: The Origins and Effects of Transnational Activities', *Ethnic and Racial Studies*, 22 (2), 1999.

Portes, A. and Bach, R., *Latin Journey*, Berkeley, University of California Press, 1985.

Portes, A., and Borocz, J., 'Contemporary Immigration: Theoretical Perspectives on Its Determinants and Modes of Incorporation', *International Migration Review*, 23 (3), 1989.

Post Office London Directory 1971, London, Kelly's Directories, 1972.

Post Office London Directory 1961, London, Kelly's Directories, 1961.

Post Office London Directory 1951, London, Kelly's Directories, 1951.

Prestwich, M., 'The Huguenots under Richelieu and Mazarin', in I. Scouloudi (ed.), *Huguenots in Britain and Their French Background 1550–1880*, Basingstoke, Macmillan, 1987.

Proceedings of Hugenot Society of Great Britain and Ireland, 1888–91, Vol. III, London, Spottiswoode & Co., 1892.

Race Relations, Spring/Summer (no place of publication nor publisher (1970)).

Rapport, N. and Dawson, A. (eds), *Migrants of Identity: Perceptions of Home in a World of Movement*, Oxford, Berg, 1998.

Ravenstein, E.G., 'Laws of Migration', *Journal of the Royal Statistical Society*, 52, 1889.

Register of the Church of Saint Jean Spitalfields, London, Huguenot Society of London, Vol. XXXLX, 1928.

Ressinger, D.W., *Memoirs of the Reverend Jacques Fontaine 1658–1728*, London, The Huguenot Society of Great Britain and Ireland, 1992.

Rex, J., *Race, Colonialism and the City*, London, Routledge and Kegan Paul, 1973.

Rickard, P., *A History of the French Language*, London, Unwin Hyman, second edition, 1989.

Robinson, V., 'Indians', in C. Peach (ed.), *Ethnicity in the 1991 Census*, Vol. 2, London, HMSO, 1996.

Roth, C., *A History of the Jews in England*, Oxford, Clarendon Press, 1979.

Rothstein, N., 'Huguenots in the English Silk Industry in the Eighteenth Century', in I. Scouloudi (ed.), *Huguenots in Britain and Their French Background, 1550–1800*, Basingstoke, Macmillan, 1987.

Rubinstein, W.D., *A History of Jews in the English Speaking World: Great Britain*, Basingstoke, Macmillan, 1996.

Rudé, G., *Paris and London in the Eighteenth Century: Studies in Popular Protest*, New York, Viking, 1971.

Russell, C. and Lewis, H.S., *The Jew in London: A Study of Racial Character and Present-day Conditions*, London, T. Fisher Unwin, 1900.

Saggar, S., *The 1997 General Election: Ethnic Minorities and Electoral Politics*, London, CRE, 1998.

Sassen, S., 'Rebuilding the Global City: Economy, Ethnicity and Space', in A. King (ed.), *re-Presenting the City: Ethnicity, Capital and Culture in the 21st Century Metropolis*, Basingstoke, Macmillan, 1996.

Scott, J.H., *Spitalfields*, London, 1894 (no publisher cited).

Scouloudi, I. (ed.), *Huguenots in Britain and Their French Background, 1550–1800*, Basingstoke, Macmillan, 1987.

Sheppard, F.H.W. (ed.), *Survey of London, Vol. XXVII Spitalfields and Mile End New Town*, London, London County Council, 1957.

Shorter Oxford English Dictionary, Oxford, Oxford University Press, 2002 edition.

Sims, G.R., *Living London*, London, Cassell, 1902.

Skidelsky, R., *Oswald Mosley*, Basingstoke, Macmillan, 1981.

Smith, A., *A City Stirs*, London, Chapman and Hall, 1939.

Smith, G., *Language, Ethnicity, Employment, Education and Research: The Struggle of Sylheti-speaking People in London*, CLE/LMP Working paper No. 13, Community Languages and Education Project, London, University of London Institute of Education, 1985.

Smith, G., 'Can Jews Be Patriots?' *Nineteenth Century*, London, May 1878.

Smith, H.L., *The History of East London from the Earliest Times to the End of the Eighteenth Century*, London, Macmillan, 1939.

Smith, J., 'The Jewish Immigrant', *Contemporary Review*, LXXXVI, London, 1899.

Smith, R., 'Financial Aid to French Protestant Refugees 1681–1727: Briefs and the Royal Bounty', *Proceedings of the Huguenot Society of London*, Vol. XXII, London, Huguenot Society of Great Britain and Ireland, 1976.

Spiro, R., 'Post-biblical Jewish History – the London Vista', in D. Englander (ed.), *The Jewish Enigma*, Milton Keynes, Open University, 1992.

Statt, D., *Foreigners and Englishmen: The Controversy over Immigration and Population 1600–1760*, London and Toronto, Associated University Press, 1995.

Stedman Jones, G., 'The "Cockney" and the Nation', in D. Feldman and G. Stedman Jones (eds), *Metropolis London*, London, Routledge, 1989.

——— *Outcast London*, London, Penguin, 1983.

Stow, J., *Survey of London*, Oxford, Clarendon, 1908 edition.

Sutherland, N.M., 'The Huguenots and the Edict of Nantes 1598–1629', in I. Scouloudi (ed.), *Huguenots in Britain and Their French Background 1550–1880*, Basingstoke, Macmillan, 1987.

——— *The Huguenot Struggle for Recognition*, New York and London, Yale University Press, 1980.

Sutherland, S. and Clarke, P. (eds), *The Study of Religion, Traditional and New Religion*, London, Routledge, 1991.

Swift, R. and Gilley, S. (eds), *The Irish in Britain*, London, Pinter Publishers, 1988.

Thompson, E.P., *The Making of the English Working Class*, London, Penguin, 1968 edition.

Thurlow, R., *Fascism in Britain: A History 1918–1985*, Oxford, Blackwell, 1987.

Tomalin, C., *Samuel Pepys: The Unequalled Self*, London, Penguin, 2002.

Vertovec, S., 'Conceiving and Researching Transnationalism', *Ethnic and Racial Studies*, 22 (2), 1999.

Vigne, R. and Littleton, C., *From Strangers to Citizens*, Brighton, Sussex Academic Press, 2001.

Visram, R., *Ayahs, Lascars and Princes*, London, Pluto Press, 1985.

Walker, C., 'The Impact of Homelands upon Diaspora', in G. Sheffer (ed.), *Modern Diasporas in International Politics*, Beckenham, Croom Helm, 1986.

Wallace, I., *The Global Economic System*, London, Unwin Hyman, 1990.

Waller, W.C., 'Early Huguenot Friendly Societies', *Huguenot Society Proceedings VI*, 1898–1901, Aberdeen, Aberdeen University Press, 1902.

Wallerstein, I., *The Modern World System*, Vol. 1, New York and London, Academic Press, 1974.

Walter, B., ' "Shamrocks Growing out of Their Mouths": Language and the Racial-isation of the Irish in Britain', in A. Kershen (ed.), *Language, Labour and Migration*, Aldershot, Ashgate, 2000.

Weber, M., *The Protestant Work Ethic and the Spirit of Capitalism*, London, Unwin, 1938.

Webster, W., *Imagining Home: Gender, 'Race' and National Identity, 1945–64*, London, UCL Press, 1998.

Weinreb, B. and Hibbert, C. (eds), *London Encyclopaedia*, Basingstoke, Macmillan, 1983.

Weinreich, M., *History of the Yiddish Language*, Chicago and London, University of Chicago Press, 1973.

White, A. (ed.), *The Destitute Alien in Great Britain*, London, Sonnenschein & Co., 1892.

White, J., *Rothschild Buildings*, London, Routledge & Kegan Paul, 1980.

White, S.C., *Arguing with the Crocodile*, London, Zed Books, 1992.

White, V., 'Health Advocacy in Medicine', in A. Kershen (ed.), *Language, Labour and Migration*, Aldershot, Ashgate, 2000.

Williams, J. Lloyd and Chowdhury, M.R., *Ten Sylheti Poems*, London, Sylheti Trans-lation and Research, 1998.

Wirth, L., *The Ghetto*, Chicago, University of Chicago Press, 1928.

Zangwill, I., *The Children of the Ghetto*, Woking, Leicester University Press, 1977 edition.

Zborowski, M. and Herzog, E., *Life Is with People: The Culture of the Shtetl*, New York, Schocken, 1970.

Zipperstein, E., *Business Ethics in Jewish Law*, New York, Ktav, 1993.

Zolberg, A.R., 'The Next Waves: Migration Theory for a Changing World', *International Migration Review*, 23 (3), 1989.

Government papers

Committee on Lotteries 1808, (182) II, 147.

Decennial Census 1891, PP 1893–4, CVI.

Dwellings of the Poor, report of the Dwellings Committee of the Charity Organisation Society, London, 1881.

First Report from the Home Affairs Committee, *Bangladeshis in Britain*, Session 1986–7, Vol. 1, London, HMSO, 1986.

Home Affairs Sub-Committee on Race Relations and Immigration, *Bangladeshis in Britain*, Vol. II, London, HMSO, 1986.

London County Council, *Minutes of Proceedings*, Report of the Housing of the Working Classes Committee, 17 March 1903.

Minutes of Evidence of the Petition of the Ribbon Weavers, 1818, (134) IX.5.

Report of the Select Commission on the State of the Handloom Weavers II, 1840, Vol. XXIII, London, p. 147.

Report to the Board of Trade on the Sweating System at the East End of London, 1887, PP LXXXIX, London, 1887.

Royal Commission on Aliens, 1903, PP 1903, X, q 18968.

Select Committee on Handloom Weavers 1834–5, Analysis of Evidence, 1835 (492)XIII.343.

Unpublished sources

Theses

Garbin, D., 'Migration, territories diasporiques et politiques identitaires: Bengalis musulmans entre "Banglatown" (Londres) et Sylhet (Bangladesh)', unpublished Ph.D. thesis, University of François Rabelais de Tours, 2004.

Glasman, J., 'London Synagogues and the Jewish Community c.1870–1900', unpublished M.Sc. thesis, Bartlett School of Architecture, London University, 1981/82.

Gwynn, R., 'The Ecclesiastical Organisation of French Protestants in England in the Later Seventeenth Century, with Special Reference to London', unpublished Ph.D. thesis, University of London 1976.

Kalman, R., 'The Friendly Societies of London 1793–1911; with particular reference to the East End of London', unpublished MA dissertation, University of London, 1990.

Keating, M., 'The Huguenots as Exemplary Incomers: Did the Huguenots Set the Agenda by Which Future Incomers Have Been Measured', unpublished M.Phil. dissertation, University of London, 1998.

Schwarz, L.D., 'Conditions of Life and Work in East London, 1770–1815', unpublished D.Phil. thesis, University of Oxford, 1976.

Sundstrom, R., 'Aid and Assimilation: A Study of Economic Support Given French Protestants in England 1680–1727', unpublished Ph.D. thesis, Kent State University, 1972.

Vaughan, L., 'Clustering, Segregation and the "Ghetto": The Spatialisation of Jewish Settlement in Manchester and Leeds in the 19th Century', unpublished Ph.D. thesis, Bartlett School of Architecture, University of London, 1999.

—— 'The Jews in London 1695 and 1895', unpublished M.Sc. thesis, Bartlett Graduate School, University College London, 1994.

Reports

Carey, S., 'Brick Lane, Banglatown: A Study of the Catering Sector: Final Report', unpublished report, May 2002.

—— 'Looking for the Buzz: Heroin – the Drug of Choice: Drug Use amongst Bangladeshi Youths on the Ocean Estate', unpublished report, produced for the London Borough of Tower Hamlets, October 2000.

Shah, P., 'Bangladeshis in English Law', unpublished paper presented at 'Bangladeshis in Britain' workshop, 25 May 2002.

Webber, J., 'Islam in Bangladesh', Introductory notes for CCBI's Conference, 'Movements in Islam' undated, unpublished paper.

Newspapers

Arbeiter Fraint
Daily Telegraph
East End News
East London Advertiser
East London Observer
Eastern Post
Evening Standard
Guardian
Guardian Education
Jewish Chronicle
Jubo Barta
Lancet
Morning Star
Observer
Polishe Yidel
Sunday Times
The Times

Electronic sources

http://www.census2001.gov.uk/cci/nugget.asp?id.–260 (accessed 2 June 2004).
http://www.eastlondon-mosque.org.uk/html/history/htm (accessed 30 June 2002).
http://www.file:C:\SUBMISSION.htm (accessed 12 January 2004).
http://www.homeoffice.gov.uk/n_story.asp?item_id-587 (accessed 3 September 2003).
http://www.cweb2.loc.gov/frd/cs/bangladesh/bd_appen.html (accessed 17 June 1996).
http://www.icweb2.loc.gov/frd/cs.Bangladesh/bde_appen.html (accessed 17 June 2002).
http://www.ind.homeoffice.gov.uk/default.asp?pageId=3784 (accessed 20 May 2004).
http://www.movinghere.org.uk/stories/story57/htm (accessed 15 February 2004).
http://www.odci.gov/cia/publications/factlook/geos.bg.html (accessed 17 June 2002).
http://www.statistics.gov.uk/census 2001_1991 (accessed 16 February 2004).

Index

443910

Lightning Source UK Ltd.
Milton Keynes UK
UKOW05f1053040417
298290UK00006B/67/P